# CATALYZING DEVELOPMENT

# CATALYZING DEVELOPMENT

## A New Vision for Aid

HOMI KHARAS, KOJI MAKINO, AND WOOJIN JUNG

EDITORS

BROOKINGS INSTITUTION PRESS
*Washington, D.C.*

*Library of Congress Cataloging-in-Publication data*
Catalyzing development : a new vision for aid / Homi Kharas, Koji Makino,
and Woojin Jung, editors.
       p.      cm.
   Includes bibliographical references and index.
   Summary: "Provides analysis of how the field of international aid is
changing with new approaches necessary because of new actors providing
assistance, including middle-income countries, private philanthropists, and
the private sector, and new challenges, including climate change and the large
number of fragile states"—Provided by publisher.
   ISBN 978-0-8157-2133-8 (pbk. : alk. paper)
   1. Economic assistance.   2. Technical assistance.   3. Economic
development—Planning.   I. Kharas, Homi J., 1954–   II. Makino, Koji.
III. Jung, Woojin.
   HC60.C333 2010
   338.91—dc22                                              2011012920

9 8 7 6 5 4 3 2 1

Printed on acid-free paper

Typeset in Adobe Garamond

Composition by R. Lynn Rivenbark
Macon, Georgia

Printed by R. R. Donnelley
Harrisonburg, Virginia

# Contents

# *Preface*

In November 2011 participants from more than 150 countries, including ministers of developing and developed countries, heads of bilateral and multilateral development institutions, and civil society representatives will take part in the fourth High-Level Forum on Aid Effectiveness in Busan, Republic of Korea. This meeting is intended to take account of the development community's successes and failures in achieving greater impact through aid and to redefine the aid effectiveness agenda to adjust to a changing global landscape.

Considerable work is under way to prepare for Busan, most notably under the auspices of the Working Party on Aid Effectiveness of the Development Assistance Committee of the OECD. This volume provides fresh analytical studies to complement the Working Party discussions with in-depth academic analysis. It is the outcome of a year-long research program led by researchers at the Brookings Institution, the Korean International Cooperation Agency, and the Japanese International Cooperation Agency. The editors of this volume hope that a wide process of consultation and discussion will help to refine the ideas and ultimately lead to concrete recommendations and actions at Busan.

The eleven chapters in this volume have undergone a rigorous review process, which has served to elevate both the quality and relevance of the research. The papers that formed the chapters were discussed at a two-day workshop held in Washington in July 2010. The participants in that workshop included academics and representatives of many aid organizations, public and private. They gave generously of their time, and this volume reflects their many contributions.

Each chapter has also been peer reviewed, and the authors have benefited from these comments. A conference volume containing drafts of the papers was prepared and discussed on the occasion of the Fourth ODA International Conference, held in Seoul, Korea, on November 29, 2010. The chapters reflect the views of their authors and not the official position of any specific organization.

The editors would like to express their gratitude to the chapter authors, the participants in the July workshop, the peer reviewers, and to Janet Walker, Diane Hammond, and Susan Woollen of Brookings Institution Press.

This project would not have been possible without the financial support of the Korean International Cooperation Agency and the Japanese International Cooperation Agency, both of which also made substantive and intellectual contributions to the volume.

# Catalyzing Development

# 1

## Overview: An Agenda for the Busan High-Level Forum on Aid Effectiveness

HOMI KHARAS, KOJI MAKINO, AND WOOJIN JUNG

Today's world is shaped by growing economic integration alongside growing economic divergence. Over two dozen developing economies are expanding at rates that previously appeared miraculous, reducing poverty at unprecedented rates. Conversely, thirty-five developing countries with a combined population of 940 million can be classified as "fragile," or at risk of suffering debilitating internal conflict.[1] The potential for globalization to act as a positive force for development contrasts with the prospects for globalization to threaten, or be unable to protect, development through a failure to deal with the challenges of hunger, poverty, disease, and climate change. Many developing countries have neither the safety nets nor the macroeconomic institutions to manage global economic shocks. Developing countries today are quite differentiated in terms of the challenges they face and their capacity to respond.

International support for global development is now couched in terms of a broad strategic vision of long-term engagement to assist countries to sustain progress and evolve into partners that can help build a stable, inclusive global economy. This support is built on three pillars:

—An understanding that the responsibility for sustained development lies principally with the governments and institutions of each developing country, with foreign assistance playing a supportive, catalytic role.

---

1. See chapter 6, this volume, for the definition of fragility and the classification methodology used in this chapter.

—A recognition that a broad array of engagements between countries contribute to development, principally through trade, investment, finance, and aid.

—A desire to fashion an improved operational model for development cooperation that reflects the differential challenges of sustainable development, the diversity of state and nonstate development partners, and the dynamics of sustained development.

Aid must be understood in this context. It can only play a catalytic role, not a leading role, in development. Development will not happen because of aid, but aid can make a difference. Developing countries are responsible for their own development. Aid is but one of many instruments of development, and the catalytic impact of aid is often seen when other forces like trade and private investment are unleashed because of better economic policies and institutions supported by aid programs.

There have been many visible improvements in the operational model for aid since the late 1990s—untying, greater alignment with global priorities such as the Millennium Development Goals, more decentralized operations, use of country systems and budgets, and better donor coordination. But other problems with the operational model have emerged:

—The mandates for aid have expanded—growth, debt relief, humanitarian assistance, anticorruption and governance, delivery of public services, state building, and climate change adaptation, to name a few. With such broad mandates, there are no simple metrics of success by which to measure the impact of aid. Some suggest the need for a new architecture, in which aid is measured in a different way and oriented toward specific targets.[2]

—Aid is terribly fragmented, with the number of official development assistance (ODA) projects surpassing 80,000 annually, delivered by at least 56 donor countries, with 197 bilateral agencies and 263 multilateral agencies.[3] The number of tiny aid relationships is daunting and, with more players, aid is becoming less predictable, less transparent, and more volatile. Despite an advisory from the Accra High-Level Forum on Aid Effectiveness to "think twice" before setting up new multilateral aid agencies, the number continues to grow. Only one multilateral development agency is known to have closed since World War II (the Nordic Development Bank). Alongside this, a new ecosystem of private development agencies has emerged—philanthropic foundations, international NGOs, church groups, corporations, and universities which command significant and growing resources. The actions of these groups are little understood, and they remain on the fringes of official development cooperation.

—The governance of aid is seen as bureaucratized and centralized at a time when more attention is being focused on the quality of aid because of pressures

---

2. Severino and Ray (2009).
3. World Bank (2008).

on some large donors to cut back on (or slow growth in) aid volumes. The result is overlap, confusion, and a lack of leadership in some areas.

Against this background, a major international forum on aid effectiveness will convene in November 2011 in Busan, Korea, under the auspices of the Development Assistance Committee of the OECD (OECD/DAC). The Busan meeting comes at an important juncture. Because aid is clearly not sufficient to achieve development, it is sometimes misconstrued as being unnecessary, despite the growing evidence that aid is working at both micro and macro levels.[4] The simple conclusion that aid does not work, while true in selected cases, is crowding out the more complex story of how aid helps in numerous different—but often unmeasurable—ways. Aid, as a government-to-government form of development cooperation, can also be perceived as an inferior alternative to private sector, market-determined processes and hence less relevant for development in today's world. Against this antiofficial aid movement, the Busan meeting must recapture the idea that ODA is a major instrument of development cooperation and can be made more effective if the right lessons are learned and if operational models are improved.

The goals of the Busan meeting are ambitious. They are nothing less than an attempt to generate a better understanding of how to improve the human condition—a twenty-first-century charter for global development cooperation by generating sustainable growth, achieving the Millennium Development Goals, and investing in a range of global public goods, like climate mitigation. Ultimately, that means cooperating to achieve sustainable results at scale. That can be done by nation-states organizing and leading development cooperation by generating the right enabling environment for development, by promoting productive businesses in a competitive setting, and by, through an inclusive process, tapping into the energies of billions of citizens worldwide engaged with development. Figure 1-1 illustrates this proposition for better contextualizing the role of effective aid in supporting development.

## Asian Experiences with Aid and Development

In many ways, the vision for aid expressed in figure 1-1 has already been implemented in much of Asia (although Asian countries have not had to confront climate change until recently). In a number of Asian countries, the development experience shows a limited, yet pivotal, role played by aid. The host country for the Busan High-Level Forum (HLF4), the Republic of Korea, perhaps best exemplifies the contributions that aid can make when targeted in the right way and tailored to country circumstances. Korea brings a unique perspective in moving

4. Rand and Tarp (2010).

Figure 1-1. *A New Vision for Aid: Catalyzing Development*

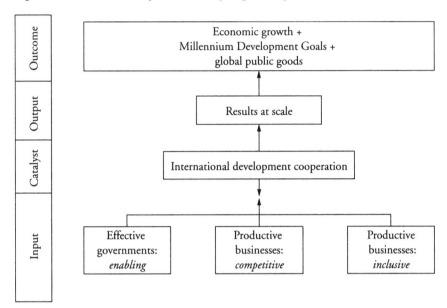

through the entire spectrum of aid, from being a major recipient to being a major donor within a span of fifty years (see the case study for Korea in box 1-1).

Other Asian experiences also provide a reminder that the lessons drawn from Korea's experiences with aid are applicable to other countries; a sustainable development trajectory must encompass self-reliance, the building of local capacity, and the evolution of development assistance to fit changing development priorities. Brief case studies of Cambodia (emerging from a fragile state), Indonesia (a large country trying to scale up development), and Vietnam (development partner with a strong national strategy) show aid working successfully in very different environments (see boxes 1-2 to 1-4 below). These studies reveal common themes and lessons that illustrate three important principles of the successful use of aid to catalyze development, despite vastly different circumstances and economic policy approaches by recipient governments.

First, *diverse aid* providers can bring complementarities, resources, and expertise, and Asian countries benefited from the broad array of development partners. At times they were able to secure assistance from one partner even when another was unconvinced of the development approach. Such "competition" among development partners goes back to U.S.-Japanese differences in approaches in Korea, World Bank–IMF differences in approaches in Vietnam, and the division of labor among donors in Indonesia. In each Asian case study, aid has been leveraged with private corporate sector investments and an emphasis on trade as a key development strategy.

Box 1-1. *Republic of Korea*

Aid to Korea has been adapted to changing country circumstances. Before and immediately after the Korean War (1950–53) aid to Korea was focused on military support and humanitarian relief, which was crucial for the survival of the country. As Korean institutions became more stable and capable after the 1960s, development interventions were scaled up, first by graduating from grants to concessional credits, then to nonconcessional financing, and finally to private finance (appendix table 1-1). Korea was fortunate to have two stable long-term donors—the United States and Japan—providing financial and technical cooperation. Recently, Korea has joined the group of OECD/DAC donor nations.

One reason for the success of Korea's experience with ODA was its strong country ownership and leadership. Korea knew what it wanted and was not intimidated into accepting donors' policy preferences. The United States put a greater emphasis on stability, which implied relatively short-lived, nonproject aid, and it was sometimes conditional, with expectations on how aid dollars would be spent. For example, using relief aid for investment was prohibited by the United States. However, the Rhee regime expressed a desire for more investments, the separation of economic aid from military aid, and long-term predictable aid in accordance with the national development plan.

Under the Park administration, the Korean government formed an Economic Planning Board to prepare five-year economic development plans. (Launched in 1961, the Economic Planning Board was responsible for development planning, annual budget preparation, and coordination of foreign aid and foreign investment.) Aid was linked to the country's planning and budget process. The Park administration maintained a policy focusing on large-scale enterprises despite the recommendations of U.S. advisers to focus more on small and medium-sized enterprises. Most of the assistance in Korea was allocated to finance the government's industrial and financial policies implemented by *Jaebeol* (a Korean form of business conglomerate), particularly in import-substituting or export-oriented, private enterprises such as the POSCO steel mill, funded mainly by Japanese repatriation payments.[1] Many of these cases were remarkably successful. The emphasis on focusing aid on investment in large economic infrastructure and services contrasted with a low aid-allocation priority for health and education, as these were financed by Korean society itself.[2] Korea and its U.S. advisers also had different approaches toward fighting corruption. Instead of penalizing corrupt businessmen, Park expropriated their bank stocks and assigned them to invest in key import-substitution industries such as fertilizers.

Country-led development was made easier by a unique organizational structure that reflected Korea's special needs. When the U.S. operation mission system (in which the American ambassador holds jurisdiction over the disbursement of aid) was deemed inappropriate for Korea, it gave rise to the creation of the Office of the Economic Coordinator (OEC). In 1956 the OEC absorbed the functions of the Korea Civil Assistance Command and the UN Korea Reconstruction Agency and became the only aid coordinating agency in Korea. Unlike an earlier period when Japanese engineers and UN personnel in Tokyo were responsible for Korean aid, the OEC was placed in Seoul and

*(continued)*

1. KEXIM (2008); Chung (2007).
2. CBO (1997).

Busan, hiring almost 900 Koreans along with 300 foreigners.[3] A decentralized structure enabled the OEC to formulate harmonized and home-grown assistance policies among key donors (appendix figure 1-1).

Throughout the aid process, Korea worked on capacity building. Between 1962 and 1971 more than 7,000 Koreans received training abroad, and additionally over 1,500 experts were sent to Korea by donor nations. A high proportion of the senior personnel in government, business, and academia received foreign training. While Korea sought to improve the quality of development projects by hiring leading foreign institutes, the planning and implementation responsibilities were largely in the hands of local people. For example, for the Geongbu Expressway, general project supervision was contracted out to a foreign expert on construction technologies but implementation and feasibility studies were handled by domestic engineers. When establishing the Korea Institute of Science and Technology with U.S. assistance, Korean project managers decided the orientation of the institute and picked the most qualified advisers, instead of waiting for experts to be sent. Investment of significant local resources and time in project implementation signaled strong Korean project ownership and was in line with local efforts to learn "how to fish."

---

3. Lee (2009).

Second, *differentiated* aid approaches are needed to take into account recipients' characteristics, histories, and priorities. This is the essence of country ownership. For the most part, Asian countries have been able to receive aid in a form appropriate to their situation. This has been driven by strong expressions of country needs, expressed by government leadership of the development agenda and over aid resources.

Third, *dynamic* approaches are needed to adjust assistance over time as development conditions evolve. Graduation strategies and hard timetables can provide a sense of urgency and the need for speed in development programs. As the examples below show, aid in Asia has constantly adapted its approach to the evolving needs of countries, whether it be the move from grants to loans in Korea as the purpose of aid shifted, or the evolution of aid instruments toward budget support in Vietnam, or the sequenced approaches to capacity development in Cambodia, or the scaled-up approach to hydrological management in Indonesia.

The conclusion: aid works, when done right. That requires starting from an assessment of development needs and only then developing an aid strategy. Too often today the process is reversed, with donor-defined aid strategies driving development outcomes.

Our case studies suggest that in Asia aid has been effective in countries that have stable long-term donors who are invested in the success of their projects and in the development of their partner. The Asian examples point to the need for aid to be sustained over time but with graduated modalities to capture fully all development benefits. Strong local leadership is critical to align aid with evolving national development priorities. This does not always mean full agreement with donors on all aspects of development, but it does imply finding the right avenues for mutual cooperation. And capacity development beyond improvement of specific technical talent emerges as a key success factor in all the Asian cases.

## The Aid Effectiveness Agenda Today

Since 1960 rich countries have given $3.2 trillion in aid to poor countries, mostly through a handful of bilateral and multilateral institutions.[5] Despite misgivings as to its effectiveness, aid continues to enjoy strong political and public support in rich countries. Emerging economies also have substantial development cooperation programs. And a variety of private international NGOs (INGOs), foundations, corporations, and individuals are actively engaged. Aid has become a $200 billion industry: $122 billion from the OECD/DAC donors, $53 billion to $75 billion from private donors, and $14 billion from emerging economy donors.[6] The last two components are growing rapidly. China, India, Brazil, Venezuela, Turkey, and the Republic of Korea, to name just a few, have developed aid programs that could soon each surpass $1 billion annually.

For most of the past decade the aid agenda has focused on increasing the volume of aid flows—with considerable success. Net ODA disbursements from members of the OECD/DAC rose from $54 billion in 2000 to $122 billion in 2008.[7] This is a substantial increase even if it is not as high as hoped for when significant pledges were made at Gleneagles. The experience of the last decade is that ambitious targets for increasing aid volumes can work if there is strong leadership. Gratifyingly, prospects for aid volumes in 2010 are not as bleak as feared, despite the gravity of the public finance situation in many donor countries.[8] With the growth in aid from private and non-DAC donors, as well as resources from hybrid financing, issues about the quantity of aid revolve around questions of ensuring a better division of labor and better coordination of activities so as to avoid overlap and waste.

As scrutiny over public funding has grown, more attention has shifted to the quality of aid. Much of this agenda revolves around assisting partner countries to achieve self-reliant development. The prevailing framework for action on aid effectiveness has been articulated in high-level conferences at Rome (2003), Paris (2005), and Accra (2008). The Paris Declaration on Aid Effectiveness, endorsed on March 2, 2005, committed over one hundred countries and organizations to enhance aid effectiveness by 2010 by respecting five principles: ownership by

5. Cumulative net ODA disbursements in 2007 constant dollars.
6. OECD/DAC (various years); chapters 2 and 3, this volume.
7. OECD/DAC (various years).
8. OECD/DAC (2010).

recipient countries, alignment of development partners with country-led poverty strategies, harmonization of activities among development partners to avoid duplication and waste, results in terms of development outcomes, and mutual accountability for performance.

While there has been significant progress under the Paris-Accra agendas, a number of challenges have emerged. The growth of aid resources and aid donors has been accompanied by a fragmentation into ever smaller projects, with the mean project size falling from $2.01 million to $1.46 million between 2000 and 2008 (in real terms). Small can be good if it is innovative and later results in scaling up, but each project also has fixed costs of design, negotiation, and implementation, which reduces dollars available for final beneficiaries.

Recipient countries each received an average of 263 donor missions in 2007. Their senior finance officials spend one-third to one-half of their time meeting with donors; in the case of Kenya, Ghana, and others, governments have resorted to "mission-free" periods to allow officials time to handle their domestic obligations. The efficiency losses from this set of transaction costs are estimated at $5 billion by the OECD, prompting calls for more serious attention to be paid to issues of division of labor among donors.[9] Better division of labor would result in larger aid flows between a given donor and recipient and would reduce the number of donor-recipient aid relationships, as some donors would exit from some countries. In fact, the OECD/DAC estimates that, if half of the smallest donor-recipient relationships were abandoned, only 5 percent of country programmable aid would have to be rechanneled. In some countries with strong leadership, like Vietnam, donor coordination has made good progress, leading to more effective use of aid, but this model cannot be readily applied to all countries, especially not to fragile states (box 1-2).

In the old aid architecture, coordination at the country level was done through UN Roundtables or Consultative Group meetings. The ten largest donors could be gathered in a single room and would collectively represent 90 percent of all aid to that country. Today, the share of the largest ten donors typically covers around 60 percent of aid. It is not easy for recipient countries to host a forum that is representative and inclusive of the experiences of all development partners while at the same time being effective in coordinating, harmonizing, and prioritizing activities.

In fact excessive coordination can alienate small donors. Large recipient countries, like India and Indonesia, have already expressed their unwillingness to debate national policy issues with small donors, and several donors have reduced their support to these countries. But small developing countries cannot afford the luxury of alienating any potential donors. They need to find ways to ensure that small donors are not marginalized by building a relationship of development cooperation that is about more than just provision of money.

---

9. Rogerson (2010).

Box 1-2. *Vietnam*

Vietnam has grown fast, dramatically reducing poverty from 58.1 percent in 1993 to 12.3 percent in 2009. Vietnam's development is especially remarkable since over the last thirty years it has had to recover from war (1955–75), adapt to the loss of financial support from the old Soviet bloc, and overcome the rigidities of a centrally planned economy. While problems such as inequalities persist—for example poverty in Vietnam is concentrated among ethnic minorities in remote mountainous areas—the country is a worthwhile case study on how to develop rapidly based on economic integration, market liberalization, and the strategic use of aid.

Vietnam is one of the largest recipients of ODA, with aid volumes approaching $4 billion (compared with $1.5 billion in 1995). Although Vietnam receives a lot of aid, it is not an aid-dependent nation. ODA was only 4 percent of its GDP in 2009.

Vietnam shows strong country ownership of its aid receipts, led by the Ministry of Planning and Investment. Coordination is based on an internally drafted five-year socioeconomic development plan and a local version of the Paris Declaration called the Hanoi Core Statement. The government, rather than donor groups, has driven the poverty reduction agenda, sometimes defining priorities that are different from donors' priorities. After the 1997–98 East Asian crisis, Vietnam focused on stabilizing its economy, and reforms progressed very slowly until 2001, leading to a halt in structural adjustment lending from the World Bank. Only when the leadership felt comfortable did reforms start up again. Vietnam also allowed its program with the International Monetary Fund to lapse over disagreements with the pace of financial sector reform and audits of the central bank. It has resisted donor pressures for greater freedom of journalism and civil society development.

These examples are not meant to indicate that the decisions made by the government of Vietnam were always best from a development perspective but rather to demonstrate that a successful development partnership must be based on serious dialogue even if disagreements between development partners occur. The critical issue is to find ways of fostering cooperation in areas where agreement and progress can be made.

A result of strong country ownership is that donor aid in Vietnam has been well aligned with country priorities. With specific sectoral programs and projects working well, Vietnam has been able to organize an umbrella instrument to channel aid in support of these activities through the budget. Initially, only a few donors agreed to general budget support for Vietnam, but once it showed a track record of success, more joined in. In recent years ten or eleven co-financiers provide budget support, accounting for 25 percent of ODA.[1] All ODA provided through budget support is automatically subjected to reasonably transparent financial reporting systems. It also has been disbursed on schedule, in contrast to project disbursements.[2] In particular, poverty reduction support credits is an exemplary practice on policy dialogue in a mature development partnership. Given the leadership and capacity demonstrated by the government, the instrument provides a soft financial incentive in place of conditionality.

One challenge that Vietnam faces is that its aid is becoming more fragmented as donors are attracted by its success. Vietnam has become a donor darling, with around

*(continued)*

1. OECD (2008).
2. Ibid.

twenty-eight bilateral donors and twenty-three multilateral agencies. The Paris Monitoring Survey of 2008 reports that Vietnam hosted 752 donor missions in 2007—more than three missions per working day. The number of missions conducted by some donors appears extremely disproportionate to the amount of aid they provide. For example, UN agencies provide less than 1 percent of ODA, but the number of these agencies operating in Vietnam increased from four in 2006 to twelve in 2007. While such aid is costly, Vietnam has been able to manage donors well. Large donors, such as the Six Bank Group, finance large infrastructure, while smaller donors, such as the Like-Minded Donor Group, the European Commission, and the UN, typically work in areas not served by the larger donors, addressing problems like social inequality and exclusion. Probably having more donors is a net positive for Vietnam, although waste and overlap may be occurring.

Vietnam's relative success in using aid is based on two pillars. First, Vietnam has a strong relationship with its major donors; 60 percent of its aid comes from its top three donors: Japan, the World Bank, and the Asian Development Bank. Second, infrastructure development has been identified as the key focus of aid money. Specifically, road transportation, power generation, water supply, and sanitation systems have been prioritized and developed.

If aid is to be seen as a mechanism of development cooperation, an instrument for achieving results on the ground, it follows that aid must be governed and managed through processes within each recipient country, not just at the global level. Two types of aid relationships have matured: government to government and civil society to civil society. In each case, there is more to be done to reinforce these relationships, especially in situations where governments are weak and lack either capacity or legitimacy. But what urgently needs strengthening is links across these relationships: civil society donors to government recipients and government donors to civil society recipients. These links are weak and sometimes confrontational but cannot be ignored.

The 2008 *Survey on Monitoring the Paris Declaration* stresses that the pace of improvement had to accelerate in order to meet the targets set for 2010.[10] In particular, the report calls for strengthening and use of country systems, stronger accountability, and lowering of transaction costs for partner countries and donors in the delivery of aid. The discussions at the Busan High-Level Forum on Aid Effectiveness in 2011 will be based in part on the evidence from the third survey on achievement of the Paris Declaration targets for 2010. It is safe to say that at least some of the indicators will not be met and that a significant agenda will remain to advance the Paris principles. This agenda will need further articulation in Busan.

But equally, there must be a discussion around two other broad questions. How should other development actors, the so-called new players, who by and

10. OECD (2008).

large were absent when the Paris principles were drafted, be incorporated in a new global aid architecture? And is there a need to adapt the Paris indicators to deal with new challenges of development, in particular to the emerging discussion on climate change financing, the practical problems experienced in applying the Paris principles to aid in fragile states, and the mixed results with capacity building?

We refer to this as the Paris++ agenda for Busan. Considerable work remains to achieve the Paris Declaration targets, and a focus on this should be maintained, but at the same time other agendas are pressing. Lessons from experience need to be absorbed. For example, Cambodia could have some lessons on phasing and sequencing of aid that are more broadly applicable to countries emerging from conflict. Its future prospects are still not assured, but considerable progress is already evident, thanks in part to the generous provision of development assistance (box 1-3).

This volume offers specific suggestions for framing an agenda for Busan through ten essays on game changers for aid—actions that we believe will transform the development landscape. We do not go into the details of how to pursue the Paris Declaration targets beyond 2010, even though this is an essential part of the agenda. Those discussions are well in-train through an extensive work program under the auspices of the Working Party on Aid Effectiveness of the OECD/DAC. Instead, this volume focuses on the "plus-plus" part of the agenda.

It is already evident that the Paris Declaration is most relevant to the portion of aid that is shrinking. To start with, the Paris and Accra Accords only cover ODA from DAC countries, covering perhaps 60 percent of total aid, a share that appears likely to shrink further as non-DAC donors and private development assistance are expanding aid faster than DAC donors. The other concerns are that the Paris-Accra processes have not been fine-tuned to reflect the specific challenges of fragile states, capacity development, and climate change, each of which accounts for a large portion of today's aid.

Table 1-1 shows how most of the increase in aid since the 1990s has gone into fragile states, where ideas like reliance on recipient country ownership and alignment of donors with country preferences and practices are difficult to implement and require unorthodox approaches. Fragile states received about $15 billion a year ($21 per capita) in aid in 1995–98 and $46 billion ($50 per capita) in 2005–08.[11] Even when the exceptional cases of Iraq and Afghanistan are excluded, ODA to fragile states grew considerably. In contrast, aid to nonfragile states hardly grew at all in aggregate and fell in per capita terms over this period, from $10.3 per capita to $10.0 per capita (the same broad pattern holds excluding the dynamic large economies of China and India). The reality is that only $20 billion a year goes to nonfragile states in a fashion that is programmable by

11. See note 1.

Box 1-3. *Cambodia*

The polity and society of Cambodia are not yet free of fragility. The Khmer Rouge government, 1975–79, participated in genocide, which led to the deaths of 21 percent of the entire population. The overthrow of that regime did not end the violence, and peace efforts did not completely succeed until much later. In 1991 a cease-fire was finally agreed to by all sides. Although Cambodia attained political stability by the late 1990s, weak accountability and corruption of the government hamper the consolidation of a genuinely legitimate state. Cambodia is among the lowest countries in Transparency International's (TI) ranking of corruption. Between 2005 and 2009 Cambodia's TI ranking dropped from 130th (among 159 countries) to 158th (among 180 countries). Furthermore, due to the history of conflict, Cambodia presents a unique development challenge. In 2008 the population cohort of ages thirty through thirty-four was smaller than any other age group and had the lowest male literacy rate. The lack of middle-aged, highly skilled people is a serious problem for the management of state institutions.

Despite these drawbacks, Cambodia has achieved rapid growth, enjoying five years of double-digit growth in the decade before the 2009 global recession. It received $5.5 billion in aid from thirty-five official donors and also benefited from the activities of hundreds of civil society organizations. Foreign aid played a pivotal role in rehabilitating infrastructure and improving basic services, thereby providing the Cambodian people with peace dividends in an early stage of the peace-building process. Improved infrastructure served as a basis for the economic development in the later stage.

Because of Cambodia's poor human capital, donors have focused on state capacity building but have addressed it through funding foreign experts. Technical cooperation has been about half of ODA in Cambodia but has been criticized domestically as being mostly supply driven, poorly coordinated, and a substitution for domestic capacity rather than an addition to it.

The Royal Government of Cambodia has tried to take ownership of the aid agenda through establishment of technical working groups in nineteen sectors and thematic areas. Through this mechanism, it has aligned aid with the National Strategic Development Plan but still finds that donors are uncomfortable with program-based approaches and budget support due to poor governance in the system. New donors like Thailand and China are important but have a development cooperation process outside this structure.

In Cambodia tangible impacts of aid can be most clearly seen at the level of specific programs. One example is the case of National Maternal and Child Health Center (NMCHC), which currently functions as the country's largest obstetrics hospital as well as the national training center for improvement of public health service. In the first phase of the project (1995–2000), priority was given to building the capacity of the NMCHC staff in both organizational management and specific health care skills. Building on the achievement of the first phase, the second phase (2000–05) expanded the training program for midwives and physicians across the country. This example shows how capacity can be developed in specific areas when foreign experts and local staff engage in a process of mutual learning.

Table 1-1. *Aid to Fragile and Nonfragile States, 1995–98 and 2005–08*[a]
U.S. dollars

| Aid | 1995–98 | | 2005–08 | |
|---|---|---|---|---|
| | Billion | Per capita | Billion | Per capita |
| ODA from DAC donors | 73.3 | . . . | 119.0 | . . . |
| *Aid to fragile states* | | | | |
| Net ODA | 15.3 | 21.4 | 45.7 | 50.4 |
| Less ODA to Iraq and Afghanistan | 14.7 | 21.8 | 28.3 | 33.1 |
| *Aid to nonfragile states* | | | | |
| Net ODA | 39.3 | 10.3 | 43.5 | 10.0 |
| Less ODA to India and China | 33.9 | 20.6 | 40.1 | 20.9 |

Source: OECD/DAC, aggregate aid statistics online; World Bank, World Development Indicators online.

a. The sum of aid going to fragile and nonfragile states does not add to total net ODA because some aid is regional, not allocable by country, or used for non-country-specific purposes.

recipient countries, or about 10 percent of total aid.[12] Thus the Paris-Accra discussions are relevant to only a small portion of total aid.

Figure 1-2 highlights the changing nature of the composition of total aid. Using approximations for the volume of aid from private assistance and emerging donors, DAC development assistance was over 80 percent of total aid in 1995–98. While allocations for fragile states (19 percent) and for technical cooperation (21 percent) were significant, the bulk of DAC aid (40 percent) went for other purposes.[13] By 2005–08, the aid environment had changed significantly. Non-DAC official donors (5 percent) and private philanthropy (32 percent) became large players and are expected to grow even more. Climate change adaptation (as measured by Rio markers) emerged as a major component of total aid and is also certain to become even larger. The portion of aid going toward fragile states rose from 19 percent to 26 percent. The portion of core DAC aid shrank to just 19 percent of total aid.

In 2005, the year the Paris Declaration was signed, more than half the world's poor lived in stable, low-income countries (table 1-2). In 2010 only 10 percent of the world's poor live in such countries, while the majority live in middle-income and fragile states. The traditional aid model must respond to these changed circumstances. Aid was originally envisaged as an instrument to help low-income countries develop until such time as they could sufficiently provide

12. About 54 percent of aid is country programmable. OECD/DAC (2010).

13. Technical cooperation is used as a proxy, albeit a highly imperfect one, for capacity development—for which unfortunately time-series data do not exist. In comparing the volume of aid for various types of capacity development in the Creditor Reporting System for 2008, we find it is close to the volume for technical cooperation reported by the DAC.

Figure 1-2. *Aid Composition, 1995–98 and 2005–08*

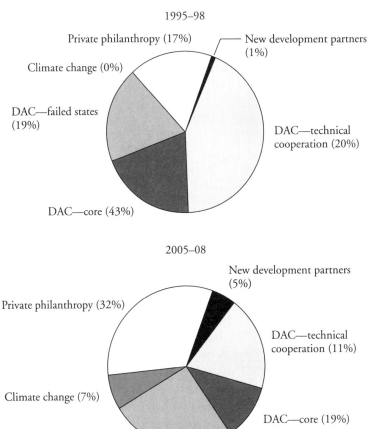

1995–98

Private philanthropy (17%) ─── New development partners (1%)

Climate change (0%)

DAC—failed states (19%)

DAC—technical cooperation (20%)

DAC—core (43%)

2005–08

New development partners (5%)

Private philanthropy (32%)

DAC—technical cooperation (11%)

Climate change (7%)

DAC—core (19%)

DAC—failed states (26%)

for the material needs of their citizens. The complication for aid policymakers is that aid is often deemed unnecessary in middle-income countries and ineffective in fragile states—precisely where today's poor people can be found. Development cooperation in these settings requires differentiated strategies, usually tailored to each specific country case.

The Paris Declaration principles and targets have been most successfully implemented, and have achieved the greatest development impact, in stable countries where donors have reliable partners and have confidence in their ability to deliver the right sorts of interventions and reforms. But as the demography of global poverty has evolved, donors will have to adjust to different environments.

Table 1-2. *Where Do the World's Poor Live?*
Percent

| | 2005 | | 2010 | |
|---|---|---|---|---|
| State | Low income | Middle income | Low income | Middle income |
| Stable | 53.9 | 25.6 | 10.4 | 48.8 |
| Fragile | 19.6 | 0.9 | 23.7 | 17.2 |

Source: Based on Chandy and Gertz (2011).

## Plan of the Book and Summary Findings

The new environment for aid depicted in figure 1-2 shows where important conversations are needed at Busan to enhance aid effectiveness and improve aid architecture. This volume is an effort to inform these conversations through research on each of the three key topic areas: new players, new challenges, and new approaches.[14]

Chapters 1 through 5 discuss the new aid ecosystem from the perspective of the new players, including non-DAC donors (chapter 2), international NGOs, philanthropists, and a vocal public engaged in thousands of civil society organizations (chapter 3), and multinational corporations (chapter 4). The existing global aid architecture, built around a few major official donors, is straining to accommodate this diversity of views and must become better networked (chapter 5). With so many interacting stakeholders, it may not be possible to have a single architecture, as in the past, but rather a set of guidelines, responsibilities, and accountabilities to shape how each group should act and interact—what might be called a new aid ecosystem.

Chapters 6, 7, and 8 describe the new challenges that must be considered today. The details of implementation, sequencing, and phasing of aid in fragile states, for capacity development and for climate change, are being vigorously debated, with no clear understanding of the best way forward.

Some thirty-seven fragile states, with one-third of the world's billion extreme poor, have development needs that are quite different from those of other countries. Already there has been a diversion of aid resources toward fragile states, where development outcomes are far harder to achieve and sustain, raising issues of scale of activities, phasing, and sequencing (chapter 6). The same risks pertain to climate change financing. Despite all the talk of additionality, there is concern that more

14. While not all aspects of this changing environment are strictly new—for instance, China has been providing aid to other countries since the 1950s, and capacity building has long been an objective of aid—they nevertheless represent a range of issues that have come to prominence in recent years and that demand greater attention in the evolving aid effectiveness agenda.

resources for climate mitigation will mean fewer resources for development and that development funds will be channeled prematurely toward climate adaptation activities. At a minimum, because climate change financing has aspects of a public good and universal implementation, it is not easy to integrate delivery modalities with development financing practices that focus on selectivity (chapter 7). In both these cases, and to achieve development more broadly, partner countries need to upgrade their technical and administrative capacity to absorb and utilize to maximum benefit the bewildering array of new resources. Yet capacity development is one of the least well understood aspects of aid, and several donors are radically rethinking their approaches in order to mainstream capacity development (chapter 8).

Chapters 9, 10, and 11 discuss several new approaches that appear promising in delivering better results. Aid must move beyond small successes, with projects to demonstrate that it can achieve results at scale. Donors can have a far-reaching impact even in large countries, as the experience of Indonesia shows (box 1-4). More donor agencies are focusing on the need for interventions that have the potential to be scaled-up in terms of impact (chapter 9). Technological change also opens up the possibility for far-reaching improvement in the transparency and quality of aid data, with benefits that could amount to $11 billion by some estimates, especially if new sources of information, like beneficiary feedback and local evaluation, are collected (chapter 10). And more recipient countries are finding that the practical experiences of their peers with implementing development programs are of enormous value. South-South cooperation has been enthusiastically welcomed (chapter 11).

Taken together, the ten chapters that follow this overview provide specific recommendations for game changers that could radically improve the development results from aid. They provide an action agenda for the Busan HLF4. Gaining consensus and developing an implementation plan will not easy, but there is a compelling need for new thinking on aid. The Busan HLF4 provides an opportunity to mobilize the political support needed to move the agenda forward.

## New Players

Chapters 2, 3, 4, and 5 look at the new players in the aid architecture.

### New Development Partners

Kang-ho Park (chapter 2) highlights the rise of new development partners, countries that are not part of the OECD and that may not have subscribed to the Paris Declaration but that are now providing significant resources for development. He estimates that these cooperation programs were tiny in 1995, accounting for only $1 billion, or 1.7 percent of ODA, but that they may now account for $15 billion; by 2015 new development partners could disburse one-fifth of ODA if their growth continues to outstrip that of developed country partners.

Box 1-4. *Indonesia*

Indonesia is the largest country in the ASEAN, and its political stability and economic development is crucial to the development of the rest of the region. As one of the East Asian miracle countries, it reduced the number of people living in poverty from roughly 50 million (about 40 percent of the population) in 1976 to approximately 20 million (about 11 percent of the population) in 1996. Development in Indonesia has been pursued along three parallel axes: growth, poverty reduction, and security. In the second half of the 1980s Indonesia implemented policy reforms in such areas as trade, foreign direct investment, and tax revenues to reduce reliance on primary commodities. These reforms were highly successful, resulting in average annual growth rates of 7 percent through the mid-1990s.

Indonesia has a strong relationship with its primary donor, Japan. Around 30 percent of the electricity used in Indonesia comes from the power plants developed or enhanced with Japan's ODA, 30 percent of dam capacity was developed with Japan's ODA, and a quarter of the rice that Indonesian people eat every day comes from paddy lands developed with Japan's ODA.

Other donors were also important but in different areas. There is evidence of a successful division of labor. The United States focused its aid mainly on education, governance, and health, while the Asian Development Bank (ADB) extended loans for infrastructure projects. The Indonesian government has taken ownership of its aid and actively coordinates its development partners. In 2009 the Jakarta Commitment was signed by the government and twenty-two donors as a local version of the Paris Declaration.

One striking feature of Indonesia's experience is the long-term engagement exhibited in some programs. For example, the Brantas River Basin development project in East Java was set up to manage a watershed of forty rivers. It was created in 1961 and continues to this day; the Japanese government has been providing assistance to the project continuously for fifty years. Every decade the plan is reviewed to see if goals are being met and updated. The gradual institutional evolution of this project, in the relationships between central and provincial authorities and other stakeholders, is at the core of the efficient water resource management seen today throughout Indonesia.

The long-term horizon taken to resolve a major development issue like water resource management encouraged supporting institutions to be developed along with the infrastructure of dams and irrigation canals. Local capacity was built; 7,000 engineers and technicians were trained through the Brantas project, for example, many of whom have gone on to work in other projects across Indonesia. Their skills were honed through a series of joint works with foreign experts on river basin development. This project showcases the synergies between hard aid (development of the actual dam) and soft aid (capacity development) and the extent of development externalities that can accompany successful projects when they operate at scale. At the same time, the Brantas project operated with strict budget constraints; social obligations were funded out of project revenues, not additional grants. Impacts, not resources, were scaled up.

As much as money, new development partners bring valuable know-how and technology to their development cooperation. They are valued by recipients for their practical experiences in overcoming development challenges and in implementing successful strategies in an environment that is close to that faced by today's developing countries. Many of the new donors present a challenge to the norms and standards of development aid. Their guiding principles are Southern solidarity, mutual benefit, and cooperation. Many are simultaneously recipients and providers of development funds. Some even reject the term *aid* as not fitting their concept of mutual benefit and cooperation. In this view, the blending of aid with other instruments to achieve economic, commercial, and political benefits for both development partners is simply how mutually beneficial cooperation functions. It is a different approach from that of traditional aid donors, which demand conditionality in return for assistance.

New development partners do not fit within the frame of the existing aid architecture. Some of the Paris concepts, such as untying of aid and provision of resources through programmatic means, go against the perceived advantages of new development partners, namely the provision of their own development experiences in a speedy way with emphasis on the how-to aspects of implementing development projects and programs. The Paris emphasis on harmonization is also seen as diminishing the new development partners' contribution, since harmonization limits the scope for alternative approaches and is dominated by larger, more powerful donors. There are no incentives for new development partners to participate in such efforts.

There is some common ground. All development partners agree on the principle of country ownership, although there may be differences in how this is interpreted. All development partners have also agreed on the Millennium Development Goals as a valuable framework for establishing country development objectives. The issue is with implementation.

Park proposes an elegant solution, based on the long-standing international principle of common but differential responsibility. Applying this solution to development assistance, he suggests that development partners be tiered into three groupings: DAC donors that have subscribed to the Paris principles but that have still to implement many of the aid effectiveness targets; non-DAC OECD or EU countries that are committed to the shared values of the OECD and hence are prepared to take the Paris principles as a reference guide; and other countries that are both recipients and providers of aid and that would abide by a more flexible, but defined, set of principles.

In Park's view the missing element in the aid architecture is any effort to develop such a tiered approach. The current dialogue tries to persuade new development partners to join the club of traditional aid donors. But there are few incentives for this, nor can the exchange of views reduce the inherent tensions of different approaches. Instead, he advocates that the Busan HLF4 be a platform for new development partners to base their own standards and responsibilities for aid effectiveness that will maximize their potential development contribution.

## Private Development Aid

Sam Worthington and Tony Pipa (chapter 3) discuss international aid that flows from private philanthropic sources in developed to developing countries.[15] This private development assistance (PDA) includes international NGOs, foundations, individual philanthropists, corporations, universities, diaspora groups, and religious congregations and networks. The key distinction of this type of private funding is that it is philanthropic in origin, as opposed to direct foreign investment or remittances, which may also have important development impact but have quite different motivations.

The scale of PDA is significant. It is estimated that private philanthropic aid from fourteen developed countries totaled $52.6 billion in 2008. Extrapolating this to all developed countries and making adjustments for underreporting, the actual figure for PDA could be in the range of $65 billion to $75[16] billion. Although many individuals contribute to PDA, it is increasingly organized, project-oriented, and consistent with international norms on delivery. PDA can no longer be caricatured as small-scale, humanitarian assistance. In a 2006 survey of InterAction's members, 73 percent of respondents identified long-term sustainable development as a primary program area.[17] The largest global INGO, World Vision International, counts 46,000 staff, manages a $2.5 billion global budget, and is larger than several official DAC donors.

International NGOs are both local and global. They regularly establish a long-term presence in poor communities, generating community trust and the expertise necessary to be effective. A 2008 five-country analysis of a hundred INGOs and local civil society organizations found that 90 percent of INGOs had been working in country for at least five years, 77 percent for more than ten years.[18] Between 90 and 99 percent of INGOs' in-country staff are local citizens.[19] Globally, networks of NGOs form a conduit for sharing development knowledge and innovations based on an increasingly extensive body of evidence. Many INGOs have entire divisions dedicated to evaluation; the 2008 survey found that 92 percent of

15. While this chapter focuses on flows from developed to developing countries, it is important to note that local NGOs and civil society organizations are beginning to raise sums from individual donors in developing countries. Many local NGOs also get significant amounts of in-kind assistance from citizens of developing countries.

16. Hudson Institute (2010).

17. InterAction (2009).

18. Long (2008).

19. In meetings with U.S. officials in 2009, InterAction members said that their staff in Afghanistan numbered 11,000, with 98 percent being local hires.

the INGOs had measurement and evaluation systems. The foundation sector is in the midst of a metrics revolution, pursuing new and better methodologies for impact assessment.[20] Unfortunately, much of this is unpublished, so the aggregate contribution of PDA to development results cannot yet be measured.

PDA is complementary to ODA, although because they have different approaches and areas of focus they are sometimes opposed to each other. PDA strives to be innovative, people-centered, long term, and grounded in local adaptation.[21] It works with communities and local civil society in the delivery of public services. In contrast, ODA grows out of, and is influenced by, the strategic political considerations of donor countries.[22] Its primary point of entry is at the national level, supporting national governments and plans, state capacity, physical infrastructure and social programs.

Taken together, PDA and ODA offer a more robust definition of "country ownership" than that suggested by the Paris Declaration. Worthington and Pipa call this taking a whole-of-society approach. They call for a greater voice for local civil society in the articulation and assessment of development programs and a formal role for NGO representatives at DAC ministerial meetings. In return, the organized PDA sector would take responsibility for developing norms of behavior and transparency to permit a more constructive dialogue with ODA agencies and recipient governments. In many ways, this proposal is similar in spirit to that of Park: recognize and seek to maximize the development contribution of new players while encouraging them to organize themselves in an agenda-setting process that provides a "grand bargain" of inviting their participation in return for specific responsibilities.

### Private Corporations

The private sector has long been seen as the key to sustained growth and development, but private corporations have traditionally been viewed as motivated solely by profit, so traditionally the relationship between the private sector and aid has been largely passive. The logic was that if aid could improve the enabling environment for business, the private sector would produce the investment and jobs that would create economic growth and alleviate poverty. Because private sector resources are so large, this logic meant that aid could be leveraged many times if properly focused on a private sector development agenda.

Jane Nelson (chapter 4) suggests that focusing on creating an enabling environment for business is essential but not sufficient. She argues that this is a simplistic picture of the private sector's evolving contribution to development. Among

---

20. See, for example, McKinsey and Co. (2010); Tuan (2008); Grantmakers (2009).

21. Many INGOs routinely plan to spend private development assistance as ten-plus-year investments into a particular program area or civil society organization.

22. This case is articulated by Alesina and Dollar (1998).

other approaches, she documents the growing concept of "impact investing" as "actively placing capital in businesses and funds that generate social and/or environmental good and at least return nominal principal to the investor."[23] Nelson cites studies suggesting that impact investments could grow to $500 billion in the next ten years. With this scale, impact investors and the networks that support them are creating effective leadership platforms featuring new development models that blend economic viability and market-based approaches with social and environmental objectives.

The private sector has not always been regarded as a champion of development, and the first priority is to ensure minimum standards that avoid exploitative types of development that have been seen in the past. One way of doing this is through the business leadership coalitions that are being formed at the country level to focus on development and on poverty alleviation. Some of these coalitions are freestanding and some are dedicated units of well-established chambers of commerce. These convene multistakeholder initiatives and mobilize private sector engagement in development at national and global levels. The contributions of the private sector are several: delivering base-of-the-pyramid products and services; building accessible, affordable, and reliable physical and communications infrastructure for remote and low-income groups; leveraging science and technology; building skills; and spreading international norms and standards. The private sector renders these contributions by making core business practices more development friendly (by establishing value chains with low-income producers for example); through corporate philanthropy; and through policy dialogue, advocacy, and institutional development.

Nelson's view is that, while there are many examples of projects in which private and official aid sectors collaborate, these are often small in scale and impact. She advocates an approach in which groups of companies and other stakeholders join forces in collective action to solve development problems.

Nelson singles out two areas for action. First, private corporations can help donor countries take an approach toward development that addresses trade, investment, and commercial ties as well as aid. Second, business leaders in recipient countries can be mobilized to champion strategies and public campaigns for inclusive and green growth. Nelson suggests targeting selected sectors—such as agriculture, forestry, health, water, infrastructure—in national multistakeholder pilots. The private sector in each pilot country would take on agreed roles and responsibilities. The innovative feature of Nelson's idea is that cooperation with the private sector be organized on a sectoral basis rather than on a donor-recipient basis. There are only a few examples of such vertical funds in the current aid architecture; expanding this to include inclusive and green growth would be a worthwhile way of showcasing the development potential of public-private partnerships.

---

23. Monitor Institute (2009).

## Aid Coordination

Ngaire Woods (chapter 5) tells powerful stories about the lack of coordination of aid and the problems caused by the asymmetrical relationship between small developing countries and powerful donors. She distinguishes between coordination and cooperation. The latter refers to joint activities, usually harmonized, to achieve common goals. But Woods suggests that cooperation is a far-off goal (as reflected in the declining share of aid channeled through multilateral agencies, one of the major instruments for cooperation). She suggests that, while cooperation may be desirable, it is unlikely to be pervasive given the rivalries and differences in approach and experiences among development partners.[24]

Woods argues that coordination is a more realistic goal because all parties stand to benefit. Coordination seeks to avoid waste and damage when the actions of any one development partner affect the outcomes of another's activities. As she says, "Coordination is not ambitious; principally it serves to prevent inadvertent damage caused when donors are ignorant of each other's actions." In Woods's view the key ingredient of coordination is information sharing. But how?

Woods describes two levels of coordination: standard setting for all donors at the international level and country-level coordination of international agencies active in any specific country. While she reports on some progress on both fronts, the pace is slow. Woods documents the problems that have emerged with trying to use meetings for coordination: far too many stakeholders (because donors have not yet developed an adequate division of labor); some of them ill informed, with only limited experience of the country; many of them with too little technical expertise and too little institutional memory. The result: limited impact, leading in a vicious cycle to less attention being given to proper planning and to attendance at meetings.

Woods proposes that aid recipients should manage the coordination process but warns that this will not be easy. Quoting the World Bank, she notes that "to date, the move to genuine country-led partnerships that effectively combine ownership and partnership is being made in only a few IDA countries, typically in one or two sectors." She lists various arguments in favor of a country-led approach, including the incentive to coordinate effectively, as citizens reap the benefits in terms of development effectiveness, and the information to make sure that coordinated approaches meet country needs. But she cautions that donor incentives work in the opposite direction and that therefore much stronger political will is required to implement a country-led coordination model. Not only must donors

---

24. The easiest way of cooperating is through multinational institutions. Yet even traditional donors are channeling a smaller share of their resources through multilaterals, showing the practical limits to cooperation in today's world.

provide resources to strengthen the capacity of countries to manage aid by themselves, but they must also make sure that well-meaning donor officials on the
ground give governments enough space to manage by themselves—even if that
means allowing them to make mistakes. Woods concludes that trust is the missing ingredient that needs to be created through high-profile political events such
as the Busan HLF4.

## New Challenges

Chapters 6, 7, and 8 present important new challenges facing development aid.

### Fragile States

Foreign aid to support economic development in fragile states is fraught with contradictions. State building is inherently an indigenous process, and foreigners
must find ways to be part of the solution, not part of the problem. The gap
between need and ability to implement successful development projects is greatest in fragile states. Many fragile states suffer the effects or aftereffects of conflict,
with destroyed infrastructure coexisting with destroyed institutions and service-
delivery mechanisms. The need for justice and security in postconflict environments means that achievement of a durable peace is the overriding objective
rather than economic development per se.

Shinichi Takeuchi, Ryutaro Murotani, and Keiichi Tsunekawa (chapter 6)
divide fragile states into two groups, those in a "capacity trap" and those in a "legitimacy trap." The former cannot deliver basic security and services to the population. The latter cannot satisfy people's expectation of enhancement of social inclusion, economic equality, and political participation. Countries that fail in either
regard risk suffering a reversal into conflict—in fact a country reaching the end of
a civil war has a 43.6 percent chance of returning to conflict within five years.[25]

Takeuchi and colleagues stress two points. First, they caution that the interdependence of traps in fragile states implies that solutions must be broad based and
long term. Quick results should not be expected; sustainability is hard to achieve.
But without significant assistance dealing with a range of development challenges,
the risk of a development collapse is high. Better metrics for measuring state
building are needed. Second, in cases in which the central government has difficulty in capacity building, a bottom-up approach may offer opportunities to construct a legitimate state. When development projects are designed and implemented with well-structured participatory approaches that protect the socially
weak, as in the case of community development councils (CDCs) in Afghanistan,
they generate trust in elected community leaders, providing the foundations for

25. Collier and others (2003).

legitimacy while also delivering priority services for the public who have a positive view of the results.[26]

But there is a warning here as well: because state building must be based on an indigenous political process, the donor community may find it hard to accelerate the pace of change simply by increasing the volume of aid resources. Finding the balance between excessive aid that is wasted and too little aid to make a systemic difference is the heart of the problem. Regional mechanisms can provide insight into the appropriate balance.

### Climate Change

Climate change poses a challenge to development aid on three counts. First, the significant resources needed to fight climate change have the potential to divert money from other forms of development assistance. Kemal Derviş and Sarah Puritz Milsom (chapter 7) point out that large new bilateral funds have sprung up recently, most notably Japan's Hatoyama Initiative, which has pledged $11 billion (of which $7.2 billion is ODA) over three years (2010–12) for mitigation and adaptation efforts. Under the Copenhagen Accord, rich countries promised to provide "fast-start financing" to developing countries for 2010–12 of approximately $30 billion and to try to mobilize $100 billion a year by 2020, almost as much as total ODA today.[27]

It is evident that all climate financing cannot be in the form of ODA, considering the costs to address climate change are unprecedented: the UN Framework Convention on Climate Change (UNFCCC) estimates costs for adaptation alone to be between $40 billion and $170 billion a year.[28] Rather, the scale of climate financing needs requires a hybrid approach, where aid is leveraged with nonconcessional resources as in the Global Environment Facility model.

The second challenge is that climate change adds to development needs, and developing countries worry that climate concerns could slow their growth and poverty reduction trajectories. This is especially true in the large emerging economies—India and China—that depend heavily on coal to power their development. Both adaptation and mitigation activities are costly for development.

Third, climate change requires verification and accountability or, more broadly, strong governance. The mutual accountability processes developed in the aid archi-

---

26. Of the respondents who were aware of CDCs in 2009, 78 percent expressed their satisfaction with the performance of their local CDCs. Furthermore, 81 percent believed that their CDCs are capable of representing their interests before the provincial authorities, while 62 percent believed that they are capable of doing so before the national government. Rennie, Sharma, and Sen (2009, pp. 80–84).

27. As of June 2010 fast-start commitments were about $28 billion, but it is unclear if these are additional to prior development assistance. The question is the credibility of these commitments. This year marks the end point for achievement of the Gleneagles targets of increasing aid to Africa by $25 billion. Only half that target is likely to be achieved.

28. IPCC (2007).

tecture are "soft." They revolve around debate, an exchange of views, inclusive participation of many stakeholders, and sharing of experiences. Accountability in the
aid world is more about relational approaches than about substantialist, regulatory,
or legal processes. In fact, the latter (also termed *conditionality*) have been largely
discredited as a tool of effective development cooperation.

But climate change requires verification. If parties cheat on climate emissions
(and the incentives to cheat are significant because of the trade-off seen between
long-term, sustainable growth and faster, short-term, "dirty" growth), the whole
world suffers. It is imperative that climate funding be combined with a verification strategy. Conversely, the incrementality of climate funding also needs to be
verified, something that is conceptually hard to do given the intrinsic link
between adaptation and poverty reduction and practically hard to do with the
rudimentary state of transparency and "statistical markers" of aid.

Derviş and Puritz Milsom wrestle with these issues, complicated by ethical
overtones. Climate mitigation funding is considered by some as a "compensation," paid to developing countries by rich countries for their past pollution trans-
gressions, and by others as an incentive to participate in the provision of a global
public good for the mutual benefit of the world. Their proposed solution is a two-
track approach. Track one would be global, with efforts to identify the cheapest
way of reducing worldwide carbon emissions by sector and country and to evaluate progress made. This should be kept separate from development assistance.
Track two would be sectoral, seeking limited agreement on specific proposals
rather than a single undertaking. For example, moving toward an agreement on
forest conservation may be more palatable in terms of the impact on economic
development. This track needs to be implemented at the country level through
National Adaptation Programmes of Action (NAPAs) and Nationally Appropriate Mitigation Actions (NAMAs).

Derviş and Puritz Milsom argue forcefully that climate mitigation is not aid
but rather a payment for a global service and should be accounted separately from
development assistance. Help for adaptation, on the other hand, is more like
other development assistance and can be accounted as such.

## Capacity Development

Akio Hosono, Shunichiro Honda, Mine Sato, and Mai Ono (chapter 8) describe
the evolution of thinking on capacity development (CD). Although CD was
highlighted in the Paris Declaration as a key crosscutting theme for development
effectiveness, it has not been easy to construct a consensus on good practices on
the basis of existing experience. At times CD has been conceived of as a means to
facilitate new aid approaches of general budget support and sectorwide programs.
This led to one focus on strengthening of public financial management systems;
use of these systems became part of the Paris Declaration targets.

But this focus of capacity has now been recognized as too narrow. The Accra Agenda for Action highlights the need to broaden CD to actors beyond the national government (local governments, civil society organizations, media, parliaments, and the private sector) and to areas beyond financial management. This trend of broadening the scope of CD is also in line with the most widely cited definition, from the DAC, viewing capacity as a holistic and endogenous process of people, organizations, and society as a whole.

With this broader scope, new analytical frames have been applied to capacity. The key insights are that capacity cannot be viewed as a simple technical gap but rather as an evolutionary process of systemic change. The former requires clear specification of the gap; the latter allows more room for flexibility, learning by doing, and adaptation to a constantly changing external environment. Time and space are needed, and must be consciously created, for mutual knowledge and learning creation.

Based on selected case studies of successful CD, the authors discuss a set of success factors: the enabling environment and context (such as decentralization and autonomy of local institutions); ownership, awareness, and determination as the fundamental drivers of an endogenous CD process (like the demand for better schools in Niger); specific triggers and drivers that give impetus to capacity (like an innovative mechanism to remove bottlenecks hampering local collective action); mutual learning and trust building for cocreation of innovative solutions; scaling up good-practice CD pathways; and the role of external actors in supporting CD.

The conclusion: CD is too important to be left as something to happen spontaneously. External assistance can yield significant results, even in difficult environments, but these must be based on an appropriate analytical understanding and on well-articulated, yet flexible, pathways. Reading between the lines, there is a tension between the slow pace and flexibility needed for successful CD and the increasingly short-term, metric-focused orientation of a results focus for aid.

The Busan HLF4 can help with the formalization, institutionalization, and mainstreaming of CD. There are several global networks on CD, such as the CD Alliance and the Learning Network on CD (LenCD), as well as country-level initiatives and sector-specific initiatives (for example, education). This learning should be supported and extended through further rigorous case studies, development and refinement of CD analytical tools (including national CD strategies, assessments, guidelines, and indicators), and expansion of mutual learning opportunities through dialogue and field-based experimentation.

## New Approaches

The final chapters, 9, 10, and 11, offer new approaches to delivering aid.

## Scaling Up

The past decade has seen a tremendous spurt of innovation in piloting new approaches to development, exemplified by processes like the World Bank's Development Marketplace. This has been accompanied by a renewed emphasis on evaluation in an academically rigorous way through randomized trials and case studies. But the search for effective development interventions has not yet resulted in an institutionalized approach to scaling up to maximize the development impact. That, argues Johannes Linn (chapter 9), is because scaling up is typically an afterthought in development projects. He suggests that evaluating the scaling-up potential in partner countries should be a major focus of attention for aid donors.

Linn defines scaling up as "expanding, replicating, adapting, and sustaining successful policies, programs, or projects in geographic space and over time to reach a greater number of people." Linn separates two common failures in scaling up. A type 1 error is when a successful innovation or activity is not scaled up and a type 2 error is when scaling up is done but is inappropriate or done wrong.[29] The novelty of his argument is that the large development banks (and some countries) often try to go to scale but on the basis of insufficient piloting, testing, and learning as well as on inappropriate phasing, resulting in problems with effective operation.

Like capacity development, scaling up can be formalized in analytical frameworks that identify key drivers, spaces, pathways, and intermediate indicators. But Linn notes that few agencies have undertaken systematic scaling-up reviews to assess how their internal incentives and procedures facilitate or hinder scaling up, although some recognize the need to scale up to translate experiences and lessons into broader policy and institutional change.[30] Sometimes termed the micro-macro linkages, scaling-up pathways have received little attention in the follow-up to small pilots.

Scaling up is easier when outcomes are narrowly measured and projects are simple. That is the experience with vertical funds. But what is a strength to the program can be a challenge in other areas. Vertical fund evaluations comment on the substitution of resources from other priority areas (and complications with ensuring long-term fiscal sustainability), on the limited attention to capacity

29. Even successful projects may not be appropriate for scaling up. Some projects are "gold-plated" to ensure their success, but the cost is so high that scaling up becomes infeasible or would entail too high an opportunity cost in terms of forgone development in other areas. One World Bank evaluation summarizes the problem as follows: "By and large, what is being scaled up has not been locally evaluated." Ainsworth, Vaillancourt, and Gaubatze (2005, p. 62).

30. The International Fund for Agricultural Development is the only identified agency to have conducted such a review.

development and to broader policy formulation and implementation, and on the difficulties in partnering with others once the model to be scaled up is determined.

Linn argues that the scaling-up agenda cannot move forward unless there is greater political support. If development partners would agree to introduce the objectives of scaling up explicitly into their mission statements and operational policies, as well as into evaluations, then there is a better chance that the range of development pilots now being undertaken can be leveraged into sustainable development progress.

### Transparency

At Accra transparency and accountability were emphasized as essential elements for development results. The International Aid Transparency Initiative (IATI) was launched to provide improved information on what donors were doing. But Homi Kharas (chapter 10) points out that the consensus on the importance of transparency has not translated into an urgency for action. Despite the new ecosystem of aid players, transparency is restricted to a small group of traditional donors and has largely bypassed new development partners or PDA. Kharas warns that the development community is losing the war in communicating a compelling story of successful aid interventions and that lack of transparency, especially at the partner country level, is an obstacle to better development impact.

Transparency is a vital tool for mutual accountability. It is most useful when rule enforcement is difficult, as is the case between development partners. In such cases, information is not provided to implement traditional command-and-control rules (the conditionality approach) but to allow a variety of accountability structures, like parliamentary and civil society oversight, to develop norms and standards that result in improved outcomes.

Kharas emphasizes the importance of building up the demand for information. Too often transparency has been approached from the supply side, with agencies supplying information that is never used or databases being established without a clear understanding of what is required. Overreporting is costly and has led in many cases to reporting fatigue. Nevertheless, significant information gaps still exist, because the current process of providing data is not demand driven.

At the global level, too few donors provide adequate information. The IATI is a useful start, but only half of the aid provided by DAC donors is covered by IATI signatories, and only the Hewlett Foundation subscribes to the IATI among PDA and new development donors. Coverage is therefore around one-third of total ODA. A critical objective is to improve this, either through more signatories to IATI or through donors developing their own similar functionality. Aid data at the global level need to be understood as a public good. All donors would benefit in terms of better strategies if they properly understood the three Ws of transparency: Who is doing what where.

But it is at the local level where gaps are most acute and the benefits likely to be largest. There are now several aid databases at the recipient country level, but data quality is poor and access often limited. Donors have little incentive to provide information and occasionally are unable or unwilling to respond to country requests. Resource predictability, links with budgets, prioritization to minimize gaps between resources and needs, and better analysis of development impact through beneficiary assessments are among the benefits to be had from greater local transparency of aid.

Kharas emphasizes the opportunity provided by new IT tools and systems. Open-source data exchanges can allow local databases to be seamlessly linked to global databases and can permit aggregation of unique agency databases, without the need for a single, comprehensive database, which is viewed as impractical. Geo-referencing can overlay aid resources with survey data showing development needs. Mobile telephony can provide real-time beneficiary feedback in a way that yields extraordinary development impact improvements in some controlled experiments and gives a voice to those demanding better information.

Many of these tools are already being piloted by official and private donors alike, but there is no systematic process for constructing an information spine to support development. Kharas suggests that the benefits of such an effort would be considerable, citing estimates of the gains from transparency that are upward of $10 billion annually, compared to one-off costs of only tens of millions of dollars.

## South-South Knowledge Exchange

South-South cooperation (SSC) was introduced as a global topic involving debate among developed and developing countries during the Accra HLF. Hyunjoo Rhee (chapter 11) defines it as developing countries working together to foster sustainable development and growth. She also relates it to triangular cooperation: OECD-DAC donors or multilateral institutions providing development assistance to Southern governments with the aim of assisting other developing countries.

Rhee shows that significant benefits can be gained from SSC, often related to broader programs of regional integration and to knowledge sharing and advice based on practical experiences with implementing projects or resolving development issues. The regional dimension is critical to maximizing the development impact because it permits nonaid instruments to be used. Rhee gives the example of the Greater Mekong subregion, where transport corridors have been built to connect countries in Southeast Asia. The impact has been raised by knowledge sharing on the soft infrastructure of customs procedures, trade facilitation, visa processing, cross-border trucking agreements, and the like, subjects that are inherently South-South in nature simply because of the geography of the region.

Rhee emphasizes appropriate knowledge exchanges through SSC. Recipient needs may be better understood by other Southern countries that have experienced similar situations. Language and cultural familiarity make knowledge transfers more effective. Costs are lower, so "value for money" is perceived as higher. But against this, SSC results in greater donor fragmentation and is often a top-down process driven by political considerations rather than development needs. There is limited monitoring and evaluation, although informal feedback appears positive.

The most significant constraint is the lack of information about the potential for SSC. Recipients are not aware of experiences that others have been through, and development partners may not have extensive cooperation agreements with all countries. There is no process for matching supply and demand. Rhee proposes formalizing SSC at the Busan HLF4, starting with universally agreed definitions. She proposes using regional organizations to match supply and demand.

There already exist a number of global platforms for South-South exchange, including the World Bank Institute, the UNDP, and sector funds.[31] Rhee argues that we should build on these and on her proposed new regional platforms, linking them into a global network for South-South cooperation, with four pillars: an information and networking pillar, a technical pillar for matching supply and demand, a financial pillar to match resources and needs, and an advisory pillar to help formulate better SSC projects and evaluate the experiences.

## Next Steps for Busan: An Actionable Agenda

Aid effectiveness may be considered a narrow topic, but there are few issues in the world today where there is a near consensus on goals (sustainable growth plus the MDGs, broadly defined, plus global public goods) shared between multinational corporations, civil society, and rich and poor country governments. The consensus on goals among diverse players in the new aid ecosystem is the greatest strength of the global aid architecture.

The chapters in this volume focus on game changers that could significantly improve aid and development effectiveness. Each chapter considers case studies in order to make practical recommendations for improving aid effectiveness. Taken together, the recommendations would make a material difference in the lives of millions of people. Table 1-3 illustrates the main elements of the proposed Paris++ agenda for Busan. It suggests the shape of an effective division of labor between aid actors, shown in the columns, along with how these actors could be organized in networks to coordinate their activities. The table also suggests, in each row, how each actor might take a differentiated response to key issues. Taken together with suggestions for better ways to implement new approaches in terms of transparency and scale, the result should be a significant improvement in aid effectiveness.

31. The Alliance for Financial Inclusion, for example, funded by the Bill and Melinda Gates Foundation and GTZ, operates a program to share South experiences with microfinance.

Table 1-3. *Paris ++ Agenda for Busan*

| Issue | DAC donors | New development partners | New players | | |
|---|---|---|---|---|---|
| | | | Private aid | Corporations | Organizing networks |
| *Core development activities* | Meet Paris Declaration targets | Provide low-cost infrastructure | Support social development | Improve investment climate | Country-based, country-led |
| *New challenges* | | | | | |
| Fragile states | Focus on capacity and legitimacy | Focus on capacity and legitimacy | Protection of vulnerable populations | Implement OECD/ UN guidelines | Country-based, donor-assisted |
| Capacity development | Holistic approach | Organize South-South knowledge exchange | Build local civil society capabilities | Skills training supply chains | Global, regional, and national platforms |
| Climate change | Separate mitigation from aid; support NAPA and NAMA | Separate mitigation from aid; support NAPA and NAMA | Advocacy; community resilience | Suppport Green Growth Institute; new funds and technologies | Global and sectoral organization; national plans |
| *New approaches* | | | | | |
| Transparency | Provide up-to-date complete data linked to budgets | Meet minimum agreed data standards | Publish aid volumes and evaluation lessons | Endorse transparency standards | Establish standards and databases, globally and nationally |
| Results at scale | Include scaling up in mission statements | Provide hybrid financing partnered to investments | Mobilize Southern civil society | Support base of pyramid and inclusive business modes | MDGs (UN-led), growth (G20-led), climate change (UNFCCC-led) |

But in implementing this agenda, the chapters in this volume also contain notes of caution. Aid can only be a catalyst, not a driver of development. Aid can work, and has achieved notable successes in even the most disadvantageous country settings. But it is not a panacea. In particular, there are six warnings that recur:

—Do not expect fast results. In many places, the impact of aid is felt in the long-term and results are not achieved in a linear fashion. Patience, along with sequenced interventions, is needed. Long-term interventions must be the norm. More resources cannot always accelerate the pace of change; indeed, sometimes too much external funding can inadvertently damage weak domestic institutions.

—Successful pilot projects are not enough of a game changer. Aid must change development processes, whether through capacity building, transparency, or scaling up.

—Country ownership cannot be equated with government ownership. Broader concepts of "whole of society" are needed, as well as judgments on responsible governments, and these inevitably involve political calculations. Aid cannot be treated as an apolitical activity.

—Harmonization has its limits: the diversity of challenges and development partners and approaches should be celebrated, not excoriated.

—Verification of development results, especially in climate change, will inevitably return. This should not be interpreted as new conditionality but as part of a broader process of dialogue toward shared development objectives.

—Aid, as a concept, is becoming blurred, and hybrid financing systems are being developed. The aid architecture must link with other resources for development.

*Ten Actionable Game-Changer Proposals for Seoul*

The Busan HLF4 can be a significant milestone in aid effectiveness. As a dialogue forum, it can bring together a number of new players on an equal footing to debate development issues. That would already represent a break from the past. But it would be disappointing if the Busan HLF4 concluded without actions. The chapters in this volume put forward concrete proposals to help focus international negotiations and to promote internal thinking within development agencies. The proposals need to be debated and tested, consensus needs to be built, and implementation issues considered. They must be costed and subjected to value-for-money analysis. The proposals are as follows:

1. Establish a three-tiered approach to aid effectiveness principles with minimum standards (including on ownership/alignment, capacity development, information sharing, and an ODA-GNI target) to be developed by new development partners.

2. Add Northern and Southern civil society representation to the OECD/DAC ministerial from groups committed to establishing and implementing PDA norms and responsibilities.

3. Add private sector representation to the OECD/DAC ministerial from business groups that are partnering with donors and governments to drive inclusive

and sustainable growth. Select pilot countries and sectors to implement and evaluate such collaborative platforms.

4. Promote aid coordination led by aid recipient governments.

5. Provide broad-based, long-term support to fragile states, focusing on the formation of a legitimate state. Regional approaches could be promising.

6. Further mainstream the capacity development perspective in policies of partner countries, donor organizations, and other new development actors and promote it through flexible, long-term, and sequenced approaches that specify capacity "for what."

7. Link aid and climate change financing in a "resources for development" framework. Develop a two-track approach to climate change financing: a global approach to minimize the cost of carbon reduction by selection of least-cost country and sector interventions; and a narrow approach to sector-specific agreements, starting with forest conservation and country-based adaptation and mitigation plans.

8. Encourage aid agencies to introduce scaling up into mission statements, operational guidelines, internal incentives, and evaluations.

9. Develop regional approaches to South-South cooperation that can then be linked into a global network for South-South cooperation, with two pillars: a technical pillar to match supply and demand and a financial pillar to match resources with needs.

10. Commit all aid providers to promote transparency, development evaluation, and beneficiary feedback at the recipient country level by systematic use of new IT tools and open, web-based provision of information.

Appendix Table 1-1. *Role of Aid in Korea's Development*

| Period | Purpose and needs | Form and modalities | Sector and composition[a] | Reliance on aid | Major donors[b] |
|---|---|---|---|---|---|
| 1942–52 Korean War | Short-run relief | Grants (100%), relief goods | Education, land reform, consumer goods | Only foreign savings[c] | U.S. |
| 1953–61 Rhee | Defense, stability, rehabilitation | Grants (98.5%), commodities, technical cooperation | Agriculture, nonproject aid, military aid, consumer and intermediary goods | Heavily dependent on aid[d] | U.S., UN |
| 1962–75 Park | Transition, long-term growth | Concessional loans (70%), technical cooperation, volunteers[e] | Social-overhead capital, import-substituting and export-oriented large industries, project aid, intermediary and capital goods | Diminution of the absolute and relative importance of aid[f] | U.S., Japan |
| 1976–96 Chun, Roh T. W. | Balance between stability and growth | Nonconcessional financing | Sector loans | Removal from the IDA lending list | Japan, Germany, international financial institutions |
| 1997–2000 Kim Y. S. | Financial crisis | IMF bailout packages | Structural adjustment program | Graduation from ODA | IMF, IBRD |

Source: OECD statistics; Chung (2007); KDI (1991); Mason and others (1980).

a. Food, beverages, and manufactured items are classified as consumer goods; crude materials, fuels, and chemicals are intermediate goods or raw materials; and machinery and transport equipment are classified as capital goods. The majority (77 percent) of project aid was allocated to public overhead capital reconstruction and modern industrial sectors such as manufacturing, mining, transportation, and communication. Non-project aid consists of surplus agricultural commodities provided under Public Law 480 and development loans that were used to purchase agricultural commodities.

b. From 1953 to 1961, 83 percent of all assistance and 99 percent of bilateral aid came from the United States. During the period 1962–75, the share of U.S. assistance was reduced to 61 percent, while Japan became the second-largest donor, accounting for 29 percent of total aid. During 1976–90 Japan provided 63 percent of total aid. Significant increases in aid were also recorded by Germany over this period.

c. The average annual per capita aid for 1945–53 was $5.50 (10 percent of per capita income). Total aid over this period was $853 million, averaging $105 million a year.

d. Korea relied heavily on aid for day-to-day needs, defense, and reconstruction. Aid as a share of GDP averaged 14 percent, making up almost 100 percent of foreign savings and 72 percent of imports. More than half of tax revenue (54.1 percent) in 1957 came from a counterpart fund derived from the sales of foreign aid supply.

e. The Peace Corps started to serve in Korea in 1966 to promote social reform, empowerment, and local capacity building.

f. Overall assistance declined over this period, after peaking in 1957 at $383 million. By 1962 it had fallen to $232.3 million. Average annual economic aid during 1962–67 was $155 million, or $3.60 per capita. In the 1970s the Korean government maintained cordial relationships with the IFIs but did not count on them for substantial financing, even during the of 1973 oil crisis. Given growth rates of 10 percent, the long delays generally experienced in approving and implementing foreign assistance projects were seen as more of a drag than a help to Korea's development.

Appendix Figure 1-1. *Flow Chart, Office of the Economic Coordinator*

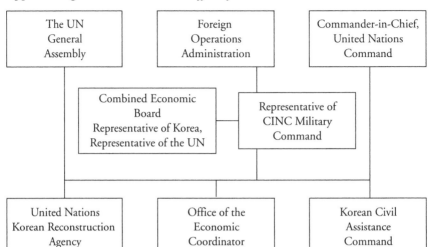

## References

Ainsworth, Martha, Denise Vaillancourt, and Judith Hahn Gaubatz. 2005. *Committing to Results: Improving the Effectiveness of HIV/AIDS Assistance.* Washington: World Bank.

Alesina, Alberto, and David Dollar. 1998. "Who Gives Foreign Aid to Whom and Why?" Working Paper 6612. Cambridge, Mass.: National Bureau of Economic Research (June).

CBO (Congressional Budget Office). 1997. "The Role of Foreign Aid in Development: South Korea and the Philippines." September (www.cbo.gov/doc.cfm?index=4306&type=0).

Chandy, Laurence, and Geoffrey Gertz. 2011. "Poverty in Numbers: The Changing State of Global Poverty from 2005 to 2015." Brookings.

Chung, Young-Iob. 2007. *South Korea in the Fast Lane: Economic Development and Capital Formation.* Oxford University Press.

Collier, Paul, and others. 2003. *Breaking the Conflict Trap: Civil War and Development Policy.* Oxford University Press.

Hudson Institute. 2010. *Index of Global Philanthropy and Remittances: 2010.* Santa Barbara, Calif.

InterAction. 2009. "The Other Partner: NGOs and Private Sector Funding for International Development and Relief." Washington.

IPCC. 2007. *Climate Change 2007: Synthesis Report.* (Contribution of Working Groups I, II, and III to the Fourth Assessment Report of the Intergovernmental Panel on Climate Change.)

KDI (Korea Development Institute). 1991. *Forty Years of Korean Finance.* Vol. 4.

KEXIM (Korea Export and Import Bank). 2008. "International ODA Trend."

Lee, Heonjin. 2009. Research Paper P-3, "Economic Aid Policies of the United States for the Republic of Korea 1948-1960." Seoul: Hye An.

Long, Carolyn. 2008. "Foreign Assistance Reform Monitoring Initiative: Final Report." Inter-Action.

Mason, E. S., and others. 1980. *The Economic and Social Modernization of the Republic of Korea.* Harvard University Press.

McKinsey and Co. 2010. "Learning for Social Impact: What Foundations Can Do." April.

Monitor Institute. 2009. "Investing for Social and Environmental Impact: A Design for Catalyzing an Emerging Industry."

OECD. 2008. *Survey on Monitoring the Paris Declaration: Making Aid More Effective by 2010* (www.oecd.org/dataoecd/55/34/42056862.pdf).

OECD/DAC (Organization of Economic Cooperation and Development, Development Assistance Committee). 2010. "Getting Closer to the Core" (www.oecd.org/dataoecd/32/51/45564 447.pdf).

———. 2006. *The Challenge of Capacity Development: Working toward Good Practice.* Paris.

———. Various years. "Aggregate Aid Statistics" (www.oecd.org/dataoecd/50/17/5037 721.htm).

Rand, John, and Finn Tarp. 2010. Working Paper W. "Firm-Level Corruption in Vietnam." World Institute for Development Economic Research.

Rennie, Ruth, Sudhindra Sharma, and Pawan Sen. 2009. "Afghanistan in 2009: A Survey of the Afghan People." Asia Foundation (www.unodc.org/documents/afghanistan).

Rogerson, Andrew. 2010. "2010 DAC Report on Multilateral Aid" (www.oecd.org/dataoecd/23/17/45828572.pdf).

Severino, Jean-Michel, and Olivier Ray. 2009. "The End of ODA: Death and Rebirth of a Global Public Policy." Working Paper 167. Center for Global Development, March.

World Bank (Resource Mobilization Department). 2008. "Aid Architecture: An Overview of the Main Trends in Official Development Assistance Flows."

———. Various years. *World Bank Indicators.*

# 2

## New Development Partners and a Global Development Partnership

KANG-HO PARK

Over the last few years, a number of new economic powers have become important players in the global aid system. Because of their growing economies and their increasing influence as regional and global players, they have gained much attention worldwide. Significantly, the volume of official development assistance (ODA) from these powers is rising. Some are more important players in aid today than smaller traditional donors. China, India, Saudi Arabia, Republic of Korea, Turkey, Brazil, and Venezuela, among others, have been increasing their outward flows of aid at a remarkable rate. While the OECD Development Assistance Committee (DAC) remains the core of the global aid system, its monopoly over world ODA is eroding with the rise of the so-called new development partners. These partners now have growing influence on issues affecting global development. This chapter examines the rise of these partners and their impact on the aid architecture and asks how a global development partnership can be forged to improve effectiveness across the newly expanded donor community. It concludes with several important recommendations for the Fourth High-Level Forum on Aid Effectiveness.

The author would like to thank Laurence Chandy of the Brookings Institution for his suggested changes to a draft of this chapter. This chapter is the author's own view and does not represent the position of the Korean government.

## The Rise of New Development Partners

The composition of global aid is changing, with many new players becoming active. Global philanthropies, international NGOs, and private corporations are maturing into major private aid players. Emerging, or reemerging, donors (described in this volume as "new development partners") have become significant sources of finance for many poor countries. Traditional donors that form the OECD/DAC can no longer claim to speak for the world's donor community.

In 2008 Saudi Arabia reported ODA outflows of $5.6 billion, making it a larger contributor of aid than fifteen of the twenty-three DAC members (table 2-1). In the same year, China provided more ODA ($3.8 billion) than eleven DAC members, and Korea and Turkey each gave more ODA than four DAC members. Together, these four new development partners contributed over $11 billion in aid.

Net ODA disbursements from new development partners increased from $1 billion to $14.5 billion between 1995 and 2008, moving from 1.7 percent of global aid flows to 12 percent over the same period (figure 2-1). Early evidence indicates that the global financial crisis has had no discernible effect on this trend. Underlying this trend is the rapid economic and political maturation of emerging economies. As these economies grow, so will their flows of trade, aid, and investment with the rest of the developing world. According to one estimate, total South-South cooperation alone could surpass $15 billion this year.[1] Based on existing global growth projections, a conservative estimate is that new development partners will provide about 20 percent of the world's ODA by 2015.[2]

New development partners bring different types of financing and skills to the development community (table 2-2). Their contributions are typically well managed and relevant and draw on their own development experience. The experience of successful late developers is especially relevant because the challenges faced by developing countries are more likely to mirror that of recently emerging countries than those of countries that developed a century or more ago.[3] New development partners have valuable know-how and technology that suit their partner countries. Responsiveness and speed are seen as signs of their strength. The development of new technological capacities in new development partners has created the potential for further cooperation. Many new development partners prefer not to be seen as donors and consider their development assistance to be a form of economic and technical cooperation, mutually benefiting both donor and recipient countries.

1. OECD (2010b, p. 136).
2. Based on global growth projections from the Wolfensohn Center for Development at Brookings, if all non-DAC G20 donors commit 0.15 percent of GDP to ODA in 2015, this would represent $26 billion in aid.
3. UNDP (2009, p. 3).

Table 2-1. *ODA Disbursement, Twenty-Five New Development Partners, 2005, 2007, 2008*[a]

$ million

| Development partners | 2005 | 2007 | 2008 |
|---|---|---|---|
| *OECD members* | | | |
| Korea[b] | 752 | 699 | 802 |
| Turkey | 601 | 602 | 780 |
| Poland | 205 | 363 | 372 |
| Czech Rep. | 135 | 179 | 249 |
| Hungary | 100 | 103 | 107 |
| Slovak Rep. | 56 | 67 | 92 |
| Iceland | 27 | 48 | 48 |
| Mexico | n.a. | n.a. | n.a. |
| *New EU members* | | | |
| Estonia | n.a. | 16 | 22 |
| Latvia | n.a. | 16 | 22 |
| Slovenia | n.a. | 54 | 68 |
| Lithuania | n.a. | 48 | 48 |
| Romania | n.a. | n.a. | 123 |
| Arab countries | | | |
| Saudi Arabia | 1,005 | 2,079 | 5,600 |
| Kuwait | 218 | 110 | 283 |
| UAE | 141 | 429 | 88 |
| *Other donors* | | | |
| China | 1,337 | 2,596 | 3,800 |
| India | 1,000 | 1,000 | 1,000 |
| Brazil | n.a. | 437 | n.a. |
| Venezuela | n.a. | n.a. | n.a. |
| Taiwan | 483 | 514 | 435 |
| Israel | 95 | 111 | 138 |
| Russia | n.a. | 210 | 220 |
| South Africa | n.a. | 40 | n.a. |
| Thailand | n.a. | 67 | 178 |
| Liechtenstein | n.a. | 20 | 23 |
| Total | 6,155 | 9,808 | 14,498 |

Source: OECD/ DAC data; Brautigam (2009); Chinese annual statistics; interviews with Chinese officials and Indian officials; author's calculations.

a. Figures do not include debt cancellation.

b. In 2010 Korea joined the OECD/DAC but is considered as a new development partner rather than a traditional donor.

n.a. = Not available.

Figure 2-1. *ODA Disbursements, New Development Partners, 1995–2010*

$ billion

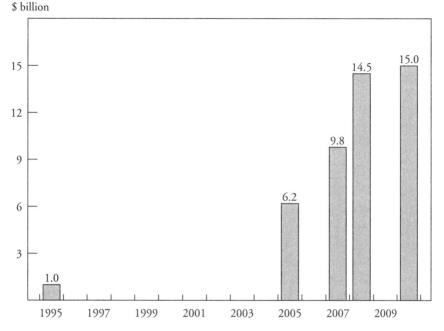

Source: OECD/DAC; author's calculations.

Triangular cooperation presents an opportunity for joining efforts and using the comparative advantages of traditional donors and new development partners to support development in beneficiary countries. New development partners are perceived as credible intermediaries between traditional donors and aid recipients. At the same time, they challenge traditional donors' authority in setting the standards and norms of development aid.[4] A view of new development partners' aid as complementing traditional aid flows is captured in the Buenos Aires Plan of Action, the 2008 Accra Agenda for Action, and the 2010 Bogota statement, "Toward Effective and Inclusive Development Partnerships."

Of all the new development partners, China generates the most interest among traditional donors, the world's media, and aid recipients. China has long been a donor and an aid recipient. China's aid program began in an ad hoc fashion in 1950 with the transfer of grain, medicine, cotton, and other industrial materials to North Korea during the Korean War. From then on, support for socialist countries and Marxist independence movements marked the early years of China's aid.[5] China was the first developing country to establish an aid program.

4. Kragelund (2010).
5. Brautigam (2009, p. 30).

Table 2-2. *Types of New Development Partners' Aid, Nine Donor Countries*

| Donor | Type of aid |
| --- | --- |
| China | Project-based aid, in-kind aid, technical cooperation, debt relief |
| India | Project-based aid (including technical cooperation), with some program-based approaches in Bhutan, Nepal, and Afghanistan; some debt relief |
| Korea | Technical cooperation grants, project/program grants, other grants, bilateral loans |
| Turkey | Project-based and programmable aid, technical cooperation |
| Brazil | Technical cooperation, debt relief, food/emergency assistance |
| Saudi Arabia | Project-based aid (but not technical cooperation) with a small amount of programmable aid, some budget support and debt relief |
| Kuwait | Project-based aid and technical cooperation, some budget and balance-of-payments support, debt relief |
| UAE | Project-based aid and technical cooperation, debt relief, some budget support |
| South Africa | Almost all aid channeled through multilateral systems (NEPAD, African Renaissance Fund), some debt relief |

Source: UN ECOSOC (2008).

In 1964 Premier Zhou Enlai visited ten African countries. In a speech in Ghana, he outlined eight principles that still to this day guide China's foreign aid: equality and mutual benefit; no interference in internal affairs and no conditions; interest-free loans with easy rescheduling; emphasis on self-reliance; income generation, rapid construction, and quick results; top-quality equipment at prices competitive with the market; maximum transfer of technology; and technical assistance experts who live by local standards with no special treatment. China strictly follows these eight principles and fully respects recipient countries' stated priorities and needs. In the spirit of national ownership and the demand-driven principle, China selects and designs its aid programs through consultations, which put host countries in control. China regards the satisfaction of local people as a measure of the quality and effectiveness of its foreign aid programs.[6]

China does not publish complete data on its ODA. The Chinese Ministry of Finance publishes grant aid budgets in its annual finance statistics, reporting a total of $1.9 billion (12.8 billion yuan) to developing countries in 2008. In contrast, information on concessional loans is provided only on a piecemeal and occasional basis, when the government releases, via the press, details of the number of projects, countries, and approximate size of concessional loan programs. In January 2007 China's Commerce Ministry announced ahead of President Hu Jintao's tour of Africa that China would lend African nations $3 billion in preferential credit between 2007 and 2009. Recently, a Chinese official of the Ministry of Commerce said in an international workshop that in 2008 China provided

6. Yu (2008).

almost the same amount of concessional loans as grant aid to developing countries. Therefore, we can estimate that China's total aid budget amounted to around $3.8 billion in 2008.

Chinese aid expenditure tripled over the last decade. After the 2007 announcement of concessional loans to Africa, Prime Minister Wen Jiabao followed this up in November 2009, pledging $10 billion in concessional loans to African countries over the next three years—a more than threefold increase—which provides a sense of the pace with which China's aid budget is growing, particularly aid to Africa. Between 2000 and 2003, 44 percent of Chinese aid went to Africa.[7]

China's aid is disbursed in the form of grants (Ministry of Commerce), interest-free loans (Ministry of Commerce), concessional loans (Exim Bank), scholarships (Ministry of Education), medical technical assistance (Ministry of Health), and multilateral donations (various ministries). The main sectors for China's assistance are agriculture, infrastructure, education, and health. Within these sectors, China focuses on construction projects, technical cooperation, provisions of general goods, human resources development, emergency humanitarian assistance, youth volunteers, and debt relief.

China's aid is mostly tied. One of the required criteria for receiving concessional loans is that "Chinese companies shall be selected as the project contractor. And for procurement projects, equipment supply shall come from a Chinese exporter in principle; priority shall be given to equipment, materials, technology or services from China. In principle, no less than 50 percent of total procurement shall be made in China."[8] This may provide part of the explanation for why China does not publish complete data on its ODA, especially on its concessional loans.

China Exim Bank's reluctance to reveal details of its concessional loans may reflect a desire to protect the commercial confidentiality of Chinese exporters. Or it may be that full disclosure would disqualify Chinese concessional loans from counting as ODA, when assessed against the guideline of the OECD/DAC.[9] The advice given to exporters on applying for concessional loans suggests that the primary purpose of the loans is to provide capital to Chinese exports, which is at odds with the definition of ODA provided by the DAC, which specifies that assistance must have the promotion of economic development and welfare as its main objective.

India has been a provider of development assistance since its independence, but its prominence as a donor has risen more recently as a result of its growing economic and political influence in the global community. In 2007 India announced annual expenditure of around $1 billion for development cooperation, comprising a mixture of grants and loans to foreign governments representing $500 million each. The Indian Technical and Economic Cooperation Division of the Ministry

7. Li Zhaoxing (2003).
8. China Exim Bank (2009).
9. Hubbard (2008, p. 227).

of External Affairs is responsible for the delivery of approximately half of the Indian ODA budget, reflecting an emphasis on technical assistance. Other government agencies responsible for ODA are the Ministry of Finance's Department of Economic Affairs, which delivered around 44 percent of the country's aid in the form of bilateral grants, and the Exim Bank.[10]

In terms of geographical distribution, most assistance is provided to India's neighboring and regional countries, including Nepal, Bhutan, and Afghanistan. During the India-Africa Forum Summit in 2008, India promised to double its existing level of credit to Africa and to allocate $5.4 billion in lines of credit over the following five years. India also announced that the Ministry of External Affairs' aid to Africa would be enhanced with grants in excess of half a billion dollars, with human resources development and capacity building as critical areas of focus. Ever since India began to provide ODA—to Nepal in the 1950s and through the Indian Technical and Economic Cooperation scheme from the mid-1960s—there has been a clear emphasis on unconditional, technical, project-based cooperation. Assistance is consistently framed as a partnership, in the spirit of South-South cooperation.[11]

The Republic of Korea made a full transition from aid recipient to aid donor over the space of a single generation—a result of rapid and sustained economic growth and poverty elimination. Emerging from conditions similar to those faced by poor countries today, Korea's development has been viewed as a successful model for other developing countries to follow. Understanding that sharing its successful development experience with developing countries is the most effective means of assistance, Korea has concentrated its efforts on human resource development through technical cooperation and on economic development, inspired by the Korean growth model. For example, each year Korea hosts 4,000 people from developing countries for training in Korea and sends experts and volunteers into the field to transfer development know-how. Last year, the Korean government and the United Nations Development Program (UNDP) agreed to establish the Seoul Policy Center for Global Development Partnerships, which will focus on transferring Korea's development knowledge to developing countries.

In 2008 Korea spent 56 percent of its gross bilateral aid in Asia, of which two-thirds was focused on East Asia. Korea has recently increased its ODA to Africa, doubling its support to the region through its Initiative for Africa Development. Korea's ODA has been increasing steadily; in 2008 it amounted to $802 million, or 0.09 percent of Korea's GNI. Korea plans to increase this share to 0.25 percent by 2015, the target year for the UN's Millennium Development Goals. Besides increasing its total aid flows, Korea is doubling its efforts to improve its aid quality. Tied aid has long been considered a key test of donors' commitment to effec-

10. OECD (2009b, p. 141).
11. Price (2005).

tive aid and a crucial component of the aid paradigm envisaged by the DAC. Historically, Korea's ODA has been heavily tied. In 2007 only a quarter of Korean aid was untied, well below the average for existing DAC members. Korea has now committed to untying 75 percent of its ODA by 2015.

In 2008 Turkish ODA amounted to $780 million, representing a tenfold increase since 2002 (up from $73 million). Turkey focuses its aid on countries in Central Asia—more than 80 percent of Turkish ODA goes to Asian countries—with high outlays to Afghanistan, Kyrgyz Republic, Azerbaijan, and Pakistan. Turkey is planning to increase its assistance to other regions, however, especially to Africa. The Turkish International Cooperation and Development Agency is the principal body responsible for the administration of Turkish aid, with coordination offices in twenty countries. Most Turkish aid takes the form of projects and technical cooperation. The focal sector of Turkish aid is education, including a large share reserved for scholarships for study in Turkey.

Brazil is an increasingly important actor in development cooperation, most notably in its own neighborhood of Latin America and the Caribbean. It is, however, also engaging beyond the continent; approximately half of its development cooperation programs are implemented in Africa, in particular in Portuguese-speaking countries. The bulk of Brazil's aid takes the form of financial and technical cooperation; it stood at $437 million in 2007, according to DAC data. However, *The Economist* magazine estimates that total Brazilian ODA was almost three times this size in 2008, and this excludes the significant value of public commercial loans issued to Brazilian firms working in poor countries, which approximates $3.3 billion since 2008.[12]

Technical cooperation is coordinated through the Brazilian Agency for Cooperation. Brazil's technical cooperation with other countries is rapidly growing and is one of the priorities of foreign policy under the current government. The main objectives that can be identified for Brazil's aid are to strengthen Brazil's foreign relations and international presence, to open and consolidate markets for Brazilian goods and services, and to consolidate Brazilian science and technology capabilities. Brazil has also specialized in the provision of triangular cooperation, which simultaneously has served to deepen its political and economic ties with other emerging market countries, specifically South Africa and India. Sectorally, there has been a special focus on health, agriculture, and human resource development. Aid to support the development of global energy markets, especially ethanol, has emerged as another area of focus, although actual projects in this area remain minimal to date.[13]

The three oil-rich Gulf States of Saudi Arabia, Kuwait, and the United Arab Emirates are the main Arab givers of ODA. Three standout features of aid from the

12. "Brazil's Foreign Aid Program: Speak Softly and Carry a Blank Cheque," *The Economist*, July 15, 2010.
13. Costa Vaz and Inoue (2007).

three major Arab donors is that it is predominantly bilateral (around 85 percent), it mostly takes the form of loans, and a large share (about 50 percent of national and multilateral Arab aid) is devoted to other Arab countries. The Ministry of Finance in each of the Arab donor countries is the lead institution responsible for aid delivery, but they tend to provide little information publicly as to the details of their aid programs. Arab aid has also been very volatile, due both to the volatility of Arab countries' revenue from their oil and gas exports and to their strategic use of aid to support changeable, short-term, foreign policy goals. Much aid has gone to build and maintain allies in the Arab world and to reward supporters during military conflicts, including the Iran-Iraq War and the Gulf War. Other focuses important to Arab donors include domestic commercial interests and Islamic countries. The latter should be separated from the large flows of nonofficial aid focused on promoting Islam.[14]

## Aid Policies of New Development Partners

The previous section demonstrates that there is considerable variation among new development partners. Nevertheless, one can identify common features that stand in strong contrast to traditional aid giving. These features are connected not only by the objectives driving new development partners but also by the various influences that shape their incentives. Together, these features add up to a different theory of aid, or aid model. Five of these features are explored in this section:
    —Aid is foreign policy driven and mutually beneficial.
    —Aid is tied and not given as general budget support.
    —Aid is channeled bilaterally rather than through the multilateral system.
    —Aid is focused close to home, allowing relevant experiences to apply.
    —Aid is not subject to conditions and there is less emphasis on transparency.

### Foreign Policy–Driven and Mutually Beneficial Aid

New development partners, like traditional donors, are political actors and tend to use their aid strategically. New development partners' aid strategies are shaped by political and economic factors. Aid has been used to strengthen relations with other developing countries in order to gain support for foreign policy objectives, such as the One-China policy, or India's and Brazil's bid to gain a permanent seat on the UN Security Council. According to Chinese official sources, China's new aid commitments in 1990 rose by 68 percent as a direct result of deepening diplomatic battles with Taiwan.[15] Aid has also been directed to particular developing countries that are of special economic interest, usually to gain access to strategic markets and raw materials. As the aid budgets of new development partners have

14. Villanger (2007).
15. Brautigam (2009, p. 67).

grown, the influence of economic strategy in shaping their aid flows has become increasingly evident. For example, in recent years China's and India's various concessional loans from their export-import banks to resource-rich African countries such as Angola, Nigeria, Sudan, Tanzania, and Zambia have been largely driven by energy security objectives and other industrial policy objectives.[16]

The development cooperation policies of many new development partners are based on a more holistic approach than classic ODA policies, in the sense that the provision of development assistance is not strictly separated from countries' trade and investment activities.[17] New development partners have a greater willingness to merge policy instruments in the pursuit of common objectives. In particular, China does not treat ODA separately from other instruments. Trade relationships, export promotion, and development cooperation are all handled by the Ministry of Commerce. The Chinese link business and aid in innovative ways, such as using aid to subsidize Chinese companies' establishment of agro-technical demonstration stations.[18]

A more openly foreign policy–driven approach to aid does not necessarily imply that aid will be managed and delivered in a way that is contrary to recipients' interests. Rather, this approach allows new development partners to convincingly present aid as being of mutual benefit to both parties. Recipients then have the sense of being treated as equal partners and can assess the value of aid based on a simple cost-benefit approach.

## Tied Aid without General Budget Support

One of the implications of a more foreign policy–driven approach to aid is the preference for aid tying. The majority of new development partners tie their aid to the procurement of goods and services from suppliers in the donor country.[19] For instance, development partners' technical assistance usually involves sending its nationals as experts to partner countries, funding partner country students to study at institutions or to participate in training events located in the donor country, and providing emergency shipments of domestically produced goods and national medical experts to recipient countries.

Tied aid is criticized on two grounds. First, it undermines local markets in beneficiary countries. This is undoubtedly true for both traditional donors and new development partners. Second, tied aid is associated with higher unit costs, given that the provision of aid is subject to no or less competition. While this criticism is often leveled at traditional donors, it is argued that the price premium associated with tied aid is less applicable to new development partners, which have low

16. In the 1970s and 1980s traditional donors also gave more aid to important trade partners. See Claessens, Classimon, and Van Campenhout (2009).

17. Chahoud (2008).

18. Brautigam (2009, p. 310).

19. Arab donors are an exception to this trend. Their bilateral aid is by and large untied.

capital and labor costs and shorter deadlines and eschew the cumbersome procedures demanded by traditional donors. Furthermore, in the case of Chinese aid
where Chinese workers often migrate permanently to recipient countries after
completing contracts, there may be added benefits to aid tying associated with
knowledge transfer and developing market chains.

In the same vein, new development partners have also shown relatively little
interest in general budget support, preferring to exert direct control over their aid
dollars. While traditional donors leverage general budget support to deepen
opportunities for policy dialogue and influence over recipients' public expenditure choices, this is not a strategy that new development partners are likely to follow. As latecomers to general budget support, their influence over policy decisions
would almost certainly be diminished. Instead, new development partners have
gone to the other end of the spectrum, focusing on project-based aid, and specializing in turn-key projects that operate entirely independent of recipient governments. This enables new development partners to demonstrate their ability to
deliver, while relieving recipients of undue interference and burden.

### Preference for Bilateral Aid over the Multilateral System

The proportion of assistance devoted to multilateral contributions is, on average,
below that of traditional donors. Multilateral shares presently average 18 percent
among new development partners, compared to 30 percent for the DAC.[20] This
overall trend masks a high degree of variance across new development partners. A
recent report shows that non-DAC EU members provided a higher proportion of
multilateral aid than DAC members in the three years from 2006 to 2008, led by
Latvia, which gave 87 percent of its aid in multilateral contributions.[21] In contrast, all other non-DAC members provide less multilateral aid, including the
large BRIC countries and Saudi Arabia.[22] The humanitarian aid sector is one area
where new development partners are increasing their use of the multilateral system.[23] However, overall new development partners have increased their bilateral
aid at a faster rate than their multilateral giving.

The tendency for new development partners outside the EU to show less
support for the multilateral system is easy to understand given their underrep-
resentation in the governance of multilateral institutions, especially the World
Bank and the IMF (table 2-3). Though the Bretton Woods institutions have
repeatedly stated their commitment to meaningful governance reform, change
has been painfully slow. A major transformation is required if the current aid
architecture is to evolve sufficiently to establish a credible and legitimate gov-

20. Davies (2010, p. 6).
21. OECD (2010a).
22. The BRIC countries are Brazil, Russia, India, and China.
23. GHA Report (2009, p. 48).

ernance mechanism that represents new development partners as well as traditional interests.[24]

## Focus on Neighbors and Application of Relevant Experience

New development partners tend to focus their aid on neighboring regions or subregions, although some, most notably China, have forayed further afield. This close-to-home preference means that new development partners better understand the needs of its recipients, often share language and culture, have opportunities to deepen trade ties, and can deliver aid at lower cost.

These recipients provide new development partners with a setting in which the lessons and know-how from their own development experiences are particularly relevant. Their aid—both in terms of modalities and sectors—is directly shaped by these experiences, which new development partners are keen to impart and from which recipients are keen to learn. New development partners provide almost all of their aid in the form of projects and technical cooperation, since these are the most effective modalities for knowledge transfer. Furthermore, their focus is largely on economic sectors, swimming against the tide of social sector spending that has dominated traditional donor increases over the past decade (figure 2-2). However, the preferences of these new development partners mirror the public expenditure of their own economies as they were developing.

China in particular has supported partner countries' priorities for infrastructure and economic development. Drawing from its own experience in domestic poverty reduction programs, it prefers to focus on developing poor people's productive capacity and places less emphasis on the provision of services and cash transfers.[25]

## No Conditions and Less Transparency

Unlike traditional donors, new development partners do not impose policy conditions on their aid recipients. This reflects their respect for recipient sovereignty and their rejection of what they perceive as an interventionist approach. This makes aid from new development partners more attractive to recipients, especially those unable to easily meet traditional donors' conditions. China imposes a single condition on its aid by insisting that recipients observe the One-China policy. This overt and narrowly drawn foreign policy goal stands in stark contrast to the typical conditions imposed by traditional donors, conditions that concern either shaping the environment in which aid is delivered, to increase its effectiveness, or spreading free market orthodoxy and democratic governance. New development

24. Hammad and Morton (2009).

25. OECD (2009a). However, other new development partners have displayed trends similar to traditional donors in terms of sector prioritization. Turkey and Korea direct more than half of their aid toward social sectors, and Russia's health sector support accounts for half of its bilateral aid (Davies 2010, p. 12).

Table 2-3. *Selected New Partners' Contributions to Multilateral Agencies, 2008*
$ thousand

| Agency | Brazil | China | India | Kuwait | Mexico | Russia | Saudi Arabia | South Africa | UAE |
|---|---|---|---|---|---|---|---|---|---|
| UNDP | 550 | 3,817 | 4,553 | 570 | 0 | 774 | 4,000 | 1,564 | 324 |
| UNICEF | 3,012 | 1,290 | 2,800 | 200 | 0 | 1,000 | 2,500 | 25 | 13,938 |
| UNRWA | 200 | 80 | 20 | 2,500 | 5 | 0 | 40 | 148 | 5,337 |
| WFP | 1,441 | 9,576 | 17,130 | 0 | 50 | 15,000 | 503,753 | 315 | 50 |
| UNHCR | 0 | 652 | 10 | 2,000 | 102 | 2,000 | 112 | 146 | 54 |
| UNFPA | 0 | 900 | 222 | 50 | 0 | 300 | 300 | 23 | ... |
| UNIFEM | 25 | 30 | 20 | 20 | 60 | ... | 100 | ... | 50 |
| IFAD | 2,639 | 5,000 | ... | 2,800 | 1,000 | ... | 3,500 | ... | 650 |
| GFATM | ... | 2,000 | ... | 1,000 | ... | 78,405 | 6,000 | 146 | ... |
| IADB | 10,859 | ... | ... | ... | 6,980 | ... | ... | ... | ... |
| AfDB | ... | 40,613 | ... | 3,384 | ... | ... | ... | 3,633 | ... |
| AsDB | ... | 7,500 | ... | ... | ... | ... | ... | ... | ... |
| World Bank/IDA | 42,051 | ... | ... | 9,650 | 3,449 | 19,515 | 16,666 | 5,513 | ... |
| Total | 60,776 | 71,457 | 24,756 | 22,174 | 11,647 | 116,994 | 536,971 | 11,513 | 20,403 |

Source: OECD (2010a, b).

Figure 2-2. *Traditional Donors, Aid to Economic and Social Sectors, 1980–2006*

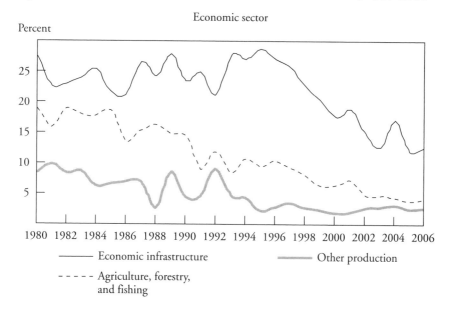

Economic sector

Percent

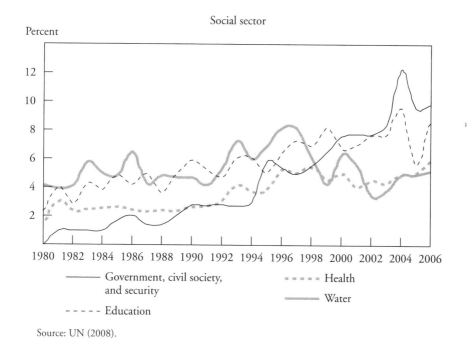

Social sector

Percent

Source: UN (2008).

partners' rejection of aid conditionality extends to performance-based aid, reflecting their long-term perspective, which places emphasis on improving capacity over securing immediate development results.

Many new development partners do not publicize their development assistance, undermining the ability of recipients to manage their aid flows and of the broader donor community to coordinate effectively as well as removing a key instrument for accountability. The exclusion of new development partners from the DAC means their aid does not appear in most aggregated aid databases.[26] This lack of transparency has fueled speculation in Africa that the provision of Chinese loans to governments could reverse the achievements of debt relief from the past decade.

## Aid Effectiveness and New Development Partners

The rise of new development partners has shaken up the existing aid system. The size of their collective resources and their choice of particular aid modalities, sectors, and recipients are reshaping the pattern of global aid flows and forcing traditional donors to take notice. The difference in their resource allocation model is providing recipients with greater choice and increasing their bargaining power while reducing the control once exerted by traditional donors.[27] As relative outsiders to the donor community that socialize together in recipient countries, they do not feel compelled to conform to traditional donor norms, which prompts scrutiny of what purposes these ultimately serve.

By falling outside the purview of the Paris Declaration, new development partners, through no fault of their own, undermine what both that declaration and the Accra Agenda for Action can hope to achieve. While single-donor, incremental steps toward implementing the Paris Declaration should be welcomed, they cannot deliver a coherent, coordinated, and efficient aid system as long as Paris only partially covers today's aid actors.[28]

Nevertheless, there is no evidence that new development partners are any less concerned about the effectiveness of aid than traditional donors. New development partners have been enthusiastic supporters of the Millennium Development Goals since their inception, while a number of traditional donors have taken years to fully embrace this results-focused and aid-centric agenda. Moreover, the principles enshrined in the Paris Declaration, and the motivations that underpin them, resonate with new development partners and the delivery of their aid. However, since new development partners tend to subscribe to a different aid

---

26. The new AidData database is an exception, in which some, though not all, new development partners are included.

27. Kragelund (2010).

28. This would equally apply if all aid actors were signatories to the declaration but implementation were only partial.

Table 2-4. *Implementation of Paris Declaration*

| Paris principles | DAC/traditional donor implementation | New development partner implementation |
|---|---|---|
| Ownership | Use national development strategy (or PRSP) to outline priority areas for donors, based on technical discussions.[a] | Ministers/senior officials articulate specific projects for cooperation through high-level political dialogue. |
| Alignment | Use and strengthen recipient institutions and procedures where feasible; discourage tying of aid. | Deliver turnkey projects in short run; make capacity building the long-term strategy; tying is permissible and widely used. |
| Harmonization | Use common arrangements to minimize burden on recipients; encourage multilateralization of aid. | Minimize burden by avoiding cumbersome bureaucratic processes; use multilateral system where judged to be in own interest. |
| Managing for results | Use recipient-led performance assessment; support performance-based budgeting; promote international best practice. | Focus on delivering aid quickly and at low cost; use own development experiences and how-to knowledge. |
| Mutual accountability | Make aid transparent and hold each other accountable for Paris principles via targets and indicators. | Ensure that aid is mutually beneficial; agree to respect each other's sovereignty and eschew policy conditionality. |

Source: Author.
a. PRSP = Poverty Reduction Strategy Paper.

model from that of traditional donors, their approach to how these principles should be implemented varies accordingly (table 2-4).

Both traditional donors and new development partners recognize the importance of recipients exerting ownership of their own development agenda and of the allocation of foreign aid within their country. Traditional donors attest that such ownership is most effectively manifested through the articulation of detailed strategy documents that link to expenditure frameworks and budgets. This represents a highly rationalist approach, which donors can then engage through technical discussions. By contrast, new development partners look for more direct guidance for the use of their aid dollars, through the identification of specific projects by ministers or other high-ranking officials.

Traditional donors argue that aid should be aligned to recipient institutions and procedures as a way of reinforcing and building up systems and instruments of governance. In the same vein, donors should untie their aid to support the development of local procurement markets. New development partners take a different tack, delivering turnkey projects in the short run to address recipients' immediate needs and to unleash their economic potential, while emphasizing capacity building as a long-term strategy for strengthening recipient institutions and moving toward greater self-reliance. In contrast to traditional donors, new development partners view the tying of aid as legitimate, since their approach is one of development cooperation yielding mutual benefit, as opposed to development aid, which implies one-way benefit.

In recognition of the burden placed on recipients by differentiated donor procedures, traditional donors have supported moves toward greater harmonization of aid, whereby common arrangements are adopted across the aid community or aid channeled through multilateral agencies. By contrast, new development partners see the root of this problem in the enforcement of cumbersome donor processes. They minimize bureaucratic demands on recipient institutions and use the multilateral system only where it is judged to be in their interest.

Both traditional donors and new development partners focus on results, while differing in terms of how they believe results can best be achieved. Traditional donors again stress the value of bureaucratic tools such as (recipient-led) performance assessment frameworks and results-based budgeting, consistent with the rationalist paradigm to which they subscribe, while looking to identify and promote international best practice in aid. New development partners focus more directly on delivering aid quickly and at minimal cost and look to their own development experiences and know-how to support similar transformations in recipient countries.

Traditional donors understand that aid cannot be made effective without recipient cooperation and therefore seek to share responsibility for making aid work better by negotiating joint commitments and targets with beneficiary governments and monitoring indicators for their success. New development partners recognize equally the importance of aligning incentives with recipients but do so by framing aid relationships as being of mutual benefit to both parties. They seek to establish a sense of partnership with recipients by stressing respect for each other's sovereignty and eschewing policy conditionality.

In practice, both traditional donors and new development partners deviate from the Paris principles, regardless of which approach they subscribe to. For traditional donors, this is evidenced by the disappointing performance so far vis-à-vis the Paris targets. However, it is the aspirations of both groups that are of concern here, as these are central to negotiating development cooperation agreements and the defining of future commitments.

The differences between traditional donors and new development partners on how best to operationalize the Paris principles are in some cases significant and cannot be ignored. Those who assume that new development partners will eventually alter their position in line with the thinking of traditional donors may face a long wait. New development partners have little obvious motive to sign on to the Western aid model. Its legitimacy and that of the DAC is undermined in their eyes by the fact that it was initially conceived and driven by traditional donors, with developing countries only brought into the process later. The incomplete achievement of the Paris targets only makes this worse; new development partners have no desire to subscribe to DAC aid arrangements given the evident weaknesses of the current system. For new development partners, the prospect of DAC membership means being latecomers to the process, a position from which they cannot expect to exert much influence over the agenda. These problems of legitimacy, efficacy, and inclusion are similar to those facing the broader aid architecture, including the governance of the Bretton Woods institutions.

This is not to say that no progress has been made at bringing the new development partners into the discussion on aid with traditional donors. The DAC has taken steps to deepen mutual understanding of the evolving priorities of international development cooperation through regular and sustained dialogue and to promote an exchange of good practice among all assistance providers. A policy dialogue meeting cohosted by the Mexican government in September 2009 and the establishment of the Task Team on South-South Cooperation, a Southern-led platform hosted by the DAC Working Party on Aid Effectiveness, are clear evidence of the DAC's willingness to engage other providers of assistance based on a recognition of their specific strengths.[29]

On the more fundamental issue of institutional governance, the United Nations' Economic and Social Council (ECOSOC) launched the Development Cooperation Forum (DCF) in 2007, giving it a broad mandate including the promotion of more effective development cooperation. In 2009 the OECD Working Party on Aid Effectiveness (WP-EFF) was expanded to eighty members, with a substantial representation of developing countries, converting it into a parity platform for North-South negotiation. The establishment of the DCF and the redesign of the WP-EFF are positive moves precisely because they allow traditional donors and developing countries to discuss aid delivery issues on a more equal basis.

For many new development partners, however, the establishment of the DCF and changes to the WP-EFF are unlikely to provide the type of democratization of the aid architecture that they are looking for. Moreover, the changes are unlikely to provide sufficient incentive for new development partners to decide to operate within the norms and conventions of the existing aid architecture and to sign up as donors to agreements on aid effectiveness, such as the Paris Declaration. The Busan High-Level Forum on Aid Effectiveness in 2011 will provide a chance to clarify this picture and may serve as a starting point for different providers of assistance and recipients to cooperate on a stronger foundation.

29. OECD (2010b, p. 15).

## Building a Global Development Partnership: A Common Vision for Development and Variations in Responsibilities

Traditional donors and new development partners have a shared interest in ensuring that aid is effective and that it contributes to the achievement of partner country development objectives, including the MDGs.[30] It is undoubtedly true that there is room for new development partners to improve aid effectiveness, as is the case for traditional donors. While new development partners are still learning about best practices, they should be subject to the same level of scrutiny as traditional donors.[31] It is unlikely that this will occur, however, as long as they do not participate in global aid agreements as recognized providers of aid.

If efforts to establish a truly global agreement on aid, inclusive of new development partners, are to be successful, they should avoid making two false assumptions. The first false assumption is that new development partners can be shoehorned into the Western-dominated institutions and agreements that currently oversee aid flows from traditional donors, without altering the shape of the shoe in the process. Many new development partners adopt a different aid model from traditional donors and therefore cannot be expected to apply the principles set down in Paris and echoed in Accra in the same way as is currently designated by the DAC.

The second false assumption is that the push toward greater aid effectiveness among new development partners should come from traditional donors. There is little reason to believe that new development partners will respond positively to such demands when the current aid architecture is perceived as a product of the West and thus as inherently biased in favor of traditional donors. Besides, new development partners perceive their aid narrowly in terms of a bilateral agreement with recipients, a relationship in which traditional donors play no essential part.

What then is the right approach to establishing a new global agreement in which new development partners participate meaningfully and willingly? Rather than shoehorning new development partners into the existing aid effectiveness agreements, the development community should look to establish a new system of common but differentiated targets, whereby donors are assigned different commitments according to their type.

Donors could be divided into three categories: one, traditional donors who are members of the OECD/DAC; two, those OECD or EU donor countries who have yet to join the DAC; and three, all other new donors. Based on this categorization, category three countries would agree to a less restrictive set of commitments that are consistent with their model of aid. In addition, these countries may be allowed a higher degree of flexibility in the application of targets to encourage

30. Davies (2010).
31. North-South Institute (2008).

their participation and in recognition of the particular circumstances many face as being a donor and recipient of aid at the same time. For category two the Paris principles and targets have not been binding in the past but have nevertheless served as implicit, aspirational targets. Going forward, these donors would be set a similar set of targets to category one, given their participation in existing Western institutions and their willingness to develop their aid more closely on the Western model.[32] As with the existing aid effectiveness agenda, international development institutions would then be charged to ensure the application of the guidelines through well-established procedures such as peer review, regular reporting, and the publication of progress reports.

A downside of this approach is the unavoidable dilution effect that the tiering will bring on the effectiveness of the commitments. However, the global community must ultimately make a choice between no commitments and modified commitments for new donors. We also have to remind ourselves that the concept of common but differential responsibility is well established in other policy dialogues, such as with regard to environmental protection. Furthermore, there is no reason why negotiators should limit themselves to a static concept of the tiering mechanism. Regular and inclusive policy dialogue could result in new developing partners adopting stricter standards over time.

One conspicuous advantage of such an arrangement is that the international donor community will end up with a set of minimum standards for all donors. These standards would come to represent a common vision for development that applies equally to both Western and Eastern aid models, while being accommodative of important differences.

Another important component of establishing a global agreement on aid effectiveness is that the inclusion of new development partners results from a clear expression of recipient demand. This is both the most legitimate and the most effective means of bringing new development partners on board. The effectiveness of this strategy derives from the readiness of new development partners to respond to recipient preferences. In fact, this characteristic on the part of new development partners reinforces the case for decentralizing responsibility for a large component of the aid effectiveness agenda to the country level, where efforts toward greater donor coordination and the establishment of a division of labor among donors are more likely to succeed.

Ultimately, a successful global agreement on aid effectiveness will require a high level of trust between traditional donors and new development partners. That level of trust will be achieved only through a closer and more open dialogue. It is important to acknowledge the differences that new development partners have in terms of their experiences, resources, and level of economic and political development. Exchanging views, rather than giving lectures, on lessons learned

---

32. Kragelund (2008).

and approaches to aid and cooperation could lead to better collaboration within the aid community. By establishing greater trust and understanding in the donor community, not only might a global agreement on aid effectiveness be possible but it could be the beginning of a global development partnership in which aid donors and recipients and other important stakeholders collaborate to accelerate development and the achievement of the MDGs.

## Conclusions and Recommendations

ODA from new development partners and its overall impact on poor countries is rapidly growing. New development partners represent fresh funds and expertise that partner countries appreciate. Their aid catalyzes other flows, such as trade and investment, which may have an even larger impact on the partner countries than aid flows alone.

The rise of new development partners increases the need for new mechanisms that enable donors to share and coordinate information about aid. Traditional donors can continue to invite new development donors to take part in peer reviews of DAC members' aid performance as well as in global forums for development. However, engaging them fully faces much greater hurdles. New development partners are still generally underrepresented in the global decisionmaking architecture, a system whose establishment they were largely excluded from. This exclusion makes them reluctant to stand shoulder to shoulder with traditional donors.[33] To engage new development partners, the aid community must provide the appropriate incentives.

What should be the incentives to engage new development partners? First, it is important for traditional donors to acknowledge the differences that new development partners have in terms of their experiences, resources, and level of economic and political development. Many new development partners do not see themselves strictly as donors and consider their development assistance to be a form of economic and technical cooperation, benefiting both countries. This amounts to a different aid model, one in which the Paris principles still resonate but are implemented in a different way from that envisaged by the DAC. If the global community wishes these new donors to abide by global aid guidelines, we must allow for greater flexibility. In particular, not all new development partners should be measured against the same bar as traditional donors. Instead, some minimum standards should be identified that are appropriate across the donor community.

Second, the pressure for new development partners to commit themselves to greater aid effectiveness should come not from the traditional donor community but from recipient governments. If recipients make clear their interest in the aid

33. Leipziger and O'Boyle (2009, p. 72).

effectiveness agenda and in having donors cooperate with one another, new development partners are likely to heed this request.

Third, a more inclusive process for setting standards needs to be developed, in which the voices of new development partners are heard. This will signal to new development partners that they are not simply acceding to Western standards but that traditionally Western-dominated institutions are evolving to accommodate the rise of new development partners.

Just as traditional donors are serious about making their aid more effective, new development partners also care about the effectiveness of their aid. We need to keep in mind that new development partners' ultimate goals for aid are not so different from those of traditional donors. Efforts should focus on identifying how different donors can benefit from the lessons of others, potentially leading, in the longer run, to a merging of combined best practices replacing current approaches.[34] If the traditional donor community is willing to acknowledge and respect the useful role of new development partners, to allow flexibility to newcomers in the application of new effectiveness guidelines, and to engage new development partners in agenda setting, a global development partnership could be agreed, which could significantly enhance the impact of aid throughout the developing world. The Busan HLF4 might be a turning point in a transition toward more equitable decisionmaking in aid, if these recommendations are followed:

—New development partners should be fully engaged in agenda setting on aid effectiveness.

—Partners should be given flexibility in the application of commitments and targets.

—Common guidelines or minimum standards should be established among all donors. The following could be considered as common guidelines or minimum standards:

*Ownership and alignment:* supporting national ownership should be a key guiding principle shared by all donors; to support ownership, all donors should align their assistance to partner country priorities.

*Information sharing:* information on who does what at the country level needs to be shared by all donors and by recipient countries; agreement is needed on definitions and methodologies for how to measure volumes and impact of different types of development assistance.

*ODA-GNI target:* all government donors should commit 0.15 percent of GNI to ODA by 2015.

## References

Abdel-Malek, Talaat. 2009. Remarks, Policy Dialogue on Development Cooperation, Mexico City, September 28–29.

34. Abdel-Malek (2009).

Alesina, Alberto, and David Dollar. 2000. "Who Gives Foreign Aid to Whom and Why?" *Journal of Economic Growth* 5: 33–63

Brautigam, Deborah. 2008. "China's African Aid; Transatlantic Challenges." Paper. German Marshall Fund.

———. 2009. *The Dragon's Gift: The Real Story of China in Africa.* Oxford University Press.

Chahoud, Tatjana. 2008. "Southern Non-DAC Actors in Development Cooperation." Briefing Paper 13/2008. German Development Institute.

China Exim Bank. 2009. "Chinese Government Concessional Loan and Preferential Export Buyer's Credit" (http://english.eximbank.gov.cn/businessarticle/activities/loan/200905/9398_1.html).

Claessens, Stijn, Dammu Cassimon, and Bjorn Van Campenhout. 2009. "Evidence on Changes in Aid Allocation Criteria." *World Bank Economic Review* 23, no. 2 (2009): 185–208.

Costa Vaz, Alcides, and Cristina Yumie Aoki Inoue. 2007. "Emerging Donors in International Development Assistance: The Brazil Case." International Development Research Center (http://publicwebsite.idrc.ca/EN/Documents/12447281201Case_of_Brazil.pdf).

Davies, Penny. 2010. "A Review of the Roles and Activities of New Development Partners." CFP Working Paper 4. Washington: World Bank.

GHA Report. 2009 (www.globalhumanitarianassistance.org/report/gha-report-2009).

Hammad, Lama, and Bill Morton. 2009. "Non-DAC Donors and Reform of the International Aid Architecture." Issues paper. North-South Institute.

Hubbard, Paul. 2008. "Chinese Concessional Loans." In *China into Africa,* edited by Robert I. Rotberg. Brookings.

Kragelund, Peter. 2008. "The Return of Non-DAC Donors to Africa: New Prospects for African Development?" *Development Policy Review* 26, no. 5.

———. 2010. "The Potential Role of Non-Traditional Donors' Aid in Africa." International Center for Trade and Sustainable Development.

Leipziger, Danny, and William O'Boyle. 2009. "The New Economic Powers." *World Economics* 10, no. 3: 43–78.

North-South Institute. 2008. "Does Aid Work? Can It Work Better? Crucial Questions on the Road to Accra and Doha."

OECD. 2009a. *Development Partnership for Growth and Poverty Reduction.*

———. 2009b. *2009 Development Cooperation Report.*

———. 2010a. *DAC Report on Multilateral Aid.*

———. 2010b. *2010 Development Cooperation Report.*

Price, Gareth. 2005. "Diversity in Donorship: The Changing Landscape of Official Humanitarian Aid: India's Official Aid Program." Asia Program. London: Chatham House.

UN. 2008. *Trends and Progress in International Development Cooperation: Report of the Secretary-General.* E/2008/69.

UNDP. 2009. *South Report 2009, Perspectives on South-South Cooperation for Development.*

UN ECOSOC. 2008. *Trends in South-South and Triangular Development Cooperation.* Background study, Development Cooperation Forum.

Villanger, Espen. 2007. "Arab Foreign Aid: Disbursement Patterns, Aid Policies, and Motives." CMI (www.cmi.no/publications/file/2615-arab-foreign-aid-disbursement-patterns.pdf).

Yu, Myung-hwan. 2008. Remarks. G8 Development Ministers' Meeting, "Expanding Partnership for Development." Tokyo, April 5.

Zhaoxing, Li. 2003. "Report by H. E. Mr. Li Zhaoxing, Minister of Foreign Affairs of the People's Republic of China to the Second Ministerial Conference of the China-Africa Cooperation Forum." Addis Ababa.

# 3

## Private Development Assistance: The Importance of International NGOs and Foundations in a New Aid Architecture

SAMUEL A. WORTHINGTON AND TONY PIPA

Nonstate entities are increasingly providing significant resources for international development and in some countries and localities are dwarfing the presence of even the largest donor governments of the Development Assistance Committee of the Organization for Economic Cooperation and Development (OECD/DAC), the traditional source of official development assistance (ODA).[1] With their growing scale, scope, and nature, nongovernmental organizations (NGOs), local civil society organizations (CSOs), and other private groups active in development—together referred to as private development assistance (PDA)—are rapidly transforming the basic architecture of the international aid system.

The effectiveness framework developed through the Paris Declaration and the Accra Agenda for Action has been a significant catalyst for improving the delivery and management of official aid. However, while there has been recognition of the important contributions of international NGOs (INGOs), foundations, and local civil society organizations and a commitment to creating an enabling environment

The views in this chapter are the authors' and not necessarily those of InterAction or its members.

1. More and more middle-income countries—such as Brazil, China, and India—have become significant donors but are not members of the DAC. Official development assistance (ODA) provided by donor governments flows by way of bilateral relationships as well as through multilateral institutions and financing mechanisms. OECD, "Is It ODA?" (www.oecd.org/document/0/0,3343,en_2649_34447_42398912_1_1_1_1,00.html) provides the full definition of ODA used by DAC donors for reporting purposes.

to maximize those contributions, these groups have had no formal role as donors during the development of these cooperative agreements.[2] While formal CSO development effectiveness principles have recently been established, these diverse groups have not been subject to the same sort of accountability mechanisms to improve the effectiveness of their own interventions.[3]

The effectiveness of the aid architecture in promoting development and achieving the Millennium Development Goals (MDGs) would be enhanced by the formal recognition and integration of the intellectual capital, financial resources, technical capacity, and decades-long experience embodied by private aid flows. INGOs in particular have a direct interest as large global donors in participating in and shaping the evolution and rules of a broader, more comprehensive framework for the global aid architecture.[4] Their programs often complement and leverage ODA flows while fitting into the development strategies of nation-states. Any serious effort to improve development effectiveness must address both ODA and PDA actors.

This chapter examines the scope and defining characteristics of the PDA provided by a range of nonprofit actors, contrasting it with the ODA provided by donor governments. It explores the distinctive contributions of these nonprofit entities to development, including the size and reach of their resources, the level of their services, the innovations they produce, and the role they play in enhancing the voice of beneficiary communities. While the chapter provides a general overview of PDA, greater emphasis is placed on the role of the INGO community engaged in service delivery. It concludes with several recommendations to advance development effectiveness by leveraging the capacity of INGOs and formally including them in global cooperative negotiations and agreements, starting with the 2011 High-Level Forum on Aid Effectiveness.

An important condition for the full inclusion of PDA at the 2011 forum is establishing a dialogue between the ODA and PDA actors, something that has arguably been deficient in the past. PDA typically flows directly from INGOs to local communities and institutions in developing countries, bypassing central governments, some of which see this investment in local civil society as undermining their ownership of national development efforts. Meanwhile, some civil society advocates remain uniformly and vocally critical of governments and official aid. This chapter argues that, despite these differences, there exists a largely unexplored space for high-level collaboration to enhance the complementary nature of ODA and PDA; to leverage the different strengths of these comple-

2. The Accra Agenda for Action, paragraph 21, does acknowledge the importance of civil society to development.

3. See Istanbul Principles: Framework for CSO Development Effectiveness, October 2010.

4. INGOs are nonprofit institutions that work across borders to advance a mission. They often work with, and through, local civil society organizations or national nonprofit organizations operating in a developing country. The funding of INGOs comes primarily from the populations of developed countries.

mentary operational aid flows; to shape the effectiveness of both public and private aid flows; and to design a global aid architecture that better reflects the current reality of all aid flows. This chapter, then, aims to expand and build this constructive dialogue.[5]

## A Major Shift within the Aid Architecture

As defined by the World Bank, aid architecture is the set of rules and institutions governing aid flows to developing countries. While there is a global aid architecture, there is no central architect; the structures and rules governing an increasingly diverse aid industry have evolved over time without a master plan.[6] Until recently, member governments of the DAC have been the primary sources of aid flowing from developed to developing countries. The architecture of the Paris Declaration and the Accra Agenda for Action owes its original conceptualization to this premise, with the primary objective to effectively and efficiently deliver the ODA contributed by these countries' governments.

Despite a fairly circumscribed set of sources, the aid agencies and channels through which ODA resources flow have expanded dramatically, with as many new actors created between 1996 and 2006 as during the previous fifty years. A 2006 World Bank analysis lists over 230 international organizations, funds, and programs, and the United Nations Development Program (UNDP) estimates more than a thousand financing mechanisms at the global level. Levels of ODA from DAC countries have experienced a global resurgence over the past decade, growing from approximately $75 billion (in constant 2008 dollars) in the last half of the 1990s to $123 billion in 2009.[7] The commitments explicit in the Paris Declaration were a welcome recognition of the hazards accompanying the growing complexity of the system and have been catalysts for rationalizing the delivery of official aid and for taking concrete steps to increase its effectiveness.

Yet the changes associated with ODA are only part of the transformation that the aid architecture is undergoing. Aid flows from private sources and non-DAC governments are growing rapidly. These new actors bring to the aid system distinctive values, expertise, partners, and motivations, dimensions that expand the potential of the system beyond the simple addition of their financial resources.

---

5. This chapter is not meant to provide a comprehensive overview of the strengths and weaknesses of private development actors nor to assess the challenges that INGOs or local civil society development programs pose to official development efforts undertaken by developing country governments. To a large extent, civil society efforts are viewed in official aid circles as advocacy voices that try to influence and critique ODA rather than as colleagues engaged in a common development enterprise. This advocacy voice—which is often loud—can be perceived as illegitimate, even though civil society groups, including INGOs, are increasingly recognized as important global development actors in their own right.

6. International Development Association (2007).

7. OECD (2010).

*Definition and Scope of PDA*

The term *PDA* means the international aid that flows to developing countries from private philanthropic sources in developed countries.[8] These include INGOs, foundations, individual philanthropists, corporations, universities, diaspora groups, and religious congregations and networks. In this usage PDA does not include private capital investments or remittances, though these also have development impacts.

The scale of PDA is significant. It is estimated that private philanthropic aid from fourteen developed countries totaled $49 billion in 2008.[9] The United States was the predominant source, with $33.7 billion in both cash and gifts-in-kind disbursed.[10] The global economic crisis has made a dent in PDA flows estimated to have caused losses of more than $1 billion in the U.S. INGO community, costing more than 10,000 jobs.[11] However, it is believed that PDA flows have since resumed their growth.

Total ODA from DAC countries in 2008 reached a record $121 billion, a total 2.5 times larger than PDA. However, only a portion of that ODA is available to developing countries for the infrastructure projects and social programs that these countries identify as development priorities, since ODA is also used for debt relief, the administrative costs of aid agencies, and humanitarian relief.

The OECD has begun to calculate the levels of country programmable aid (CPA) available for long-term development, defining it as ODA excluding flows for humanitarian aid and debt relief; flows not spent in the recipient country and applied toward purposes such as administration or research; and flows not discussed between the donor agency and recipient governments, such as food aid.[12] Other analysts go further, deducting funds for technical cooperation.[13] CPA from official assistance has been decreasing steadily, even as absolute amounts of ODA have experienced a resurgence.[14] In 2008 the OECD calculated that only 54 percent ($62.6 billion) of the total $116 billion of ODA was left for CPA. After reasonably deducting the funds spent on technical cooperation (since that money is

8. Although this chapter focuses on flows from developed to developing countries, it is important to note that local NGOs and CSOs are beginning to raise sums from individual donors in developing countries. Many local NGOs also get significant amounts of in-kind assistance from citizens of developing countries.

9. The $49 billion amount represents a lower bound, since it counts "identified flows" only. Hudson Institute (2010).

10. Ibid. The Hudson Institute assigns a value to volunteer labor and includes it in their estimation of U.S. PDA. To focus specifically on financial flows, we deduct this amount, which totaled $3.6 billion in 2008. Nation-states and the OECD/DAC often question the total amount of PDA. While there are grounds for further analysis, the total private resources raised by INGOs continues to grow. For InterAction members, private donations currently stand at around $8 billion a year.

11. From a confidential survey of InterAction member CEOs. InterAction (2009).

12. Benn, Rogerson, and Steensen (2010).

13. Kharas (2007); Reality of Aid Network (2006).

14. Kharas (2007).

Table 3-1. *U.S. Private Development Assistance*

Units as indicated

| Source | US$ billion | Percent |
|---|---|---|
| International NGOs | 11.8 | 35 |
| Foundations | 4.3 | 13 |
| Corporations | 7.7 | 23 |
| Religious congregations[a] | 8.2 | 24 |
| Universities | 1.7 | 5 |
| Total | 33.70 | 100 |

Source: Hudson Institute (2010).

a. These figures are contributions from congregations directly to either local civil society organizations or support missions. Contributions to faith-based NGOs, such as World Vision International and Catholic Relief Services, are represented in the international NGO category.

also unavailable to be applied toward country programs), the amount falls to 39 percent ($45.55).

The incomplete nature of the data makes an exact accounting of the CPA within PDA more difficult, but a significant proportion of PDA associated with INGOs and foundations supports development programs in country. A conservative estimate that includes solely INGOs, foundations, and corporations—and that deducts humanitarian aid—nears $30 billion for 2008. While the numbers may not be exact, the implications are clear: the orders of magnitude of ODA and PDA available for CPA are much more equivalent than their aggregate totals suggest.

*Ecology of PDA*

While data regarding private flows are difficult to gather and aggregate with accuracy, reporting requirements and research methods are maturing in the United States. Table 3-1, showing the sources of U.S. PDA, provides an introduction to the ecology of PDA.

Together, foundations, corporations, and INGOs make up 70 percent of PDA provided by the United States. Most of this assistance represents organized, project-based aid, consistent with the norms, protocols, and best practices associated with the organized aid architecture. This is often not the case for the other sources, which are all nonprofit entities. A portion of the contributions by religious congregations goes to short-term missions, such as trips by church groups to tackle time-limited projects. Universities support scholarships for international students to study in the United States.

Corporations, as for-profit organizations, have pressures, motivations, and goals that diverge from the dominant mission orientation of the other sources; they receive focused attention in another chapter in this volume. It should be noted that corporations tend to have limited capacity for measurement, evaluation, and service and often rely on NGOs for these activities. There is increasingly, however, a strong link between corporations and INGOs. InterAction members, in a 2006 internal survey, identify over 800 corporate partners that either fund their development efforts or are partners in joint efforts.

The segment of PDA that comes from INGOs and foundations, which together comprise almost half of total U.S. PDA, closely conforms to the practices of the aid architecture. The projects of these groups are managed by a professional infrastructure that, while not directly shaped by the architecture of the Paris Declaration and the Accra Agenda for Action, is increasingly focused on its own scale, effectiveness, accountability, limitations, and challenges. Its goals, such as the building of local capacity over simple service delivery, mirror those of ODA while remaining distinct and often focused on poor or vulnerable populations. It is this segment of PDA that is the focus of this chapter.

## Distinctive Contributions of PDA

It is a mistake to assess the importance of PDA solely in terms of financial resources. The reach, characteristics, and distinctive approaches of INGOs and foundations add important dimensions to the aid system that improve its development effectiveness and potential for impact. Much of this value derives from the close relationship of INGOs to local CSOs and to community leaders in developing countries, often the source of innovation, knowledge, and experimentation.

### International Nongovernmental Organizations

Historically, INGOs have had North American or European roots, but increasingly they are a global phenomenon.[15] Many of the largest are part of international federations and alliances such as CARE International, Oxfam International, World Vision International, Caritas, Plan International, and Save the Children Federation. All have been experiencing rapid global growth. Estimates put the number of INGO secretariats at around 18,000, and the development-focused revenues of the sector now exceed those of the UN system.

It has been common to think of INGOs as implementers of ODA, using donor government support to provide public services. Over the past decade, however, shifts in their funding structure have made them independent actors in their own right.[16] Their revenue breakdown now is close to 70 percent private contributions and 30 percent government funding, though the ratio of ODA to PDA

15. For example, BRAC, a massive Bangladesh INGO, now has a significant U.S. presence and programs in Africa and throughout the subcontinent. Major INGOs now operate with donations from such diverse publics as those of the United States, Canada, Mexico, Brazil, the European Union, India, South Africa, Hong Kong, Australia, New Zealand, and Japan.

16. It is important to distinguish the INGO community from for-profit international development contractors. International development contractors currently deliver the vast majority of U.S. ODA and often implement effective development programs. They do not, however, count any significant PDA funds

varies widely across organizations.[17] The number of contributors is remarkable: in 2006 members of InterAction, the U.S. NGO platform, received funds from 13.6 million U.S. donor groups, or an estimated 40 million Americans.[18]

INGOs have also traditionally been characterized as humanitarian operations, primarily providing emergency relief, but increasingly they have shifted their focus to long-term efforts to reduce extreme poverty and address social disadvantage. In a 2006 survey of InterAction's members, 73 percent of respondents identified long-term, sustainable development as a primary program area.[19] The most recent reliable estimate sets the level of humanitarian assistance of U.S.-based INGOs at 36 percent of aggregate programming.[20] U.S. INGOs organize their services around one or more MDGs, with the largest INGOs actively engaged across multiple sectors. As the INGO community matures, its programs are increasingly focused on support for local capacity, alignment with government development priorities, and attempts to achieve greater scale. This evolution will take time and can only benefit from a greater sharing of lessons and practice across the ODA-PDA divide.

The bulk of INGO resources are concentrated in a small number of organizations, and all the major actors are actively engaged in coordinating their efforts around the world. InterAction finds that its nine largest members account for 47 percent of all revenue, compared to 1.17 percent for the sixty-three smallest.[21] The top thirty-four InterAction members each manage individual budgets of over $100 million a year. The largest INGO, World Vision International, counts 46,000 staff and a $2.57 billion global budget, over 80 percent coming from private funding.[22] At least twenty INGOs employ more than 5,000 staff; typically 97 percent of these are local. Independent, nonpartisan, and committed to mission above all else, these professional organizations are committed to delivering development programs that are driven by poor people themselves, with the goal of creating lasting social change. INGOs prefer to fund their work through and with local community-based groups and local governments. The major INGOs have extensive project monitoring and evaluation capacity, often far more extensive than the governments of their home countries. They have thousands of highly technical employees, their global infrastructure is overwhelmingly staffed by local

---

as a portion of their project portfolios. Contractors rarely have long-term, locally managed development infrastructure, and their primary clients remain ODA donors; they also lack the freedom to experiment, which access to PDA provides. Since several large INGOs manage significant sums of ODA, the two types of organizations are often erroneously conflated.

17. Kharas (2009).
18. InterAction (2009).
19. Ibid.
20. Kerlin and ThanaSombat (2006).
21. InterAction (2009).
22. Internal strategic planning analysis of InterAction member data, completed September 2010.

personnel, and their relationships with local governments and civil society often are founded on decades of joint project work.

These organizations play several different roles, depending upon the context. They act as donors, directly funding civil society organizations in the countries where they are active. They provide technical assistance and capacity-building support; offer training, learning, and management support to help local civil society and municipal governments strengthen their capabilities; and deliver high-quality, effective programs. They advocate at the national and global levels and assist in building the advocacy capacity of local civil society to enhance the voice of the poor in global policymaking. They play a central role in pushing governments in their home countries to increase their levels of ODA. In certain instances they deliver social services directly, though they predominantly act as enablers, assisting local actors to deliver social services.

## Foundations

From 1980 to 2008 the number of active foundations in the United States increased from just over 22,000 to almost 76,000.[23] The proportion of its resources contributed to international causes has also accelerated rapidly, increasing more than 70 percent between 2002 and 2007, with 72,000 foundations—95 percent of active U.S. foundations—involved in making grants.[24] And between 2001 and 2005, the number of public benefit foundations in thirteen EU member countries increased by more than 50 percent—to 95,000.[25] But although the number of foundations worldwide is increasing rapidly, their resources are fairly concentrated. In 2008 only twenty-five U.S. foundations accounted for almost 25 percent of total giving.[26] Also in 2008 the top ten foundations in thirteen EU countries held almost 25 percent of foundation assets.[27]

Some of this growth has been driven by a wave of successful entrepreneurs entering the world of philanthropy, seeking to apply to social problems the calculated risk taking, business discipline, and drive for scalable solutions that served them well in their for-profit ventures. Notable among these have been Bill and Melinda Gates and Warren Buffett, whose combined contributions have made the Gates Foundation the world's largest and whose annual grant disbursements in 2007 exceeded about half of the DAC members' level of ODA.[28] This movement, described sometimes as venture philanthropy and at other times as philanthro-

23. Lawrence and Mukai (2010).
24. Foundation Center (2008); Lawrence and Mukai (2010).
25. European Foundation Centre (2008).
26. Foundation Center (2008).
27. European Foundation Centre (2008).
28. Tomlinson (2008).

capitalism, extends across the world from Carlos Slim Helu in Mexico to Jack Ma and Huang Rulun in China.[29]

While few hard data exist regarding the impact of their attempts to inject a business sensibility into grant giving, there is little doubt that such activity has significantly raised the profile of philanthropy among the world's wealthiest.[30] The Gateses and Buffett have just embarked on an effort to convince the members of the Fortune 400 to set aside 50 percent of their wealth for charitable causes, which would roughly equal $600 billion. A 1999 study by the Social Welfare Research Institute at Boston College conservatively forecast wealth transfers of $41 trillion in the United States over the next fifty-five years, estimating that between $6 trillion and $25 trillion could go toward philanthropy.[31]

## Unique Value of PDA

As the resources and reach of INGOs and foundations continue to grow, both bring unique value to the aid system.

### Innovation

As mission-driven organizations, legally accountable only to a governing board of directors whose bottom line is social improvement, foundations and INGOs enjoy considerable independence and flexibility, providing them with wide latitude to develop and test new approaches. Foundations are particularly free from constraint and often describe their resources as social venture capital, especially when their assets come from a single party. The entrepreneurial mind-set of the newest philanthropists has heightened the focus on identifying, testing, and scaling promising new approaches. For example, the Bill & Melinda Gates Foundation has pioneered new collaborations (such as the GAVI Alliance) and new approaches (such as advance market capitalizations) to accelerate the development of vaccines for infectious diseases affecting developing countries; the Ford Foundation has for decades seeded the capacity of social change and justice organizations around the world; and a collaboration of prominent foundations is currently investing in the creation of African-based think tanks.

The commitment of INGOs to benefit the world's poorest often fosters internal practices to increase accountability to the populations they serve. The combination of this ethos and their drive to establish comparative advantages within a competitive marketplace acts as an engine for innovation and new practices (not that INGOs are the single source of such advances: they often build upon the

---

29. Letts, Grossman, and Ryan (1997); Bishop and Green (2008).
30. For a healthy dose of skepticism, see Edwards (2008).
31. Social Welfare Research Institute (1999).

experimentation and small-scale innovations of local civil society, leveraging their long-term partnerships with local leaders). Many essential development practices—such as participatory development, rights-based approaches, gender-based practices, microfinance, and a focus on smallholder farmers—were originally championed by the INGO community.

A recent commitment by U.S. NGOs to stimulate innovation in food security highlights this ambition. Technical staff from about sixty organizations came together to establish best practices and develop criteria for innovative approaches, and INGOs submitted their projects before a panel composed of INGO and official UN and bilateral aid representatives.

## From Local to Global

With their objectives firmly rooted in social change and progress, INGOs place a high priority on identifying promising ideas and leaders that emerge at the community level, often investing in smaller-scale efforts grounded in a local context and culture. They also regularly establish a long-term presence in poor communities, given the levels of community trust and expertise necessary to be effective. A 2008 five-country analysis of a hundred INGOs and local civil society organizations finds that 90 percent of the INGOs had been working in-country for at least five years and 77 percent for more than ten years.[32] Depending on the organization, 90–99 percent of the in-country INGO staff are local citizens.[33]

While their programs are intensely local, INGOs have a global presence and global networks that act as conduits for sharing development knowledge and innovations within and across countries. They are well placed to identify promising new practices in one community that emanate from local civil society or their own efforts, spread knowledge throughout their networks, and adapt those innovations to new cultural and geographic contexts. At their best, they are interested less in advancing proprietary methods than in maximizing the reach and application of effective programming, however it originates, to as many communities as possible. They do so with levels of professionalism that rival official aid agencies or global corporations. As an illustration, in the area of microfinance, the major INGOs focused on developing and replicating programs as the characteristics of high-performing programs were identified and defined. For example, Plan International now operates programs with partners in twenty-seven countries; a majority of the funds are high-performing loans, with a rate of repayment comparable to that of a formal bank. INGOs also adopted child survival methodologies deemed of high caliber by the U.S. government whether or not their programs were funded by the U.S. government.

32. Long (2008).

33. In meetings with U.S. officials in 2009, a group of InterAction members shared details on their staff: in Afghanistan it numbered 11,000; 98 percent of them were local hires.

Foundation investments often support such cross-pollination by prioritizing the development and testing of successful models that can be scaled up and replicated for wider application. In 1981 Grameen Bank, the pioneering microfinance organization created by Muhammad Yunus, capitalized its initial five-year expansion only after receiving an $800,000 loan guarantee from the Ford Foundation, which was willing to take the risk when commercial banks refused.[34]

New philanthropic platforms allow those individual donors too small to fund a foundation to bypass intermediary INGOs and faith-based networks and take their investments directly to the grassroots level. The Global Greengrants Fund and the Global Fund for Children, both created in the 1990s, pool the funds of many contributors, distribute small sums to promising grassroots leaders, and monitor progress. Online sites such as Kiva.org, globalgiving.org, charitywater.org, and SeeYourImpact.org, all less than a decade old, allow small donors to choose the specific individuals, programs, and communities that will receive their support.

*Impact*

The flows that compose PDA are manifestations of their donors' personal aspirations to make tangible improvements in the lives of the poor. This bespeaks a focus on measurable results, and as PDA has grown, so has the capacity and sophistication of its sources to discern impact and translate learning from past efforts into improved methods and approaches. Many INGOs have entire divisions dedicated to evaluation: 92 percent of the INGOs and civil society organizations surveyed in 2008 had measurement and evaluation systems. The foundation sector is in the midst of a metrics revolution, pursuing new and better methodologies for impact assessment.[35] InterAction's monitoring and evaluation working group currently has a partnership with Harvard University and another with 3ie, a foundation-supported evaluation initiative based in Cairo, Egypt.

INGOs have decades' worth of project assessments, and foundations routinely monitor outcomes on a per-grant basis. Admittedly, much of this is project-level information and unpublished, which makes impact across organizations and sectors difficult to aggregate. Nevertheless, the evaluation capacity of PDAs is underestimated: the data that are captured make INGOs, foundations, and other private groups valuable sources of information and knowledge for other development actors.

Just as a focus on outcomes has replaced the focus on outputs that previously dominated assessment practices, the field is in the midst of an evolution to move from project-specific to program-and-organization-level impact, and several

---

34. Lawry (2009). INGOs then played a key role in exporting and adapting the microcredit concept to communities in other cultural and geographic contexts, helping spread microfinance across the globe and providing a platform for public and private investments to take it to scale.

35. See for example McKinsey & Co. (2010); Tuan (2008); and Grantmakers for Effective Organizations (2009).

efforts are under way to make data more comparable and comprehensible across organizations and sectors.

## Challenges Facing PDA

PDA resources, to some extent, align through a decentralized marketplace organized under the framework of the MDG. Yet foundations and INGOs have a long way to go before individual efforts are aligned to compose a whole greater than the sum of its parts.

### Coordination

Coordination of PDA actors remains a real challenge, not least because of the fragmentation of PDA resources. A vivid example is provided by the ongoing relief efforts in Haiti, where approximately one thousand INGOs are registered with the UN Office for the Coordination of Humanitarian Affairs. At the same time, the claim that private aid actors are too diffuse or numerous to coordinate ignores the reality of the market that shapes PDA. A concentration of resources makes coordination among this community possible. Of the thousand INGOs in Haiti, fifteen account for over 90 percent of resources, and among these organizations there is a clear willingness to work within the evolving donor coordination rules.[36]

Over the past twenty-five years, INGOs have increasingly organized into collective membership alliances, creating national NGO platforms such as Bond in the United Kingdom, Coordination Sud in France, JANIC in Japan, InterAction in the United States, and ACFID in Australia, among many others. Similar NGO platforms have also emerged throughout the developing world, from VANI in India to ABONG in Brazil. These platforms represent thousands of NGOs around the world. In 2008, 82 national NGO platforms came together to form a global alliance, the International Forum of National NGO Platforms, to serve as a permanent space for cooperation and joint initiatives. The NGO Forum, facilitated by a steering group of NGO leaders from France, Chile, India, Brazil, South Africa, the United States, North Africa, and others, has initiated a number of efforts to advance NGO diplomacy around the world.[37]

These efforts try to align interests within the decentralized NGO and civil society marketplace. The International Forum of National NGO Platforms launched an initiative to establish global development norms for nonstate devel-

---

36. InterAction (2010).

37. The term *NGO diplomacy* is now commonly used within the INGO community to describe diplomatic efforts to influence donor governments, the United Nations, the G8, and others. The concept was created by Henri Rouille d'Orfeuil, "La Diplomatie Non Gouvernemontale: Les Ong Peuvent-Elles Changer Le Monde?" Editions de l'Atelier, March 2, 2006. Henri Rouille d'Orfeuil served as the president of Coordination Sud, the French NGO platform, until 2008.

opment actors. The Open Forum for CSO Development Effectiveness conducted a global consultation on development effectiveness norms involving civil society groups and national NGO platforms in more than eighty countries. The Open Forum's global leadership met in Istanbul in October 2010 and drafted the first formal CSO development effectiveness principles; these were endorsed by all participating NGO platforms, including groups with significant PDA such as Inter-Action (U.S.), Coordination Sud (France), BOND (U.K.), among others.[38]

In the past, the complex nature of the NGO community has hindered the ability of bodies like the OECD/DAC to engage. However, the INGO system has now evolved so that selecting a limited number of representatives who can both speak for and represent a broader community is possible.

## Information Sharing

A lack of standardized data, limited resources to invest in the generation of aggregated data, and difficulty in opening INGO databases to public use have hampered attempts to organize PDA. The field, however, is pursuing various efforts, with the most significant innovations coming from U.S. and European INGOs and foundations. Southern NGO platforms suffer from an acute lack of resources, and the willingness of official donors to fund these organizations remains mixed.[39]

At InterAction, the U.S. national platform, a mapping project is being conducted that will detail where INGOs are investing in food security efforts around the world. Not only will the effort detail where investments are being made and capacity exists, it will also capture best practices and innovations through a process that encourages rigorous documentation and reporting. Meanwhile, the Foundation Center, which gathers data on U.S. foundations, has developed Philanthropy In/Sight, a tool that maps grants and patterns of giving overlaid with over a hundred demographic and socioeconomic data sets for a particular locality.

The response to the 2010 earthquake in Haiti demonstrates the opportunity and drive for better coordination within the NGO community. InterAction, with ICVA (the International Council of Voluntary Agencies, based in Geneva), opened an NGO coordination office within two weeks of the disaster. The office is housed in the UN compound, involves all major INGOs, and works closely with the leadership of the UN coordination effort. InterAction has also mapped the efforts of thirty-eight INGOs that are investing $974 million in PDA into Haiti's relief and reconstruction efforts.

38. The following eight principles guide the work and practices of civil society organizations in both peaceful and conflict situations, in work from grassroots to policy advocacy, and in a continuum from humanitarian emergencies to long-term development: Respect and promote human rights and social justice; embody gender equality and equity while promoting women's and girl's rights; focus on people's empowerment, democratic ownership, and participation; promote environmental sustainability; practice transparency and accountability; pursue equitable partnerships and solidarity; create and share knowledge and commit to mutual learning; and commit to realizing positive sustainable change.

39. USAID efforts to support national NGO platforms in Africa ended in 2007.

*Power Imbalance*

One challenge that remains largely intractable is the power difference between Northern INGOs and their Southern partners. INGOs control significant resources and function primarily as donors to local partners, balancing conflicting accountabilities that include responsibilities to their donors (individuals as well as foundations), missions, and the poor themselves. A significant number of the larger INGOs are trying to address these North-South tensions within their own organizations by becoming transnational organizations with multiple boards of directors, including boards in Southern countries. While this trend continues to unfold, most INGOs have a limited percentage of board members from the global South. Fiduciary responsibility remains largely with the boards of INGOs located in OECD countries.

## Relationship between PDA and ODA

For the most part, the channels through which ODA and PDA flow remain separate. There are a small number of public/private mechanisms, such as the Global Fund to Fight AIDS, Tuberculosis, and Malaria, and INGOs program a limited percentage of overall ODA.[40] Still, ODA channels are dominated by public funds and government-led decisionmaking, whether through bilateral channels or by the boards of multilaterals. PDA flows predominantly through civil society organizations, with INGOs and foundations funding a wide array of local civil society groups.

*Complementarity*

Yet PDA and ODA intersect in substantive ways, and an examination of their relationship helps to draw a comprehensive picture of the aid system and its potential for development outcomes.[41] PDA strives to be innovative, people-centered, long term, and grounded in local adaptation.[42] ODA seeks to work at scale and build state-centered capacity.

ODA grows out of, and is influenced by, the strategic political considerations of donor countries.[43] Its primary point of entry is at the national level, supporting national governments and plans and building physical infrastructure as well as social programs. PDA, primarily mission driven, represents the personal engagement of private citizens in social issues. Its primary focus begins at the community level, supporting local civil society and municipal and provincial governments and investing in the poor themselves to develop human capacity to

40. Approximately 10 percent, according to a recent estimate by the OECD/DAC secretariat.
41. Desai and Kharas (2007).
42. Many INGOs routinely plan to spend PDA as ten-plus-year investments into a particular program area or civil society organization.
43. This case is articulated in Alesina and Dollar (2000).

overcome poverty, environmental degradation, and human rights violations. Taken together, ODA and PDA present a more robust definition of country ownership than that suggested by the Paris Declaration.

## Political Interdependence

As country-to-country aid, ODA is drawn from tax revenue. Decisions about its deployment are made by elected and public officials, and its continuation depends upon their political will. Though all taxpayers nominally contribute to ODA, citizens have limited, if any, direct agency over the direction of those resources.

PDA represents the ideals of a large group of private citizens. These groups can be as disparate as community organizations, corporations, faith-based institutions, and youth service groups. Nearly three-quarters of U.S. religious congregations give directly to U.S.-based development and relief INGOs; in fact many major denominations have INGO networks directly affiliated with, and receiving substantial and regular contributions from, their congregations.[44]

PDA can be characterized as less "democratic" than ODA, in that it derives its force from self-selected donors and their particular motivations, ideas, and interests. PDA results from donors choosing to give and represents their judgments about the strengths of a particular INGO, what communities or people should benefit from their aid, and in what way. It provides an outlet for a set of compelling motivations and values and creates public demand in donor nations for development themes that touch people. The advocacy of its proponents significantly influences the public agenda for development.

Over the past two decades, the NGO community in Europe and North America has emerged as a major advocate for increased levels of ODA. Ongoing efforts to raise resources from private sources, including the public at large, have led INGOs to spend millions of dollars on public education programs, to build strong constituencies among the general public in OECD countries, and to launch advocacy efforts aimed at increasing the level of ODA. In many ways, government support for ODA reflects the impact of a growing advocacy effort to engage the public around global poverty issues. Groups like ONE, and other global brands like Save the Children, have developed extensive partnerships with celebrities, who serve as spokespeople for the international development community.

## Substitution

The official aid architecture is based on the notion that governments are the primary providers of social services. In many instances, however, governments have been unable to successfully provide basic public goods to all citizens. Civil society, supported by PDA funding, has evolved to fill some of these gaps.

---

44. Note that methodologies of data collection and analysis were consciously designed to avoid double counting these contributions.

These resources tend to flow from Northern INGOs to Southern civil society actors and at times to the frontline services of municipal governments, bypassing the national infrastructure. Admittedly, this is not an ideal situation for strengthening state governance and delivery of services. INGOs have been accused of acting as the "new colonialists," benefiting from insufficient state capacity, and growing their own organizations while limited resources are targeted to build the viability of the state to replace them as primary providers of these services.[45] Pointed criticisms, for example, were surfacing about the role of INGOs in Haiti before the January 2010 earthquake, accusing them of creating a parallel system of social services that left the government perpetually weakened and unable to meet its duties.

INGOs generally acknowledge that state institutions are necessary for providing and sustaining social services over the long term. For example, after the January 2010 earthquake, members of several major INGO platforms—including InterAction, CONCORD, Coordinadora de ONG, Canadian Council for International Cooperation (CCIC), Coordination Sud, and platforms in Brazil and Chile—developed principles to guide the reconstruction of Haiti that include a focus on building Haitian institutions and a commitment to aligning INGO activities with the Haitian government's rebuilding plans. This is complicated by the responsibility of INGOs—both to their donors and to their program beneficiaries—to apply their resources, first and foremost, to meet people's needs, even while the long-term process of building state sustainability is under way. In Haiti, for example, INGO commitments depend on the willingness of the Haitian government to decentralize power and support the capacity of municipal governments to play an active role in the rebuilding.

Governments in developing countries often try to structure or regulate the services being provided by civil society, to bring them under the jurisdiction of the state. There is also the misperception that INGOs are receiving funds that could go to developing country governments. The vast majority of the millions of contributors that provide PDA, however, would never accept that their donations should instead fund a central government. The impetus for their support is to assist development programs that directly touch poor communities. While the services that INGOs provide may fill gaps in state services, the private resources themselves are far from substitutable. Nevertheless, the marketplace of private aid flows could be better encouraged to align itself with the development plans of a particular state.

*Divergence*

In the United States over the past fifteen years USAID and other U.S. ODA donors have steadily moved away from funding U.S. NGOs that raise significant private funds. The only primarily privately funded U.S. NGO among USAID's

---

45. See Cohen, Kupcu, and Khanna (2008) for the term *new colonialists*.

top twenty vendors for 2009—Catholic Relief Services—ranks sixteenth on the list, which is steadily becoming dominated by for-profit contractors.[46] At the same time, private aid funding has grown significantly within the NGO community, with InterAction members experiencing a tripling of private funds since 2001—to over $6 billion in 2006.

The two funding streams in the United States have significantly diverged from one another. This poses the risk of the development of two parallel aid systems, however interdependent in practical terms, with separate norms, methodologies, and standards of effectiveness.

## Voice

As Southern civil society grows in its capabilities to provide services and support communities, it provides a platform for everyday citizens to engage in political processes and push the state to increase its capacity to deliver social services and protect human rights. This creates demand-side accountability, with citizen groups and independent entities focused on holding their governments to account.[47]

The relationship to Northern INGOs and foundations often helps to grow this capacity, through funding, technical assistance, and other types of direct interactions. In Malawi, Oxfam has worked with a national intermediary and a network of CSOs to increase their ability to analyze the expenditures of the national budget in four social sectors—health, education, agriculture, and water and sanitation—and track whether allocations have reached intended beneficiaries at the community level.[48]

Increasingly, Northern NGOs also assist by amplifying and representing the concerns of the poor during policymaking discussions at their national and global levels. This occurs through public advocacy campaigns, such as the Make Trade Fair Campaign, representation on decisionmaking bodies and in bilateral and collective dialogue with national government and multilateral leaders.

## A Twenty-First-Century Development Effectiveness Agenda

The PDA community has undergone a quiet revolution in recent years in four important respects.

First, its resources have grown to represent a significant source of capital flows from rich to poor countries, valued at no less than $49 billion. While this figure is significantly below the total flows represented by ODA, the two sources are nearly equivalent when stripped down to what is available for use by recipient countries for actual development programs.

46. Ranking from USAID (2010).
47. Burnley (2010).
48. Oxfam (2010).

Second, PDA is increasingly devoted to core development activities, aimed at improving the long-term prosperity and resilience of recipient countries and their people. Where once PDA focused on immediate development needs, concentrating on relief work, it has expanded its focus to include innovations—often in conjunction with local governments—that can be scaled up to address underlying development challenges.

Third, PDA actors are adopting professional approaches to manage and deliver their assistance, whether using tracking devices to monitor the use of funds or conducting impact evaluation to assess the results of their interventions.

Fourth, while the PDA community is diffuse, it has demonstrated an ability to organize and to appoint representatives to speak on behalf of the community. Among other things, this allows the PDA community to better engage with other development actors, at both a national and a global level.

Together, these four changes represent a maturation of the PDA community into an impressive, skilled, and respected entity within the broader development sector, and one that can and should be engaged in relevant high-level discussions that affect the aid architecture. With this maturation also comes a desire to focus on results and effectiveness.

The problems of effectiveness within the PDA community are well documented. Despite some examples of good practice, coordination within the community varies from country to country, and successful models of coordination are not easily replicated. While resources remain concentrated among a small number of large INGOs and foundations, the fragmentation among small parties is an ongoing problem, which has shown no signs of letting up as publics in the North continue to express their desire to engage in development efforts. Transparency within the PDA community, beyond reporting by individual organizations, is deficient, making it difficult to determine who is doing what, where. Finally, accountability within the community needs to be improved to eliminate instances of bad practice. These are some of the very same challenges facing the ODA community, which are being addressed through the Paris Declaration and the Accra Agenda for Action and will be taken up again at the 2011 High-Level Forum.

It is evident from the above that now is the time for the PDA community to be brought into the High-Level Forum discussions. However, the lack of trust between the PDA and ODA communities, as well as recipient governments, provides an obstacle to this sort of engagement. Indeed, the problem of trust has undermined previous attempts to bring the different communities together in development effectiveness discussions, such as at Accra. How can this obstacle be overcome?

Below, we set out a possible way forward that could be taken up at the 2011 High-Level Forum. This takes the form of a "grand bargain," whereby the PDA community, the ODA community, and recipient governments each pledge separate commitments that would enable the beginnings of a common effectiveness agenda. An agreement to these commitments would provide the right blend of incentives for each party to work together and to claim a stake in this joint agenda.

### PDA Commitment 1: Defining PDA Principles, Norms, and Commitments

Building on the existing global effort to define CSO principles, the PDA community should, over time, define its own agreement on effectiveness, consisting of commitments, targets and indicators, following an approach similar to that of the Paris Declaration. This agreement would be built on the Istanbul CSO Development Effectiveness Principles and would reference and reflect the core principles of the Paris Declaration.[49] For instance, "harmonization" and "alignment" should add urgency to the emerging efforts to rationalize and map PDA.

The definition of objectively verifiable, time-bound, financial commitments would enhance the accountability of the PDA community for its effectiveness. This could result in the establishment of group rankings of PDA actors, based on their performance against indicators of effectiveness. PDA-related standards have a long history, and any effort to group PDA actors would need to take into account and build on existing certification regimes.

### PDA Commitment 2: From Translucency to Transparency

Information sharing and communication between the PDA and ODA global infrastructure are hampered by the incomplete nature of data related to PDA. Tracking PDA flows in terms of size, application, and geographic distribution is challenging. Legal obligations typically require just a basic level of reporting, and these obligations vary across countries. While INGOs are committed to transparency and routinely publish financial data far beyond their legal requirements, the variances in their individual frameworks complicate the compiling and aggregating of relevant information.

To date there are no global PDA data collection efforts, and the national efforts that have emerged are privately funded. A global initiative to gather, analyze, and map data regarding PDA flows, in partnership with NGO platforms worldwide, would be an important step forward. Such an effort—which supports and builds on the work done by the Hudson Institute, the Brookings Institution, and Inter-Action in the United States—would advance the standardization of PDA data, leading to a better understanding of the size and impact of PDA on the aid system.

In addition, a focus on development effectiveness entails going beyond the facilitation of more complete data on PDA flows to the creation of a robust and open marketplace of information regarding impact. The intellectual capital that foundations and INGOs possess—the depth and breadth of analysis and knowledge

---

49. The Istanbul principles were adopted at the Open Forum for CSO Development Effectiveness in October 2010.

about development successes, failures, and best practices——is intrinsic to their distinctive value, but this intellectual capital is underutilized. One global INGO alone has over ten internal databases containing data related to progress on its projects and activities. If development assistance groups, working together, managed to open, link, and unleash such data (that is, made it available to the overall aid system, including the donor public and intended beneficiaries), they would establish a culture of sharing and the potential for deepening our understanding of effective development.

## ODA Commitment: A Seat at the Table

The Inter-Agency Steering Committee, which guides the coordination of global humanitarian efforts, demonstrates the value of integrating public and private actors in policy decisionmaking. Composed of the heads of UN agencies and nonstate groups, including InterAction, ICVA, the Red Cross movement and representative INGOs, this body has enabled a dialogue at the leadership level and helped the international NGO community to integrate its PDA humanitarian efforts with official global efforts. No comparable leadership space currently exists in the development realm. Previous efforts to engage civil society have focused on the voice of CSO groups as advocates interested in influencing ODA. Although this outreach to civil society is positive, it has not engaged INGOs or foundations as PDA donors interested in building a global aid architecture that leverages private aid flows.

An official relationship that links the leadership of major PDA institutions with the OECD/DAC and its ministerial-level dialogues should evolve, not simply on an ad hoc basis but more formally within the structure of the global aid system. One concrete solution is to add six "observer" seats—but defined as active participant seats—at the OECD/DAC ministerial table: three representing PDA donors from the North and three representing their civil society counterparts from the South.

Global civil society has proven its ability to select its own formal representatives in a transparent and inclusive manner. Recent examples are the inclusion of civil society representatives in the World Bank's multidonor trust fund for food security and the INGO representative seated on the board of the Interim Haiti Reconstruction Commission (IHRC).

## Recipient Government Commitment: Whole-of-Society Approach

Donor countries have begun to develop whole-of-government approaches to development, recognizing the broad range of policy tools——including not only aid but also trade, climate policy, and migration——that shape development outcomes. This approach acknowledges that improving the delivery and effectiveness of aid is only one factor in improving outcomes; it seeks to leverage the multiple ways a donor country's resources and policies affect developing countries.

On the same basis, a whole-of-society approach is warranted when considering the various actors that contribute to development outcomes in developing countries. This means expanding the definition of country ownership to include—but also to go beyond—recipient country governments to incorporate local civil society groups. The approach necessitates engagement with all actors within the aid system, both public and private, creating the space to deepen understanding of their respective roles and strengths and to explore ways to tap and leverage the potential of PDA.

To operationalize this whole-of-society approach, the following three steps should be taken by recipient country governments:

—Expand existing ODA donor steering committees to incorporate major private donors. This government-hosted ODA-PDA donor group would help coordinate and align programs with the plans and societal needs of the recipient government

—Create a broader ODA-PDA group based on technical expertise, to offer knowledge, best practices, and capacity on particular issues and initiatives

—Institute regular town hall consultations with representatives of local civil society and other international NGOs investing or working in the country.

# References

Alesina, Alberto, and David Dollar. 2000. "Who Gives Foreign Aid to Whom and Why?" *Journal of Economic Growth* 5:33–63.

Benn, Julia, Andrew Rogerson, and Suzanne Steensen. 2010. *Getting Closer to the Core—Measuring Country Programmable Aid*. Paris: OECD Development Cooperation Directorate.

Bishop, Matthew, and Michael Greene. 2008. *Philanthrocapitalism: How the Rich Can Save the World*. Bloomsbury.

Burnley, Jasmine. 2010. "Twenty-First-Century Aid: Recognising Success and Tackling Failure." Briefing Paper 137. Oxfam International.

Cohen, Michael, Maria Figueroa Kupcu, and Parag Khanna. 2008. "The New Colonialists." *Foreign Policy*, June 16.

Desai, Raj M., and Homi Kharas. 2007. "Do Philanthropic Citizens Behave Like Governments? Internet-Based Platforms and the Diffusion of International Private Aid." Working Paper 12. Wolfensohn Center for Development, Brookings.

Edwards, Michael. 2008. *Just Another Emperor: The Myths and Realities of Philanthrocapitalism*. New York: Demos.

———. 2010. *Small Change: Why Business Won't Save the World*. San Francisco: Berrett-Koehler.

European Foundation Centre. 2008. *Foundations in the European Union: Facts and Figures*. Brussels, May.

Foundation Center. 2008. *International Grantmaking IV: An Update on U.S. Foundation Trends* (with Council on Foundations). Washington.

Grantmakers for Effective Organizations. 2009. *Evaluation in Philanthropy*. Washington.

Hudson Institute. 2010. *Index of Global Philanthropy and Remittances: 2010*. Center for Global Prosperity. Santa Barbara, Calif.

InterAction. 2009. "The Other Partner: NGOs and Private Sector Funding for International Development and Relief." Washington.

InterAction. 2010. "Haiti Footprint." Washington.

International Development Association. 2007. "Aid Architecture: An Overview of the Main Trends in Official Development Assistance Flows." Washington.

Kerlin, Janelle, and Supaporn ThanaSombat. 2006. "The International Charitable Nonprofit Subsector: Scope, Size, and Revenue." Policy Brief 2. Washington: Urban Institute.

Kharas, Homi. 2007. "Trends and Issues in Development." Working Paper 1. Wolfensohn Center for Development, Brookings.

———. 2009. "Development Assistance in the 21st Century." Wolfensohn Center for Development, Brookings.

Lawrence, Steven, and Reina Mukai. 2010. Foundation Growth and Giving Estimates. Washington: Foundation Center.

Lawry, Steven. 2009. "Effective Funding: How Foundations Can Best Support Social Innovators." Stanford Social Innovation Review (Spring 2009).

Letts, Christine W., William Ryan, and Allen Grossman. 1997. "Virtuous Capital: What Foundations Can Learn from Venture Capitalists." Harvard Business Review, March–April 1997.

Long, Carolyn, 2008. "Foreign Assistance Reform Monitoring Initiative: Final Report." Washington: InterAction.

McKinsey & Co. 2010. "Learning for Social Impact: What Foundations Can Do." New York.

OECD. 2010. "Methodological Work: What Is ODA, How Is It Counted, and Who Qualifies for It?" (www.oecd.org/document/0/0,3343,en_2649_34447_42398912_1_1_1_1,00.html).

Oxfam. 2010. "Twenty-First-Century Aid: Recognising Success and Tackling Failure." Briefing paper.

Reality of Aid Network. 2006. "Reality of Aid 2006: Focus on Conflict, Security, and Development Cooperation." Quezon City, Philippines.

Social Welfare Research Institute. 1999. "Millionaires and the Millennium: New Estimates of the Forthcoming Wealth Transfer and the Prospects for a Golden Age of Philanthropy." Boston College.

Tomlinson, Brian. 2008. "World Aid Trends: Donors Distorting the Reality of Aid in 2008." Quezon City, Philippines: Reality of Aid Network.

Tuan, Melinda. 2008. "Measuring and/or Estimating Social Value Creation: Insights into Eight Integrated Cost Approaches." Seattle: Gates Foundation.

USAID. 2010. "Where Does USAID's Money Go?" (www.usaid.gov/policy/budget/money).

# 4

## The Private Sector and Aid Effectiveness: Toward New Models of Engagement

JANE NELSON

Private corporations, financial institutions, social enterprises, and business associations and coalitions are becoming significant players in international development, both individually and through a variety of collaborative mechanisms.[1] This trend has important implications for both the quantity and quality of resources being mobilized for development and for the aid effectiveness agenda. Ongoing efforts to improve aid effectiveness should place support for shared economic growth at their core and should call for a more coordinated approach to market development among donors, one that is focused on enabling vibrant and diversified domestic private sectors and on catalyzing more and better foreign private resources.

The domestic and foreign private sector plays an increasingly important role not only in driving economic growth and job creation but also in determining how resilient, inclusive, and environmentally sustainable this growth will be.

---

1. There is no commonly accepted definition of the private sector. A number of definitions combine for-profit enterprises, nongovernmental organizations, philanthropic foundations, academia, and social movements. According to the OECD statistical glossary, "The private sector comprises private corporations, households, and nonprofit institutions serving households." For the purpose of this chapter, the terms *private sector* and *private enterprise* are used to describe either for-profit firms or enterprises that exclusively or primarily employ market-based solutions to achieve their core objectives, even when those objectives have an explicit social or environmental dimension (for example, social enterprises, social businesses, and socially responsible investors). The terms also include bodies that provide a representative or collective platform on behalf of for-profit private enterprises. This chapter is drawn from Nelson (2010).

Although aggregate data are not available, evidence suggests that private enterprises provide a growing source of commercial, philanthropic, and hybrid financial resources, managerial capacities, scientific and technological innovation, and market-based solutions for achieving development goals in many developing countries and sectors. Market-based approaches can also be a valuable platform for scaling development interventions. At the same time, there is clear evidence that private investment can result in negative development impacts, especially in fragile states and situations of weak governance. These negative impacts can range from human rights abuses, environmental degradation, poor labor standards, corruption, rent seeking, and tax avoidance to situations in which foreign direct investment, portfolio flows, and tied aid crowd out or undermine the capacity and resilience of the domestic private sector and domestic institutions.

As donor and partner governments review the policies and mechanisms for engaging with the private sector, it is essential that they focus both on catalyzing the positive development multipliers of private investment and market-based solutions and on mitigating negative impacts. It is also essential that they focus on strengthening domestic private sector players and country-led public-private initiatives as well as on engaging with multinational corporations and global partnerships.

## Defining Private Sector Engagement

The private sector covers a range of actors, from smallholder farmers and microenterprises to small and medium-sized firms to large domestic and multinational corporations. It ranges from firms and financiers driven by the motive to maximize profits to companies, social enterprises, and impact investors that employ market-based approaches with explicit social or environmental objectives. It also includes business associations, enterprise networks, producer cooperatives, and business leadership coalitions. As the United Nations Commission on the Private Sector and Development notes in its seminal report to the UN secretary general:

> Large companies are a vital part of the private economy, but the poor are an equally important part. They are often entrepreneurs themselves—frequently of necessity, operating informally, trapped in subscale enterprises. We endorse the view that market-oriented business ecosystems comprise many forms of private enterprise coexisting in a symbiotic relationship. The ecosystem generally includes multinational corporations, large domestic companies, cooperatives, small and medium enterprises and microenterprises with formal and informal players. It thus encompasses the farmer in the field as much as the multinational company.[2]

2. UNDP (2004).

Small and medium-sized enterprises, employing less than 250 people, are the main drivers of job creation and growth, accounting for over 90 percent of businesses worldwide.[3] In many developing countries, due to well-documented market failures and governance gaps, up to 80 percent of these enterprises operate in the informal economy.[4] As such, they are unable to benefit from the opportunities and protection that the law provides, and they have minimal economic resources, bargaining power, or political voice to influence public policy and market outcomes. One of the most important actions that donors can take is to work with partner governments, other private sector actors, and nonprofit organizations to overcome these obstacles to entering the formal sector. In particular they can help to catalyze the so-called missing middle of small and medium-sized firms that operate between microenterprises and large companies and are often essential in building a vibrant middle class.

There are other private sector actors, both domestic and foreign, that do have considerable resources, influence and organizing capacity. The following groups of private sector actors can play a particularly important role in determining development outcomes, both positive and negative: corporations, private financial institutions, social enterprises, and business associations and coalitions.

*Corporations*

Large domestic companies employing over 250 people are, along with local capital markets and financial institutions, key drivers of private investment. A vibrant and diversified domestic private sector is an essential foundation for job creation, economic growth, and poverty alleviation. According to the UN Commission on the Private Sector and Development, "Domestic resources are much larger than actual or potential external resources."[5]

At the same time, multinational or transnational corporations are responsible for substantial flows of private capital from developed to developing countries and, increasingly, among developing countries. Foreign direct investment (FDI)—equity investment, intracompany loans, reinvested earnings, and portfolio investments—can also be a source of new ideas, scientific advances, technologies, resources, skills, and business models. Despite this potential, research on the development benefits of FDI shows a mixed record, with marked variations among industry sectors and performance often dependent on the quality of governance and regulatory environments in home countries and host countries.

There is therefore a dual imperative for partner governments and donors to catalyze domestic private investment and FDI, while also aiming to minimize

3. For definitions of different sizes and types of enterprise, see the *OECD Glossary of Statistical Terms* (http://stats.oecd.org/glossary/).

4. World Bank (2011).

5. UNDP (2004, p. 9). In the 1990s domestic private investment averaged 10–12 percent of GDP, domestic public investment, 7 percent, and foreign direct investment, 2–3 percent.

negative impacts arising from large-scale corporate activities. Foreign and domestic corporations that operate in sectors and value chains that are essential to economic growth and poverty alleviation—either directly supporting it or potentially undermining it—have an especially important role to play. These include companies in infrastructure; energy; water and sanitation; oil, gas, and mining; agriculture and forestry; health care and nutrition; financial services; information and communications technology; professional services; and tourism.

Three trends in FDI are particularly worthy of note. First, half of global FDI inflows are now going to developing and transition economies. While the global economic crisis resulted in large declines in both FDI and portfolio investments into developing countries, UNCTAD'S *World Investment Report 2010* notes:

> FDI inflows to developing and transition economies declined by 27 percent to US$548 billion in 2009, following six years of uninterrupted growth. While their FDI contracted, this grouping appeared more resilient to the crisis than developed countries, as their decline was smaller than that for developed countries (44 percent). Their share in global FDI inflows kept rising: for the first time ever, developing and transition economies are now absorbing half of global FDI inflows.[6]

Second, FDI, along with other sources of private finance, now dwarfs official development assistance (ODA) from developed countries. According to the U.S.-based Hudson Institute, private capital investment, together with global philanthropy and remittances, accounted for 75 percent of the developed world's economic dealings with developing countries in 2009.[7] Despite the economic crisis, FDI from the United States to developing countries grew to $54 billion in 2009, and U.S. corporations gave an estimated $7.7 billion in philanthropic contributions, including both cash and product donations (largely from health care companies). As a comparison, UNDP's total income has been around $5.5 billion a year over the past three years. It should be noted, however, that most FDI flows go to middle-income or natural-resource-rich developing countries. ODA remains the major source of external capital flows for most of the least developed countries and fragile states. Donor initiatives to catalyze domestic private sector development and investment are arguably even more essential in these countries.

Third, one of the most important trends in the past decade is the number of corporations from China, India, Brazil, Russia, Mexico, South Africa, Korea, Turkey, Malaysia, and other emerging economies that are growing dramatically in their domestic markets and spearheading greater South-South and regional

6. UNCTAD (2010, pp. xviii–xix).
7. Hudson Institute (2010).

investment. They are especially active in sectors such as agriculture, infrastructure, banking, retail, mobile telecommunications, and natural resources. UNCTAD estimates that there were 82,000 transnational corporations worldwide in 2008. Some 28 percent of them are in developing and transition economies, compared to less than 10 percent in 1992, making them major players in their own domestic markets as well as drivers of growing South-South private investment flows.[8] UNCTAD notes that rankings by the *Financial Times* and *Fortune* magazine note an even larger percentage of transnational corporations from developing and transition economies entering the global stage.

## Private Financial Institutions

Participation in capital markets and affordable and reliable access to finance are necessary for almost every successful development outcome, whether at the household, community, firm, or national levels. Private financial institutions have a vital role to play in this process, from commercial banks, insurance companies, private equity investors, venture capitalists, pension funds, and stock exchanges to for-profit microfinance intermediaries and community development funds.

The past two decades have seen the emergence of new types of financial players and asset classes, the creation of public-private and philanthropic-commercial funding coalitions, and the transformational impact of the convergence between information and communication technologies and financial intermediation. These have facilitated fundamental changes in finance, from the emergence of twenty-four-hour global trading, which shifts trillions of institutional dollars around the globe daily, to mobile money services for the poor, which facilitate individual access to ten dollars or less in remote rural communities.

The global financial crisis has demonstrated the risks and costs associated with a complex and interdependent system when private financial innovation outpaces the ability of public accountability mechanisms, national regulators, and international institutions to keep up with the rate and complexity of change. Yet this should not prevent ongoing efforts to explore innovative private and public-private financing models for development. In particular, efforts are needed to

—Develop market-based solutions for delivering financial services and risk management tools directly to the poor and to invest in and regulate the microfinance intermediaries that serve them.

—Fund small and growing businesses, especially those owned by women entrepreneurs.

—Increase pension fund and private equity investments in developing country corporations and improve the social, environmental, and governance performance of these investments.

8. UNCTAD (2010, p. 5).

—Leverage additional private finance for development. This can range from millions of small donations, investments, and remittances made by individuals to multimillion-dollar commitments made by large institutional investors, corporations, and private foundations toward financing global public goods such as climate mitigation and adaptation and global health funds.

The burgeoning field of what is being termed *impact investment* offers potential for innovations in development finance. A 2009 study, *Investing for Social and Environmental Impact,* defines impact investing as "actively placing capital in businesses and funds that generate social and/or environmental good and at least return nominal principal to the investor."[9] The report identifies three types of investor: financial-first investors, who aim to optimize financial returns with a floor for social and environmental impact; impact-first investors, who seek to optimize social or environmental impact with a floor for financial returns; and yin-yang deals, which blend capital, motivation, and performance. The concept of impact investing (also referred to as blended-value finance) includes a range of investment vehicles and instruments, from global health funds and clean technology funds to pension funds that adhere to socially responsible investment criteria to small and medium-sized enterprise funding, microfinance, and community development banks.[10]

Major banks, investment funds, and insurance companies from both developed and developing countries are starting to establish units or funds that fit the impact-investing category. The Monitor Institute estimates that these investments could reach approximately $500 billion within a decade.[11]

Private equity funds, especially those targeted at specific sectors or geographies, also offer potential for leveraging increased private finance for development. Although private equity deals were dramatically cut following the financial crisis, over the past five to ten years a number of firms have emerged that are specializing in developing economies. In 2004 a few of these firms created the Emerging Markets Private Equity Association (EMPEA) with the belief that "private equity and venture capital can be critical drivers of economic growth in emerging markets while simultaneously generating strong returns for investors."[12] Less than five years after its creation EMPEA had more than 250 members, with nearly $500 billion under management focused on high-potential companies in the emerging markets of Africa, Asia, Europe, Latin America, and the Middle East. Over 75 percent of these firms or funds have been established since 2000. Even those that are part of well-established commercial banks or fund management entities such as Absa Bank and Standard Bank have been created as specialized units within the past decade.

9. Monitor Institute (2009).

10. World Economic Forum (2005).

11 Monitor Institute (2009).

12. Emerging Markets Private Equity Association (www.empea.net).

## Social Enterprises

The past decade has also seen the emergence of the field of social entrepreneurship. Social enterprises have an explicit social or environmental mission and use innovative, often market-based, approaches to achieve impact at scale. Some of them are for-profit entities. Many of them have the ambition to achieve systems change. They assume a variety of legal and operational models. A 2010 report by Brookings drawing on work by the Schwab Foundation identifies the following categories:[13]

—Leveraged nonprofits that capitalize on the performance requirements of a variety of investors or donors to secure ongoing support based on a diversified funding portfolio.

—Enterprising nonprofits that have a self-financing component contributing to the organization's sustainability.

—Hybrid enterprises that combine aspects of the for-profit and nonprofit legal models, either through an innovative legal structure or by using a for-profit subsidiary to support the social activities of the nonprofit.

—Social businesses that aim to deliver profitable financial performance and competitiveness while expressing an equal or greater commitment to a social aim.

Despite their relatively small numbers and size, social enterprises and the private foundations, impact investors and networks that support them have been effective in making the case for development models that blend economic viability and market-based approaches with explicit social or environmental objectives. Leading players such as the Grameen network of enterprises, BRAC, Ashoka, PATH, Acumen Fund, TechnoServe, Root Capital, and E+Co, to name just a few, have become credible practitioners of and advocates for these new approaches. In 2009 the Aspen Network of Development Entrepreneurs was established as a member-driven global network of these and other organizations focused on supporting small and growing businesses that create economic, social, and environmental benefits for developing countries.

## Business Associations and Coalitions

Business associations and coalitions include traditional representative bodies such as chambers of commerce, employers' organizations, trade and industry associations, and small enterprise and smallholder producer associations. These representative private sector organizations focus primarily on promoting the direct business interests of their members. Over the past decade, a few of them, such as the Confederation of Indian Industry and the U.S. Chamber of Commerce, have established dedicated units focused on supporting development goals. Many of them have also established units to support small-enterprise development.

---

13. Abdou and others (2010). See also Schwab Foundation for Social Entrepreneurship: Outstanding Social Entrepreneurs 2010 (www.schwabfound.org).

Collective business efforts also include business leadership coalitions that have been established with the explicit and dedicated purpose of leveraging private sector resources to address development challenges on either a global or a national basis or organized around specific industry sectors or development challenges. These business-led coalitions are increasingly important as platforms for engaging with donor and partner governments, convening multistakeholder initiatives, and mobilizing private sector engagement in development.

Global and regional examples include the World Economic Forum, the World Business Council for Sustainable Development, the International Business Leaders Forum, Business for Social Responsibility, Business Action for Africa, the Initiative for Global Development, and the Global Business Coalition on HIV/AIDS, Tuberculosis, and Malaria. National examples include Philippine Business for Social Progress, the Thai Business Initiative for Rural Development, Instituto Ethos in Brazil, and the National Business Initiative in South Africa. With a few exceptions, most of these business leadership coalitions have been created in the past two decades.

The U.K.-based Business in the Community manages a global network of national and regional business coalitions focused on corporate social responsibility. This network includes some 100 organizations from sixty countries, approximately half of them in Asia, Latin America, Africa, and the Middle East.

## The Private Sector as a Development Actor

There is now broad recognition within the donor community of the vital development role played by the private sector and of the need to promote domestic private investment and growth as well as FDI and foreign portfolio flows. The World Bank concluded in its *World Development Report 2005*:

> Private firms are at the heart of the development process. Driven by the quest for profits, firms of all types—from farmers and microentrepreneurs to local manufacturing companies and multinational enterprises—invest in new ideas and new facilities that strengthen the foundation of economic growth and prosperity. They provide more than 90% of jobs, creating opportunities for people to apply their talents and improve their situations. They provide the goods and services needed to sustain life and improve living standards. They are also the main source of tax revenues, contributing to public funding for health, education, and other services. Firms are thus central actors in the quest for growth and poverty reduction.[14]

Box 4-1 summarizes some of the potential contributions of the private sector as a development actor. In each of the areas listed in box 4-1 it is also possible to

14. World Bank (2004).

Box 4-1. *Private Sector Contributions to Development*

*Generating jobs and income:* The private sector drives job creation, income generation, asset accumulation, and productivity gains, which are crucial to economic growth and to providing opportunities for people to lift themselves out of poverty.

*Delivering products and services:* Private enterprises develop and deliver many essential products and services to low-income producers and consumers, from productivity-enhancing inputs to smallholder farmers and enterprises to basic consumer products such as health and nutrition, energy, water and sanitation, housing, education, and finance.

*Building infrastructure:* The private sector plays an important role in financing and building physical and communications infrastructure. These can make products and services more accessible, affordable, and reliable for low-income producers and consumers, improve access to markets, and underpin green growth, both in remote rural locations and in rapidly urbanizing ones.

*Leveraging science and technology:* The private sector is at the heart of scientific and technological breakthroughs in areas such as information and communications technology, life sciences, and clean technology. Transferring and adapting such technologies to meet the needs and capacities of developing countries and making them directly available to the poor is having a transformative impact on development in a number of sectors.

*Mobilizing financial resources:* Private enterprises are a major source of taxes and other public revenues. They pay local employees, suppliers, and distributors and make philanthropic contributions and social investments. Some are delivering microfinance (credit, savings, and insurance) and small business services to low-income enterprises and households. There is growing private engagement in innovative financing-for-development mechanisms at the global level in areas such health, education, and carbon finance.

*Investing in human capital and workforce development:* Private firms offer education, training and skills development, and in some cases health services through a combination of employee programs, supply chain initiatives, and community investment or philanthropic activities.

*Spreading international norms and standards:* Companies that have global operations and supply chains play a role in spreading norms and standards in areas such as human rights, labor, the environment, product and occupational safety, and anticorruption measures.

Source: Nelson (2003, 2010).

identify risks and potential negative impacts—both intentional and unintentional—associated with private sector engagement, especially in the case of large corporations. These might include responsibility for or complicity in human rights abuses; unsafe labor and environmental standards; rent seeking and corruption in the case of large investments and infrastructure projects; exploitive interaction with low-income producers, employees, or consumers; transfer of inappropriate technologies; bringing in external workers and failing to develop local human capacity and skills; and crowding out local private investment. Certain industries, such as extractives and infrastructure, and certain situations or locations, such as conditions of weak governance and fragile states, are especially vulnerable to such negative impacts.

Therefore, in addition to catalyzing private sector engagement there is a need for both the public and private sectors to consider the broader development impacts of this investment, with the aim of minimizing negative impacts and leveraging positive ones. In the context of improving development outcomes, three modalities of private sector engagement are of particular relevance: core business operations and value chains; strategic philanthropy and community investment; and public policy dialogue, advocacy, and institution building.[15]

Far and away the greatest impact that the private sector has on development, both positive and negative, is through core business operations and value chains. These include the company's commercial activities and relationships in the workplace, the marketplace, and along its value chain, whether global, regional, or local. The main contribution that any company can make to development is through carrying out its core business activities in a profitable, productive, and responsible manner. In addition, companies can work both individually and collectively to

—spread global norms and standards for compliance with responsible business practice in areas such as human rights, labor standards, ethical and anticorruption measures, environmental standards, and product safety;

—build more inclusive markets and business models that include the poor as producers, consumers, and employees (also described as base-of-the-pyramid models); and

—develop innovative technologies and financing mechanisms to deliver scalable or replicable solutions to development challenges, such as mobile money and other information technology solutions, low-carbon clean technology, life sciences to improve health outcomes, and so on.

Strategic philanthropy and community investment should be aimed at mobilizing not only money but also the company's people, products, and premises to help support and strengthen local communities and nonprofit partners. If the social investments made by companies and their foundations are aligned with the company's core areas of competence and interest, they are more likely to achieve scale and impact and to be sustainable over the longer term.

Companies, either on an individual basis or on a collective basis, can also participate in public policy dialogues and advocacy platforms and help governments to build public capacity, strengthen institutions, and deliver public goods. This is best done in a transparent manner. Transparency also matters in the more traditional activities of corporate lobbying and political campaigning.

15. Adapted from Nelson (1996).

While many companies engage in development activities through their corporate philanthropy programs, relatively few are focused on understanding and managing the broader development impact of their core business operations and value chains. This is starting to change, in part as a result of alliances with or demands from governments, public donors, foundations, social enterprises, and nongovernmental organizations. A growing number of global corporations are engaging in individual and joint efforts to minimize negative impacts arising from their core business operations in areas such as human rights, corruption, conflict, health, safety, and the environment. A few are also starting to experiment with innovative market-driven approaches, public-private partnerships, and multi-stakeholder accountability mechanisms to address development challenges that have traditionally been the responsibility of the public sector.

In summary, growth in the volume and variety of private sector engagement in development has been driven by a combination of commercial interest (as companies explore new markets and business opportunities and manage their risks in developing economies) and changing public expectations of the social responsibility and accountability of the private sector. As a result, private sector engagement ranges from commercially viable business models, equity investments, and portfolio flows to corporate philanthropy, volunteering, and community investments. It encompasses project-based interventions, industrywide alliances and accountability mechanisms, and business engagement in public policy dialogue.

From the perspective of ODA and aid effectiveness, the central question for donors is what role they should play in catalyzing private sector investment and growth and in directly supporting efforts to make this private investment more inclusive and environmentally sustainable, while also mitigating the negative impacts of private investment.

## Official Development Assistance and Private Sector Engagement

In its 2008 *Private Sector Development Strategy*, the Department for International Development (DFID) of the United Kingdom made a clear case for donor intervention in markets and private sector development:

> Just because private sector development is successful it does not necessarily follow that poor people benefit. Private markets can exclude the poor, especially those who have nothing to buy or sell. Social or economic barriers can exclude groups such as ethnic minorities, migrants, or women. . . . It is justifiable for donors to support government interventions in markets where there are significant failures and inefficiencies which limit private sector growth and prevent the participation of poor men and women.[16]

16. DFID (2008).

Similar arguments can be made about the need to address environmental sustainability, especially water shortages and other implications of climate change. Well-documented market failures and barriers identified by DFID and others include market power through monopoly or imperfect competition, uneven access to information or lack of information generation, social exclusion, incomplete or missing markets, coordination failures, and externalities and public goods. Added to these are challenges of corruption and weak corporate or public governance structures.

A 2008 study undertaken by the UN Development Program offers similar conclusions on the need for donors and other development actors to play an active role in overcoming market failures and constraints on integrating the poor into formal sector markets and value chains.[17] Drawing on extensive research, the study focuses on five main constraints: limited market information, ineffective regulatory environments, inadequate physical infrastructure, missing knowledge and skills, and restricted access to financial products and services. It illustrates ways in which private sector companies can collaborate with other actors to overcome these constraints.

Although little in-depth or comparative analysis has been undertaken on the evolving relationship between ODA and the private sector, evidence suggests that most bilateral and multilateral donors and development finance institutions have increased the quantity and the variety of their engagement with the private sector over the past decade. The following examples offer only a glimpse into the rapidly expanding and diversifying landscape of institutional engagement between the private sector and donor community. Motives and mechanisms vary depending on the donor agencies and private sector entities in question, but the vast majority of them focus on addressing one or more of the following three objectives:

—Catalyzing domestic and foreign private investment and innovation
—Promoting better corporate governance, responsibility, and accountability
—Including private sector representatives in development policymaking.

## Catalyzing Domestic and Foreign Private Investment and Innovation

Donors are supporting initiatives that aim to improve the overall enabling environment for private sector investment and innovation and they are also supporting programs that target private sector resources more directly at achieving specific development objectives such as poverty alleviation and environmental sustainability. In the first case, their focus tends to be on the private sector as a desired development outcome and in the second case on the private sector as a desired development partner.

Over the past two decades many donors have provided policy support to governments in developing countries to improve the overall business climate for

17. UNDP (2008).

investment. Some have also provided financial and advisory support directly to private firms, from large corporations to small and medium-sized enterprises and producer associations.

In its first public report on developing the private sector, published in 1989, the World Bank argued that private sector development requires three main elements:[18]

—A supportive (or enabling) business environment consisting of a stable macroeconomic setting, economic incentives that promote efficient resource allocation by the private sector, and laws and regulations that protect the public interest but do not unnecessarily interfere with private initiative.

—Services in infrastructure and human resource development necessary to permit private enterprises to function effectively.

—A financial system that provides the incentives and institutions needed to mobilize and allocate resources efficiently.

These elements remain essential today, though they are still inadequate in many countries. At the same time there has been growing recognition of the importance of specific business laws and regulations in enabling or hindering private sector development, especially that of small and medium-sized enterprises. Launched in 2001, the World Bank's Doing Business project has established an empirically rigorous framework for assessing ten sets of such microeconomic indicators. These are now tracked in 183 countries and provide a benchmark against which partner governments, donors, and private investors can assess progress.

In addition to supporting overall private sector development, a growing number of donors have implemented programs to leverage the private sector as a partner in achieving more inclusive and sustainable growth. They have provided catalytic financing, convened multistakeholder initiatives, developed tools, and undertaken capacity building to increase the broader development impact of private sector investment and philanthropy. These activities include efforts to engage companies and social enterprises in achieving the Millennium Development Goals and in promoting green growth and job creation.

Humanitarian agencies are also working more strategically with the private sector to mobilize private resources for responding to humanitarian crises with both immediate aid and help in longer term recovery. Corporate philanthropy and product donations have a long-standing role, but there is increased emphasis on harnessing core business capabilities such as logistics and information technology to improve the coordination and effectiveness of humanitarian assistance.

## Promoting Better Corporate Governance, Responsibility, and Accountability

Donors can also play a valuable role in spreading responsible business standards and practices. Donor engagement regarding corporate governance, responsibility, and accountability ranges from long-standing efforts such as the ILO's Core

18. World Bank (1989).

Labor Standards and the OECD's Guidelines on Multinational Enterprises to such newer initiatives as the UN Global Compact and the UN secretary general's special representative on business and human rights. The efforts also include ODA funding for nongovernmental organizations, trade unions, and the media in their capacity as watchdogs and campaigners for more responsible and accountable private sector behavior.

### Including Private Sector Representatives in Development Policymaking

Multilateral and bilateral agencies have taken measures to engage private enterprises and their representative bodies more systematically in global policy dialogues and as formal advisers to major donor programs. The World Bank Group and a number of UN agencies and bilateral development organizations such as the Millennium Challenge Corporation have established external councils to advise either on overall strategy or on specific programs. Although no mapping or analysis has been undertaken of the composition, mandates, and impact of such advisory mechanisms, anecdotal evidence points to most of them having some level of input from the private sector. Donors have also encouraged and supported the creation of advisory councils or business-ministerial forums at the country level in certain recipient countries.

## Examples of Donor-Business Engagement

The following section offers a brief overview of some of the evolving mechanisms for donor engagement with the private sector. This is an area that has not been comprehensively mapped or analyzed and one that warrants further research.

### Bilateral Donors

Members of OECD's Development Assistance Committee have employed a variety of new strategies, engagement models, and financial and technical assistance facilities to promote private sector development and to leverage private resources in efforts to meet the Millennium Development Goals and enhance humanitarian assistance.

A 2009 study by the U.S.-based Business Civic Leadership Center reviewed the private sector engagement strategies of ten bilateral agencies that account for some 75 percent of ODA. It found that all of these agencies had increased the resources focused on the private sector and that a majority had established dedicated units, funds, and initiatives to partner with business.[19] A few of these, such as GIZ's Public-Private Partnerships Program, USAID's Global Development Alliance, and DFID's Challenge Funds have now been under way in different formats for ten years and have catalyzed some 4,500 projects among them. They

---

19. Corporate Citizenship (2009).

have undertaken or are in the process of undertaking evaluations on what has worked in partnering with the private sector. This remains a work in progress, but the findings should feed into the fourth High-Level Forum on Aid Effectiveness when completed.

The long-standing Donor Committee on Enterprise Development continues to provide a platform for shared learning in the area of small enterprise development, and the OECD's Business and Industry Advisory Committee (BIAC) has served as a representative business body providing advice and counsel to the OECD for nearly fifty years. Although development issues are relevant to or integrated into a number of BIAC's policy groups, it does not have a policy group that is dedicated to development or aid effectiveness, and to date there is no common hub in OECD or elsewhere for joint research, evaluation, and learning with the private sector to achieve broader development goals. Informal networks, however, have started to emerge both globally and at the country level.

At the UN Millennium Development Goals summit in September 2010 eleven bilateral donors, supported by the International Finance Corporation and the UNDP, launched a joint bilateral donors' statement in support of private sector partnerships for development (see appendix for full statement). In this statement, the donors make the point, "Rather than viewing the private sector merely as resource providers, we choose to recognize the private sector as equal partners around key development issues and will enter into partnerships with local and international companies of various sizes." This document provides a useful framework for mapping bilateral donor engagement with the private sector and commits the participating donors to explore how the principles of aid effectiveness intersect with their partnerships with the private sector.

## United Nations

Many UN agencies, funds, and programs have increased the level and quality of their private sector engagement. New systemwide initiatives such as the United Nations Global Compact (UNGC) have also been created. Established in 2000 under the leadership of the secretary general, the UNGC has become the world's largest corporate citizenship initiative, with over 6,500 signatories (of which some two-thirds are from developing countries and approximately thirty national or regional networks). Funded primarily by bilateral donors and governed by a multistakeholder board, the UNGC requires corporate signatories to commit to a set of ten principles in the areas of human rights, labor, the environment, and anticorruption and to report publicly on progress. The UNGC works with other agencies to engage companies and investors in finding innovative solutions to development and to global challenges such as climate change and water security.

In 2005 the UN secretary general also appointed the first-ever special representative with an exclusive focus on business and human rights. John Ruggie was appointed with a mandate to propose measures that would strengthen the human rights performance of the business sector around the world. In 2008 the UN Human Rights Council was unanimous in welcoming a policy framework Ruggie proposed for that purpose. The council extended the mandate for a further three years, asking the special representative to build on and promote the framework so as to provide concrete guidance for states, businesses, and other social actors. The three-part framework can be summarized as the state's duty to protect human rights, the corporate responsibility to respect human rights, and access to remedy.

The UNDP's Growing Inclusive Markets Initiative and its Business Call to Action are two other new initiatives that are mobilizing the private sector to support development goals globally and at the country level. Growing Inclusive Markets is an empirically driven effort to improve understanding on how the private sector—especially domestic companies in developing countries—can contribute to human development and the Millennium Development Goals in commercially viable ways. The initiative is supported by a global advisory board of over twenty major bilateral and multilateral donors, academic and research institutions, and business leadership coalitions. It has created a network of Southern-based researchers and is working with a number of partner governments to improve their enabling environments for inclusive business. Building on the initial work of this initiative, in 2011 the Turkish Government and UNDP announced the creation of the Istanbul International Center for Private Sector in Development.

The Business Call to Action is a commitment-driven effort that calls on individual corporations to make specific commercially viable commitments to the millennium goals. As of July 2010 some twenty corporations were participating in the initiative. In October 2010 the UNDP launched an open-access, knowledge-sharing platform aimed at supporting efforts by companies to fight poverty. It contains more than 120 in-depth business case studies, together with contacts for more than 250 supporting actors at the local, regional, and global levels that can provide financing, technical assistance, information, and policy advice to support more inclusive business models. These include government entities, academic institutions, development agencies, multistakeholder platforms, and nonprofit organizations.

The United Nations Foundation, working through the U.N. Office for Partnerships and other agencies, is another example of a relatively new entity (established in 1998) that has leveraged donor, philanthropic, and private investment from a wide variety of sources to fund and scale programs in areas such as women, population, climate, and energy.

Space does not permit a summary of all the new private sector engagement mechanisms being employed in the UN system or the way in which long-standing structures have evolved, as in the case of the ILO. Suffice it to say some forty UN funds, programs, and agencies participate in the UN's Private Sector

Focal Points network, which was established in 2004. Their modes of engagement and motivations for working with the private sector vary, depending on the UN entity in question, but in almost all cases the level and variety of private sector engagement has increased over the past decade. In 2009 the UN's Guidelines on Cooperation between the United Nations and the Business Sector were revised and updated with the aim of facilitating greater cooperation that is mutually accountable, beneficial, and effective.

## Development Finance Institutions

Development finance institutions, such as bilateral and multilateral development banks, have also increased the level and range of financial and advisory services offered to the private sector. The International Finance Corporation (IFC), as the World Bank's private sector arm, offers a useful barometer. Its investments grew from $5.3 billion in 2005 to an anticipated $12.6 billion in 2010, and its projects have more than doubled, from about 236 in 2005 to an anticipated 528 in 2010. It now operates in sixty International Development Association countries, compared with twenty-nine five years ago. It is extending services to small and microenterprises and is financing market-based solutions to deliver health, housing, education, and financial services for the poor.[20] In 2010 the IFC established a unit within its advisory services group focused on inclusive businesses.

In addition to increasing the size and reach of its portfolio, the IFC is focusing more explicitly on the development impact of its clients' business operations. Its performance standards on social and environmental sustainability were instituted in 2006 and have become a global benchmark. Similar approaches have been adopted by more than thirty OECD export credit agencies, some fifteen European development finance institutions, and more than seventy financial institutions that are signatories of the Equator Principles, which cover some 75 percent of all project financing in developing countries.

Regional development banks demonstrate similar trends and actions. According to the World Bank, since 2000, nonsovereign lending by the multilateral development banks has been their fastest-growing portfolio, albeit from a small base.[21]

## New Multistakeholder Institutions and Initiatives

An important trend over the past decade has been the establishment of new multistakeholder institutions, initiatives, and funds financed and governed by a combination of donor agencies, philanthropic foundations, companies, and business associations. Some were established as or became independent entities; others are housed within existing public or nonprofit institutions. Many are global, while others are regional or sector specific.

---

20. Information provided by communications department, International Finance Corporation, July 12, 2010. See also www.ifc.org/ifcext/annualreport.nsf/content/AR2009.

21. World Bank (2009).

Some of these institutions are focused on mobilizing innovative funding mechanisms, harnessing market forces, overcoming market failures, or addressing governance gaps to achieve greater scale in tackling complex, systemic challenges in areas such as global health and nutrition, food security, financial services for the poor, and climate change mitigation and adaptation. The Global Fund to Fight AIDS, Tuberculosis, and Malaria; the Global Alliance for Improved Nutrition; the Clinton Global Initiative; and the Alliance for a Green Revolution in Africa are four notable examples, catalyzed by funding from public donors, corporations, and philanthropic foundations such as the Bill & Melinda Gates Foundation and the Rockefeller Foundation.

Other multistakeholder initiatives are focused on improving sectorwide accountability and transparency for social, environmental, and human rights performance in industries and supply chains that have a major influence on development—such as extractives, manufacturing, agriculture, electronics, pharmaceuticals, and construction. Examples include the Extractive Industries Transparency Initiative and the Voluntary Principles on Human Rights and Security, which focus on oil, gas, and mining; the Fair Labor Association, focused on the apparel sector; the Equator Principles, focused on project finance; the Marine Stewardship Council, focused on fisheries; and many fair trade and sustainability certification programs in agriculture and consumer goods.

## Toward New Models of Engagement and Effectiveness

Despite progress in the relationship between ODA and the private sector, there is room for improvement. The percentage of ODA targeted at catalyzing private enterprise—whether as a desired development outcome or as a development partner—remains low. There is insufficient coordination and little shared learning about donor strategies, modalities, and instruments to engage the private sector and about the business models and financing mechanisms employed by private enterprises. There is a need to expand but also to move beyond project-based cooperation between donors and private enterprises to more systemic and transformational solutions. Few private enterprises or their representative bodies have participated in the High-Level Forums on Aid Effectiveness. The Paris Declaration and the Accra Agenda for Action barely mention the private sector.[22]

While there are now thousands of individual project-based development partnerships between companies, donors, foundations, and NGOs, these are often small in scale and impact. Many replicate effort and reinforce challenges of country-level coordination, alignment, and accountability. There are untapped opportunities for companies, donors, and other development actors to collaborate in a

---

22. The OECD convened an informal meeting in Paris on June 22, 2010, to share lessons and experiences with the private sector and explore ways to address the issue of the private sector in the context of aid effectiveness as a contribution to the fourth High-Level Forum.

more collective manner to achieve systemwide change and increase the scale and impact of joint efforts.

The aforementioned multistakeholder initiatives are examples of systemic collaboration. These multistakeholder efforts are not easy to establish or sustain. They require new modes of thinking and new operating models. They require leaders who can broker agreements between diverse and sometimes mutually distrustful institutions and individuals. Yet they are worthy of increased attention, analysis, and experimentation.

The following presents recommendations, in three areas of collaboration: increasing private investment, improving corporate accountability, and enhancing policymaking.

### Recommendation 1: Increasing Private Investment

Much can be done to improve the enabling environment and incentives for private sector investment and innovation in developing countries. Donors, companies, and foundations should create joint financing, technical assistance, and data collection facilities to improve business climates for private investment. By focusing regionally, nationally, or subnationally, these initiatives can prioritize key productive sectors and leverage resources for fragile states. The private sector contribution should involve not only funding, but also market-driven technical input, training, and capacity building. The Africa Investment Climate Facility, the Middle East Investment Initiative, and the Emerging Africa Infrastructure Fund offer three examples. The Center for Global Development has proposed a Doing Business facility that would draw on the empirical foundation of the World Bank's Doing Business project to deliver concrete financial incentives for the best business climate reformers.[23] The value of the Doing Business project could be further enhanced by undertaking additional data collection and benchmarking related to policy reforms that support investment and growth in key productive sectors.

Lessons on catalyzing private investment for development can also be drawn from the challenge and innovation funds that have been established by a number of bilateral donors, notably DFID, AusAid, GIZ, and Danida, especially those that have focused on specific sectors or geographies. To date no comparative analysis has been undertaken on these models of catalytic funding. Other incentive and recognition models include award programs and platforms such as the World Bank's Development Marketplace, the G20 SME Finance Challenge, and the Marketplace on Innovative Financial Solutions for Development, which was cohosted in 2010 by the Agence Française de Développement (AFD), the Bill & Melinda Gates Foundation, and the World Bank.

Donors, governments, companies, social enterprises, and philanthropic foundations should collaborate to make investments in key value chains more inclusive

---

23. Moss (2010).

of the poor and environmentally sustainable. The need and the potential are especially great in sectors such as agriculture, health, water and sanitation, energy, housing, and financial services. Although such approaches are at an early stage, especially where corporations play a leadership role, there are interesting models that could be learned from, adapted, experimented with, and where relevant, scaled up.

In agriculture, for example, corridor initiatives, such as those that are being spearheaded by the World Economic Forum's "New Vision for Agriculture" and partner governments in Tanzania and Vietnam, and commodity value chain initiatives being cocreated by agribusiness companies and organizations, such as the Bill & Melinda Gates Foundation and TechnoServe, offer collaborative models for the way forward. Progress has also been made in collaborative efforts to make financial service value chains more inclusive, especially mobile money and microfinance. There are opportunities to do more in this area, especially developing more collaborative approaches to financing small and medium-sized enterprises.

There are also opportunities for donors, foundations, and private enterprises to cooperate on initiatives to strengthen domestic business organizations, producer associations, and market intermediaries that enhance the productive capacity and increase the economic power of low-income producers, employees, and consumers.

A number of initiatives to mobilize public, private, and philanthropic resources already exist in global health and nutrition. Companies in a variety of industries, not only health care, are active in collective business initiatives: the Global Fund, the Global Business Coalition on HIV/AIDS, TB, and Malaria (GBC), and the Global Alliance for Improved Nutrition (GAIN). The Global Fund, GBC, and GAIN have all established country-level collaborative mechanisms that have mobilized domestic private sector leadership in tackling specific disease burdens and nutritional challenges. These and other multistakeholder global health partnerships offer innovative models for leveraging private finance, technology, and networks to serve the poor, both globally and at the country level. These vertical initiatives also provide lessons for launching country-led alliances aimed at strengthening health systems in a more integrated manner. To date, although some mapping has been undertaken, little comparative analysis has been done on country-led coalitions and how they relate to the global partnerships. Similar vertical or sector-focused multistakeholder partnerships are emerging or being proposed in the areas of energy, agriculture, forestry, tourism, water, and education.

There is also a need for better data collection, research, monitoring, and evaluation of market-based solutions and collaborative alliances among companies, donors, partner governments, foundations, and NGOs. There are opportunities to undertake impact assessments that draw on methodologies from both the development community and the private sector. Foundations, private enterprises, and donors can also cooperate in building the capacity of local research institutes and scholars in developing countries to enable them to better advise governments and domestic companies on how to design more inclusive, market-oriented policies and inclusive business models. In particular, there is a need for increased research and analysis on the role of South-South private sector capital flows and cooperation. The recently established Istanbul International Center for the Private Sector in Development and the Global Green Growth Institute in Korea both have the potential to play an important role in this area.

The costs and benefits of tied aid remain an ongoing point of debate and contention. The Accra Agenda for Action includes a commitment to "relax restrictions that prevent developing countries from buying the goods and services they need from whomever and wherever they can get the best quality at the lowest price." This commitment needs to be fulfilled, together with ongoing dialogue between new and traditional donors and partner governments to address this issue.

## Recommendation 2: Improving Corporate Accountability

There is a need to implement more consistent principles and standards in the areas of corporate responsibility, accountability, and transparency. International conventions and declarations directed mainly at governments but with applicability to business need to be strengthened. These include the Universal Declaration of Human Rights, the ILO Conventions and Declaration on Fundamental Principles and Rights at Work, and the OECD Convention on Combating Bribery of Foreign Officials in International Business Transactions. They also include officially agreed or recognized guidance, such as the OECD Guidelines for Multinational Enterprises, international finance institution (IFI) safeguard policies, the UN Global Compact, ISO standards for quality, safety, the environment, and corporate social responsibility, and the "Protection Respect and Remedy" framework on business and human rights. The private sector in both developed and developing countries has been active in consultations associated with the development or revision of most of these cross-industry initiatives and instruments. In all cases there is an ongoing need for collaborative efforts, consultation, and capacity building to ensure their effective implementation in practice along global supply chains and in developing countries.

There are also opportunities for donors, companies, foundations, and NGOs to scale up or strengthen some of the industrywide voluntary accountability mechanisms that have been established over the past decade and to ensure their effective implementation at the country level. Initiatives such as the Extractive Industries Transparency Initiative, the Roundtable on Sustainable Palm Oil, the Fair Labor Association, the Ethical Trade Initiative, and the Access to Medicines Index offer very different financing and governance models for promoting responsible business practices and transparency in strategic industry sectors. Some

promote greater public sector transparency in addition to private sector accountability. They warrant detailed analysis and collective effort to scale or replicate.

In all cases, whether corporate responsibility standards and initiatives are
mandatory or voluntary, their implementation on the ground in developing
countries depends not only on the responsibility and capacity of the companies
involved but also critically on the monitoring and sanctioning capacity of government ministries and civil society organizations. In many cases, there is also a
need for grievance mechanisms at either the project or the national levels. Working with partner governments and relevant business associations and civil society
organizations, donors can play a vital role in helping to build this on-the-ground
capacity.

## Recommendation 3: Enhancing Policymaking

Within developing countries there is the need to explicitly broaden the concept
of country ownership to include private sector leaders and leaders from civil society; not only representative business groups but some of the top business, civic,
and academic leaders in the country. These leaders should be invited to form
high-profile consultation mechanisms that could help government ministers to
identify priorities for inclusive and sustainable growth and to develop implementation strategies and public campaigns.

Lessons can be learned from the country coordinating mechanisms of the
Global Fund and from initiatives such as South Africa's Business Trust, which is
jointly governed by government ministers and corporate CEOs to harness business resources for development, and Brazil's Fome Zero, a national food security
policy that established formal mechanisms and criteria for engaging the private
sector and civil society. Business-government dialogue structures have been created in a number of developing countries to discuss economic development and
growth strategies. The governance, constitution, and effectiveness of these public-
private policy mechanisms need to be mapped and evaluated and, where relevant, replicated. At the same time, donors can play an essential role in building
the capacity of domestic economic institutions and traditional business associations, including small-scale producer associations.

Within donor countries there is an opportunity to scale business engagement
in advocacy and public awareness efforts to support international development.
In the United States, for example, networks such as the Initiative for Global
Development, the U.S. Leadership Council, the Modernizing Foreign Assistance
Network, and the Ad Council have brought together corporate leaders with their
NGO counterparts to raise public awareness of development issues and to advo-
cate for aid and trade reform in the U.S. government. The Millennium Challenge
Corporation and USAID have also established external councils to advise on over-
all strategy; both of them include private sector perspectives. Other bilateral and
multilateral donors have created similar external multistakeholder advisory bod-

ies. Once again, almost no mapping or comparative analysis has been undertaken on these advisory and consultation structures or on their impact on enhancing the quality of development policymaking and aid effectiveness. Such analysis needs to be undertaken.

The private sector is increasingly engaged in most major United Nations, World Bank, G8, and G20 conferences and dialogues. This engagement occurs through a combination of representative business bodies, such as the International Chamber of Commerce and International Employers Organization, which are accredited to participate in selected ministerial dialogues, and through the hosting of high-level private sector side events and forums alongside such meetings.

Despite increased private sector participation in global and regional ministerial dialogues, to date there has been almost no private sector engagement in the previous High-Level Forums on Aid Effectiveness and little emphasis placed on the importance of economic growth. The 2011 forum offers an opportunity to rectify this gap. It should place support for shared economic growth at its core and call for a more coordinated approach to market development among donors— one that is focused on enabling vibrant and diversified domestic private sectors and on catalyzing more and better foreign private resources. The following five suggestions focus specifically on the way the HLF can support more effective business sector engagement in the aid effectiveness agenda.

—*Support better research and data collection on the role of the private sector in development.* The HLF could support and extend the research mandate of the OECD/DAC work stream on the role of the private sector in aid effectiveness. Established in 2010, this work stream offers a useful platform for coordinating private sector engagement in the HLF process, including but not limited to input from the OECD Business and Industry Advisory Committee. Among other activities, the work stream is undertaking research on the different incentives and modalities for private sector cooperation with donors and partner governments. Lack of credible aggregate data and rigorous analysis of different donor approaches to working with the private sector remains an obstacle to scaling business engagement in achieving development goals and improving aid effectiveness. The OECD work stream, together with the UN Global Compact and recently established research centers such as the Istanbul International Center for the Private Sector in Development and the Global Green Growth Institute, could underpin an ongoing research and learning network focused on improving data collection and on evaluating and sharing lessons on different donor modalities for engaging the private sector in improving development outcomes. Such a network could draw on evaluation methodologies and knowledge management approaches from both the development community and the private sector. The 2011 High-Level Forum could be used to announce the creation of this research and learning network.

*—Emphasize the links between development and climate change and call for market-based solutions to address them.* The recent establishment of the Global Green Growth Institute in Korea offers a potential platform for engaging leaders from the private sector. Leading companies, chief executive officers, and business associations could be invited to collaborate with donors and partner governments in joint research, policy dialogue, and on-the-ground projects to strengthen the links between the development effectiveness agenda and the climate change agenda. The Global Green Growth Institute has the potential to become an incubator for testing more integrated approaches to economic development and climate mitigation and adaptation, drawing on the combined financial resources, technologies, and expertise of both the public and private sector.

*—Call for increased business participation in donor-supported leadership platforms such as the United Nations Global Compact and the Business Call to Action.* The 2011 HLF should publicly reinforce calls for companies from all countries and sectors to sign up to and adhere to the Ten Principles of the UN Global Compact (focused on universally agreed principles in the areas of human rights, labor, the environment, and anticorruption) and to participate in the UNDP-hosted Business Call to Action, which engages companies to support the MDGs through their core business activities. The 2011 HLF, with Korea as the host, offers particular potential to engage business leaders from other key emerging markets in Asia, Africa, Latin America, and the Middle East, in addition to OECD-based multinationals.

*—Increase donor support for the Bilateral Donors' Statement in Support of Private Sector Partnerships for Development.* Announced at the 2010 United Nations General Assembly, this joint statement recognizes the private sector as a partner around key development issues and commits donors to fostering a more robust role for the private sector in development (see appendix to this chapter). Already endorsed by a number of bilateral donors, multilateral institutions, and business organizations, this statement can help shape a common understanding of the relative roles of the public and private sectors in development and illustrate the types of interventions that can stimulate inclusive and sustainable economic growth. In the lead-up to HLF 4 this statement should be circulated for broader adoption.

*—Identify a small number of pilot countries to build collaborative public-private mechanisms focused on improving development outcomes.* In the lead-up to the HLF, donors, partner governments, and business groups could identify five to ten countries that already demonstrate effective dialogue between the private sector, civil society, government, and donors. These countries could be announced at the 2011 HLF meeting as incubators for developing more systemic, multistakeholder, collaborative initiatives at the country level. These initiatives would be country-led and supported by public and private donor funding and impact investors. They would set strategic priorities, allocate responsibilities, and agree on metrics

and mutual accountability for achieving more inclusive and sustainable growth in, for example, agriculture and tourism, the strengthening of health systems, and local processing and beneficiation of natural resources.

## Conclusion

Private sector contributions and market-based approaches to development are by no means a panacea. Governance gaps, market failures, and bad business practices undermine the potential. Some of these obstacles can be overcome by collaboration with other development actors. Others call for regulatory oversight or vigilant nonprofit watchdogs and an open media. There will always be a need for governments, donors, philanthropists, and NGOs to provide social services, cash transfers, and safety nets to the poorest, most vulnerable communities.

Simultaneously, the private sector is an important part of the solution, as the driver of economic growth and job creation and as a partner in improving development outcomes and stretching limited ODA and philanthropic dollars. As such, the donor community should increase its collaboration efforts with businesses at the operational and policy level, domestically and globally. There is great potential to jointly develop financing mechanisms, technologies, and business models that deliver more inclusive and sustainable economic growth in developing countries—and in doing so, support the goals of the aid effectiveness agenda.

## Appendix: Bilateral Donors' Statement in Support of Private Sector Partnerships for Development

As members of the international bilateral donor community, we recognize the tremendous impact that private sector actors can have on development and we commit to working together to meet the Millennium Development Goals (MDGs). These objectives have been previously outlined in the Millennium Development Goal, Develop a Global Partnership for Development. In the ten years since the MDGs were established, the international community has made great progress in developing partnerships with business and we come together today to renew and give greater meaning to our commitment.

1. We recognize that the private sector is the engine of economic growth and development—creating jobs, goods and services and generating public revenues essential to achieve the Millennium Development Goals. Through our individual institutions we are engaging actively with both local and international businesses on development projects and we have many successes to demonstrate the value of those relationships.

2. We also recognize the important role that multilateral institutions and business organizations, including the UN Global Compact, continue to play in advancing sustainable business models and markets to build an inclusive global economy.

3. Rather than viewing the private sector merely as resource providers, we choose to recognize the private sector as equal partners around key development issues and will enter into partnerships with local and international companies of various sizes. We aim to collaborate with companies that focus not only on profit margin but also on social and environmental impact, and whose work harmonizes with our developmental goals.

4. We recognize there are many different ways to engage with the private sector:

    a. We work with the private sector to implement inclusive business models—sustainable, market-based solutions that are commercially viable and can deliver measurable, impactful, and scalable development results for those at the base of the pyramid.

    b. We work with the private sector to promote responsible business practices in areas such as human rights, labor, environment, and anticorruption.

    c. We work with the private sector to address operational and humanitarian challenges through corporate social responsibility programs that serve both development interests and long-term business interests, improving not only the quality of life in developing countries but also the competitive environment for companies, their license to operate, and their reputational capital.

    d. We actively engage the private sector in public-private policy dialogue and advocacy around issues of global and national importance, including achieving the MDGs, addressing climate change, improving the investment climate, and enhancing aid effectiveness.

5. While there are various ways of engaging with the private sector, we recognize certain common elements exist throughout all our partnerships. In particular, we believe that true partnerships must leverage the skills, expertise, and resources of all parties and that all parties must share in the risks and rewards of the partnership.

6. We recognize the important role donors can play to help businesses overcome the challenges they face in contributing to the MDGs, including the culture shift required in balancing development objectives against maximizing return on investment, moving to inclusive business models, managing risk, and measuring impact.

7. To foster a more robust private sector role in development, we as donors commit to:

    a. Share the risk of investment to spur and leverage the creative investments of private capital through the use of catalytic and innovative financing, including matching grants, loans, equity, and guarantees, and develop new partnership mechanisms to improve our collaboration.

    b. Work with developing country governments to establish a supportive enabling environment through policy and regulatory frameworks that create incentives for stronger private sector participation in development.

    c. Facilitate stronger relationships between private sector actors and other national stakeholders, including governments, civil society, and local small and medium enterprises to support country ownership.

    d. Promote partnerships that improve the lives of both men and women in order to secure equal opportunities.

    e. Build the capacity of local private sector partners to develop socially responsible business initiatives by providing targeted technical assistance.

    f. Increase awareness through facilitating dialogue, developing tools, and supporting learning that showcases the powerful and positive role that well-functioning inclusive markets can play in achieving the MDGs.

8. We recognize the important role that science and technology play in spurring creative and effective development solutions. The private sector is a key driver of innovation, and we will work to integrate these innovations into our programs.

9. We recognize that partnerships with the private sector have the greatest impact when they are strategic; programs become scalable and sustainable when they are integrated into broader strategic initiatives.

10. We are committed to working with the least developed countries and countries struggling in conflict and fragility, as well as with middle-income countries with thriving private sectors.

11. We are committed to the Principles of Aid Effectiveness as detailed in the Paris Declaration and Accra Agenda for Action and will explore how these principles intersect with the work of these partnership communities.

12. We encourage the private sector to commit to an ever increasing role in and responsibility for international development and invite businesses to further shape our understanding of the roles they can play as development partners, so that jointly we can promote a lasting global partnership for development.

This statement was announced at the 2010 United Nations Millennium Development Goals Summit. As of September 2010 it had been endorsed by the following bilateral donors, with input also provided by the United Nations Development Program (UNDP) and International Finance Corporation (IFC):

Austrian Development Agency
Danida, Denmark
Ministry for Foreign Affairs of Finland
Federal Ministry for Economic Cooperation and Development, Germany
Japan Official Development Assistance

Ministry of Foreign Affairs, The Netherlands
Norwegian Ministry of Foreign Affairs
United States Agency for International Development (USAID)
Department for International Development, United Kingdom
Swedish International Development Cooperation Agency
Swiss Agency for Development and Cooperation

## References

Abdou, Ehaab, and others. 2010. "Social Entrepreneurship in the Middle East: Toward Sustainable Development for the Next Generation." Middle East Youth Initiative Report. Silatech, Dubai School of Government, and Wolfensohn Center for Development, Brookings.

Brainard, Lael, ed. 2006. *Transforming the Development Landscape: The Role of the Private Sector.* Brookings.

Brainard, Lael, and Derek Chollet, eds. 2008. *Global Development 2.0: Can Philanthropists, the Public, and the Poor Make Poverty History?* Brookings.

Center for the Advancement of Social Enterprise. 2008. *Developing the Field of Social Entrepreneurship.* Duke University Press.

Corporate Citizenship. 2009. "Partnering for Global Development: The Evolving Links between Business and International Development Agencies."

Corporate Social Responsibility Initiative, International Business Leaders Forum, and World Economic Forum. 2005. "Partnering for Success: Business Perspectives on Multistakeholder Partnerships." Report 4. Corporate Social Responsibility Initiative, Harvard Kennedy School.

Davies, Robert, and Jane Nelson. 2003. "The Buck Stops Where? Managing the Boundaries of Business Engagement in Global Development Challenges." Policy Paper 2. International Business Leaders Forum.

DFID (Department for International Development, U.K.). 2008. *Private Sector Development Strategy: Prosperity for All—Making Markets Work.*

Hudson Institute. 2010. *2010 Index of Global Philanthropy and Remittances.*

Jenkins, Beth. 2007. "Expanding Economic Opportunity: The Role of Large Firms." Report 17. Corporate Social Responsibility Initiative, Harvard Kennedy School.

Jenkins, Beth, and Eriko Ishikawa, with others. 2010. "Scaling Up Inclusive Business: Advancing the Knowledge and Action Agenda." Harvard Kennedy School.

Monitor Institute. 2009. *Investing for Social and Environmental Impact: A Design for Catalyzing an Emerging Industry.*

Mosbacher, Robert, Jr. 2010. "A New Strategy to Leverage Business for International Development." Working Paper 41. Center for Global Economy and Development, Brookings.

Moss, Todd. 2010. "A Doing-Business Facility: A Proposal for Enhancing Business Climate Reform Assistance." Final report. Supporting Business Climate Reforms Working Group, Center for Global Development.

Nelson, Jane. 2010. *Expanding Opportunity and Access: Approaches That Harness Markets and the Private Sector to Create Business Value and Development Impact.* Harvard Kennedy School.

———. 2006. "Leveraging the Development Impact of Business in the Fight against Global Poverty." Working Paper 22. Corporate Social Responsibility Initiative, Harvard Kennedy School.

———. 2003. "Economic Multipliers: Revisiting the Core Responsibility and Contribution of Business to Development." Policy Paper 4. International Business Leaders Forum.

———. 2002. *Building Partnerships: Cooperation between the United Nations System and the Private Sector.* United Nations Department for Public Information.

———. 1996. *Business as Partners in Development: Building Wealth for Countries, Companies, and Communities.* World Bank, UNDP, and International Business Leaders Forum.

Nelson, Jane, and David Prescott. 2006. "Business and the Millennium Development Goals: A Framework for Action." International Business Leaders Forum and United Nations Development Program.

Nelson, Jane, and Noam Unger. 2009. *Strengthening America's Global Development Partnerships: A Policy Blueprint for Better Collaboration between the U.S. Government, Business, and Civil Society.* Brookings.

Prahalad, C. K., and Allen L. Hammond. 2002. "Serving the World's Poor, Profitably." *Harvard Business Review* 80, no. 9: 48–58.

Prahalad, C. K., and Stuart L. Hart. 2002. "The Fortune at the Bottom of the Pyramid." *Strategy + Business Magazine*, no. 26, first quarter.

Rangan, V. Kasturi, and others. 2007. *Business Solutions for the Global Poor: Creating Social and Economic Value.* Hoboken, N.J.: John Wiley & Sons.

UNCTAD (United Nations Conference on Trade and Development). 2010. *World Investment Report 2010: Investing in a Low-Carbon Economy.*

UNDP (United Nations Development Program). 2008. "Creating Value for All: Strategies for Doing Business with the Poor."

———. 2004. "Unleashing Entrepreneurship: Making Business Work for the Poor." Report of the Commission on the Private Sector and Development.

United Nations General Assembly. 2005. "Strengthening the Role of the Private Sector and Entrepreneurship in Financing for Development." Report of the Secretary-General, 59th Session, May 19.

USAID (United States Agency for International Development). 2006. *The Global Development Alliance: Public-Private Alliances for Transformational Development.*

Witte, Jan Martin, and Wolfgang Reinicke. 2005. *Business Unusual: Facilitating United Nations Reform through Partnerships.* United Nations Global Compact.

World Bank. 2011. "About *Doing Business:* Measuring for Impact" (www.doingbusiness.org/about-us).

———. 2009. "A Development Emergency." Global Monitoring Report 2009.

———. 2004. *World Development Report 2005: A Better Investment Climate for Everyone.*

———. 1989. "Developing the Private Sector: A Challenge for the World Bank Group." Findings of the Private Sector Development Review Group.

World Economic Forum. 2008. "The Next Billions: Unleashing Business Potential in Untapped Markets."

———. 2005. "Private Investment for Social Goals: Building the Blended Value Capital Market."

# 5

## Rethinking Aid Coordination

NGAIRE WOODS

Should aid be better coordinated? And if so, how? The case for aid coordination is a powerful one. As aid poured into Haiti in the wake of a massive earthquake in January 2010, television coverage around the world broadcast two different realities. One story was about well-organized aid givers collecting record donations and dispatching food and medical equipment by the ton to Haiti. The other was a story about aid stymied by a lack of coordination. Television crews depicted Haitian families and children complaining that none of the food, medical assistance, or shelter was reaching them. The president of Haiti soon spoke out: "I am not in a position to criticize anybody, not in the least people who have come here to help me," René Préval said. "What I am saying is, what everybody is saying is, we need better coordination."[1]

The failure to coordinate was soon apparent to all. A few days after the crisis, Médecins Sans Frontières announced that international coordination of the relief effort "is not existing or (is) not sufficient."[2] A month or so later, an assessment by Refugees International concluded that "coordination and communication

I am indebted to Barbara Lee, Jonathan White, Alan Gelb, Ezra Suruma, and Brenda Killen for their excellent comments on the first draft of this chapter, and to Christina Ward for her research assistance.

1. Patricia Zengerle and Jackie Frank, "Haiti Aid Needs Better Coordination," Reuters, January 2, 2010.

2. The Haiti manager of Médecins Sans Frontières, Benoit Leduc, speaking in Port-au-Prince, was cited on NPR, January 1, 2010.

between Haitian civil society and UN and international NGOs are largely miss-ing, with both sectors operating along parallel and separate lines."[3] Many local organizations were unable to access meetings at the UN compound in Port-au-Prince: they were either unaware of their meetings, did not have proper photo-ID passes for entry, or did not have the staff capacity to spend long hours at the com-pound. Yet their inclusion in coordination was crucial to avoid overlap and to maximize outreach and coverage.[4] The result was a situation familiar to all con-cerned with humanitarian relief. Foreign governments, UN agencies, and some 900 international NGOs trying to coordinate among themselves, often ineffec-tually, and mostly in the absence of Haitian groups trying to work in their own communities.

Coordination failure in Haiti reflects long-standing problems, not unique to Haiti. Three years before the earthquake, the World Bank convened a technical meeting about Haiti to discuss how better to coordinate development assistance. The records of that discussion highlight a core question that affects outside assis-tance to countries: Who should coordinate whom and how?

Haiti proposed to the World Bank's 2007 technical meeting that its own Min-istry of Planning and External Cooperation should be the main coordinator of assistance and proposed a plan for strengthening and restructuring the ministry to permit it to coordinate aid strategically, sectorally, and geographically.[5] Haiti's proposal reflects an approach to which donors have long paid lip service. In the Paris Declaration of 2005 over a hundred aid providers committed to ensuring that development assistance would be provided in a manner that permits devel-oping countries to set their own strategies and objectives, with donors aligning behind these objectives and using local systems.[6] In practice, however, other donor priorities intervene.

In Haiti after the 2010 earthquake there were daily discussions with the gov-ernment, but the government was very clearly not in charge. It may have seemed necessary to sideline the country's government, which itself had been devastated by the quake, but this sidelining has a longer history. Back in 2007 Haiti's plan to strengthen its capacity and take over coordinating external assistance met with little support. Donors agreed to "meet at the representative level in Port-au-Prince to consider and coordinate the assistance they could provide" in order to strengthen Haiti's capacity. The donors' main concern was to ensure that they coordinated among themselves, including distributing tasks between donors and

3. Duplat and Parry (2010).
4. At the UN compound in Port-au-Prince, UN agencies and international NGOs had established "task-specific cluster groups to improve communication across operating agencies, discuss specific needs, and coordinate activities in order to avoid overlap and maximize outreach and coverage of a response." Ibid.
5. World Bank (2007b).
6. OECD (2005).

presenting common positions on key issues. They agreed to more regular and structured meetings with the government of Haiti. However, donors firmly reasserted their own leadership of efforts to coordinate assistance: in-country led by the resident coordinator of the UN System, with the World Bank leading among capitals.[7]

Donors' preoccupation with their own coordination was further entrenched as international NGOs poured into the country. The Haitian president, accused of not ensuring that aid reached the needy, said, "The Haitian government has not seen one cent of that money that has been raised for Haiti. I presume that that means the money is going to NGOs."[8] The president is referring to approximately 900 international NGOs involved in delivering relief to Haiti after the earthquake (see chapter 3, this volume). As noted above, the efforts of these groups to coordinate among themselves, facilitated by the UN, tended not to include Haitian groups.

Haiti is but one example of coordination failure. Another rather different example is Mozambique. Far from sidelining the government, donors have flocked to Mozambique because they like and trust the government to the extent that some describe the country as a "donor darling." Nevertheless coordination problems have been rife.

Mozambique is the subject of a study by independent experts called "Perfect Partners?" The researchers conclude that, in spite of efforts to improve donor coordination, donors were failing to reduce "the overall burden on capacity-starved institutions."[9] At least one donor mission was arriving in Mozambique every working day (the authors were unable to calculate the full number because so few donors complied with the reporting requirements of Mozambique's Department of International Cooperation). The picture they depict of aid flowing into Mozambique is one of donor-generated chaos. They estimate that half of total public spending was grant aid, spent off budget, and coming into the country through a multitude of uncoordinated, donor-driven, development and technical assistance projects that did not add up to a coherent whole.[10] Aid directed to government ministries, such as the Ministry of Agriculture, was negated by "fragmented donor interventions and the continuing strength of established individual niches and of the interests (and rent-seeking) that such fragmentation often creates."[11]

An ostensible solution to coordination failure in Mozambique has been attempted in recent years, by persuading donors to deliver aid in the form of general budget support. In theory, this should be a way to resolve the coordination

7. World Bank (2007a).
8. Zengerle and Frank, "Haiti Aid Needs Better Coordination."
9. Killick, Castel-Branco, and Gerster (2005, p. 35).
10. Ibid., p. 46.
11. Ibid., p. 47.

problems described above, putting the government at the center of the coordination of external assistance. Interestingly, the results are not as obvious as might be expected. One study of budget support provided to Mozambique reports that the process began rather promisingly.[12] The original group of six donors willing to give budget support was small and active and tried to enter into genuine policy dialogue with the government, including on governance issues. But the growing influence of the group and its access to senior government officials soon provoked envy among other donors.

Mozambique's budget support donors' group soon grew from six to eighteen, as donors that had not been part of the initial process bought a seat at the table by contributing (even quite small amounts) to the budget support program. A memorandum of understanding spells out the terms under which these eighteen donors provide aid as general budget support, the arrangements for periodic performance reviews, and the reciprocal obligations with which the parties undertake to comply. A regular cycle of annual and midterm reviews was set up based on twenty-four sectoral and thematic working groups, which meet regularly to accompany the formulation and implementation of government policies, including reforms contained in the performance assessment framework—a summary matrix that forms the basis of policy dialogue.

The process of dialogue with the government is, as described above, a cumbersome one, which gives donors a voice (in the various working groups) across all parts of government. Further exacerbating this, the increase in donor participation in budget support increased the costs and damage of donor activity.[13] Meetings with the government became larger and less expert. The larger number of donors brought different priorities to the table, including HIV/AIDS, the investigation and prosecution of past corruption, and land privatization. These problems were compounded by the rapid turnover of donor staff, whose average stay of two years or less rarely gives time to understand the underlying issues.

Problems of coordination in Mozambique persist, according to the 2010 review of Mozambique's program aid partners.[14] Their interviews with government officials and other partners reveal a breakdown in donor-government dialogue. They depict an atmosphere of mutual accusations, where legalism is used to pursue agendas outside the memorandum, and open discussion is being replaced by the use of written responses to mutual accusations. They write that mutual evaluations are being turned into a kind of tribunal to try the government of Mozambique. Even the new memorandum of understanding, held up by donors as a positive milestone in their relationship with the government, is perceived by partners in Mozambique as asymmetrically in favor of the donors, produced under great pressure, and accepted by the government in order to ensure disbursements.

12. De Renzio and Hanlon (2007).
13. Ibid.
14. Castel-Branco, Ossemane, and Amarcy (2010, p. 4).

The cases of Haiti and Mozambique highlight that rethinking the coordination of aid requires a more radical reappraisal of basic premises than is present in most current debates. From outside, donors seem mired in discussions of how to improve the processes they use to inform each other of their respective efforts. More recently, they have branched out into discussions of how to include China and emerging donors in those discussions.

This chapter seeks to crack open the premise upon which the debate is structured—the notion that what the aid system needs is "more coordination." This chapter argues that we should begin by carefully distinguishing coordination from cooperation in development assistance. The fundamental goal of coordination is to ensure that the efforts of one donor do not stymie the efforts of another donor. In the end, this chapter asks whether this can only be achieved by ensuring that coordination is rooted in, and managed by, the government receiving the development assistance.

## Redefining, Coordinating, and Cooperating

A few years ago a budget director of Uganda reflected on the deluge of donor delegations with whom she was having to contend. It struck her as ludicrous that she was in fact observing a parade of the same half dozen countries, simply coming under different guises: as DFID, USAID, AFD, CIDA, SIDA, Norad, the World Bank, the IMF, the UNDP, the FAO, UNEP, and so on.[15] Her point was simple: Why do donors create institutions for cooperation in development assistance and then so often ignore them and pursue their efforts one by one?

I propose that coordination in development assistance is almost always used to describe activities that paper over a deeper failure to cooperate.[16] Consider that the United Kingdom, the United States, Japan, and Canada (and 183 other countries) could cooperate in providing development assistance by channeling all their contributions to the World Bank. The bank could then use pooled information and the established rules and procedures for working with a developing country government to provide the assistance. No further coordination would be required.

But the situation is otherwise: each of these countries pursues development assistance goals through a multiplicity of actors and programs, including various domestic agencies, NGOs, international programs and international organizations. For this reason, coordination is important.

### Cooperation

Cooperation in development assistance I define as donors working together to plan and deliver aid, such as by creating an international institution to pool fund-

---

15. Cited in Welsh and Woods (2007).

16. This is very different from the approach that political scientists take to the concepts of coordination and cooperation. Keohane (1984); Aggarwal and Dupont (2004).

ing, information, and expertise and to collectively make decisions. Examples of such institutions are the International Bank for Reconstruction and Development and the International Development Association. The argument for cooperation is that it enables donor governments, by pooling resources and knowledge, to deliver development assistance that has some degree of mutually recognized stability, neutrality, and autonomy. Cooperation can reduce the number of donors or ensure a single or dominant donor with which a recipient government can work, an oft-cited factor in the success of aid to Taiwan and Botswana.[17]

To cooperate in such a way, states need to create institutions or agreed norms and rules so that each understands what it should do and what others are likely to do. By creating institutions, states can emphasize longer term aims and goals and also reduce their transaction costs.[18] In practice, cooperation in development assistance is relatively limited compared to the bilateral (or nonmultilateral) activities of governments. In spite of having created international institutions for cooperation, the longest-standing OECD/DAC member states continue to channel the lion's share of their development assistance through their own bilateral programs. The OECD/DAC reported in September 2010 that, in the period 1989–2008, the multilateral share of total overseas development assistance stayed relatively stable, ranging from 27 percent to 33 percent, excluding debt relief. However, when the contributions of EU member states to the EU (which have risen faster than other components) are excluded, one sees that the share of multilateral overseas development assistance has declined, from 22 percent in 1989 to 20 percent in 2008.[19] Put another way, about 80 percent of aid is still delivered through bilateral agencies.

Why do states not cooperate in development assistance? Four sets of reasons stand out. First, there are national reasons. There are vested interests in programs delivered in ways that benefit national companies, nongovernmental organizations, and particular government agencies. Public support for aid is widely thought to be sustained by stamping the national flag on projects, funds, and activities. Accountability to national taxpayers is thought to require the use of national auditing procedures and projects and policies achieved and reported within the fiscal year and within the electoral cycle.

A second set of reasons is about values and the genuine philosophical differences about what aid should aspire to. For example, should poverty reduction trump infrastructure development? Should HIV/AIDs treatment trump maternal health? Should indigenous rights trump growth and energy strategies? Donors often disagree about these priorities. The result is that they pursue different goals.

The third set of reasons encompasses genuine disagreements about what works and where. The evaluation of aid is plagued with both methodological and political difficulties. The protracted time frames involved in achieving development

17. Brautigam (2000); Azam, Devarajan, and O'Connell (1999).
18. Abbott and Snidal (1998); Keohane and Martin (1995).
19. OECD (2010).

results create a problem with short-run evaluations. This problem is compounded by inherent difficulties in establishing causation between expenditures and outcomes. As a result, bilateral donors often prefer to deliver aid where they are most convinced of the merits of their interventions and where they can quickly change course if it seems to pose reputational or other risks to the responsible minister or administration overseeing the aid program.

The fourth set of explanations relates to the perceived weaknesses of multilateral agencies: cumbersome and time-consuming procedures, lack of transparency, high overhead costs (with higher absolute costs and salaries), and a lack of accountability. More generally, major donors argue that there is insufficient evidence of the effectiveness of multilateral aid, particularly as regards development impact and value for money, despite agencies' high levels of investment in evaluation, assessment, disclosure, and communications systems.[20] That said, several new donors—Korea and Central and Eastern European countries—are now giving the largest share of their aid multilaterally.[21]

## Coordination

Coordination in development assistance is not the same as cooperation. It does not involve governments working together to plan, deliver, and achieve a common goal. When two donors join forces to plan and build a well, they are cooperating. Coordination, by contrast, refers to organizing activities harmoniously so as not to thwart one another. Coordination ensures that two wells are not built side by side or that two different agencies avoid vaccinating the same child twice. Coordination is not ambitious; principally it serves to prevent inadvertent damage caused when donors are ignorant of each other's actions.

Coordination is important because so little cooperation takes place. Large numbers of donors, each doing their own thing in developing countries, give rise to a need for coordination to ensure that all of these activities take place in harmony. The problem is not a new one. In 1981 Lesotho was said to have sixty-one separate donors financing 321 projects.[22] In 2002 Vietnam was said to have twenty-five official bilateral donors, nineteen official multilateral donors, and about 350 international NGOs, accounting for more than 8,000 development projects.[23] The costs of such multiplicities of donors include reversible costs, such as duplication and waste, as well as irreversible costs, such as undermining the quality of governance or retarding the development of public sector capacity.[24] The debate about coordination arises as donors seek to reduce such costs.

20. Ibid., chap. 6.
21. Ibid.
22. Morss (1984).
23. Acharya, Fuzzo de Lima, and Moore (2003).
24. Knack and Rahman (2004).

Through coordination donors seek to lessen the risks of one agency's actions being inadvertently rendered more costly, useless, or damaging by the actions of another agency. It involves sharing information about at least three things:

—What is being planned: donors' current and future projects and their financing.

—With whom and when it is being planned: ensuring mechanisms for working with a country or a community to avoid bottlenecks, overstretch, and paralysis.

—What has been delivered: past interventions and their impact.

Too often coordination is seen as an ex post process—mostly meetings—in which disjointed activities and varying interests are cobbled together before being imposed on a government by donors. The evaluation of Mozambique's program aid partners proposes that, instead, coordination should be ex ante—coordination around the needs of the government's program instead of subsequently trying to coordinate studies determined by several partners individually and according to their own agendas.[25] It argues that coordination is linked with strategies and plans rather than with meetings. Figure 5-1 links the timely sharing of information with adjustments to policy. When information is exchanged ex post, it typically incurs much greater cost.

Even information sharing is not easy. This is reflected in an evaluation by the World Bank that examines repeated failures to share information about current and future projects.[26] This outcome may mean a suboptimal allocation of resources from the perspective of both donors and recipients.

## International Donor Model of Coordination

Attempts to create an international donor-driven model of coordination have been led by the OECD/DAC at two levels: standard setting for all donors at the international level; and country-level coordination of international donors active in any one country, for which the DAC is trying to set standards and create a norm of monitoring and enforcement. At the core of the DAC's traditional coordination role is an international reporting and standard-setting system, whereby members commit to report their official development assistance to the organization and agree to abide by tight definitions as to what constitutes overseas development assistance. In creating and protecting this definition of official development assistance, the DAC has been successful.

At the international level, the OECD/DAC process is also about ensuring cooperation among multilateral and bilateral donors. Although only about 20 percent of official development assistance is channeled through multilateral agencies, even this much aid poses serious coordination problems because 81 percent of it flows

25. Killick, Castel-Branco, and Gerster (2005).
26. Halonen-Akatwijuka (2004).

Figure 5-1. *Cooperation and Coordination from Donors' Perspectives*

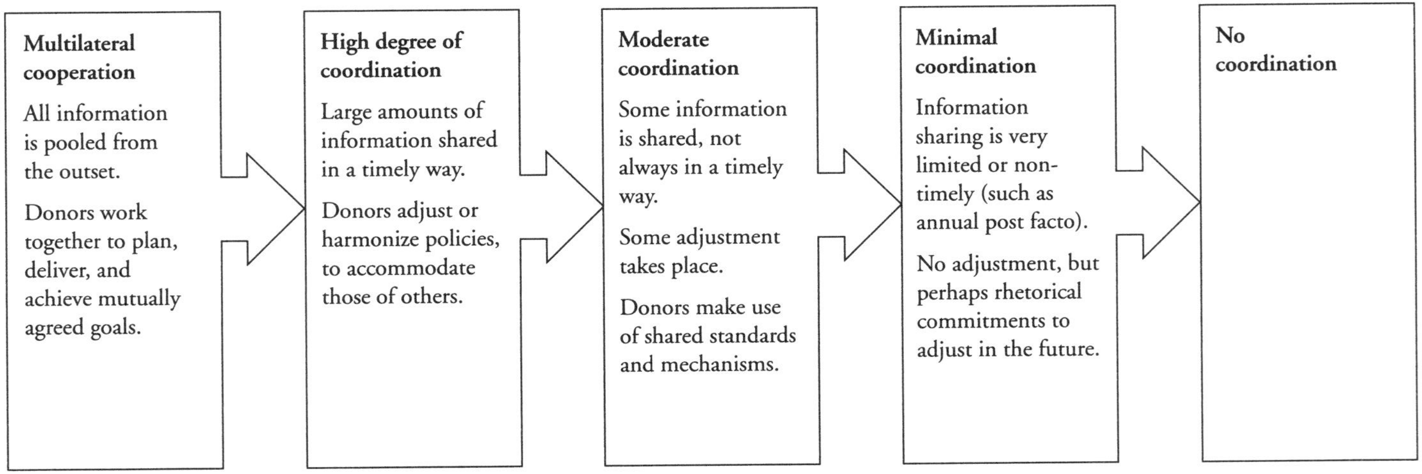

**Multilateral cooperation**

All information is pooled from the outset.

Donors work together to plan, deliver, and achieve mutually agreed goals.

↗

**High degree of coordination**

Large amounts of information shared in a timely way.

Donors adjust or harmonize policies, to accommodate those of others.

↗

**Moderate coordination**

Some information is shared, not always in a timely way.

Some adjustment takes place.

Donors make use of shared standards and mechanisms.

↗

**Minimal coordination**

Information sharing is very limited or non-timely (such as annual post facto).

No adjustment, but perhaps rhetorical commitments to adjust in the future.

↗

**No coordination**

to six clusters of international organizations: EU institutions (37 percent), the International Development Association (21 percent), UN funds and programs (10 percent), the Global Fund (6 percent), the African Development Bank (4 percent), and the Asian Development Bank (3 percent). Beyond these clusters of organizations lie another 200 or more multilaterals to which the rest flows. The result is significant competition by multilateral agencies for funding, for influence, and for a lead coordination role on the ground.

In recent years the DAC has facilitated a multilateral process to enhance the effectiveness of aid by setting standards in relation to donor actions with one another as well as in-country. The Paris Declaration and the Accra Agenda for Action set out a series of commitments by donors for better practice.[27] These include working to better harmonize development assistance by donors coordinating with one another, simplifying procedures, and sharing information. Along with these commitments are interlocking commitments to ensure ownership, alignment, results, and accountability. These mean that developing countries would set their own strategies for reducing poverty, for improving their institutions, and for tackling corruption; that donors would align behind these objectives and use local systems; that developing countries and donors would focus on measurable development results; and that donors and partners would be mutually accountable for development results.

Most observers agree that progress in ownership is at best modest. Of the subset of donors who give general budget support to Mozambique, only 58 percent were using the national systems for audit by 2010.[28]

At the country level ex ante coordination is sometimes required (such as of analysis, as argued above, before goals are set). Meetings need to be of well-prepared and well-functioning groups: the Mozambique annual review argues that "to improve the functioning/effectiveness of working groups it may be necessary to rationalize them, simplifying their architecture in a very substantial way, having far fewer people in each group (which requires specialization of the Program Aid Partners), and allocating staff with technical expertise to discuss each group's specific matters."[29] The people involved in meetings need to have knowledge (or institutional memory) of their agency's history with the government, prior advice, and formal and informal commitments. Too often this is missing: both the 2010 Mozambique review and a 2007 study note the problems posed in this regard by donors' regular rotation of staff.[30]

Having created a coordination framework, the long-standing OECD/DAC members would now like to induct emerging economies and other "new" (as they

---

27. OECD (2005, 2008a).
28. Castel-Branco, Ossemane, and Amarcy (2010).
29. Ibid.
30. Ibid.; de Renzio and Hanlon (2007).

see it) donors. The OECD/DAC countries are concerned that China, for example, is avoiding their carefully crafted standards on issues such as export credits,
debt sustainability, corruption, and governance. That said, the evidence suggests
that the gap between China's actions and the actions of OECD/DAC donors is
not as wide as is often assumed.[31] Three obstacles stand in the way of expanding
the OECD/DAC process.

The first is that argued by Kang-ho Park (chapter 2, this volume): many new
partners believe that the Paris Declaration lacks legitimacy because it was conceived and driven by traditional donors, with developing countries only brought
into the process later.

A second obstacle is that emerging economies do not see the OECD/DAC
process as having been effective in improving the performance of aid. To quote
Deborah Brautigam: China does not participate in donor-led groups (the Paris
Club, Consultative Groups, the DAC process on coordination) not least because
"they generally do not see aid from the West as having been very effective in
reducing poverty in Africa."[32] Brautigam also argues that China is cognizant of
the importance of transparency and, if asked, will share with African governments
the amount of aid development finance it is providing.

Third, the international donor-led coordination process does not speak to the
issues that emerging donors prioritize. Their way of delivering aid is different and
(with China skewing the picture) more closely aligned with recipient government
priorities. The emerging donors do not impose conditionality. The fact that
China, India, Brazil, Korea, and Thailand have all been recipients of aid shapes
their approach. China, for example, does not set up project implementation units.
Its eight principles of aid set out a strong framework of mutuality, including at a
practical level.[33]

The aid of emerging donors tends to be far less fragmented than that of
OECD/DAC donors. OECD/DAC donors typically offer small amounts of
funding to many projects across several sectors (in each of which they impose
their own, different reporting requirements), with health and education being
particularly popular.[34] And the problem is getting worse, not better. The Accra
Agenda for Action highlights the costly fragmentation of aid and duplication of
initiatives. By contrast, emerging donors tend to focus on fewer sectors and less
fragmented sectors (such as infrastructure). For example, in a report on aid effectiveness in Cambodia, the government reports that in 2006 alone, there were sev-

31. Brautigam (2010); Woods (2008).
32. Brautigam (2010, p. 31).
33. Among China's principles: the experts dispatched by China to help in construction in the recipient countries will have the same standard of living as the experts of the recipient country; Chinese experts
are not allowed to make any special demands or enjoy any special amenities; and in providing technical
assistance, the Chinese government will see to it that the personnel of the recipient country fully master
such techniques.
34. Knack and Rahman (2004).

enteen aid projects in the health sector at once, in contrast to the road and transport sector, where, over twenty years, a group of eight donors financed more than fifty projects.[35]

In sum, the international donor coordination system has achieved some modest successes in setting standards of reporting among DAC donors. However, significant obstacles remain.

## Country-Led Coordination Model

The problem with the internationally driven model of coordination is that in practice it can crowd out local processes of priority setting, of delivery and implementation, and of evaluation and feedback. Simply put, the donor's agenda and attention become focused on inter-donor relations and negotiations. Consultative group and country coordinating mechanism meetings take place, in which the country's representatives listen to donors argue. To quote a World Bank evaluation: "To date, the move to genuine country-led partnerships that effectively combine ownership and partnership is being made in only a few IDA countries, typically in one or two sectors."[36]

Tellingly, almost all suggestions for improvements in processes focus on donors. The World Bank proposes that donors could better share information, cofinance projects, jointly take part in strategic programming for countries, and have donor coordination meetings. The OECD/DAC proposes more coherence among multilateral donors, using common arrangements, shared analysis, and complementing each other's activities. Neglected is an analysis of how aid coordination could be rooted in, and managed by, governments receiving development assistance. The rationale for investigating this rests on three hypotheses.

First, the aid-receiving government is probably the most likely repository of the necessary information (even accepting the problems all governments have in accessing and using the information at their disposal). This is increasingly true as the number of donors (public and private) increases, the rotations of staff remain short (and therefore their access to information is limited and short term), and the number of countries, communities, and sectors in which donors operate increases.

Second, the incentives to ensure effective coordination are likely to be stronger within the aid-receiving government (even when they are relatively weak) than within donor agencies, which have very strong incentives not to coordinate. This chapter outlines some of the reasons that donors prefer not to cooperate and, equally, prefer to limit coordination. I would add to these that the costs of noncoordination are more likely to be concentrated at the local level. By contrast, the

35. Royal Government of Cambodia (2007).
36. See World Bank, 2001, p iv.

benefits of noncoordination are strong for donors seeking to meet other objectives (speedy disbursement, quick results, domestic political priorities).

Finally, development effectiveness (which provides the rationale for efforts to improve coordination) requires effective government. Here the most important part of the OECD/DAC agenda are the links between coordination, ownership, and alignment. This link is emphasized in the Accra Agenda for Action. That agenda highlights country ownership and the support of country systems: "We will strengthen and use developing country systems to the maximum extent possible" and respect "countries' priorities, investing in their human resources and institutions, making greater use of their systems to deliver aid, and increasing the predictability of aid flows." Making this a reality surely requires having developing country governments lead in coordinating aid in their own countries and focusing efforts on enhancing their capacity so to do.

## Some Implications for the High-Level Forum

In November 2011 the OECD will convene a High-Level Forum on Aid Effectiveness. This is the fourth such forum and the continuation of a process that began in Rome in 2003, when major donors agreed to harmonize procedures and practices among themselves. In Paris in 2005 donors and developing countries agreed on a set of principles to improve aid effectiveness and on specific targets to be reached by 2010. The Paris Agreement was further endorsed in Accra in 2008. In Busan participants will take stock of progress toward the targets set out in the Paris Declaration.

This chapter proposes that the fourth High-Level Forum needs to address or catalyze a country-led approach to coordination. Countering such an approach is the view that a lack of trust prevents donors from embracing a country-led approach to coordination and that trust is best built up (slowly) through the Paris process. This chapter argues that a more urgent approach is needed.

The lack of trust argument requires close scrutiny. For example, among the targets to be assessed in Busan are those relating to the second Paris principle concerning alignment. It sets out standards for countries' improvements in public financial management and procurement systems.[37] The implicit assumption is that if countries improve on these measures (that is, by their ability to use and account for aid), donors will trust them more and align more of their aid. Yet anecdotal evidence suggests that countries improving their country systems have been receiving less, not more, budget support.[38] What does the wider evidence tell us? Further evidence could be revealed from information about the use of public

---

37. These are measured by the World Bank's Country Policy and Institutional Assessments.
38. OECD (2008b).

financial management systems and use of country procurement systems. It might well be the case that, irrespective of donors' trust in national institutions, they simply like to maximize their own control over projects and programs for reasons of their own changing interests, accountability, and public relations. For this reason, serious moves toward a country-led agenda would need a push from the highest political level, so as to cut through the countering incentives.

Another Paris target under scrutiny in Busan is to reduce by two-thirds parallel project implementation units (PIUs). This is a worthy and important goal. A caveat must be lodged, however. The experience of Mozambique with general budget support is sobering. Although Mozambique freed itself from some aid with PIUs attached, it soon found itself embroiled with twenty-four donor-created working groups overseeing its use of budget support. As donors giving budget support acquired greater influence, so too more donors began to contribute and take a place at the table. There is little or no evidence of donors stepping back with anything like such alacrity. Put simply, donors find it difficult to genuinely withdraw from influencing policy and projects in country. To quote a senior aid official, "We just can't keep our hands off things." This is a further reason that a more country-led approach to coordination is as necessary as it is difficult to achieve.

The simplest philosophical principle underlying the Paris process of standard setting is to get donors to focus more on what countries need rather than on what donors wish to give. In this the Paris target on technical cooperation is telling, because it reveals how much technical cooperation is about what donors wish to supply—and how little it is about what a country needs. The target set in 2005 is for 50 percent of technical cooperation flows to be implemented through coordinated programs consistent with national development strategies. It would be pleasing to see the Busan High-Level Forum treat this issue seriously. At the heart of it lies the reality that much donor technical assistance diverts developing country governments away from their own priorities, sapping their ability to meet the challenges that donors would (in theory) like them to address and to plan around. The positive opportunity is for countries to receive assistance, of the kind Haiti called for in 2007, to genuinely strengthen their capacity to coordinate external assistance coming into their country.

# References

Abbott, K., and D. Snidal. 1998. "Why States Act through Formal International Organizations." *Journal of Conflict Resolution* 42, no. 1: 3–32.

Acharya, Arnab, Ana Fuzzo de Lima, and Mick Moore. 2003. "The Proliferators: Transactions Costs and the Value of Aid." Institute of Development Studies.

Aggarwal, Vinod, and Cédric Dupont. 2004. "Collaboration and Coordination in the Global Political Economy." In *Global Political Economy*, edited by John Ravenhill. Oxford University Press.

Azam, Jean-Paul, Shantayanan Devarajan, and Stephen A. O'Connell. 1999. "Aid Dependence Reconsidered." Policy Research Working Paper 2144. World Bank.

Brautigam, Deborah. 2010. *The Dragon's Gift: The Real Story of China in Africa*. Oxford University Press.

———. 2000. *Aid Dependence and Governance*. Almqvist & Wiksell.

Castel-Branco, Carlos Nuno, Rogerio Ossemane, and Sofia Amarcy. 2010. "Mozambique: Independent Evaluation of the PAPs' Performance in 2009 and Performance Trends in the Period 2004–2009." Instituto de Estudos Sociais e Economicos.

de Renzio, Paulo, and Joseph Hanlon. 2007. "Contested Sovereignty in Mozambique: The Dilemmas of Aid Dependence." Working Paper 2007/25. Global Economic Governance Program, Oxford University.

Duplat, Patrick, and Emilie Parry. 2010. "Haiti: From the Ground Up." Field report. Refugees International.

Halonen-Akatwijuka, Maiji. 2004. "Coordination Failure in Foreign Aid." Policy Research Working Paper 3223. World Bank.

Keohane, Robert O. 1984. *After Hegemony: Cooperation and Discord in the World Political Economy*. Princeton University Press.

Keohane, Robert O., and Lisa L. Martin. 1995. "The Promise of Institutionalist Theory." *International Security* 20, no. 1: 39–51.

Killick, Tony, Carlos N. Castel-Branco, and Richard Gerster. 2005. "Perfect Partners? The Performance of Programme Aid Partners in Mozambique. 2004." Report to the Program Aid Partners and Government of Mozambique.

Knack, Stephen, and Aminur Rahman. 2004. "Donor Fragmentation and Bureaucratic Quality in Aid Recipients." Policy Research Working Paper 3186. World Bank.

Morss, Elliott. 1984. "Institutional Destruction Resulting from Donor and Project Proliferation in Sub-Saharan African Countries." *World Development* 12, no. 4: 465–70.

OECD (Organization for Economic Cooperation and Development). 2010. "2010 DAC Report on Multilateral Aid."

———. 2008a. "Accra Agenda for Action."

———. 2008b. "Assessing Progress on Implementing the Paris Declaration and the Accra Agenda for Action."

———. 2005. "Paris Declaration on Aid Effectiveness."

Royal Government of Cambodia. 2007. "The Cambodia Aid Effectiveness Report 2007." Cambodian Rehabilitation and Development Board, Council for the Development of Cambodia.

Welsh, Jennifer, and Ngaire Woods, eds. 2007. *Exporting Good Governance*. Wilfred Laurier University Press.

Woods, Ngaire. 2008. "Whose Aid? Whose Influence? China, Emerging Donors, and the Silent Revolution in Development Assistance." *International Affairs* 84, no. 6: 1205–21.

World Bank. 2007a. "HAITI: Technical Meeting on Aid Coordination and Budget Support." Summary of Discussion and Agreements Reached. Friday, March 23, 2007 (http://site resources.worldbank.org/INTHAITI/Resources/March23Mtgsummary.pdf).

———. 2007b. "Strengthening Aid Coordination and Results Monitoring in Haiti: A Framework for Discussion." Discussion paper, March 23, 2007, technical meeting.

———. 2001. "OED IDA Review of Aid Coordination in an Era of Poverty Reduction Strategies." IDA 10-12. Operations Evaluation Department.

# 6

## Capacity Traps and Legitimacy Traps: Development Assistance and State Building in Fragile Situations

SHINICHI TAKEUCHI, RYUTARO MUROTANI, AND KEIICHI TSUNEKAWA

Dealing with fragility and fragile situations is one of today's most critical international challenges, a challenge closely related to the problems of conflict prevention, poverty reduction, and global security. There have been many attempts at defining "fragility," or "fragile states."[1] In the present chapter we conceptualize fragility as a situation in which human security is under continuous threat, with armed conflict and chronic poverty as its most prominent features. We adopt this definition in part because we want to avoid punctilious debates over definitional matters and in part because conceptual simplicity highlights the true source of the problem: governments unwilling or unable to protect their people from violence and destitution. This means that the process of state building—the formation of an effective and legitimate state—should be at the center of the agenda for overcoming fragility, as called for in the OECD/DAC "Principles for Good International Engagement in Fragile States and Situations."[2]

In considering the state-building process, it is important to keep in mind differences in historical context between the standard paradigmatic state builders, typified by the European countries, and contemporary developing countries. In Europe state formation was a long-term evolving process of coercive power

---

The authors would like to express many thanks to the participants for their valuable comments on an earlier version of this chapter. Errors and omissions are our own.

1. For example, Stewart and Brown (2009); OECD (2008b).
2. See OECD (2007a). The same argument appears in OECD (2008a, 2008b, 2010a).

accumulation.[3] By contrast, among the postcolonial, independent countries we find cases in which the process of state formation was impeded by the colonial powers. These countries obtained independence before a cohesive state structure could be consolidated.

This initial impairment aggravated poverty and violence within societies and deepened fragility.[4] As news of humanitarian tragedy spread rapidly via high-tech media, the international community could not justify waiting for some "natural" process of state building to unfold. In addition, in many cases, fragility in an individual state caused harmful effects in regional and global contexts.[5] Against this backdrop, international engagement with state building was strengthened. While the consequences often have been criticized as inadequate, the need for state building, and for international engagement in the state-building process, is now widely accepted.[6]

DAC donors, in fact, have increased ODA to states in fragile situations as well as to states in the process of overcoming fragility, which is one of the main reasons for the ODA resurgence of the 2000s. According to our calculation, the receipt of ODA by these states expanded from $9.3 billion (16 percent of total ODA) in 2000 to $42.9 billion (33 percent of total ODA) in 2008.[7] This ODA has tended to be concentrated in a small number of countries. The top five—Iraq, Nigeria, Afghanistan, Democratic Republic of Congo (hereafter the DRC), and Ethiopia—accounted for 56 percent between 2003 and 2008.[8]

ODA from DAC donors is, however, only one part of the resources provided to fragile states. Humanitarian aid and peacekeeping expenditures also are expanding. In 2007 peacekeeping expenditures in Côte d'Ivoire, the DRC,

3. Tilly (1992).

4. Buzan (1983).

5. Weiner (1996); Fukuyama (2005).

6. For criticism of the consequences of state building, see Chandler (2006). Literature that accepts the need for state building includes Fearon and Laitin (2004); Krasner and Pascual (2005); and Paris and Sisk (2009a).

7. We first compiled a list of thirty-three fragile states on the basis of seven existing indexes: IDA resource allocation index, Country Indicators for Foreign Policy Fragility Index, Brookings Index of State Weakness in the Developing World, Fund for Peace Failed States Index, Institute for Economics & Peace Global Peace Index, George Mason University State Fragility Index, and USAID Fragility Alert Lists. We ourselves added Bosnia and Herzegovina and the West Bank and Gaza. Our resultant list differs only slightly from the one prepared by OECD (2010c). We used WDI data to calculate the amount of ODA to these countries.

8. It is said that debt relief represents a large share of the ODA to fragile states. In 2005 and 2006 debt relief to Iraq and Nigeria did, in fact, inflate the fragile states' share in ODA; however, apart from those two years, the share of total ODA to fragile states does not change much with or without debt relief. It was 18 percent ($8.4 billion) in 2000 and 31 percent ($34.3 billion) in 2008. The share of the five largest recipients, however, drops to 41 percent in 2003–08 if debt relief is excluded (OECD, OECD International Development Statistics, various years). We must also attend to the possibility that in postconflict situations, the cost of security for aid personnel or large per diems for hazard pay can inflate unit costs considerably. Aid used in the field may consequently be less than the announced amount.

Liberia, and Sudan exceeded the ODA that each received.[9] In some countries, such as Afghanistan and Iraq, external military forces themselves deliver aid to security sectors and to local communities. In addition, assistance from emerging donors and from global thematic funds and private foundations now constitutes an important part of resources for fragile states.[10]

In spite of the huge flow of aid to these countries, state-building efforts still face many challenges. One source of difficulty lies in a contradiction inherent in externally supported state building. State building is an endogenous process in which people come to have a sense of belonging through their own experience. It is impossible for national sentiment to be imposed.[11] OECD's Statebuilding Guidance and the g7+ statement by the group of fragile states both recognize this point, and acknowledge the importance of ownership by local actors.[12]

A second difficulty comes from the fact that, while fragile states are the need-iest recipients of foreign aid, by definition they lack the political and social con-ditions that would allow them to use aid effectively to reduce their fragility. This lack of state capacity hinders donors from applying the principles of the Paris Declaration, as is evident in the low average use of country systems (such as pub-lic financial management [PFM] and procurement).[13] To maximize resource use efficiency and development effectiveness, donors tend to assume a major part of recipient government tasks themselves and to rely on pool funding, such as mul-tidonor trust funds. These practices, however, may actually discourage ownership and delay the nurturing of national legitimacy.

Many analysts have discussed the challenges of state building in fragile situa-tions.[14] Donors and development practitioners try to enhance engagement with fragile states through the OECD/DAC International Network on Conflict and

9. OECD (2010c, p. 41).

10. OECD (2010d, 2010e). According to an OECD estimate (2010e), financial flows to fragile coun-tries include $7.1 billion for peacekeeping operations, $626 million assistance from emerging donors (excluding China and India), $127.8 million from Education for All FTI, $2.6 billion from the Global Fund to Fight AIDS, Tuberculosis, and Malaria, and $6.2 billion from U.S. private foundations.

11. Paris and Sisk (2009b, pp. 306–09) note five dilemmas faced by external actors involved in state building that are concerned with this contradiction: footprint dilemmas (to what extent should external actors be engaged with the domestic affairs of the host state?); duration dilemmas (how long should exter-nal actors continue their engagement?); participation dilemmas (who should decide on the participants of political processes in state building, and by what criteria?); dependency dilemmas (how can local actors' dependency on, as well as antagonism against, external actors be avoided?); coherence dilemmas (how can external actors be coherent among themselves, and how can a balance be struck between local and external values?).

12. OECD (2011). The grouping of fragile states calls itself "small g7," in contradistinction to the "large G7" of advanced industrialized countries. "Plus" is added as the number of member states has increased beyond seven.

13. This is a finding of the Paris Declaration survey. OECD (2008d, p. 40).

14. Ghani and Lockhart (2008); Jarstad and Sisk (2008); Paris and Sisk (2009c); Newman, Paris, and Richmond (2009).

Fragility (INCAF), which encourages international dialogue with developing countries and civil society. The results of these dialogues are reflected clearly in the Dili Declaration of April 2010. Their arguments and findings, however, are either very general (in the sense that their theoretical frameworks presumably are applicable to all fragile states) or very specific (in the sense that their analyses remain single-country studies). Considering the endogeneity of the state-building endeavor, it is important to be sensitive to the local contexts of individual countries while at the same time avoiding a piecemeal approach that would impede meaningful policy planning. What is required is a study with an intermediate-level focus, which balances theoretical generalization and context-specific policy discussion.

With this in mind, the present chapter categorizes state-building experiences in fragile situations into two theoretical types. Capacity trap countries are those that have failed to improve state capacity to provide security and social services and that consequently have failed also to establish state legitimacy. Legitimacy trap countries are those that have demonstrated a high capacity to provide security and services to the population but that suffer from shaky legitimacy due to expanding inequalities and authoritarian management. Some of these countries are no longer in fragile situations as defined above; however, the risk remains that continued deterioration in legitimacy could make them fragile once again.

After presenting our theoretical framework, we offer case study analyses of four postconflict countries: Afghanistan, the DRC, Cambodia, and Rwanda. The first two represent capacity trap cases, while Cambodia and Rwanda are legitimacy trap cases. We chose postconflict countries because fragile situations are most often found in those countries in which armed conflicts have destroyed the institutional and physical infrastructure for protecting people.

Policy implications based on the analyses are discussed in the concluding section of this chapter. The chapter insists that fragile state problems should be tackled from a perspective focusing on state building as a long-term process, that international aid players should consider the two types of fragility when they elaborate their policies, and that regional mechanisms and strategies should be strengthened when measures to tackle fragility are designed.

## Capacity and Legitimacy in State Building

In exploring our theoretical state-building framework, we start with an examination of Alain Whaites's conceptualization.[15] Whaites posits state building as a cyclical process of political settlement (or peace), service delivery by the state, and reactions from the society. Political settlement, understood as agreement among

---

15. Whaites (2008).

political elites to settle differences by peaceful means, influences and determines the capacity of the state to fulfill core competencies, among which provision of security is foremost.[16] People's reaction to the state depends on the quality of public services provided to them. The quality may be better than expected, or worse. A strong state performance will strengthen the political settlement; by contrast, if the state fails to meet social expectations, political settlement may be threatened by violent challenges to the incipient state.

As also argued by Whaites, the present chapter argues that the formation of a capable and legitimate state ("responsive state-building" is Whaites's term) is necessary to avoid a recurrence of violence and to sustain peace in postconflict societies. The fact that a country reaching the end of a civil war faces an approximately 43.6 percent risk of returning to conflict within five years underscores the importance of legitimacy for sustainable peace.[17] In this sense peace building and state building are two overlapping processes. A UN document refers to peace building as a range of measures targeted "to reassemble the foundations of peace and provide the tools for building on those foundations something that is more than just the absence of war."[18] Other work agrees on the point that peace building is about ending or preventing war.[19] To achieve "something that is more than just the absence of war," however, we must build a capable and legitimate state.

Whaites's argument points to a dialectic between the state's capacity (to provide security and social services) and its legitimacy in the eyes of its citizens. The importance of capacity and legitimacy in state building is also emphasized by other analysts and organizations.[20] The OECD understands state building to be "an endogenous process to enhance capacity, institutions, and legitimacy of the state driven by state-society relations."[21] Richard Manning and Alexandra Trzeciak-Duval emphasize the importance of enhancing the state functions of ensuring justice and security, delivering basic social services, and providing core economic governance while they warn that "functional capacity and political will, on their own, may be insufficient to achieve stability."[22] They insist that "legitimacy is also needed to ensure effective state-society relations."

16. Di John and Putzel (2009, p. 4) define political settlement as "the balance or distribution of power between contending social groups and social classes, on which any state is based." This is a definition from a more historical and structural point of view. While a short-term agreement among political elites may or may not correspond with the distribution of power among social groups, the long-term stability of the agreement will most probably depend on the extent of correspondence.

17. Collier and others (2003).

18. United Nations (2000, par. 13).

19. See Stedman, Rothchild, and Cousens (2002); Wyeth and Sisk (2009); United Nations (2009b). These two concepts are used in the official title of the Dili Declaration (International Dialogue on Peacebuilding and Statebuilding 2010), although the declaration does not clearly demarcate the two.

20. Chandler (2007); Roberts (2008); OECD (2010a); DFID (2010).

21. OECD (2008a, p. 1).

22. Manning and Trzeciak-Duval (2010, p. 109). Manning was chair of the DAC from 2003 to 2007; Trzeciak-Duval is head of policy coordination in the DAC Secretariat.

Applying the framework of dynamic capacity-legitimacy interactions to our analysis of postconflict state building, we discern two patterns.

In the first pattern, a fragile state cannot ensure security, which weakens the government's capacity for social service delivery. The failure to fulfill this function hampers improvement in state legitimacy, which in turn impedes improvement in state capacity to provide security and social services. We call this vicious circle a capacity trap.

In the second pattern, even if a state succeeds in gaining capacity and legitimacy in the early phase of state building, it might still face new challenges in the next phase. Once basic human security is assured, people's expectations can expand to encompass demands such as fairness in terms of social inclusiveness, economic equity, and political participation. A state that has been successful tends to respond slowly to such new expectations precisely because it has established firm authority over the country. Achievement of relatively high legitimacy in the early phase will impede quick response to new challenges; consequently, the state risks declining legitimacy. We call this situation a legitimacy trap.

These two patterns are discernible in figures 6-1 and 6-2. The vertical and horizontal lines of these diagrams are the political stability indicator and the voice and accountability indicator, respectively, of the world governance indicators.[23] Political stability is a proxy for state capacity to maintain public order, while voice and accountability is one of the sources of state legitimacy. The diagrams locate each country in two different time points: the year in which armed conflict ended (or 1996, the year for which the oldest data are available) and the year for which the most recent data are available. In order to secure comparability among the countries, however, the length between the two time points is limited to ten years. If one country takes 1996 as the starting point, the end point is 2006.

Figure 6-1 shows four countries (Afghanistan, Iraq, Sudan, and the DRC) for which both indicators stagnated or deteriorated between the two time points. These are regarded as countries that have fallen into a capacity trap. The countries in figure 6-2 improved their capacity to maintain security but failed to ameliorate democratic legitimacy (voice and accountability). They face a legitimacy trap. In this chapter, we examine Afghanistan and the DRC as typical capacity trap cases and Cambodia and Rwanda as representative legitimacy trap cases.

## Breaking out of the Capacity Trap: Afghanistan and the DRC

The capacity trap problem involves a vicious circle between the lack of capacity to ensure public security/social service delivery and the difficulty in establishing state legitimacy. The lack of capacity to provide security hinders the state from enhancing its capacity to deliver other basic services and consequently from estab-

23. Kaufmann, Kraay, and Mastruzzi (2009).

Figure 6-1. *Four Postconflict Countries in a Capacity Trap*

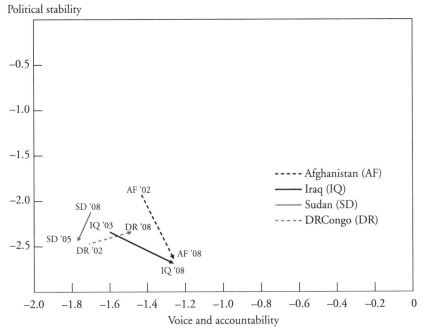

Source: Kaufmann, Kraay, and Mastruzzi (2009).

lishing its legitimacy. An attempt at bottom-up state building is examined in the final part of this section as a possible escape from this trap.

*Lack of Capacity to Ensure Security*

Below we discuss the social, historical, and geographic sources of weakness. Included is a look at the dispersion of armed power, with its reliance instead on external forces for security.

SOCIAL, HISTORICAL, AND GEOGRAPHIC SOURCES OF WEAKNESS. Although Afghanistan and the DRC started to reconstruct their states eight and seven years ago, respectively, both countries are still struggling to ensure public security, one of the most fundamental functions of the state. The aftereffects of recent armed conflict are undoubtedly among the major causes of the problem. However, it cannot be ignored that for social, historical, and geographic reasons a territorially integrated administration has never been established in either of the two countries.

Afghan society is traditionally composed of numerous microsocieties, or associations, delineated along tribal, ethnic, linguistic, and sectarian lines and coalescing around influential leaders who claim religious powers or who are able to distribute material and security benefits on a patrimonial basis. Traditional community elders or local power holders once handled most local affairs, but these

Figure 6-2. *Five Postconflict Countries in a Legitimacy Trap*

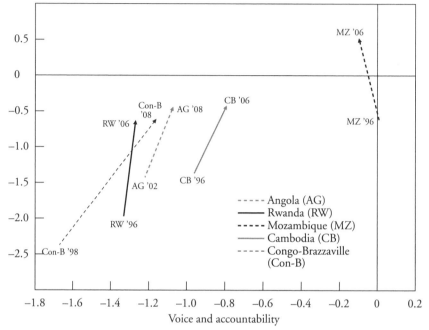

Source: Kaufmann, Kraay, and Mastruzzi (2009).

have gradually been replaced by armed commanders or local men of influence, now commonly known as warlords.[24]

Similarly, the DRC, a country that is "challenged by geography," is typical of those African states that have failed since the precolonial era to consolidate their power over distance.[25] This area, in the center of Africa and as vast as the whole of Western Europe, was kept intact largely because its numerous rivers and thick forests obstructed intrusion by colonial powers. It was recognized as de facto personal property of King Leopold II of Belgium in the aftermath of the 1884–85 Berlin Conference, but its territorial integration was not advanced. Apart from historical happenstance, there is no reason why this territory should constitute a single sovereign state.

After independence, consecutive episodes of political turbulence devastated what little economic and social infrastructure existed in the DRC. The capacity of the Congolese/Zairian state to provide public goods was extremely limited.[26]

24. Saikal (2005, pp. 195–200).
25. Hurbst (2000, p. 145).
26. Young and Turner (1985).

During the Mobutu era (1965–97), national budgets for local development were scarce and never appropriately allocated. In fact, since its birth this artificially created state has never functioned well, compelling its people always to live in fragile situations.

Due to their geographic locations and lack of territorial integrity, both Afghanistan and the DRC have also been subject to intervention by outside forces. Located at the crossroads of continental Asia, with porous borders that make it susceptible to the movement of drugs, weapons, and armed militants, Afghanistan has experienced active intervention by neighboring countries and global powers. Still today neighboring countries pursue strategic interests across the border via their own networks of support and control.[27]

The DRC, for its part, has suffered two military intrusions by Rwanda. The Tutsi-led government of Rwanda, insisting that Hutu rebels who fled in 1994 into eastern DRC threatened its security, decided in 1996 to intervene militarily across the border. Some years later, the Rwandan government's support for Tutsi-led rebel groups in DRC fueled armed clashes, which were repeated even after the conclusion of a peace agreement in 2002.[28]

DISPERSION OF ARMED POWER AND RELIANCE ON EXTERNAL FORCES FOR SECURITY. At the beginning of the political process no single group could impose hegemonic power over others in Afghanistan and DRC. Many warring parties maintained armed forces of their own. The efforts for disarmament and demobilization have not yet solved the problem of power dispersion.

In Afghanistan the initial disarmament, demobilization, and reintegration (DDR) program, implemented in 2003–05, demobilized 62,376 soldiers of the northern Afghan Military Forces (AMF), but some ex-AMF commanders who had been unable to obtain satisfactory positions in the civil service or in the new security forces tried to retain influence through "unofficial" militias. The government introduced another program, called the Disarmament of Illegal Armed Groups (DIAG), and disbanded 382 illegal armed groups in 2005–08. But most of these groups were ex-AMF; non-AMF illegal groups have continued to be security threats, particularly in the southern regions.[29] In some locales, where there are

27. There are regular reports of Pakistani military and intelligence support to insurgents. See Sherman (2008, p. 314). Armstrong and Rubin (2005) also point out the importance of a regional perspective.

28. For details, see Reyntjens (2009) and Prunier (2009). The Tutsi is a tiny ethnic group in the DRC, but it formed the most powerful rebel group called Rassemblement congolais pour le démocratie with the assistance of Rwanda. During the transitional government, between 2003 and 2006, its access to political posts was ensured by the peace accord, which stipulated a strict power-sharing scheme. When Congolese Tutsis lost such privileges after the elections held at the end of the transitional period, a number rebelled against the government, claiming the right to defend themselves from Hutu rebels and the Hutu-sympathetic government.

29. According to a UN estimate, some 1,800 illegal militias, including both ex-AMF commanders' groups and non-AMF fighters, exist throughout the country, especially in remote areas far from the capital. Sherman (2008, p. 321).

no effective national police on the ground, militias are generally accepted as local security forces.[30]

The DRC government faces a similar dilemma. The power-sharing transitional government did not have an integrated leadership to carry out a meaningful DDR program.[31] In the face of years of intransigent refusal by Tutsi-led rebels against the national DDR program, the government, with support from the international community including the UN, promoted a policy of "rapid integration" of various armed groups into the national army, but the result so far has been problematic.[32] Under the rapid integration policy, former rebel groups, including Tutsi-led CNDP (Congrès national pour la defense du peuple), were integrated into the national army without waiting for disarmament and demobilization. This allowed the armed groups to retain their own integrated command structures. As a result, CNDP, which had benefited from the power-sharing agreement, was able to acquire even more power by establishing control over some mineral-rich locations in the name of counterinsurgency operations.[33]

Their weak security capacity forced the governments of these countries to rely on external actors to establish and maintain public security. In Afghanistan the government was itself put in place by external forces in the context of the U.S.-led "war on terror," and deep dependence on foreign military forces has continued since then. The training of Afghan national military forces is progressing, though slowly. Unless national security forces assume major responsibilities for the maintenance of security, it will be difficult to connect the attained security with state legitimacy. Meanwhile, "collateral" civilian casualties caused by foreign military forces have adversely affected state legitimacy.

In the DRC, the role of foreign militaries has been more limited, but Operation Artemis, conducted by EU forces in 2003, is believed to have contributed critically to the stabilization of the country's Ituri region. And despite fierce criticism of its ineffectiveness from some corners, the role played by MONUSCO (United Nations Organization Stabilization Mission in the Democratic Republic of the Congo) in DRC peace building and state building should not be underestimated.[34] This foreign assistance, however, has not yet been accompanied by the formation of a capable and legitimate state.

## Limited Capacity for Service Delivery

The lack of security hinders the delivery of humanitarian aid and other services to the people. In both the DRC and Afghanistan the international community has been trying to help the governments to secure the necessary resources and to

---

30. Higashi (2008); Sherman (2008); Bhatia and others (2009).
31. Edmonds, Mills, and McNamee (2009); Mobekk (2009); Onana and Taylor (2008).
32. United Nations (2009a).
33. International Crisis Group (2009); United Nations (2009a).
34. Tull (2009).

Table 6-1. *Health and Education Indicators, Afghanistan and the DRC, Various Years*

Units as indicated

| Indicator | Afghanistan | | DRC | |
|---|---|---|---|---|
| | *2000–01* | *2008* | *1999–2002* | *2008* |
| Life expectancy at birth (years) | 41.93 (2001) | 43.95 | 46.72 (2001) | 47.65 |
| Infant mortality rate (per 1,000 live births) | 148.1 (2000) | 135.2 | 125.8 (2000) | 125.8[a] |
| Literacy rate, adult total (percent of people ages 15 years and above) | n.a. | n.a. | 67.17 (2001) | 66.6 |
| Immunization, DPT (percent of children aged 12–23 months) | 44 (2001) | 85 | 46 (2001) | 69 |
| Immunization, measles (percent of children aged 12–23 months) | 46 (2001) | 75 | 49 (2001) | 67 |
| Net primary school enrollment rate (percent) | n.a. | n.a. | 32.41 (1999) | n.a. |
| Gross primary school enrollment rate (percent) | 21.90 (2001) | 106.12 | 58.82 (2002) | 90.39 |

Source: World Bank, *World Development Indicators,* various years.

a. Infant mortality rate in the DRC is reported as 125.8 in 1990, 1995, 2000, and 2005–09. This suggests that the database uses data from the nearest available year when year-specific data are unavailable.

n.a. = Not available.

build institutional capacity for planning and implementing various public service programs. The resultant performances vary among different subsectors, however, as shown in table 6-1.

Gross primary school enrollment and immunizations show large improvements. But these are subsectors that can be improved quickly by a massive infusion of foreign aid. In contrast, social indicators such as life expectancy, infant mortality, and literacy have scarcely been ameliorated over the past seven years. These are areas where change for the better requires long-term government effort. As a whole, the living conditions of ordinary people remain poor. The Congolese and Afghan Human Development Index rankings in 2007 were 176 and 181, respectively, among 182 countries.[35]

The DRC government has tried to improve the situation by strengthening the capacity of its state machinery. The Congolese national strategy paper on economic growth and poverty reduction emphasizes the necessity of developing state capacity in peace building, good governance, and macroeconomic management.[36]

35. UNDP (2009).

36. RDC (2006). The strategy paper sets five pillars: promote good governance and consolidate peace; consolidate macroeconomic stability and growth; improve access to social services and reduce vulnerability; combat HIV/AIDS; and promote local initiatives.

Characteristically, however, the document does not contain a strategy for the conflict-prone eastern areas, where improvement in public services is especially needed.[37] These services have so far been provided by donors and NGOs in an allegedly uncoordinated manner.

Afghanistan receives six times more net ODA per capita than the DRC, which explains its better performance in both school enrollment and immunizations in spite of the unstable security situation.[38] Although there remain problems such as geographic variations and low female enrollment, public service coverage of the population has been enhanced across the country. However, this enhancement has been accompanied by only limited improvement in state institutional capacity and state legitimacy. One reason for this is that Afghanistan's public finance is heavily dependent on external resources. Domestically sourced revenue for 2004–05 covered only 8 percent of the total national budget; the rest came from donor funding.[39] Another reason is that 80 percent of the assistance provided by donors was spent outside government channels.[40] For the most part, it has been external donors, NGOs, or contractors that have delivered public services to the people. Although these foreign experts may have managed donors' funds effectively, nonetheless this practice impedes the capacity development of the Afghan state machinery. Furthermore, lack of control by the Afghan government undermines its legitimacy in the eyes of the Afghan people.[41]

The same impediment applies to an even greater degree to direct aid administered by foreign military forces. While it may be effective in implementing service delivery operations in the short run, it does not help to improve the capacity and legitimacy of the national government. Furthermore, there is considerable doubt

37. Another explanation for the poor performance of the DRC is the nature of external aid during the postconflict years. Foreign aid increased drastically in 2003, but 94.2 percent of bilateral ODA was directed at "actions related to debt." OECD (2007b). The debt relief operation was inevitable due to the huge debt accumulated since the Mobutu era. It meant, however, that the amount of new external resources available for the transition government was more limited than it appeared to be.

38. Afghanistan received $167.64 per capita net ODA (current $) in 2008, compared with $25.05 for the DRC. World Bank (various years).

39. See Suhrke (2009, pp. 231–32). Heavy dependence on external resources has not changed over time: domestic revenue as a percentage of operating expenditure remained at 61 percent in 2008–09. Islamic Republic of Afghanistan (2009, pp. 11–12). Compared to 64 percent in 2004–05. Suhrke (2009, p. 232).

40. OECD (2010b, p. 35). Other figures also show a lack of Afghan government ownership. The rate of ODA channeled through national systems and managed by the government remains low: 11.6 percent in 2007–08, 25.4 percent in 2008–09, and an expected 31.0 percent in 2009–10. Share of discretionary funds decreased, from 12.5 percent in 2007–08 to 4.2 percent in 2008–09, as donors increasingly express sectoral and regional preferences and earmark their ODA. OECD (2010b, pp. 21–22).

41. A similar situation is observed in the health sector. Health services in Afghanistan have been contracted out to NGOs. This practice has been successful in the sense that cost-effectiveness and service quality have improved. Ghani and Bizhan (2009, pp. 105–06). However, because the primary health care units, the final points of service delivery, are built, manned, and managed by international and national NGOs, health service delivery has been associated with international players, rather than with the state. OECD (2010b, pp. 23–24).

about the sustainability of aid projects conducted or protected by foreign military forces.[42]

## Capacity Trap against Legitimacy Building

As shown above, the Afghan and Congolese states have suffered from inadequate improvement in their security and services delivery capacities. The inadequate capacity hinders the state in building legitimacy; weak legitimacy, in turn, obstructs the maintenance of public security and consequently the delivery of social services to the citizens.

In the case of the DRC, the state's low capacity for service delivery has been aggravated by an illegal exploitation of mineral resources, which reinforces bad governance practices based on strong patrimonialism. Investigations by the United Nations as well as by other organizations reveal that Congolese mineral resources such as diamonds, coltan, and cassiterite have been systematically and illegally exploited by a number of foreign and national armed groups, including the Congolese national army (Forces Armées de la République Démocratique du Congo).[43] A vicious circle is already clear: the lack of nationwide public security leads to low government capacity to control national resources potentially usable for better services delivery; the low capacity of the Congolese state to control illegal activities and to deliver social services diminishes state legitimacy and renders the establishment of security more difficult.

The Afghan state also suffers from patrimonial and factional divisions. The slow growth of state capacity on the one hand and corruption and inefficiency on the other reinforce each other. Although the Afghanistan National Development Strategy identifies three pillars of objectives (security, rule of law and good governance, and social and economic development), progress is slow in the area of rule of law and good governance, which adversely affects the performance of the other two pillars.

The peculiarity of the Afghan experience, however, resides in its heavy dependence on external forces, both for the assurance of security and for the improvement of service delivery. It has indirectly obstructed legitimacy building by delaying improvement in the capacity of state machinery.[44] Low state legitimacy aggravates the security situation, which compels continuation of external dependence in both security and service delivery.

In both Afghanistan and the DRC, we observe a vicious circle among low security, limited service delivery, and low legitimacy.

---

42. OECD (2010b).

43. United Nations (2001, 2002, 2008, 2009a); Global Witness (2005, 2009). Illegal mineral exploitation was observed not only in the eastern part of the country, where antigovernment armed groups have established control, but also in government-controlled areas where government forces and their allies carry out such illegal activities. United Nations (2002).

44. Rubin (2005, 2006).

*An Attempt at Bottom-Up State Building*

To break the vicious circle of the capacity trap, we must find a point to interrupt the circle. In the countries where powerful contenders against the government are active, the struggle is not only on the battlefield but also in people's hearts and minds. To win their support, the state must meet the immediate needs of everyday life. When the capacity of a national government is low, or when the government is distrusted by its people, service delivery at subnational levels may supplement tasks undertaken by the national government and may eventually serve as a first step toward bottom-up state building. Here we briefly examine Afghanistan's National Solidarity Program (NSP) to show how this might develop into such an endeavor.[45]

The NSP is a community-driven development program. Although it was initiated by the Ministry of Rural Rehabilitation and Development (MRRD) and the World Bank, its implementation has been outsourced to international and national NGOs or consultants. Under this program, as of May 2010, 22,257 community development councils (CDCs) were established, covering approximately 70 percent of Afghanistan's rural communities.[46] Through the creation of the CDCs, "the NSP initiated the formation of the first democratic local institutions at the community level, thereby encouraging capacity building, collective discourse, and inclusive decision making."[47] According to one survey, the public awareness of CDCs is rising, and 78 percent of the respondents who were aware of CDCs in 2009 expressed their satisfaction with the performance of their local CDCs.[48] Furthermore, 81 percent and 61 percent believe that their CDCs are capable of representing their interests before, respectively, the provincial authorities and the national government.[49] The high trust that people give to the CDCs may indicate that they could serve as building blocks of a legitimate state formed from below. The MRRD itself is now trying to strengthen communications with CDCs through its provincial offices.

On the basis of this success, JICA and the MRRD have started an attempt to cluster several CDCs into higher level groupings. The project, called Intercommunal Rural Development Project (IRDP), was launched in 2005 for the purpose

45. See the program's website (www.nspafghanistan.org).
46. NSP website (www.nspafghanistan.org).
47. Narayan, Tas, and de Mercey (2010, p. 468).
48. At the national level, the awareness of CDCs was 37 percent in 2006, 32 percent in 2007, 42 percent in 2008, and 44 percent in 2009. In rural areas, where CDCs actually operate, 49 percent of the people are aware of them. Rennie, Sharma, and Sen (2009, p. 81).
49. Ibid., pp. 80–84. Another survey, a randomized impact evaluation in six provinces, indicates that the creation of the CDC and the ensuing selection and implementation of rehabilitation projects have been successful, particularly in strengthening the authority of village councils in local decisionmaking and in changing the perceptions of villagers toward government figures such as the president and central government officials. Beath and others (2010).

of implementing larger scale infrastructure projects (such as intervillage roads, drinking water supply networks, and irrigation dams) that require intercommunal cooperation.[50]

Although neither CDCs nor CDC clusters have yet been endorsed as local administrative units by the government, this clustering might serve not only to foster intervillage solidarity but also to push the state-building effort one step upward by making local public institutions accountable to ordinary Afghans. What is most important in capacity trap countries is to build a legitimate state by gradually fostering people's trust in public institutions. For this purpose, CDCs and CDC clusters could be promising starting points.

## Challenges of Strengthening Legitimacy: Cambodia and Rwanda

The following passages examine the initial success, with international assistance, of Cambodia and Rwanda in security consolidation and service delivery and illustrate potential sources of legitimacy gaps.

### Consolidation of Security

Unlike the two countries examined in the previous section, the governments of Cambodia and Rwanda have both demonstrated high capacity to ensure public security and deliver basic social services to their populations. Their initial success is based on two factors: control over the military and the government and suppression of antigovernment voices and movements.

CONTROL OVER THE MILITARY AND THE GOVERNMENT. First, Cambodia and Rwanda have not suffered from a lack of social and geographic cohesiveness as seriously as have Afghanistan and the DRC. Cambodia and Rwanda are geographically small and integral, although their borders have never been free from penetration from outside. Cambodia has ethnic and religious minority groups, but the great majority of its population is Buddhist Khmer. The establishment of national public security should be easier in a homogeneous society like Cambodia's. Rwanda has a highly divisive society but is different from the mosaic Afghan and Congolese societies. The social structure in Rwanda is less entangled in the sense that it is composed of two major ethnic groups: Hutu and Tutsi. If one of them establishes full control over the other, nationwide security is easily established. This is exactly what happened in 1994, when the Tutsi-led Rwandan Patriotic Front (RPF) won a decisive victory over the Hutu-led government.[51]

---

50. Wakamatsu (2010).

51. During the rest of the 1990s, the Rwandan government—now dominated by the Tutsi—conducted forceful counterinsurgency operations against Hutu militias on both sides of the Congolese border. The operations resulted in a significant number of fatalities on both sides. The first government attack was directed against former military members of the Hutu government in refugee camps in eastern DRC, triggering a civil war. As a result, hundreds of thousands of refugees went missing or were massacred. Adelman

Second, in both counties, at the end of armed conflict one of the warring parties emerged as overwhelmingly powerful in terms of the coercive forces it controlled. These forces were used to maintain public security and also to control the government. In Rwanda the RPF's complete military victory gave the government a free hand in the postconflict state building. In Cambodia the civil war ended before the Cambodian People's Party (CPP) established a decisive hegemony over other military and political forces. As a result, the CPP was forced to share governmental power with the royalist FUNCINPEC party, when the latter won the largest number of congressional seats in the 1993 election. However, the CPP was able to maintain a strong hold over vast areas of national territory thanks to its control over security forces, control it had never relinquished since the mid-1980s.[52] The CPP also wielded strong influence in courts and over subnational provincial authorities. After violent clashes in 1997, the power-sharing scheme with FUNCINPEC was cancelled, and the CPP consolidated its domination of the Royal Cambodian Armed Forces and the government.

Third, the firm grip on the military by the CPP in Cambodia and by the RPF in Rwanda, together with international assistance, helped the DDR process to proceed smoothly in the two countries. In 1999 the Cambodian government launched a World Bank–supported program to demobilize some 45,000 combatants from the Royal Cambodian Armed Forces. It also disarmed former Khmer Rouge soldiers by offering them generous amnesty measures, bringing about the final surrender of former Khmer Rouge combatants in 1999.[53] In Rwanda, during the second stage of the Rwanda Demobilization and Reintegration Commission (RDRC) operations, which lasted from 2001 to 2008 with full international support, 29,641 ex-combatants were demobilized, 44,366 received a transition allowance, and 43,669 received reinsertion support.[54] According to the World Development Indicators, the size of the Rwandan armed forces declined from 80,000 in 2002 to 35,000 in 2007. As a result of these activities, both the Cambodian and Rwandan governments were able to reduce their financial burdens without alienating soldiers or militias.

SUPPRESSION OF ANTIGOVERNMENT VOICES AND MOVEMENTS. In parallel with consolidation of military control, the two governments successfully created

---

(2003); Umutesi (2004). In 1997–98 government forces attacked Hutu militia who had returned to Rwanda from the DRC under the guise of civilian returnees. During this operation, a number of Hutu civilians were allegedly slaughtered. An international NGO estimates that at least 6,000 civilians were killed between January and August of 1997. Amnesty International (1997).

52. Richardson and Sainsbury (2005, p. 287). Although the RCAF was created anew in 1994 by integrating troops of warring factions, CPP officers and soldiers remained at the core of the organization. Hendrickson (2001, pp. 68–72).

53. Bartu and Wilford (2009, pp. 14–22).

54. According to MDRP, these figures are equivalent to 80–90 percent of the original targets (www.mdrp.org/rwanda.htm).

political institutions that favor ruling parties and deprive opposition parties and antigovernment forces of opportunities to freely voice dissatisfaction or to compete for government power.

The primary control mechanism in Cambodia is the patronage network, which the CPP installed in local communities. During the 1980s the CPP (then the KPRP) selected and appointed village heads for political and administrative purposes. Since that time dense patronage relations have been developed and maintained between the CPP and village chiefs and between village chiefs and villagers.[55] According to one survey, 41 percent of respondents replied that village chiefs have the greatest influence on their daily lives. This percentage exceeds the 28 percent who believe that the prime minister is the most influential.[56] Support from village chiefs, therefore, is indispensable to the CPP's retention of its hegemonic position in Cambodia. For more than twenty years, the informal support base of the CPP-led government has remained intact in the form of networks of personal allegiances, which exist in parallel with formal democratic procedures and structures.[57]

In Rwanda, as in Cambodia, government supporters were appointed to the leading positions in local administrative units—but only after the end of the civil war. The RPF government, however, introduced peculiar institutional arrangements to facilitate its hold on power despite the Tutsi status as a minority ethnic group. The new constitution, written under government auspices and adopted by referendum in 2003, includes a clause stipulating that "propagation of ethnic, regional, racial or discrimination or any other form of division is punishable by law" (article 33). The RPF government turned the vague term *division* to its advantage by interpreting this clause to be a prohibition against any expression of ethnicity.

The law punishing "genocide ideology" has a similar function.[58] Terms such as *division, divisionism,* and *genocide ideology* are often used in Rwanda when the government criticizes its opponents. It is now virtually impossible in Rwanda to organize a political party based on the support of the Hutu majority. Before the first postconflict election of 2003, the biggest Hutu opposition party was ordered to dissolve itself because of its "divisive ideology." In April 2010 a Hutu woman who had declared as a rival candidate in the next presidential election was arrested and charged with "association with a terrorist group, propagating the genocide ideology, revisionism, and ethnic division."[59]

55. The CPP village chiefs kept their positions even after the introduction of democratic elections into local politics. In the 2002 direct elections for commune councils, the CPP won the majority of seats in 98.58 percent of the commune councils. They then reappointed long-serving village chiefs in almost all the villages. Yamada (2009, pp. 27–28).

56. IRI (2008).

57. Blunt and Turner (2005, p. 77).

58. Law 18/2008 stipulates punishment against the crime of genocide ideology.

59. *New Times,* April 23, 2010.

*Service Delivery with International Assistance*

On the basis of secure political order, the Cambodian and Rwandan governments took advantage of generous international assistance to improve the provision of social services to their populations.

Rwanda had always depended on foreign assistance to support its public finances, and this dependence has deepened since the end of the civil war. Foreign grant aid accounts for 30 percent to 50 percent of total fiscal revenues.[60] Social sectors have received the biggest share. From 2001 to 2006, on average 50 percent of total bilateral ODA commitments were concentrated on "social infrastructure and services," which covers education, health, and population as well as water supply and sanitation.[61] The education sector, which has been the largest recipient of the social sector budget, was praised by the UNDP as "an example of what well-planned, coordinated, and targeted investments can achieve in terms of human and economic development."[62] The health sector too has benefited from foreign assistance, with the Ministry of Health receiving 96 percent of its 2008 development budget from external sources.[63]

International assistance has played a similarly significant role in Cambodia. One of the best examples is UNHCR's refugee resettlement program. Between March 1992 and April 1993 the organization helped to repatriate 362,209 refugees by repairing 238.5 kilometers of roads, twenty-two bridges, 1,362 wells, and other basic infrastructure that would benefit returnees.[64] The Cambodian government also used foreign aid to improve the capacity of the state institutions that deliver basic services such as water supply and maternal health.[65]

In both countries remarkable improvements in security and service delivery have been followed and reinforced by relatively high economic growth. Cambodia increased its GNI per capita (PPP, current international dollar) from $640 in 1995 to $1,820 in 2008, while Rwanda experienced an annual GDP growth as

60. The average ratio of foreign grants versus total fiscal revenue between 1995 and 2006 was 43 percent, while between 1981 and 1993 it was 25 percent. World Bank, *World Development Indicators,* various years.

61. OECD (2007b, 2008c).

62. UNDP (2007a, p. 22).

63. Republic of Rwanda (2007).

64. UNHCR (1993, pp. 4, 18).

65. In the early postconflict period, the Phnom Penh Water Supply Authority implemented an emergency rehabilitation program with assistance from UNDP and France. Simultaneously, it worked with JICA to formulate a medium/long-term master plan, on the basis of which financial and technical assistance was secured from France, Japan, the ADB, and the World Bank to improve and extend water supply facilities. JICA (2008, pp. 140–41). As a result, the water supply coverage in Phnom Penh improved from 25 percent in 1993 to 90 percent in 2006, while nonrevenue water dropped to 6 percent in 2006, the lowest figure in Southeast Asia. Asian Development Bank (2007). In the health sector, while the Cambodian government allowed donors and NGOs to deliver emergency assistance directly to the grassroots, it also started a capacity development effort at the National Maternal and Child Health Center in Phnom Penh with financial and technical assistances from JICA. The center started as a local hospital but grew to become a national center to train midwives and physicians for the entire nation. Murotani (2010, pp. 12–13).

high as 7.6 percent between 1998 and 2008 and doubled its GNI per capita (PPP, current international dollar) from $570 to $1,110.[66]

All these factors explain the noticeable improvement in social indicators over the past fifteen years (table 6-2). The rate of improvement in Cambodia's life expectancy and infant mortality for 1993–2000 was not as significant as for 2000–08, probably reflecting the fact that effective political stability was not achieved until 1999. Overall, however, Cambodia and Rwanda have experienced much greater advancement than Afghanistan and the DRC in the areas that require long-term efforts to achieve success, such as life expectancy, infant mortality, and literacy.

### Sources of a Legitimacy Gap

Ensuring public security and delivering basic social services have laid the foundation for state legitimacy in Cambodia and Rwanda. An opinion survey conducted in Cambodia in 2008 shows that 82 percent of the people believe that the country is moving in the right direction and that 73 percent of this 82 percent indicate "more roads built" as one reason why they believe so. A large number of respondents consider the construction of schools and clinics as equally important.[67] A majority of the Cambodian people apparently regards improvements in social infrastructure as important peace dividends, and they accept the current government as legitimate.

However, the story does not end here. Once human security has more or less been attained, people's expectations and attention may shift to qualitatively different aspirations. Respecting local traditions and practices is one thing; but treating people in fair, inclusive, and transparent ways is another. Several worrisome phenomena have emerged in Cambodia as well as in Rwanda that cast shadows on their state legitimacy.

First, increasing economic disparities are observed in both countries. Whereas the consumption of goods and services per capita per day rose by 32 percent in real terms between 1994 and 2004 in Cambodia, the poorest quintile group had only an 8 percent increase, compared to 45 percent for the richest quintile. Similarly, rural living standards rose more slowly than those in Phnom Penh and other urban centers. The Gini coefficient rose from 0.35 in 1993–94 to 0.40 in 2004.[68] Similarly, despite the rapid economic growth, "poverty levels in Rwanda remain well above pre-war levels."[69]

---

66. This rapid economic growth has been mainly export driven. It is important to notice that not only traditional export goods (coffee and tea) but also new export goods (mineral resources) have sharply increased over the past several years. The military intervention in the eastern part of the DRC has thus had a significant effect on the Rwandan economy.

67. IRI (2008).

68. World Bank (2007, p. iii). This is the figure for that part of the national sample corresponding to the 1993–94 sampling frame. If the full national sample is covered, the Gini in 2004 is 0.42.

69. UNDP (2007a, p. 7). The Head Count Index under the national poverty line (about $0.44 a day in nominal terms) was 56.9 in 2006, compared with 47.5 in 1990. The Gini coefficient has worsened from

Table 6-2. *Health and Education Indicators, Cambodia and Rwanda, Various Years*[a]

| | Cambodia | | | Rwanda | | |
|---|---|---|---|---|---|---|
| *Indicator* | *1991–98* | *2000–04* | *2008* | *1991–95* | *2000–01* | *2008* |
| Life expectancy at birth (years) | 55.52 (1993) | 56.88 (2000) | 60.97 | 26.41 (1993) | 43.00 (2000) | 50.13 |
| Infant mortality rate (per 1,000 live births) | 86.3 (1995) | 79.6 (2000) | 69.3 | 122 (1995) | 108 (2000) | 73.8 |
| Literacy rate, adult total (percent of people ages 15 and above) | 67.34 (1998) | 73.61 (2004) | 77.59 | 57.85 (1991) | 64.90 (2000) | 70.3 |
| Immunization, DPT (percent of children aged 12–23 months) | 35 (1993) | 59 (2000) | 91 | 83 (1993) | 90 (2000) | 97 |
| Immunization, measles (percent of children aged 12–23 months ) | 36 (1993) | 65 (2000) | 89 | 74 (1993) | 74 (2000) | 92 |
| Net primary school enrollment rate (percent) | n.a. | 87.32 (2000) | 88.59 | 74.12 (1992) | 75.34 (2001) | 95.86 |
| Gross primary school enrollment rate (percent) | 90.31 (1991) | 102.16 (2000) | 115.92 | 79.88 (1992) | 105.36 (2000) | 150.92 |

Source: World Bank, *World Development Indicators*, various years.
a. These two countries have longer postconflict periods than Afghanistan and the DRC. Data for an intervening year are added for the sake of comparison.
n.a. = Not available.

Second, patterns of social exclusion tend to be fixed in both countries. In Cambodia those who have no access to power elites, those who have less knowledge about their legal rights, and those who belong to ethnic minority groups are increasingly subject to disadvantageous treatment by public authorities.[70] One symptom of this is a rapid increase in land tenure disputes in recent years. About 50,000 people were reportedly evicted for development projects in 2006 and 2007 alone.[71] It is estimated that since the 1980s 20–30 percent of the country's land has been transferred to less than 1 percent of the population.[72]

The situation in Rwanda is worrisome as well. After the end of the civil war, despite the government's official statement that there is no ethnic division in Rwanda, people have witnessed a number of incidents that reflect ethnic division. Hutu opponents of the government have repeatedly been accused and suppressed in the name of preventing "divisionism" and "genocide ideology." In the process of the *gacaca*, a popular, participatory transitional justice process for punishing genocide perpetrators, the "victim-ness" of Tutsi and the "perpetrator-ness" of Hutu have been widely publicized.[73] In practice, RPF soldiers also committed atrocities during the civil war, but they have rarely been judged or punished.[74] The majority of the political and military elite are former Tutsi refugees.[75] They enjoy not only political but also economic success. Considering the tragic role that ethnicity has played in Rwanda's history of armed conflict, we need to be concerned about the possibility that state legitimacy is degenerating and that ethnic grievances are accumulating among the Hutus.[76]

A third concern is the authoritarian practice of the governments. As indicated in figure 6-1, "Voice and accountability" of the political regime has scarcely improved in postconflict Cambodia and Rwanda. Political opponents have been harassed in both countries. Economic disparity, social exclusion, and political autocracy all pose fresh challenges to the consolidation of state legitimacy in Cambodia and Rwanda. Paradoxically, the success and the strength of the Cambodian and Rwandan gov-

---

0.289 in the mid-1980s to 0.468 in 2000 and again to 0.510 in 2006. UNDP (2007b); Government of Rwanda (2007).

70. In Cambodia the CPP affiliation is important in securing jobs and promotions. In certain cases, Cambodian citizens are "forced to join ruling political parties in order to access services in the local bureaucracy and institutions." The CPP is said to control twenty companies that are the "financial pillars of the system." MacLean (2006, pp. 15–16). In contemporary Cambodia, patronage-related corruption is pervasive. Transparency International ranked Cambodia at 158th among 180 countries in the 2009 Corruption Perception Index.

71. IRIN (2008).

72. Calavan, Briquets, and O'Brien (2004, p. 2).

73. Ingelaere (2007). The social impacts of *gacaca* have been enormous, as the number of suspects has exceeded 800,000. Republic of Rwanda (2008).

74. Human Rights Watch (2008).

75. Although Hutu soldiers have been integrated into the national army as a result of the demobilization program, the core officers of the Rwandan Defense Force are mostly former RPF Tutsi members.

76. See for example Reyntjens (1985) and Prunier (1995).

ernments during the first phase of postconflict reconstruction may have lowered their incentives to respond quickly to fresh challenges. If they fail to take adaptive measures, the states may lose some of the legitimacy they have attained.[77]

## Policy Recommendations for Improving Aid Effectiveness in Reducing Fragility

Fragility, defined as the chronic lack of human security, continues to torment no small part of the developing world and the foreign aid actors who engage with it. The situation in postconflict countries is especially precarious. Despite huge ODA inflows, we observe continued or recurrent armed conflict and deterioration in human security in several countries. Exploring how best to use aid to reduce fragility is one of the most urgent tasks for the development community.

Recent analyses agree that a substantive and long-term reduction in fragility is contingent on the formation of an effective and legitimate state, because in the absence of such a state violence can recur and again worsen people's living conditions. State building, however, is a complex, unpredictable, and endogenous endeavor, affected significantly by local contexts and conditions. There can be no standard formula. It progresses through mutually reinforcing interactions between the enhancement of state capacity to deliver security and services and the improvement of state legitimacy.

Considering that successful state building is crucial for overcoming fragility, but that there are limitations to external influence in the state-building process, we recommend that state-building objectives be integrated at the earliest feasible time into any plans for international engagement in fragile situations. However, we, as a development community, must be humble enough to recognize that state building is a long-term, endogenous process in which foreign aid must be understood to be at best a catalyst for local transformation.

In spite of these complexities, measures for assessing the long-term effects of aid activities are necessary if we are to develop a greater sense of the impact of interventions. The nurturing of legitimacy is an especially difficult process to grapple with. It occurs when the great majority of the people develop a certain respect and acceptance of the state to which they belong, so that few will opt for violence even when they are dissatisfied with the state's everyday performance.

The existing indicators and measures are inadequate to capture legitimacy building.[78] We therefore recommend that, in addition to the actual improvements in security and living conditions, the changing perceptions of people and their

---

77. We should remember that the collapse of an authoritarian regime has often brought on serious armed conflict.

78. Most of the existing indicators focus on rational and legal legitimacy based on democratic values, although state legitimacy actually derives from many other sources. Our chapter shares this limitation, as we used the voice-and-accountability indicator as a proxy for legitimacy. The ratio of tax revenue to GDP

relationships with their state also be closely monitored. Efforts should be increased to establish reliable and accurate measures of the state-building progress.

Highly fragile countries caught in the capacity trap do not have state machinery effective enough to ensure public security and deliver basic social services to their people. As a result, their legitimacy remains very low. This weak legitimacy, in turn, makes it difficult for the government to improve security and service delivery.

In these countries, it may even be necessary for external players to assist through direct military involvement. However, military operations alone cannot bring permanent peace. To consolidate security for the long term, efforts should focus on reconstructing and stabilizing the social and economic lives of the people at the bottom and to nurture support and trust in the state. Civilian assistance for reconstruction and development should lead development efforts. Regardless of whether the assistance is military or civilian, however, national ownership should be respected to the maximum extent possible so that the capacity and legitimacy of the partner state can be fostered.

In very fragile situations, in which the capacity trap is especially serious, donors should focus efforts on projects for rehabilitation and development at community or district levels. Deliberate efforts should be made to foster trust in public authorities through these projects and to gradually build state legitimacy from the bottom up. The political and social conditions of each state should be closely examined to determine the optimum balance between capacity development efforts at the national level and at lower levels.

Several postconflict countries have progressed to the extent that they are now in postfragility situations. Nonetheless, some of them face a legitimacy trap because initial success in strengthening human security has weakened the government's incentive to respond to the shifting aspirations of its citizens with regard to such aspects as social and economic fairness, political accountability, and transparency. If this situation is left unattended for too long, grievances may grow to the point that state legitimacy is undermined. Therefore, governments facing a legitimacy trap should be encouraged and assisted in responding to the shifting expectations of their citizenry. Aid players should help to alleviate discontent among socially weak and disadvantaged people by providing legal and social assistance and implementing targeted development projects.

Finally, a regional perspective is increasingly important to tackling challenges stemming from fragile situations. Capacity trap countries frequently suffer from geographic and social divisiveness that enables the penetration across porous borders of weapons, people, armed militias, and drugs. Both capacity trap and legitimacy trap

---

is used in OECD/DAC's "Monitoring the Principles" as a proxy for state capacity and legitimacy. OECD (2010b, par. 11). However, what taxation means in the state-building context largely depends on the nature of the specific tax, as well as on the historical and social contexts of each country. For instance, Moore (2008) distinguishes "coercive" and "contractual" taxation. His argument suggests that strong tax-collecting capacity undermines state legitimacy if the tax is of a coercive nature.

countries are generally critical of the external imposition of values and prefer working with regional peer countries to establish standards suitable for local contexts.

With respect to regional environments, in articulating regional strategies we recommend establishing or strengthening regional mechanisms that include all stakeholders. Efforts should be made to undertake reconstruction and development on a regionwide basis. All donor countries and organizations would be encouraged to participate in these regional mechanisms, closely coordinating their activities among themselves and with regional governments and organizations so that available resources can be used as effectively as possible.

## References

Adelman, Howard. 2003. "The Use and Abuse of Refugees in Zaire." In *Refugee Manipulation: War, Politics, and the Abuse of Human Suffering*, edited by Stephen John Stedman and Fred Tanner. Brookings.

Amnesty International. 1997. "Rwanda: Ending the Silence." *Amnesty International*, September 25.

Armstrong, Andrea, and Barnett R. Rubin. 2005. "The Great Lakes and South Central Asia." In *Making States Work: State Failure and the Crisis of Governance*, edited by Simon Chesterman, Michael Ignatieff, and Ramesh Thakur. Tokyo. United Nations University Press.

Asian Development Bank. 2007. "Country Water Action: Cambodia Phnom Penh Water Supply Authority, an Exemplary Water Utility in Asia" (www.adb.org/Water/actions/CAM/PPWSA.asp).

Bartu, Peter, and Neil Wilford. 2009. "Transitional Justice and DDR: The Case of Cambodia." International Center for Transitional Justice.

Beath, Andrew, and others. 2010. "Randomized Impact Evaluation of Phase II of Afghanistan's National Solidarity Program (NSP): Estimates of Interim Program Impact from First Follow-Up Survey" (www.nsp-ie.org).

Bhatia, Michael, and others. 2009. "DDR in Afghanistan: When State-Building and Insecurity Collide." In *Small Arms Survey 2009: Shadows of War*, edited by Small Arms Survey Geneva. Cambridge University Press.

Blunt, Peter, and Mark Turner. 2005. "Decentralization, Democracy, and Development in a Post-Conflict Society: Commune Councils in Cambodia." In *Public Administration and Development* 25: 75–87.

Buzan, Barry. 1983. *People, States and Fear*. Brighton, U.K.: Wheatsheaf Books.

Calavan, Michael M., Sergio Diaz Briquets, and Jerald O'Brien. 2004. "Cambodian Corruption Assessment, May-June." USAID/Cambodia.

Chandler, David. 2007. "The State-Building Dilemma: Good Governance or Democratic Government?" In *State-Building: Theory and Practice*, edited by Aidan Hehir and Neil Robinson. London: Routledge.

———. 2006. *Empire in Denial: The Politics of State-Building*. London: Pluto Press.

Collier, Paul, and others. 2003. *Breaking the Conflict Trap: Civil War and Development Policy.* Washington: World Bank.

DFID. 2010. "The Politics of Poverty: Elites, Citizens, and States—Findings from Ten Years of DFID-Funded Research on Governance and Fragile States, 2001–2010." Synthesis paper. London: DFID.

Di John, Jonathan, and James Putzel. 2009. "Political Settlements." Issues paper. Governance and Social Development Resource Centre, University of Birmingham.

Edmonds, Martin, Greg Mills, and Terence McNamee. 2009. "Disarmament, Demobilization, and Reintegration and Local Ownership in the Great Lakes: The Experience of Rwanda, Burundi, and the Democratic Republic of Congo." *African Security* 2 no. 1: 29–58.

Fearon, James D., and David D. Laitin. 2004. "Neotrusteeship and the Problem of Weak States." *International Security* 28, no. 4: 5–43.

Fukuyama, Francis. 2005. *State Building: Governance and World Order in the Twenty-First Century.* London: Profile Books.

Ghani, Ashraf, and Clare Lockhart. 2008. *Fixing Failed States: A Framework for Rebuilding a Fractured World.* Oxford University Press.

Ghani, Seema, and Nematullah Bizhan. 2009. "Contracting out Core Government Functions and Services in Afghanistan." In *Contracting out Government Functions and Services: Emerging Lessons from Post-Conflict and Fragile Situations,* edited by OECD Partnership for Democratic Governance.

Global Witness. 2009. *'Faced with a Gun, What Can You Do?': War and the Militarisation of Mining in Eastern Congo.* London.

———. 2005. *Under-Mining Peace, Tin: the Explosive Trade in Cassiterite in Eastern DRC.* London.

Government of Rwanda. 2007. *Economic Development and Poverty Reduction Strategy, 2008–2012.* Kigali.

Hendrickson, Dylan. 2001. "Cambodia's Security-Sector Reforms: Limits of a Downsizing Strategy." *Conflict, Security, and Development* 1, no. 1: 67–82.

Higashi, Daisaku. 2008. "Challenge of Constructing Legitimacy in Peacebuilding: Case of Afghanistan." Report to the Best Practices Section in the Department of Peacekeeping Operations (DPKO) at UN Headquarters.

Human Rights Watch. 2008. *Law and Reality: Progress in Judicial Reform in Rwanda.* New York.

Hurbst, Jeffrey. 2000. *States and Power in Africa: Comparative Lessons in Authority and Control.* Princeton University Press.

Ingelaere, Bert. 2007. "Living the Transition: A Bottom-up Perspective on Rwanda's Political Transition." Discussion Paper 2007.06. Institute of Development Policy and Management, University of Antwerp.

International Crisis Group. 2009. "Congo: Une stratégie globale pour désarmer les FDLR." *Rapport Afrique,* no. 151 (July).

International Dialogue on Peacebuilding and Statebuilding. 2010. *Dili Declaration: A New Vision for Peacebuilding and Statebuilding.*

IRI (International Republican Institute). 2008. *Survey of Cambodian Public Opinion, October 22–November 25.*

IRIN. 2008. "Cambodia: Questions over Legality of Evictions in Name of Development." August 18.

Islamic Republic of Afghanistan. 2009. *Afghanistan National Development Strategy: First Annual Report 1387 (2008/2009).*

Jarstad, Anna K., and Timothy D. Sisk, eds. 2008. *From War to Democracy: Dilemmas of Peacebuilding.* Cambridge University Press.

JICA (Japan International Cooperation Agency). 2008. "Zeijaku Kokka ni Okeru Chuchoukiteki na Kunizukuri—Kuni no Risuku Taio Noryoku no Kojo ni Mukete" [State building in fragile states: enhancing resilience to risks from medium- and long-term perspectives].

Kaufmann, Daniel, Aart Kraay, and Massimo Mastruzzi. 2009. "Governance Matters VIII: Aggregate and Individual Governance Indicators, 1996–2008." Policy Research Working Paper 4978. World Bank.

Krasner, Stephen D., and Carlos Pascual. 2005. "Addressing State Failure." *Foreign Affairs* 84, no. 4: 153–63.

MacLean, Lindsay. 2006. "National Integrity System Country Study on Cambodia." Country study report. Transparency International.

Manning, Richard, and Alexandra Trzeciak-Duval. 2010. "Situation of Fragility and Conflict: Aid Policies and Beyond." *Conflict, Security, and Development* 10, no. 1: 103–31.

Mobekk, Eirin. 2009. "Security Sector Reform and the UN Mission in the Democratic Republic of Congo: Protecting Civilians in the East." *International Peacekeeping* 16, no. 2: 273–86.

Moore, Mick. 2008. "Between Coercion and Contract: Competing Narratives on Taxation and Governance." In *Taxation and State-Building in Developing Countries: Capacity and Consent*, edited by Deborah Brautigam, Odd-Helge Fjeldstad, and Mick Moore. Cambridge University Press.

Murotani, Ryutaro. 2010. "State-Building in Cambodia." JICA-RI Working Paper 5. In *State Building in Fragile Situations: Japanese Aid Experiences in Cambodia, Afghanistan and Mindanao*. JICA Research Institute.

Narayan, Deepa, Emcet Tas, and Philibert de Mercey. 2010. "Post-Taliban Recovery and the Promise of Community-Driven Development in Afghanistan." In *Moving Out of Poverty*. Vol. 4, *Rising from the Ashes of Conflict*, edited by Deepa Narayan and Patti Petesch. Palgrave Macmillan.

Newman, Edward, Roland Paris, and Oliver P. Richmond, eds. 2009. *New Perspectives on Liberal Peacebuilding*. Tokyo: United Nations University Press.

OECD. 2011. *Supporting Statebuilding in Situations of Conflict and Fragility: Policy Guidance*. DAC Guidelines and Reference Series. Paris.

———. 2010a. *The State's Legitimacy in Fragile Situations: Unpacking Complexity*. Paris.

———. 2010b. *Monitoring the Principles for Good International Engagement in Fragile States and Situations*. Country Report 1, *Islamic Republic of Afghanistan*. Paris.

———. 2010c. *Transition Financing: Building a Better Response*. Paris.

———. 2010d. *Ensuring Fragile States Are Not Left Behind*. Paris.

———. 2010e. *Resource Flows to Fragile and Conflict-Affected States 2010*. Paris.

———. 2008a. *State Building in Situations of Fragility*. Paris.

———. 2008b. *Concepts and Dilemmas of State Building in Fragile Situations*. Paris.

———. 2008c. *Geographical Distribution of Financial Flows to Aid Recipients, 2002–2006: Disbursement, Commitments, Country Indicators*. Paris.

———. 2008d. *Resource Flows to Fragile and Conflict-Affected States: Annual Report 2008*. Paris.

———. 2007a. *Principles for Good International Engagement in Fragile States & Situations*.

———. 2007b. *Geographical Distribution of Financial Flows to Aid Recipients, 2001–2005: Disbursement, Commitments, Country Indicators*.

———. Various years. *OECD International Development Statistics*.

Onana, Renner, and Hannah Taylor. 2008. "MONUC and SSR in the Democratic Republic of Congo." *International Peacekeeping* 15, no. 4: 501–16.

Paris, Roland, and Timothy D. Sisk. 2009a. "Understanding the Contradictions of Postwar Statebuilding." In *The Dilemmas of Statebuilding: Confronting the Contradictions of Postwar Peace Operations*, edited by Roland Paris and Timothy D. Sisk. London: Routledge.

———. 2009b. "Conclusion: Confronting the Contradiction." In *The Dilemmas of Statebuilding: Confronting the Contradictions of Postwar Peace Operations*, edited by Roland Paris and Timothy D. Sisk. London: Routledge.

————, eds. 2009c. *The Dilemmas of Statebuilding: Confronting the Contradictions of Postwar Peace Operations.* London: Routledge.

Prunier, Gérard. 2009. *Africa's World War: Congo, the Rwandan Genocide, and the Making of a Continental Catastrophe.* Oxford University Press.

————. 1995. *The Rwanda Crisis: History of a Genocide, 1959–1994.* London: Hurst & Company.

RDC (République démocratique du Congo). 2006. *Document de la stratégie de croissance et de réduction de la pauvreté.* Kinshasa.

Rennie, Ruth, Sudhindra Sharma, and Pawan Sen. 2009. "Afghanistan in 2009: A Survey of the Afghan People." Asia Foundation.

Republic of Rwanda. 2008. *Gacaca Courts Process: Implementation and Achievements.* National Service of Gacaca Courts.

————. 2007. *Law Determining the State Finances for the 2008 Fiscal Year* (Law 64/2007 of 31/12/2007).

Reyntjens, Filip. 2009. *The Great African War : Congo and Regional Geopolitics, 1996–2006.* Cambridge University Press.

————. 1985. *Pouvoir et droit au Rwanda; Droit public et évolution politique, 1916–1973.* Tervuren: Musée Royal de l'Afrique Centrale.

Richardson, Sophie, and Peter Sainsbury. 2005. "Security Sector Reform in Cambodia." In *Security Sector Reform and Post-Conflict Peacebuilding,* edited by Albrecht Shnabel and Hans-Georg Ehrhart. Tokyo. United Nations University Press.

Roberts, David. 2008. "Post-Conflict State Building and State Legitimacy: From Negative to Positive Peace?" *Development and Change* 39, no. 4: 537–55.

Rubin, Barnett R. 2006. "Peace Building and State Building in Afghanistan: Constructing Sovereignty for Whose Security?" *Third World Quarterly* 27, no. 1: 175–85.

————. 2005. "Constructing Sovereignty for Security." *Survival* 47, no. 4: 93–106.

Saikal, Amin. 2005. "Afghanistan's Weak State and Strong Society." In *Making States Work: State Failure and the Crisis of Governance,* edited by Simon Chesterman, Michael Ignatieff, and Ramesh Thakur. Tokyo. United Nations University Press.

Sherman, Jake. 2008. "Afghanistan: Nationally Led Statebuilding." In *Building States to Build Peace,* edited by Charles T. Call and Vanessa Wyeth. Boulder: Lynne Rienner.

Stedman, Stephen John, Donald Rothchild, and Elizabeth M. Cousens, eds. 2002. *Ending Civil Wars: The Implementation of Peace Agreements.* Boulder, Lynne Rienner.

Stewart, Frances, and Graham Brown. 2009. "Fragile State." Working Paper 51. CRISE.

Suhrke, Astri. 2009. "The Dangers of a Tight Embrace: Externally Assisted Statebuilding in Afghanistan." In *The Dilemmas of Statebuilding: Confronting the Contradictions of Postwar Peace Operations,* edited by Roland Paris and Timothy D. Sisk. London. Routledge.

Tilly, Charles. 1992. *Coercion, Capital, and European States: AD 990-1992.* Malden: Brackwell.

Tull, Denis M. 2009. "Peacekeeping in the Democratic Republic of Congo: Waging Peace and Fighting War." *International Peacekeeping* 16, no. 2: 215–30.

Umutesi, Marie Béatrice. 2004. *Surviving the Slaughter: The Ordeal of a Rwandan Refugee in Zaire.* University of Wisconsin Press.

United Nations. 2009a. *Final Report of the Group of Experts on the Democratic Republic of the Congo.* S/2009/603.

————. 2009b. *Report of the Secretary-General on Peacebuilding in the Immediate Aftermath of Conflict.* A/63/881-S/2009/304.

————. 2008. *Final Report of the Group of Experts on the Democratic Republic of the Congo.* S/2008/773.

———. 2002. *Final Report of the Panel of Experts on the Illegal Exploitation of Natural Resources and Other Forms of Wealth of the Democratic Republic of the Congo.* S/2002/1146.

———. 2001. *Report of the Panel of Experts on the Illegal Exploitation of Natural Resources and Other Forms of Wealth of the Democratic Republic of the Congo.* S/2001/357.

———. 2000. *Report of the Panel on United Nations Peace Operations* (Brahimi Report). A/55/305-S/2000/809.

UNDP (United Nations Development Program). 2009. *Human Development Report 2009.* New York.

———. 2007a. *Turning Vision 2020 into Reality: From Recovery to Sustainable Human Development, National Human Development Report Rwanda 2007.* Kigali.

———. 2007b. *Human Development Report 2007/2008.* New York.

UNHCR (United Nations High Commissioner for Refugees). 1993. "UNHCR in Cambodia: A Model for Success." Repatriation special report.

Wakamatsu, Eiji. 2010. "Building State from the Bottom Up: Community-Development Projects in Afghanistan." JICA-RI Working Paper 5. In *State Building in Fragile Situations: Japanese Aid Experiences in Cambodia, Afghanistan, and Mindanao.* JICA Research Institute.

Weiner, Myron. 1996. "Bad Neighbors, Bad Neighborhoods: An Inquiry into the Causes of Refugee Flows." *International Security* 21, no. 1: 5–42.

Whaites, Alain. 2008. "States in Development: Understanding State Building." DFID working paper.

World Bank. 2007. *Sharing Growth: Equity and Development in Cambodia.* Equity Report 2007: East Asia and the Pacific Region.

———. 2005. *Afghanistan: Managing Public Finances for Development.*

———. Various years. *World Development Indicators.*

Wyeth, Vanessa, and Timothy Sisk. 2009. "Rethinking Peacebuilding and Statebuilding in Fragile and Conflict-Affected Countries: Conceptual Clarity, Policy Guidance, and Practical Implications." Discussion note, OECD-DAC International Network on Conflict and Fragility, May 15, 2009.

Yamada, Hiroshi. 2009. "Kanbojia Jinminto no Tokushitsu to Sono Henyo 1979–2008" [Characteristics of the Cambodian People's Party and its transformation 1979–2008]. Monograph 4. Institute of Asian Cultures, Sophia University.

Young, Crawford, and Thomas Turner. 1985. *The Rise and Decline of the Zairian State.* University of Wisconsin Press.

# 7

## Development Aid and Global Public Goods: The Example of Climate Protection

KEMAL DERVİŞ AND SARAH PURITZ MILSOM

Development aid has always had multiple purposes. The most openly proclaimed purpose has been to provide assistance to poor countries and vulnerable populations, with the objective of fighting extreme poverty, providing humanitarian relief, and supporting long-term development. Stated as such, this objective reflects a moral imperative and a redistributive intent: channeling resources from the more fortunate to the less fortunate, to help them survive and to help them grow. The target can be poor countries or specific poor and vulnerable populations within countries. Under this overall moral imperative, it is customary to distinguish purely humanitarian aid, such as that provided after an earthquake, from development assistance, which has a more distant horizon and focuses on building productive capacity in some form, rather than just providing immediate relief.

Besides the moral imperative based on an ethics of redistribution across borders, development aid also often reflects political, military and strategic objectives. Rich countries tend to help those among the poorer countries that cooperate with them, that are allies, or that are in danger of becoming allies of adversaries. This was particularly true during the cold war. The United States and the West helped their allies, while the Soviet Union helped countries cooperating with Soviet objectives. Often countries played one bloc off against the other, without necessarily aligning fully with either, such as Egypt in the late 1950s when the United States and the World Bank, at the time strongly influenced by the Western powers, refused to finance the Aswan Dam, and Egypt obtained finance and technical assistance from the Soviet Union.[1] In the period from the 1950s to the 1990s the Western powers provided much so-called development aid to countries run by oftentimes corrupt dictators with the only proviso that these dictators cooperate with the West's political objectives, in spite of the fact that these dictators channeled much of the aid into their own pockets and the pockets of their domestic supporters. The Soviet Union did the same.[2]

In addition to these moral-redistributional and political-strategic purposes of foreign aid has been a third major purpose—to help finance the provision of global public goods; that is, goods that benefit not only the recipients but also the donor and indeed, in some cases, the entire world. Take, for example, the case of the avian flu, which started in Southeast Asia and was threatening the whole world. Donors financed the culling of potentially infected birds, which helped people in the entire world, for if the disease mutated to human flu and spread around the world, hundreds of millions of people worldwide would have been affected.

There are many other examples of global public goods, ranging from the capacity of countries to control and prevent terrorism, to financial systems that contribute to worldwide financial stability, to institutions that allow and encourage international trade, or those that regulate air traffic. In all these cases there is the need to finance capacity building, infrastructure, knowledge, and equipment that facilitates the provision of these global public goods. Because of the externalities involved, with benefits accruing to all, even if the public good is financed by one or a few countries, there are collective action problems affecting the provision of global public goods. Consider again the case of preventing avian flu by financing the culling of affected bird populations. All countries would benefit from the result, even if only one country financed the cost. There is, therefore, an issue of burden sharing, which affects relations between and within advanced and developing countries. Thus the poverty reduction or redistribution objective and the global public good provision objective can drive development assistance separately or in an intersecting fashion (table 7-1).

Assistance programs on the ground in developing countries ("reducing poverty" on table 7-1) provide mostly local benefits, though there may be some positive indirect spillover effects for other populations in the region. Examples of development assistance of this nature include providing microcredit loans to the poor, building rural hospitals, installing weather stations, providing bed nets, and build-

1. On July 19, 1956, the United States under the Eisenhower administration withdrew offers to finance the construction of the Aswan Dam in Egypt (www.eisenhower.archives.gov).
2. Empirical studies of aid effectiveness that ignore the fact that much of aid has been driven by purely political, rather than developmental, objectives are therefore not measuring what they intend to measure. Some of these studies should perhaps have measured the effectiveness of aid in keeping friendly regimes in power. See Bulow and Rogoff (1989); Radelet (2006).

Table 7-1. *The Intersection of Two Policy Objectives: Reducing Poverty and Providing Global Public Goods*

| Issue | Objective: reducing poverty | Intersection: reducing poverty and providing a global public good | Objective: providing a global public good |
|---|---|---|---|
| Health | Compensating the poor for culling infected birds | Reducing the probability of virus mutations that could pose a global threat | Producing a vaccine against avian flu |
| Natural disasters | Building weather monitoring stations to alert local populations of inclement weather | Alerting local populations and providing reliable scientific information on climate change | Tracking changes in earth's atmosphere and forecasting climate change |
| International trade | Building rural access roads | Encouraging rural exports | A new Doha agreement |

Source: Adapted from Derviş (2008).

ing rural roads. By contrast, a global public good would provide benefits from which everybody, in all countries, would gain. A new Doha agreement, which better facilitates international trade, would be a global public good. The production of a vaccine against avian flu and the monitoring and dissemination of comprehensive data that track changes in the earth's atmosphere are other examples. Such activities provide benefits that are largely nonrival and nonexcludable: once they are supplied no country (in the case of the World Trade Organization, no participating country) could be prevented from benefiting from them, nor can the use by one country encroach upon another country's use.

There is a conceptual difference between assistance designed for poverty reduction and that designed for the provision of global public goods. But these two objectives often overlap, whereby the provision of global public goods is rooted in development assistance. For example, consider again the case of weather monitoring stations. If assistance is provided to developing countries to build monitoring stations, those countries would directly benefit by being able to warn their citizens of inclement weather, avoiding such devastating loss of life as happened with the 2004 Indian Ocean tsunami, in which an estimated 230,000 people lost their lives.[3] But monitoring stations also serve as a global public good, providing scientific data that can be used to better understand changes in the earth's atmosphere and to more accurately predict the effects of a changing climate. Financing quality control equipment for rural exports is another example of how providing a global public good intersects with direct poverty reduction. The global community benefits by the confidence that consumers have that the products they

3. CRS (2005).

buy meet certain health and quality standards, a confidence that translates into greater demand for the goods and a healthy market for the people who make the products.

## The Case of Climate Change

This chapter addresses the way the two objectives—poverty reduction and global public goods—intersect in the specific case of attempts to protect the world, as well as the potentially most affected poorer populations, from the effects of climate change. Controlling climate change is one of the most important global challenges the world faces in the twenty-first century. A key influence on climate is the concentration of greenhouse gases trapped in the atmosphere. If global warming is considered potentially harmful, then greenhouse gas emissions are a global public "bad," and their reduction, anywhere in the world—whether in Chicago, Berlin, Beijing, or Mexico City—is a global public good. Less traffic, cleaner energy, or more energy-efficient housing in any one place in the world reduces global warming everywhere. The same can be said for less deforestation in Indonesia, Brazil, or Africa and for reforestation in China and the United States, because forests absorb carbon, reducing its amount in the atmosphere. The Intergovernmental Panel on Climate Change (IPCC) estimates that the cutting down of forests accounts for a fifth of current greenhouse gas (GHG) emissions into the atmosphere and that for every acre of tropical forest that remains intact, 200 to 300 tons of carbon dioxide ($CO_2$) can be sequestered.[4] If for example the United States or Japan helps Indonesia control deforestation by providing resources to Indonesian agriculture in a way that reduces deforestation, it would both reduce poverty and provide a global public good—or what table 7-1 calls an intersection.

### Challenge of Climate Change

Climate change is a multidimensional challenge, one that requires deep scientific and entrepreneurial ingenuity, an extraordinary level of global political cooperation, and dedication to managing our ecological interdependence while simultaneously protecting populations at greatest risk. The probabilities of risk and loss associated with climate change are uncertain, but there are certain things we do know.

We know that weather patterns have become more extreme: more droughts, more storms, more heat waves, and more floods.[5] We know that the average temperature of the earth's surface has risen by 1.3 degrees Fahrenheit from its average in the nineteenth century and that annual GHG emissions due to human activity increased approximately 70 percent between 1970 and 2004. We know that climate change disproportionately harms the poor, as they lack the resources

4. UN (2009).
5. UNDP (2007).

required to adapt, tend to be located in regions that are highly vulnerable to climate change, and work in climate-sensitive jobs. We know that catastrophic, irreversible climate change is a possibility and that there is a closing window of opportunity to act to insure against it.[6]

Atmospheric concentrations of GHGs alter the energy balance of the climate system, affecting the absorption, scattering, and emission of radiation within the atmosphere.[7] Most GHGs have both natural and anthropogenic sources; however since the industrial era human activity has added significant levels of GHGs through the burning of fossil fuels and deforestation, the majority of which is $CO_2$.[8] The atmospheric lifetime of a molecule of $CO_2$ is between 50 and 200 years. This means that the gases we release into the atmosphere today will stay there for, at minimum, decades. This also means that, even if the world were to abruptly stop the emission of heat-trapping gases into the atmosphere, we have already committed ourselves to decades of a warming climate.

There is a broad consensus among scientists that it would be prudent to contain the earth's surface temperature to within 3.6 degrees Fahrenheit (or 2 degrees Celsius) of preindustrial levels in order to protect the world from the risk associated with large-scale climate-related catastrophes. Temperatures beyond this range would increase the risk of irreversible damage to our planet. (One should not interpret this temperature ceiling too rigidly; it merely gives us a reasonable target, around which there remains uncertainty.) In order to have just a fifty-fifty chance of maintaining temperatures to within this 3.6 degrees Fahrenheit threshold, scientists estimate that GHG atmospheric concentration should be stabilized at around 450 parts per million of carbon dioxide equivalent ($CO_2e$) by 2050.[9] This level of $CO_2e$ would require that the world cut its annual output of greenhouse gases in half over the next forty years. The longer we wait to cut emissions and the further we travel along the business-as-usual trajectory, the more difficult and unlikely it will be that we avoid unmanageable temperature increases (figure 7-1).

Although climate change threatens all people in all countries, developing countries are likely to bear 75–80 percent of its costs.[10] The five ways that climate change could hinder or even reverse human development in the world's poorest countries are

—Lower agricultural production and food security

—Water stress and water insecurity

6. Due to the time lag associated with the extended lifespan of heat-trapping gases (discussed in more detail in the following sections), it will become increasingly more difficult to limit global warming.

7. IPCC (2007).

8. $CO_2$ from energy represents close to 80 percent of anthropogenic GHG emissions for Annex I countries (which consists of mostly industrialized countries and economies in transition) and about 60 percent of total global emissions. IEA (2009).

9. IPCC (2007).

10. World Bank (2010b).

Figure 7-1. *Projected Annual Total Global Emissions (GtCO₂e), 2000–2100*[a]

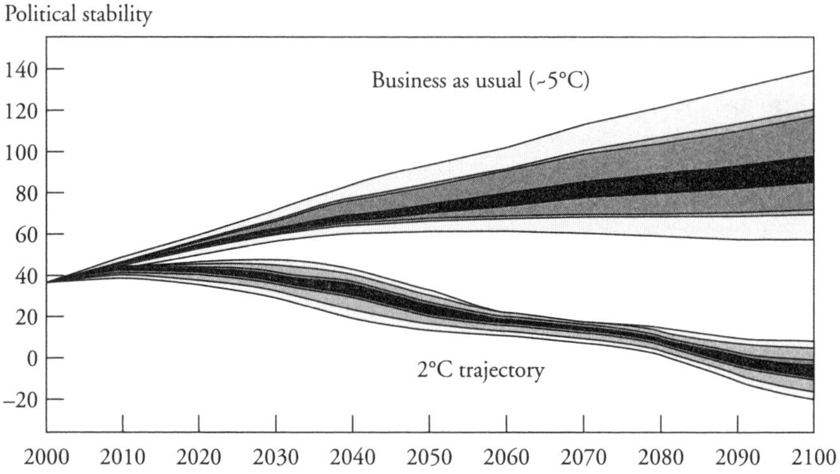

Political stability

Source: World Bank (2010b).

a. The top band shows the range of estimates across various models (GTEM, IMAGE, MESSAGE, MiniCAM) for emissions under a business-as-usual scenario. The lower band shows a trajectory that could yield a concentration of 450 ppm of $CO_2$e.

—Rising sea levels and exposure to extreme weather

—Adverse change to ecosystems and biodiversity

—Negative health impacts such as the expansion of malaria and dengue fever.[11] Climate change is thus directly linked to the fight against poverty.

Given that high-income countries have emitted the majority of the cumulative GHGs currently in the atmosphere (figure 7-2), some argue that these countries should bear the brunt of the costs associated with addressing climate change. But it is also true that given the recent and rapid growth of energy use in some developing countries, it will be impossible to meet the climate challenge without strong action by these countries, too. The IEA found that "the combustion of coal in *developing countries* drove the growth in global emissions between 2006 and 2007."[12] While developed countries are responsible for the majority of prior emissions, currently they account for only 45 percent, and this is likely to drop to 35 percent by 2030. Countries such as India and China, which rely heavily on coal, are on a path toward emitting GHG concentrations that rival those of Annex II countries.[13]

The central international framework to try to coordinate a response to climate change has been the UNFCCC, adopted in 1992 by 192 countries. In 1997 the

11. UNDP (2007).

12. IEA (2009).

13. The UN Framework Convention on Climate Change, adopted in 1992, is an international treaty wherein 192 countries joined to consider how to address global warming. Parties to the UNFCCC are classified into three groups: Annex I countries are industrialized countries

Figure 7-2. *Share of Global Emissions, Historic and 2005, by Country Income*[a]

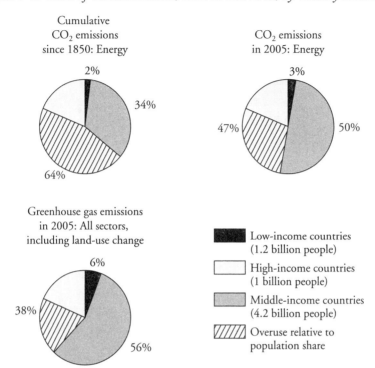

Cumulative
$CO_2$ emissions
since 1850: Energy

$CO_2$ emissions
in 2005: Energy

2%

34%

64%

3%

47%

50%

Greenhouse gas emissions
in 2005: All sectors,
including land-use change

6%

38%

56%

◼ Low-income countries
(1.2 billion people)

☐ High-income countries
(1 billion people)

▨ Middle-income countries
(4.2 billion people)

▨ Overuse relative to
population share

Source: World Bank (2010b).

a. Data cover over 200 countries for more recent years. Data are not available for all countries in the nineteenth century, but all major emitters of the one era are included. Carbon dioxide ($CO_2$) emissions from energy include all fossil fuel burning, gas flaring, and cement production. Greenhouse gas emissions include $CO_2$, methane ($CH_4$), nitrous oxide ($N_2O$), and gases with high global-warming potential (F gases). Sectors include energy and industrial processes, agriculture, land-use change, and waste. Overuse of the atmospheric commons relative to population share is based on deviations from equal per capita emissions; in 2005 high-income countries constituted 16 percent of global population; since 1850, on average, today's high-income countries constituted about 20 percent of global population.

Kyoto Protocol to the UNFCCC set binding targets for 37 industrialized countries and the European community to reduce GHG emissions, under the key principle of "common but differentiated responsibilities."[14] Though 182 countries ratified Kyoto, the United States rejected it in 2001, with the primary objection being that too much burden rested on the United States and industrialized countries and not

and economies in transition; Annex II countries, a subset of Annex I countries, are developed countries and, if they ratified the Kyoto Protocol, have committed to paying certain costs to developing countries to address climate change; and developing countries, which under the Kyoto Protocol are not expected to reduce emission levels unless developed countries supply adequate levels of funding and technology assistance.

14. For text of the Kyoto Protocol, see http://unfccc.int/resource/docs/convkp/kpeng.pdf.

enough was required from developing countries. And given the United States' size
as an emitter, any effective climate change negotiation will undoubtedly require its
buy-in. In 2007 the thirteenth Conference of the Parties to the UNFCCC met in
Bali, where the global community renewed its intentions to strengthen international coordination to fight climate change and stabilize emissions. The Bali Action
Plan outlined a course of action in which the parties, including the United States,
planned to negotiate a new treaty to succeed the Kyoto Protocol when it expires at
the end of 2012. This new treaty was to be established at the 2009 UNFCCC
meeting in Copenhagen.

More than 120 heads of state or governments participated in the Copenhagen
conference in December 2009. While some headway was made in key areas such
as financing targets for developing countries and transparency in reporting emission reduction efforts, the conference fell well short of negotiating the comprehensive, decisive way forward that the Bali Action Plan called for. The end result
was the Copenhagen Accord, a brief political declaration that sets out broad principles but does not address the key sticking points that have blocked progress in
previous negotiations, such as setting binding emissions caps or nailing down
detailed plans for financing and technology transfer. In the wake of Copenhagen
two key questions surfaced: Will the 127 countries associated with the accord be
capable of fleshing out the details of an implementation architecture to follow
through with the broad goals they supported in the declaration? And is the
UNFCCC, run under UN system rules, the appropriate central forum for negotiating international cooperative action against anthropogenic climate change?

At the sixteenth Conference of the Parties in Cancun, Mexico, in December
2010, a formal process for reporting mitigation commitments was established
(rather than the informal process agreed upon in Copenhagen). But despite this
heightened level of transparency and participation among countries, there is a
clear need for more ambitious action on the part of all countries. Even if all countries implement their emission reduction/limitation pledges, a substantial emission reduction gap will still exist.[15] More generally, the Cancun Agreements have
helped to transition the Copenhagen Accord from a letter of intent toward an
internationally coordinated package of operational measures to address climate
change, but much work remains and forward momentum hinges on country-
level implementation of existing pledges.

The second question—whether the UNFCCC can or should remain the central framework for climate change negotiations—stemmed from the difficulty in
Copenhagen to effectively negotiate under the UN system rules. The rules pro-

---

15. *Climate Action Tracker* estimates that this emission reduction gap (the gap between
pledged emissions reductions and the maximum estimated level we should maintain to stave
off earth's temperature from rising more than 2 degrees Celsius) may be around 8 billion tons
of $CO_2e$ a year by 2020 (www.climateactiontracker.org/).

vide one vote per country, and all final decisions must be made unanimously, therefore allowing any one country the opportunity to halt proceedings regardless of its population, level of emissions, or resources. Some argue that smaller, more flexible discussions might be more effective for facilitating coordinated climate action, such as the Major Emitters Forum (MEF) or the Group of Twenty (G20). It is important to underscore, however, that both the MEF and the G20 are informal governance structures and cannot produce legally binding global solutions, although experience has shown that verbal assurance from leaders on the world stage provides some political momentum for achieving progress. Another option would be to implement a two-track approach to coordinate global climate action. One track would consist of the UNFCCC annual meetings, which would have the more limited mission of encouraging countries to share and compare their plans and allow for their monitoring but would no longer try to facilitate a single "grand deal." The second track, running parallel to the annual meetings, would consist of more limited agreements, possibly by overlapping and smaller coalitions, to make collective progress of a sectoral or functional nature.

The Cancun conference, approached with much more modest expectations than the previous meeting in Copenhagen, was more successful in coordinating an international response to the climate change challenge. The Cancun Agreements, supported by nearly every member of the UNFCCC, were an important step in narrowing the trust deficit that developed in the months following Copenhagen and, moreover, have to some degree restored confidence in the UN process for addressing climate change. However this is not to say that the two-track approach is no longer needed, as discussed later in this chapter.

### Adaptation and Mitigation

When discussing resources to be deployed in the context of efforts to control climate change, a distinction is appropriate between resources to help adapt to climate change that is already occurring or will inevitably occur and resources to be used to mitigate climate change by reducing GHG emissions.

ADAPTATION. Most resources to be channeled to developing countries for adaptation are appropriately classified into the "fighting poverty" category of development assistance distinguished above. Take for example resources supporting the development and distribution of heat-resistant crops such as NERICA ("new rice for Africa"), a drought-resistant and highly productive rice variety that has been successful in West African countries. Thanks to these crops, rural populations most exposed to the increased heat waves and droughts accompanying climate change will still be able to grow food products and better resist an increase in poverty.

While the conceptual framework is clear, the heterogeneous effects of climate change across countries and the overlap in broad development needs and climate adaptation challenges make estimating the cost of climate adaptation inherently

Table 7-2. *New Climate Funds, Commitment and Time Period*
U.S.$ million

| Fund | Commitment | Period |
|---|---|---|
| *UNFCCC* | | |
| Strategic Priority on Adaptation | 50[a] | GEF3–GEF4 |
| Least Developed Country Fund | 172[a] | As of October 2008 |
| Special Climate Change Fund | 91[a] | As of October 2008 |
| Adaptation Fund | 300–600[a] | 2008–12 |
| *Bilateral initiatives* | | |
| Cool Earth Partnership (Japan) | 10,000[a, b] | 2008–12 |
| ETF-IW (United Kingdom) | 1,182[a, b] | 2008–12 |
| Climate and Forest Initiative (Norway) | 2,250 | |
| UNDP-Spain MDG Achievement Fund | 22[a] / 92[b] | 2007–10 |
| GCCA (European Commission) | 84[a] / 76[b] | 2008–10 |
| International Climate Initiative (Germany) | 200[a] / 564[b] | 2008–10 |
| IFCI (Australia) | 160[b] | 2007–10 |
| *Multilateral initiatives* | | |
| GFDRR | 15[a] (of $83 million in pledges) | 2007–08 |
| UN-REDD | 35[b] | |
| Carbon Partnership Facility (World Bank) | 500[b] (140 committed) | |
| Forest Carbon Partnership Facility (World Bank) | 385[b] (160 committed) | 2008–20 |
| Climate Investment Funds | 6,200[a, b] | 2009–12 |
| Clean Technology Fund | 4,800[b] | |
| Strategic Climate Fund, including | 1,400[a, b] | |
| Forest Investment Program | 350[b] | |
| Scaling up Renewable Energy | 200[b] | |
| Pilot Program for Climate Resilience | 600[a] | |

Source: World Bank (2010b).
a. Adaptation.
b. Mitigation.

problematic.[16] Nevertheless, there have been attempts to estimate adaptation costs, all of which indicate that these costs to developing countries are, at a minimum, tens of billions of dollars annually.[17] Funds dedicated to adaptation have multiplied in the past few years. Most are from international official flows through either bilateral or multilateral initiatives (table 7-2). Despite these developments, the estimated needs are far from being met.

The Global Environment Facility (GEF) is the traditional repository for climate funds under the UNFCCC and includes several funds allocated specifically

16. Estimates of adaptation costs have been made by the World Bank, the Stern Review, UNDP, Oxfam, UNFCCC, Project Catalyst, and the World Bank EACC.
17. Summary of estimates can be found in World Bank (2010b). Also see Schipper, Cigaran, and Hedger (2008).

for adaptation.[18] Replenishment of the GEF Trust Fund occurs every four years, when donor nations commit financial resources for supporting its operations. Funds within the GEF—the Least Developed Countries Fund, the Special Climate Change Fund, and the Strategic Priority on Adaptation Fund—are capitalized through voluntary financial contributions from parties to the convention and may occur at any time. Though contributions have increased in recent years, the unpredictability of contributions raises serious concerns as to the long-term effectiveness of the funding of the GEF.[19]

That Adaptation Fund (AF), established at the 2007 Conference of the Parties to the UNFCCC in Bali by the parties to the Kyoto Protocol, in contrast to other UNFCCC funds, uses a levy-based mechanism for capitalization.[20] The AF is capitalized through a 2 percent tax on emission reduction certificates earned through the Clean Development Mechanism (CDM), a market-based mechanism designed to mobilize mitigation efforts in developing countries.[21] This levy-based method of capitalization offers an independent resource that is entirely additional to existing assistance and therefore offers a promising vehicle for raising resources for developing countries. The AF is also unique in that it is governed by a board on which developing countries have a majority.[22] The AF also provides direct access for recipient countries to access the funds, rather than going through a UN implementation agency, which has historically been the case.[23] It is estimated that the AF could potentially raise between $300 million and $600 million over the period 2008–12, depending on the price of carbon.[24] But because the revenue to capitalize the AF relies on the scale of success within the CDM (which has it own limits and inefficiencies, discussed in the following section), the ability of the AF to provide adequate, predictable, and flexible adaptation finance to developing countries is both limited and uncertain.

The multilateral initiatives, of the World Bank in particular, have added financing instruments that are estimated to surpass the funding levels currently available under the UNFCCC. Climate Investment Funds (CIF), created in 2007, are a pooled, multidonor trust fund jointly implemented by multilateral development banks (and managed by the World Bank) to assist low-income and emerging countries in low-carbon and climate-resilient development. Funds disbursed through the CIF are in the form of grants or concessional loans.

18. Ballesteros (2010).
19. Evaluation Offices (2009).
20. Only those developing countries that are parties to the Kyotol Protocol qualify.
21. Under the CDM developed countries can invest in mitigation efforts in developing countries in exchange for certified emissions reductions (CERs). These CERs can be used in limited amounts to meet Kyotol Protocol obligations.
22. The AF board consists of two representatives from each of the five UN regional groups, one representative from a small island developing state, one representative from the least developed country parties, two other Annex 1 representatives, and two other non-Annex 1 representatives.
23. Ballesteros (2010).
24. World Bank (2010b, pp. 262–63).

Within the CIF are two trust funds, the Clean Technology Fund and Strategic Climate Fund. As table 7-2 illustrates, the World Bank's Pilot Program on Climate Resilience, included under the Strategic Climate Fund, represents a large share of the CIF's total current resources and is dedicated to adaptation programs. The program aims to facilitate the integration of adaptation into broader country development strategies and to promote climate-resilient growth and development. As of March 2010 several wealthy nations had made contributions totaling approximately $967 million, though so far total funds deposited are much less, at just over $160 million.[25] Nevertheless, this amount is a significant upsurge in climate financing dedicated to adaptation. Also interesting is the spike in CIF pledges since its 2007 inception, which are more than double contribution pledges to the GEF. The international climate financing architecture, once made up of mostly funding instruments within the GEF, is expanding rapidly, and multilateral development banks are playing a key role.[26]

Some new bilateral climate funds have also sprung up in recent years, the two largest being Japan's Hatoyama Initiative ($11 billion over the next three years, by 2012, toward mitigation and adaptation efforts, $7.2 billion of which is ODA) and Germany's International Climate Initiative (€120 million in 2008, half for mitigation and half for adaptation in emerging, developing, and transitioning economies). This rapidly expanding list of new bilateral and multilateral climate funds reflects a growing consensus that climate change poses serious risks to global sustainable development. But the upsurge of financing instruments brings with it new risks of inefficiency, such as coordination failure, lack of transparency, data gaps and reporting inconsistencies, duplication of efforts, higher transaction costs, and governance concerns.

In December 2009, at the UNFCCC Conference of the Parties in Copenhagen, some progress was made on coordinating international climate finance. Outlined in the Copenhagen Accord is a pledge by many wealthy countries to provide approximately $30 billion of fast-start financing to developing countries in 2010–12. These funds are to be "scaled-up, new and additional, predictable and adequate" and to have "balanced allocation" between mitigation and adaptation, including REDD-plus, technology development and transfer, and capacity building.[27] In addition, these countries pledged $100 billion a year by 2020 to address the needs of developing countries.

While certain aspects of the accord were a welcome development, in particular the initial pledge to mobilize climate finance through both fast-start financing

---

25. As of March 2010 the following countries had pledged contributions to the World Bank's Pilot Program on Climate Resilience: Australia, Canada, Denmark, Germany, Japan, Norway, the United Kingdom, and the United States (www.climatefundsupdate.org).

26. Schalatek (2009).

27. Copenhagen Accord, December 2009, UNFCCC. REDD is a UN program for reducing emissions from deforestation and degradation.

and long-term financing, the lack of clarity as to the details of fund delivery left many questioning the significance of the pledges. In the wake of Copenhagen it became clear that following through on fast-start finance commitments was critical for building legitimacy and trust for future climate negotiations as well as for bridging the resource gap hampering adaptation and mitigation efforts in developing countries.[28]

Leading up to the Conference of the Parties in Cancun, fast-start commitments to developing countries were approximately $29 billion, though it was not at all clear that the pledges were new and additional (above and beyond previous commitments to developing countries). The funding gap between short-term, fast-start financing and the long-term pledge of $100 billion became a key focus in Cancun. The Cancun Agreements, announced on December 11, 2010, include the establishment of a new Green Climate Fund, through which new multilateral funding for adaptation and mitigation should flow. Key to its establishment is the compromise of the new fund's governance, which will be temporarily administered by the World Bank, for a three-year probationary period, but governed by a twenty-four-member board composed of an equal number of members from developing and developed countries.[29] There is much debate surrounding the equity and efficiency of these funds, which revolves around two key subjects: additionality and governance.

Many developing countries are understandably very concerned that the resources to help them adapt to climate change and allow them to overcome its poverty-increasing effects are additional to what has already been promised as development aid rather than a redirection of existing development assistance resources (aid diversion). Aid commitments predating the Bali Action Plan did not take into account the additional burden on developing countries caused by ongoing climate change. However climate change is now globally recognized as causing new needs, due mostly to past actions of rich countries but also increasingly due to the emissions of rapidly growing emerging economies.

Given the intrinsic link between climate adaptation and poverty reduction, making the distinction between traditional ODA and climate finance for adaptation has proven extremely challenging. Take for example financing assistance for developing countries to develop efficient water irrigation systems, disease monitoring systems, or reinforced coastal defenses. These projects both reduce poverty and protect against climate vulnerabilities. How should these funds be measured and reported—as development aid, climate aid, or both? The key issue here is the lack of clarity and conformity regarding the definition of "new and additional" financing. Without a baseline to count new pledges and commitments against, it

28. See for example Project Catalyst (2010); Schalatek (2009).

29. As of March 2010 the following countries had pledged contributions to the Pilot Program on Climate Resilience: Australia, Canada, Denmark, Germany, Japan, Norway, the United Kingdom, and the United States.

is nearly impossible to determine whether climate financing is new or if it is funds diverted from other potential or pledged development efforts.

Most developing countries agree (as do some wealthy countries, such as the Netherlands and Norway) that climate finance should be classified as official development assistance only after donor countries have met the 0.7 percent of GNI target that was reaffirmed in 2005 at the Gleneagles summit. While this baseline is arithmetically straightforward, there are challenges that make this approach difficult to implement. In particular, only five of the twenty-three countries reporting official development assistance in the OECD database have met this target. In addition, not all wealthy countries have accepted this target, most notably the United States. It is therefore unlikely that this approach will garner enough political support for an international agreement. Many donor countries believe that climate adaptation is just one of many approaches to poverty reduction and that all concessional aid should be considered ODA and should count toward the 0.7 percent of GNI target.

With the AF as the exception (capitalized through a levy on the CDM), most official flows for climate assistance to developing countries are voluntary contributions and eligible under OECD rules to be counted as ODA. The definition of "new and additional" financing has strong implications for how climate resources are raised, measured, and disbursed. This was one of the major focuses and issues in the international negotiations in Cancun, Mexico, at the end of 2010.

In this context, it is important to note that the National Adaptation Programmes for Action (NAPAs; least developed countries submit to both the UNFCCC and the GEF) are not separate strategy tracks but are incorporated into poverty reduction strategies and the country's national development strategy. The NAPAs are intended to provide a process for least developed countries to identify priority activities that target urgent or immediate needs to enhance adaptive capacity to a changing climate. Once it has submitted its NAPA, the country is eligible to apply for funding for their adaptation program under the Least Developed Countries Fund. The NAPAs, designed to be action oriented and country driven, are directly linked to sustainable development; as such, they must be integrated into the overall development policy.

Another major concern of developing countries relates to the governance of the resources reserved for adaptation. They argue that these resources should be administered directly by themselves or by organizations with governance structures in which developing countries have at least equal say with donors over the management of the funds. The key moral-political argument put forward by developing countries is related to the one put forward when arguing for additionality. The developing countries were not responsible for past emissions that have created the problem that is now threatening their development, and adaptation aid is viewed as a kind of compensation. or an entitlement, due to them, rather than as a resource rooted in rich country generosity.

Recent debate within international negotiations reflects the differing perceptions of what is considered to be an appropriate governance structure for climate finance and, in particular, adaptation finance. Some countries propose that a new financial mechanism be created under the authority of, and accountable to, the UNFCCC's Conference of Parties, rather than under the Millennium Development Goals and other implementing agencies, such as the UNDP, UNEP, and IFAD.[30] On the other hand, most developed countries, as is reflected in the Copenhagen Accord, are keen on using existing institutions—and in particular the World Bank—to manage climate funds.[31] This stems from the argument that, since they are the ones providing the resources, wealthy countries should have a dominant say in the governance of the institutions using these resources. In addition, it is argued that there are practical advantages to housing climate finance within existing institutions: they have the institutional capacity to implement financing immediately, they have years of experience in handling and leveraging large amounts of money, and they have significant project-based experience.

For many developing countries, the push for a new financial mechanism under the UNFCCC is rooted in their distrust of the overall governance of the World Bank. Specifically, these countries are wary of the slow pace of reform aimed at new voting weights in the executive board and what they see as overly prescriptive conditions. Recent concern has also been raised by civil society that some of the projects funded by the bank do not reflect clean-growth policies and are heavily slanted toward fossil fuel production. The most notable example is the World Bank's May 2010 $3.75 billion loan to Eskom, $3 billion of which will be used to build the world's largest coal-fired power plant in South Africa. (The remainder is slated for renewable energy projects.)[32] World Bank vice president for the Africa region, Obiagel Ezekwesili, defended the bank's decision, explaining that "without an increased energy supply, South Africans will face hardship for the poor and limited economic growth. . . . Access to energy is essential for fighting poverty and catalyzing growth, both in South Africa and the wider subregion."[33] The Eskom project is an example of the underlying tension between the development and climate agendas.

The governance of the funds within the GEF is also disconcerting for many recipient countries. The GEF Council is the main governing body and consists of thirty-two members: sixteen from developing country constituencies, fourteen from developed country constituencies, and two from transitional economies.

---

30. "The GEF formally functions under the guidance of, and is accountable to, the Conferences of the Parties of these conventions. Over the last decade, the relationships between some of the COPs and the GEF Council have sometimes suffered from concerns that COP guidance is not fully reflected in the development of GEF operational policies." GEF (2009).

31. ActionAid (2009); UNFCCC (2010).

32. Ackerman (2009).

33. World Bank (2010a).

While all decisions are to be made by consensus, if no consensus is possible then decisions requiring formal votes are taken by a double-weighted majority. This requires 60 percent votes from council members and 60 percent majority of votes by contribution level, giving donors the edge in the decisionmaking process. In addition, the operations of the GEF take place through ten implementation agencies, including the UNDP, UNEP, UNIDO, IFAD, FAO, and the MDBs.[34] The lack of direct country access to these funds is inconsistent with the Paris Declaration and Accra Agenda for Action, which is built upon country ownership of their development policies and strategies.

The governance structure of the AF is the most popular among the developing countries and civil society. The AF is accountable to, and under the authority of, the Conference of Parties to the Kyoto Protocol and, as previously mentioned, is the only funding mechanism governed by a developing country majority. Board decisions are taken by consensus or, if necessary, by a two-thirds majority, wherein each member present gets one vote. The AF is also the only fund that does not rely on voluntary contributions and provides direct access to country governments, meaning that countries can choose implementing agencies rather than being assigned one. The main concern with the effectiveness of the AF is that its funding relies solely on the CDM, and current levels fall well short of the estimated needs.

The proliferation of climate financing instruments in recent years has resulted in a fragmented landscape, lacking a global framework. Such a framework is needed to ensure the harmonization of monitoring and reporting methods, coordination among resource channels, increased transparency and legitimacy, and more efficient and effective distribution to climate programs and projects. However, such a framework must also be flexible and allow space for national country ownership while simultaneously building trust and cooperation among donors and recipients.

The complicated landscape of adaptation financing, and the accompanying challenges of defining additionality and governance of the funds, obstruct the coordination of global climate action. Mutually acceptable adaptation financing is important not only for successful poverty reduction but also for the overall good will needed for climate cooperation, including actions related to mitigation.

MITIGATION. While the financing of adaptation, in most cases, does not provide a global public good, the financing of mitigation, anywhere in the world, does provide the global public good of reduced amounts of carbon or other heat-trapping gases in the atmosphere. Helping a developing country such as India, for example, produce electricity with cleaner energy technology is a form of resource transfer that carries with it a global public good. Such help would thus fall into the middle column of table 7-1. The invention of a carbon capture and storage

---

34. GEF Council (www.thegef.com/gef/council); ActionAid (2009).

technology for coal-fired generation plants, in itself, would fall into the third column of the table, under a global public good. Financing the incremental cost of such a plant, when compared to the cost of a plant without such clean technology, would fall into the middle column, because India would benefit from such technology ("pure" development aid), but the entire world would also benefit from reduced emissions (provision of a public good).

As described above, reaching agreement on adaptation finance is going to be difficult. However, reaching agreement on mitigation finance is going to be even more difficult because the overall amount of resources needed are even greater, and the conceptual issues relating to equity, burden sharing, enforcement, and international law, are even more complex. The discussion of how mitigation objectives should be built into development aid and cross-border resource transfers, and how these objectives should affect institutional design, is at the heart of the global climate negotiations.

To organize thought, it is useful to divide the world into three regions, or groups of countries. The advanced, "rich" countries form region A, the emerging middle- and lower-middle-income countries form region B, and the poorest, least-developed countries make up region C. There would be long-term losses from significant climate change for all three regions, but these losses will be disproportionately greater, as a percent of GDP, in region C. Oversimplifying, one can assume that whatever region C does in terms of emissions is irrelevant, as emissions from regions A and B make up more than 95 percent of total emissions. Region C simply bears the consequences of what regions A and B do, without itself contributing appreciably to the problem. Regions A and B face a prisoners' dilemma situation. It is in each region's best interest to push the maximum mitigation, and the associated short-term costs, on to the other, while benefitting from the resulting reduction in $CO_2e$ concentrations in the atmosphere. Each region would prefer to free ride on the other regions' mitigation efforts, enjoying the benefits of fewer emissions while incurring minimal costs. But if each region behaves in a noncooperative way, waiting for the other to act, they will both face the damaging outcome of rapid warming. Both regions would benefit from a cooperative solution where each would commit to mitigate, thereby keeping global warming below a certain threshold and reducing the risks of potentially very damaging temperature rises, with consequences both for themselves and the least developed countries of region C.

How is this stylized situation relevant to the debate on foreign assistance? The link lies in the fact that getting to a cooperative solution will have to involve side payments from the rich countries of region A to the middle-income countries of region B.[35] There are two distinct reasons for such side payments. First, both regions would engage in mitigation if the net benefits of mitigating at home are

35. For discussions of stylized models, see Anand (2002); Barrett (2001); Sandler (1999).

positive, even if there is no mitigation elsewhere. This may not be the case, however. It may be that it only pays to mitigate if the other region also mitigates. Or even though there may be some mitigation that brings positive net benefits to a single region without any mitigation elsewhere, the amount of such "lonely mitigation" would be much lower than the amount associated with an optimal cooperative solution where both regions commit to larger amounts of mitigation. The second reason for side payments could be one related to efficiency. It may be that it is cheaper to mitigate in one region than in another. It would then be in the interest of the region facing more expensive mitigation costs to pay the region where it is cheaper to mitigate. Assume for example that a region has decided that it is in its own interest to reduce emissions by an amount x over a certain period. Given such a decision, it would be best for that region to pay for the emission reduction wherever it is cheaper to achieve, inside or outside its borders. Such a situation too would lead to a voluntary side payment. Note the difference between the two rationales. In the first case, there is a side payment, even if the efficiency costs of mitigation are identical, to "bribe" the other region into a cooperative solution. In the second case, a least-cost solution invites such a side payment.

In our stylized three-region world, which region is likely to make side payments in its own interest? Assuming first no differences in the cost of mitigation, do the countries in region A have an incentive to make side payments—that is, provide concessional mitigation finance—to the other two regions? The answer is essentially no with respect to region C. Since whatever the poorest countries do has minimal impact on overall levels of emissions, there would be no real need to draw them into a cooperative solution, if the self-interest of the rich countries were to be the only cause of action.[36] The incentives are different when it comes to possible side payments to region B. It may well be that the outcome that is likely in the absence of side payments to them would amount to a level of overall mitigation that is clearly suboptimal from the point of view of region A countries. In the absence of side payments, the amount of emissions in region B might be so large as to cost more to region A than the side payments in question.

Whether a cooperative solution based entirely on self interest is likely to involve side payments to region B from region A, in the absence of differential mitigation costs, depends on a complex set of factors involving essentially the geographical impact of climate change and the relative value decisionmakers in the two regions place on protection from climate change compared to other social goals. These two sets of factors probably work in opposite directions. For geographical reasons, the damage that climate change could inflict may be larger in the emerging market economies such as China and India when compared to the

36. This is assuming that the only way that poor countries can retaliate against or impose costs on rich countries is through their own small emissions. There may be other costs to the rich countries however, related to the increased likelihood of state failure and associated security concerns.

United States, Canada, Europe, and Japan. On the other hand, the still much lower income levels in region B probably imply that the weight of longer term climate risks in the social welfare function of these societies, when compared to access to electricity, adequate food and shelter, and means of transport, is lower than in the richer countries. If we start disaggregating the two regions, the situation becomes, of course, much more complicated, with marked intraregional differences. The perceived cost-benefit ratios are likely to be very different between Florida and Minnesota, for example, as well as between, say, Argentina and Northern India. In the absence of mitigation cost differentials, it is not clear whether pure self-interest would lead to side payments from the rich to the middle-income countries.

But of course there are cost differentials. Lower wage levels, as well as greater opportunities to mitigate due to the relatively greater importance of new capital in the emerging economies, imply that it is generally less expensive at the margin to reduce emissions there than in the rich advanced economies.[37] This is also true for the relatively small amounts of mitigation that can be achieved in the poor countries making up region C. The relative cost advantage is a powerful incentive for side payments from the rich to the developing countries in both regions B and C, with the bulk likely to go to region B, because of its emissions.

Finally, there are the ethical arguments underpinning a certain sense of global civics that are distinct from pure self-interest. These ethical arguments affect not only adaptation, as we see above, but also the debate about mitigation. It is undeniable that between two-thirds and three-quarters of the carbon concentrations in the atmosphere have been put there by the past activities of region A countries. Many, even in region A, would agree that there is a carbon debt that these countries owe to the region C countries, a debt that has to be taken into account when trying to craft a cooperative solution. How strong this ethical argument will prove to be and how much it can affect the politics of climate negotiations remain to be seen. It exists, however, and is one of the factors in play.

In summary, a cooperative solution involving global mitigation targets will involve resource transfers from rich countries both to rapidly growing middle-income countries and to poorer developing countries. There are three reasons for this: in the absence of cost differentials, such transfers may favor a cooperative outcome; lower relative costs of mitigation in developing countries allow a globally more efficient outcome to be achieved; and ethical arguments (based on historical responsibilities as well as poverty reduction needs in developing countries) may reinforce the case for these transfers. In addition to flows driven by adaptation objectives, there will therefore have to be a substantial flow of concessional resources from rich to developing countries associated with mitigation efforts to combat climate change. These flows are conceptually distinct from traditional

37. For detailed analysis of mitigation costs, see McKinsey & Co. (2009).

ODA and may have a magnitude broadly comparable to the entire amount of traditional ODA (see below).

There are essentially two ways for these flows to materialize. The first is through the distribution or allocation of emission reduction targets and associated emission permits that are internationally tradable. Countries that agree to more ambitious emission reduction targets shoulder a larger share of the burden, which may come in the form of higher costs of energy and transport or less immediately convenient forms of land use. These costs can be reduced by "buying" emission permits from developing countries or by financing mitigation projects in these countries. In either case more actual mitigation will then take place in developing countries, but it will be paid for by the emitting enterprises in the rich countries. A second way of achieving resource transfers can be in the form of concessional finance provided by the rich countries to the developing countries in some form linked to mitigation targets agreed to by these countries. Note that the former resource flows will not appear at all in ODA statistics, while the latter will, subject to the complications of the additionality debate described above.

The estimates for mitigation costs vary widely, given the uncertainties and unknowns associated with climate change, but all estimates are very large and run into the hundreds of billions of dollars annually. The 2009 *World Economic and Social Survey* reports that most estimates range from 0.2 to 1.2 percent of global GDP a year (or between $180 billion and $1.2 trillion) by 2030.[38] With large emission reduction opportunities located in developing countries, the cheapest and most effective way to fight a changing climate is to focus resources first on these opportunities that will maximize emission reductions at the lowest possible cost.

## Summary and Conclusion

The potential importance and size of resource flows associated with efforts to fight climate change, both for mitigation and for adaptation, adds a complicated and huge new dimension to the debate on aid flows and aid effectiveness. There are and were, of course, other global public goods before climate change, particularly in the health sector, for which arguments very similar to those outlined above in the context of climate change apply. Resources spent by rich countries to fight infectious diseases in developing countries can be seen as side payments, which are similar to assistance designed to reduce carbon emissions. The benefits from these resources are shared worldwide, and they are driven both by the self-interest of the rich countries and by genuine feelings of solidarity with the citizens of poor countries.

But the size of the climate change challenge and of the resources it will take to deal with it in power generation, transport systems, housing and urban design,

38. UN (2009), pp. 154–55.

land use, and forest conservation is of an order of magnitude that has to bring the issue of a global public good into the center of the debate on aid and aid effectiveness. Both the conceptual structure of the debate and the empirical work on effectiveness has to incorporate the idea of a global public good more explicitly and rigorously, at least from an analytical point of view. It can of course be argued that there are political circumstances in which clarity does not facilitate action. It is often true that foreign aid essentially focused on poverty reduction and based on ethical impulse and feelings of human solidarity can benefit from being associated with considerations of a global public good, so that self-interest can be harnessed as a supportive argument in the political debate about foreign assistance. In the context of climate change, however, it would seem that there is an even greater need to clarify how resource flows to developing countries are essential to achieve cooperative solutions that are in the self-interest of the citizens of rich countries.

In either case, lack of clarity is not compatible with a fundamental belief in democratic principles and transparency. Citizens in democratic countries should understand what is at stake, what goals are being pursued, what the benefit-cost ratios are likely to be, and what portion of resources is dedicated to selfless poverty reduction and what portion is to finance collection action that is also entirely in their own self-interest. Confusing the objectives and obfuscating the debate is unlikely, in the long run, to work or to lead to sustainable solutions. The implication of this for the Busan Summit on Aid Effectiveness is that the financing of the global public good of mitigation should clearly be separated conceptually from development assistance. The financing of activities that benefit the whole world have a rationale that is different from that of development aid, although the two types of resources can be channeled in a coordinated way.

We conclude with some thoughts on the way forward within the international climate negotiations. Can or should one aim for a grand agreement, one comprehensive global deal, to be achieved by a near universal coalition of countries? Such a deal would take into account the self-interest of all countries but also reflect a certain amount of human solidarity, particularly with respect to the poorest. It would try to be efficient by equating the marginal cost of mitigation across sectors, countries, and regions and would involve an implicit or explicit worldwide price of carbon accompanied by side payments designed to tie the grand coalition of countries together and make the agreed mitigation and adaptation path self-sustaining. All this would be transparent, recalculated periodically in the light of new evidence or new technologies, and supported by enforcement mechanisms to discourage attempts at free riding.

To state this ideal blueprint is to acknowledge that it will not be feasible to achieve it in the form of one single undertaking, to borrow a phrase from trade negotiations. It would be far too complex to quantify all of its dimensions, to overcome empirical disagreements, and to devise mechanisms that can effectively and fairly prevent free riding. Seeking a single undertaking covering all sectors and countries, as well as all associated resource flows, as the only way forward is to condemn climate negotiations to permanent failure. The scaled back expectations in Cancun suggest that this reality is slowly being acknowledged.

Instead, what has a greater chance of success is a two-track approach. Track one would consist of a continued effort to conceptualize, design, and empirically flesh out what could be "the" grand global deal. A global mitigation cost curve à la McKinsey would be further refined and periodically updated, accompanied by a set of sectoral- and country-specific mitigation targets evolving over time.[39] Work would continue on quantifying finance flows, including concessional side payments to facilitate collective progress. All countries would continue to meet annually under the UNFCCC umbrella to review the data, debate the nature of an optimal global growth path, and exchange views on distributional issues and resource flows. However the objective of these annual meetings would not be to reach a grand all-encompassing agreement but to develop a dynamic framework within which more limited agreements could fit and to provide a comprehensive global forum to evaluate progress toward protection from the potentially devastating impacts of a changing climate.

Track two would parallel these annual meetings, aiming for more limited agreements of a sectoral, functional, or regional nature, which could be pursued by small coalitions able to reach mutually beneficial arrangements. For example, given that deforestation is the second-largest source of greenhouse gases in the atmosphere and that forest conservation may be comparatively more palatable in terms of its impact on economic growth than curbing the burning of fossil fuels, forming a cooperative coalition for the UN program REDD is much more likely in the near term. Various forms of foreign assistance flows could and should accompany these more limited agreements and help to facilitate their implementation.

Progress would be achieved by advancing on both of these tracks and through interaction between them. Of course this two-track approach, with progress made sector by sector, would not be optimal compared to one grand agreement equalizing the marginal cost of carbon reduction worldwide and across sectors; there would be a global loss of efficiency. Yet compared to doing close to nothing and being thoroughly frustrated every year by failure to achieve the "grand deal," partial cooperation in the near term, with continued efforts for more inclusive global action for the medium to long term, may be the way forward, bringing tangible progress and allowing momentum to build for more ambitious steps. Within such a strategy, resource transfers will play a very important catalytic role and thus will have to be part of the overall development aid architecture. Politically, perhaps the most important challenge will be to explain to publics in the rich countries how

39. Mckinsey & Co. (2009).

large amounts of resources to finance mitigation outside their countries' borders can in fact directly benefit themselves—by achieving emission reductions at lower cost than what would be possible at home. The Cancun meeting de facto endorsed such a two-track approach, and it is both likely and desirable that the meeting in South Africa in 2012 take place with the same overall approach.

We have two recommendations for the fourth High-Level Forum on Aid Effectiveness to be held in Busan in November 2011. First, it will be important to include the provision of global public goods in the broader development assistance debate. In terms of the amount of resources it involves, it is a very big issue. In terms of the rationale behind it, there is a clear distinction between financing a common good and providing development aid. While it may be politically expedient at times to mix the two, a sustainable democratic process should be built on clarity, not confusion. Clarity of purpose does not preclude providing both types of finance in complementary ways and even through the same institutions.

Second, and more specifically on climate, one of the most important global public goods in human history, the legitimate and indeed necessary search for a grand and universal bargain should not preclude the building of partial progress, sometimes by smaller coalitions, willing to move ahead with some financing and some agreements in some sectors. These partial and sector-focused steps should be part of a dynamic process that gets the world closer to optimal climate policies, as scientific knowledge progresses further and as political support strengthens in response to deeper understanding of the problem and a greater willingness by all nations to cooperate.

## References

Ackerman, Frank. 2009. "Financing the Climate Mitigation and Adaptation Measures in Developing Countries." G24 Discussion Paper 57. Geneva: United Nations.

ActionAid. 2009. "Equitable Adaptation Finance: The Case for an Enhanced Funding Mechanism under the UN Framework Convention on Climate Change." Johannesburg: ActionAid.

Anand, P. B. 2002. "Financing the Provision of Global Public Goods." Discussion Paper 2002/110. Helsinki: United Nations University World Institute for Development Economics Research.

Ballesteros, Athena. 2010. *From Copenhagen to Cancun: Climate Finance.* Washington: World Resources Institute.

Barrett, Scott. 2001. "International Cooperation for Sale." *European Economic Review* 45, no. 10: 1835–50.

Bulow, Jeremy, and Rogoff, Kenneth. 1989. "Sovereign Debt: Is to Forgive to Forget?" *American Economic Review* 79, no. 1: 43–50.

CRS (Congressional Research Service). 2005. "Indian Ocean Earthquake and Tsunami: Humanitarian Assistance and Relief Operations" (www.fas.org/sgp/crs/row/RL32715.pdf).

Derviş, Kemal. 2008. "The Climate Change Challenge." Annual Lecture 11. UNU-WIDER. Helinksi.

Evaluation Offices (DANIDA and GEF). 2009. "Joint External Evaluation: Operation of the Least Developed Countries Fund for Adaptation to Climate Change." Washington: Global Environment Facility.

GEF (Global Environment Facility). 2010. "Summary of Negotiations: Fifth Replenishment of the GEF Trust Fund." Uruguay.

IEA (International Energy Agency). 2009. "$CO_2$ Emissions from Fuel Combustion: Highlights." Paris (www.iea.org/co2highlights/co2highlights.pdf).

IPCC (Intergovernmental Panel on Climate Change). 2007. "Climate Change 2007: Synthesis Report." Geneva (www.ipcc.ch/publications_and_data/publications_ipcc_fourth_assessment_report_synthesis_report.htm).

McKinsey & Company. 2009. "Pathways to a Low-Carbon Economy: Version 2 of the Global Greenhouse Gas Abatement Cost Curve." New York.

Project Catalyst. 2010. "Project Catalyst Brief: Making Fast Start Finance Work." London: ClimateWorks Foundation and European Climate Foundation.

Radelet, Steven. 2006. "A Primer on Foreign Aid." Working Paper 92. Washington: Center for Global Development.

Sandler, Todd. 1999. "Intergenerational Public Goods: Strategy, Efficiency, and Institutions." In *Global Public Goods: International Cooperation in the 21st Century,* edited by Inge Kaul, Isabelle Grunberg, and Marc A. Stern. Oxford University Press.

Schalatek, Liane. 2009. *The Missing Link: Bringing Gender Equality to Adaptation Financing.* Washington: Heinrich Boll Foundation North America (www.unep.org/roa/amcen/Projects_Programme/climate_change/PreCop15/Proceedings/Gender-and-climate-change/Double Mainstreaming_Final.pdf).

Schipper, Lisa, Maria Paz Cigaran, and Merylyn McKenzie Hedger. 2008. "Adaptation to Climate Change: The New Challenge for Development in the Developing World." UNDP Environment and Energy Group.

UN (United Nations). 2009. *World Economic and Social Survey 2009: Promoting Development, Saving the Planet.*

UNDP (United Nations Development Program). 2007. "Fighting Climate Change: Human Solidarity in a Divided World" (http://hdr.undp.org/en/media/HDR_20072008_EN_Complete.pdf).

UNFCCC (UN Framework Convention on Climate Change). 2010. "Additional Views on Which the Chair May Draw in Preparing Text to Facilitate Negotiations among Parties: Submission from Parties." Document FCCC/AWGLCA/2010/MISC.2. Bonn: Ad Hoc Working Group on Long-Term Cooperative Action under the Convention (http://unfccc.int/resource/docs/2010/awglca10/eng/misc02.pdf).

World Bank. 2010a. "World Bank Supports South Africa's Energy Security Plans." News release, April 8.

——. 2010b. "World Development Report: Development and Climate Change."

# 8

## *Inside the Black Box of Capacity Development*

AKIO HOSONO, SHUNICHIRO HONDA, MINE SATO,
AND MAI ONO

In recent development discussions, capacity development (CD) has emerged as a central issue. The Accra Agenda for Action (AAA), adopted in 2008 at the third High-Level Forum on Aid Effectiveness, emphasizes CD even more strongly than does the Paris Declaration, which incorporates CD as a key crosscutting theme in aid effectiveness. The outcome document of the UN summit on its Millennium Development Goals (MDGs) in September 2010 repeatedly asserts the importance of capacity and CD; and the global initiative on management for development results identifies the development of statistical capacity as a top agenda item.

Underlying this trend is a growing recognition among donor organizations as well as the governments of donors and partner countries that lack of capacity has been and will likely remain a major obstacle in translating policy into development results.[1] Moreover, the challenges for off-track countries of attaining and sustaining development outcomes, particularly those in fragile situations, are formidable. The difficulty of their path ahead is compounded by emerging global challenges such as climate change and the increasingly volatile economic environment exemplified by the recent global financial crisis.

---

1. The launch of the Management for Development Results initiative within the global MDG campaign reflects the global development community's commitment to a stronger results orientation, both in development and in aid.

We are of the view that there is a compelling need to continue efforts at deepening our understanding of the CD process itself and the potential roles to be filled by external actors firmly grounded in real-world practice. This chapter identifies key factors in the CD process through a literature review and then applies a working analytical framework to selected case studies. This exercise can contribute to a better understanding of CD and to better CD practices, which can inform the fourth High-Level Forum on Aid Effectiveness in 2011. We focus first on perspectives that are important for improving understanding of the CD process and support to CD, presented through a brief review of key discussions and findings from previous CD studies.[2] Second, we apply CD factors to three case studies. The final sections suggest the policy implications of the case studies and discuss the way forward.

## Overview and Key Issues of Capacity Development

We begin by reviewing the body of CD literature by researchers, consultants, and practitioners that has developed since the mid-1990s.[3]

### Definitions

According to the widely cited definition from OECD/DAC, *capacity* is the ability of people, organizations, and society as a whole to manage their affairs successfully; *capacity development* is the process by which people, organizations, and society as a whole unleash, strengthen, create, adapt, and maintain capacity over time.[4] Folded into these definitions are several important features fundamental to an understanding of CD.

First, capacity development is a long-term endogenous process.[5] Second, CD is a holistic process encompassing multiple, interlinked layers of capacities. DAC, for example, builds on the basic capacity to set three analytical layers: individual, organizational, and the enabling environment.

Third, capacity embodies not only specific technical elements, such as specific health care or road construction skills, but also so-called core capacities. These include generic and crosscutting competencies and the ability to commit and engage, to identify needs and key issues, to plan, budget, execute, and monitor actions, and to acquire knowledge and skills.[6] The challenge is how to enhance

2. By capacity development studies we mean the body of research that specifically uses the current broad CD framework, both for conceptual discussions and for case studies.

3. UNDP (1995, 1998); Qualman and Bolger (1996); Lusthaus and others (1999); OECD/DAC (2006); ECDPM (2008).

4. OECD/DAC (2006). The position paper on capacity development by the UN Development Group employs this definition by DAC.

5. UNDP (2002a); Lavergne and Saxby (2001); GTZ (2003); GOVNET/DAC (2005); JICA (2006a). The UNDP (2002a) played a crucial role in raising CD discussion to the international level.

6. UNDP (1998); ECDPM (2008); JICA (2006a, 2008b).

effectively such crosscutting core capacities.[7] Various learning theories suggest that actual engagement and real-world practice in addressing specific issues in areas relevant to core capacities may be the most promising approach. Fourth, external actors cannot create capacity but can only provide support to the local CD processes.[8]

## Current Discussions

In the following we discuss the latest perspectives including systems thinking, knowledge and learning in capacity development and also the relationship of capacity development to the question, Capacity for what, for whom, and in what context?

SYSTEMS THINKING. Recent CD studies, including one from the European Centre for Development Policy Management, have begun employing "complex adaptive systems," or a systemic perspective, to derive analytical frameworks.[9] The wider acceptance of systems thinking in the current CD discussions is based on the assumption that it can better capture and explain complexities of multi-layered transformative processes in a constantly changing external (that is, development) environment.[10] Insights from systems thinking suggest that interventions will likely fail if they are fixed too rigidly in advance, whereas incremental or emergent intervention models show more promise for dealing with usually ill-defined development issues, because they allow a greater scope for an endogenous process of learning by doing.

KNOWLEDGE AND LEARNING. Closely connected with systems thinking, knowledge and learning in a CD process has increasingly been a feature of recent discussions.[11] Peter Clarke and Katy Oswald argue that mutual learning per se might even be considered to be CD.[12] CD perceived as a mutual learning process demands that we shift our idea of what knowledge is and how it can be generated away from the traditional transfer-of-knowledge model toward a co-creation-of-knowledge model.

Traditional discourse on knowledge transfer treats knowledge as a material that can be passed through planning and programs from one who teaches to one who

7. JICA (2008b).

8. Within the broad and commonly accepted framework of capacity development are variations in emphasis. One strand of studies, including the World Bank's CD strategy document for sub-Saharan Africa, puts greater focus on the macroperspective of state building. The World Bank document sets out a strategy for Africa with the "dual objectives of building effective states and forging engaged societies." World Bank (2005, p. 2). A study by ECDPM focuses more on capacity development at the level of the individual organization (ECDPM 2008).

9. ECDPM (2008).

10. The benefits of bringing systems thinking into the capacity development debate are that they highlight a focus on processes, on the interrelationships between actors, structures, and ideas, on emergence as a way to change human systems, and on an "in-built tendency towards self-organization" (ibid.).

11. Learning has increasingly been mainstreamed into various academic disciplines, including adult education and management science. Woodhill (2010); Fisher (2010).

12. Clarke and Oswald (2010).

learns. In such a model it is necessary first to identify a deficiency (a need) and then to fill it by bringing knowledge from some external source. In development assistance, debates have tended to view knowledge in terms of the transfer of technical content with little or limited consideration for context specificity, a view that reflects a simplistic understanding of knowledge generation.[13]

An emerging alternative view, by contrast, sees knowledge as a product of continuous human interaction within specific contexts. According to this view, knowledge is co-created through a mutual learning process and acquired through practical experiences.[14] The application of such a view to CD analysis helps us to capture the multilayered process of CD more effectively than the traditional and more static "capacity gap" thinking, which tends to overlook evolving interactions.[15] This alternative view also implicitly informs us that approaches and instruments to support CD can be more varied than those applied within the traditional package of technical assistance.

CAPACITY FOR WHAT, FOR WHOM, AND IN WHAT CONTEXT? According to AAA, "developing countries will systematically identify areas where there is a need to strengthen the capacity to perform and deliver services at all levels—national, subnational, sectoral, and thematic—and design strategies to address them."[16] While a holistic understanding of the dynamic process of CD is important, it poses the challenge to both partner country and external actors of how to translate such a comprehensive view into concrete practices. For this reason, it is necessary to begin by asking, Capacity for what and for whom and in what context? Answering these questions will help to clarify intervention goals.[17] To do this, we have capacity assessment tools and guidelines, developed by international donors and NGOs, that have been tested and used at various levels to better understand stakeholder needs and context.[18]

## Framework

We identify five factors, both concrete and abstract, to help in analyzing the CD process: stakeholder ownership, specific drivers, mutual learning, pathways to scaling up, and external actors. These factors are not applicable equally to all CD efforts in every context, because the CD process is much more than a simple

---

13. UNDP (2002b).

14. Nonaka, Toyama, and Hirata (2008) defines such knowledge as *phronesis,* a term coined by Aristotle, meaning the ability to determine and undertake best and collective actions in certain settings through reference to appropriate theories and technologies, as necessary.

15. Learning is not free from power relationships. Harvey and Langdon (2010) point out that when a small organization interacts with larger and more powerful institutions, its members encounter other values and rules not necessarily consistent with their own. The authors argue that more powerful institutions can influence and shape individuals' subjectivities, which sometimes results in disempowerment through learning.

16. OECD (2008).

17. OECD/DAC (2006).

18. ADB (2008); JICA (2008b); Otoo, Agapitova, and Behrens (2009); UNDP (2008).

manipulation of key factors.[19] In addition, the factors are not mutually exclusive; rather, in many cases they are mutually reinforcing and interdependent.[20]

STAKEHOLDER OWNERSHIP. Major CD studies highlight the importance of ownership; that is, the awareness, commitment, motivation, and self-determination of people and groups whose capacity is to be improved.[21] Ownership has become central, especially in the context of the global trend toward decentralization and participatory development. Experience shows that a lack of ownership, or excessive control by external actors, tends to negatively affect the sustainability of development interventions. Thus ownership is the foundation of any endogenous CD process.

SPECIFIC DRIVERS. Researchers and practitioners recognize and increasingly agree that CD is not a straightforward process but rather is a nonlinear, dynamic process.[22] Progress may be incremental at one stage and then may plateau. What generates sudden transformations in capacity or other breakthroughs likely differs from one case to another but may be a result of leadership, management system, incentive mechanisms, or organizational culture.[23] Furthermore, a change in social, political, or economic context might also bring momentum for change and open up windows of opportunity for an enhanced CD process.

Among the potential CD drivers exemplified above, leadership has been identified by many observers as one of the most influential elements. Thus leadership, informed by theories of management, now constitutes part of the standard menu for any CD analysis.[24] Leadership is important not only for organizations but for other entities as well. Strong political leadership can help promote policy changes conducive to CD and allow the time and space for testing innovative policies. In another setting, an effective community leader can enhance cohesiveness, provide vision, and give a sense of direction to his followers. Thus in various forms and at various levels, leadership is a CD catalyst.

A management system with adequate incentive mechanisms is also highlighted in a number of CD studies. This is the type of institutional factor that is critical to sustaining and scaling up innovative practices.[25]

MUTUAL LEARNING. Mutual learning is central to the endogenous CD process and for the creation of innovative solutions that address the needs of beneficiaries and other stakeholders. Peter Clarke and Katy Oswald caution, however, that in most cases the learning process does not occur automatically, because individuals and groups are usually preoccupied with the pressure they are under from their

---

19. Brinkerhoff and Morgan (2010).
20. ECDPM (2008).
21. For example, see ECDPM (2008); DAC (2006).
22. ECDPM (2008).
23. UNDP (2003); ECDPM (2008); Clarke and Oswald (2010).
24. UNDP (2003); OECD/DAC (2006); JICA (2006a); ECDPM (2008).
25. JICA (2006a); ECDPM (2008).

daily routine.[26] Under these conditions, time and space for learning must be consciously made and maintained through the values, leadership, and enabling environment that underpin and sustain mutual learning.

Ikujiro Nonaka, Ryoko Toyama, and Toru Hirata denote the time and space for learning by the Japanese word *Ba*, which they define as the essential enabling context for deep business relationships and for the creation of knowledge and value.[27] *Ba* is important both within and between organizations and can be created by both local and external actors, including donors. This has relevance to the fifth issue we examine here, the role of external actors. Learning is not limited to partner country representatives but applies also to external donors who provide CD support. The traditional assumption that external donors can fill knowledge gaps through one-way technology transfers no longer prevails. In the CD process, knowledge is an outcome of mutual learning that involves external donors acquiring local knowledge and discovering latent local capacity.

SCALING UP. Scaling up good practices is central to achieving development outcomes.[28] Several studies on both CD and scaling up suggest that there are diverse pathways to achieving results. One study differentiates three types of approaches: planned, incremental, and emergent.[29]

As there is no rigid line dividing initial experimental CD practice and the scaling-up process, most of the CD elements discussed above—drivers and the learning process—are equally relevant to scaling up.[30] Context, including commitment to the policy or program in question at a political level, matters in ensuring sufficient incentives and space for scaling up. Institutionalization of good practice by the enactment of laws or introduction of policies can become a contextual driver for the CD process. The engagement of recipient stakeholders from the outset is likely to strengthen their ownership of capacity building programs and thus enhance the effectiveness and sustainability of scaling up. Nevertheless, there is a potential risk in scaling up good practices too rapidly, without taking into account differences in local conditions. Scaling up should not be a matter of simply "filling the gap," irrespective of capacity.

DONOR AS AN EXTERNAL ACTOR. The early engagement of the broad stakeholder community, including at the national level, will increase understanding and enhance ownership. In this process, the donor as an external actor should function as a catalyst. As we note above, the role of external partners in CD is to

26. Clark and Oswald (2010).

27. Nonaka, Toyama, and Hirata (2008).

28. Hartmann and Linn (2008). These authors rightly point out that "many innovations may not be suitable for scaling up. It is precisely the experimental nature of the innovation process that needs to be recognized as important in its own right." Also see chapter 9, this volume.

29. ECDPM (2008).

30. For instance, recent literature puts strong emphasis on learning. This seems to suggest that the pathways of capacity development and scaling up have much in common and usually are continuous processes. ECDPM (2008); Hartmann and Linn (2008).

provide effective support to the locally driven process rather than to lead or control it.[31] In recent years, discussion about the role of external partners has increasingly stressed the need for humility on their part. As Derik Brinkerhoff and Peter Morgan conclude—based on their analysis of multiple case studies—"outsiders' ability to influence CD is highly circumscribed."[32] They also caution on the linkage between a single act of CD support and consequent CD improvements: "The growth of capacity may not necessarily be apparent within the timeframe of a single CD intervention."[33]

Several studies, as well as dialogues in multistakeholder forums, explore possible CD roles for external partners in greater detail.[34] At the 2004 Tokyo International Symposium on CD, in which researchers and practitioners from donor as well as partner countries participated, a list of potential catalytic roles for external partners was compiled. The roles included providers of financial resources, suppliers of knowledge, and protectors of social space for policy dialogue and civic engagement. Summarizing the discussion, the forum participants came to a consensus that the major role for external partners in CD was to serve as a catalyst.

The diversity of roles also implies that external actors can play different roles at different stages of the CD process. To facilitate mutual learning, for example, they can create a space, or *Ba*, for stakeholder interactions. They can facilitate the sensitizing of stakeholder awareness, something that can be a strong driver for a sustained CD process. They can also facilitate CD scaling up.

The question arises, then, of how to start the support. A practical approach in most cases is to find a strategic entry point by employing a broad systemic perspective to identify key stakeholders. Among the possible entry points, those constituting the core of the CD process are public institutions such as local governments, specialized public service agencies, and the clientele of these agencies, including local communities. Depending on local conditions, other stakeholders, such as NGOs, might also be important. Using this multilayered approach, societal CD may be gradually realized and long-term CD optimized.

## Case Studies in Capacity Development

We selected three CD case studies—South Sulawesi Province in Indonesia and the nations of Niger and Bangladesh—in which the local process of change bolstered by external support resulted in enhanced stakeholder capacities and, moreover, in

31. External partners can be traditional donors and also emerging donors, international NGOs, and foundations. One study urges the international community to play its part by providing support in ways that encourage, strengthen, and do not displace the initiatives of leaders and managers in partner countries. OECD/DAC (2006).

32. Brinkerhoff and Morgan (2010, p. 9).

33. Ibid., p. 5.

34. UNDP (2002a); JICA (2004); Baser (2004).

which the processes were scaled up or are being scaled up. We intentionally focus on cases of public service delivery, as improved capacity in translating national and sectoral policies into public service delivery, especially at the level of frontline services, is one of the most pressing issues for meeting and sustaining the MDGs. For reasons of information accessibility, we selected cases in which the programs and projects of the Japan International Cooperation Agency (JICA) played a central part.

## South Sulawesi Province

The case of South Sulawesi Province in Indonesia involves a pilot initiative to establish and strengthen participatory rural development mechanisms at the regency (district) level and below, engaging a broad array of stakeholders during the drastic Indonesian decentralization of the late 1990s.

Decentralization was implemented in Indonesia over an extremely short time period following the demise of the Suharto regime. After this big change, local governments (regencies), which were given broad political and administrative authority, faced a lengthy transition, best characterized as trial and error by all stakeholders—including central and local governments and communities—as they tried to come to terms with their changed roles in the new order.[35]

During the transition, the Indonesian government, with the support of JICA, undertook a pilot program aimed at improving the abilities of both government authorities and communities to plan and administer participatory rural development programs. The actual collaboration began in 1997 in four pilot villages of Takalar Regency in South Sulawesi Province. The first two years of the pilot phase were devoted to "social learning," wherein stakeholders, including local communities, government officials, and NGOs, engaged in extensive dialogue and joint activities. This mutual learning process culminated in a decision by the Takalar Regency to institutionalize an innovative, community-driven, rural development practice through regulatory enactment under a system called SISDUK (rural development support system).[36] Through this system local community groups, sensitized and equipped with the necessary skills through training, were able to access matching funds for their own projects. All through the planning, executing, and monitoring of these projects, SISDUK field officers served as catalysts, interfacing between community groups and local government administration.

Currently SISDUK remains a local mechanism of the Takalar Regency. Lessons learned from Takalar, however, are being disseminated through local CD

---

35. The big bang decentralization initiative of the Indonesia government under President Habibi has been widely reported and analyzed in a number of reports. See Hofman and Kaiser (2002); Suharyo (2003); World Bank (2003).

36. In the 1990s as well, some donors began testing approaches for engaging multiple stakeholders at various levels, such as UNDP's Capacity 21 initiative. In Indonesia the SISDUK initiative was one of the earliest multilayered and multistakeholder initiatives for decentralized rural development.

service providers. One such provider is the PLSD Indonesia Institute, a local think tank that provides training in participatory local social development, including approaches developed through the SISDUK initiative. Another provider is Hasanuddin University located in Makassar, the regional capital of South Sulawesi region, where a master's program in local social development has been established with support from JICA. These local organizations are providing support to various local CD efforts including an ongoing initiative to strengthen participatory local planning that involves both the government and local community groups in six Sulawesi regions.[37]

## Niger

The case of Niger concerns an innovative effort on the part of the government of Niger to introduce, operationalize, and nationally scale up a school-based management (SBM) initiative for primary schools, with support from multiple donors, including JICA.[38]

Niger is one of the world's poorest countries. It has very low human development indicators, including one of the lowest enrollment and literacy rates in sub-Saharan Africa. President Mamadou Tandja was elected in a historic multiparty election in 1999 and reelected in 2004.[39] In 2004 his government embarked on a sectorwide education reform program, with education decentralization as the core strategy. The program, titled PDDE (Programme Décennal de Développement de l'Education au Niger), was prepared by the Niger government in part to meet requirements for accessing the Education-for-All Fast-Track Initiative (EFA-FTI).[40]

One of the core PDDE strategies was the introduction of SBM, then a growing global trend. With donor support, the government embarked on a series of pilot SBM programs centered on the establishment and operationalization of COGES (Comités de Gestion des Establissements Scolaires), which is a local equivalent of a school management committee. Among several COGES initiatives, the government eventually adopted an approach developed through an initiative titled École Pour Tous (School for All), with a view to its replicability and sustainability. The strength of the COGES model is in what is called the COGES minimum package, consisting of several key policy instruments, including the following:

—The democratic election of COGES members by secret ballot.

—Participatory formulation and execution of school action plans.

---

37. JICA (2010a).

38. Following the success of this initiative in Niger, the Niger SBM model is being replicated in neighboring West African countries.

39. In February 2010 President Tandja was ousted in a coup. A presidential election is expected to be held in early 2011.

40. TFP Niger (2002). The ministry in charge was Ministére de l'Education de Base et de l'Alphabetisation.

—A monitoring mechanism for COGES activities including the establishment of a COGES federation at the commune level.[41]

After a joint appraisal of the first PDDE action plan confirmed the effectiveness and replicability of the initial pilots in the Tahoua and Zinder regions, the government decided to adopt the minimum package as its core policy instrument for the second PDDE action plan.[42]

With additional funding from other external sources, including that from the World Bank, Niger's SBM program has now been scaled up nationwide. COGES now function as the core multistakeholder participatory mechanism for school management.[43] Coupled with other education interventions, such as the construction of new classrooms and the provision of textbooks and education materials, COGES has contributed tangible results, including increased enrollment of girls.[44]

*Bangladesh*

The case study in Bangladesh deals with the successful capacity development of a central government department, the Local Government Engineering Department (LGED). This department is under the Bangladesh Ministry of Local Government, Rural Development, and Cooperatives (MLGRD&C) and specializes in local infrastructure development, with support from multiple donors.

The development and maintenance of rural infrastructure is a priority of the Bangladesh government. This is stated in its National Rural Development Policy (2001) and in its first (2005) and second (2008) poverty reduction strategy papers. The LGED of MLGRD&C evolved through a series of organizational changes from the Rural Works Program, which had inherited the infrastructure components of the famous Comilla model of the 1960s.[45]

The LGED has displayed remarkable progress in organizational development through a combination of effective management and donor assistance.[46] Its effective management—epitomized by the outstanding leadership and successful practices of its founding chief executive and his close associates—is characterized by the following: efficient communication with offices and staff, quick decision-making, strong work ethic, teamwork, adoption of new technologies, emphasis on staff training, and decentralized organizational structure.[47] The management

---

41. Fédération Communale des COGES. "Communes" in Niger denotes the third level administrative subdivision of the country.

42. Projet EPT (2007).

43. In spite of the ensuing political turmoil in Niger, activities of most COGES are ongoing. Projet EPT (2010).

44. JICA (2009).

45. Wilbur Smith Associates (2008); Ministry of Foreign Affairs, Japan (2006).

46. Fujita (2011).

47. ISO and others (1998); Ministry of Foreign Affairs, Japan (2006). The chief executive of LGED holds the title of chief engineer.

tactically shielded the organization from the inefficient bureaucratic practices and culture rampant within the Bangladeshi government.

A number of donors provided technical and financial resources to LGED for investment in and maintenance of rural infrastructure and for organizational development. Nordic countries (particularly Sweden) helped LGED's organizational development, particularly in the initial stage. In the late 1990s the Asian Development Bank assisted in the drawing up of a long-term organizational strategy (management capacity strengthening study, or MANCAPS), which remains the basis of the LGED's organizational architecture. Following MANCAPS' recommendations, the World Bank provided CD assistance, focusing on management issues (financial management, audit, procurement), while JICA supported technical aspects (development of geographic information systems, design of rural roads, training of staff).

During the last few decades a highly decentralized LGED established a reputation for professionalism and excellence in rural infrastructure provision and maintenance.[48] In addition, LGED is playing a growing role in the capacity development of local government and local community groups in the context of decentralization of central government functions.

## Comparative Analysis

The following analysis is based on five factors: stakeholder ownership, specific drivers, mutual learning, pathways for scaling up, and external actors.

STAKEHOLDER OWNERSHIP. Our three cases show that a strong understanding by stakeholders of their own issues, a sense of accountability and responsibility, and their determination to act have been the driving forces behind sustained CD. In South Sulawesi and Niger the fact that many communities had already taken action to address some of their issues even before the start of external interventions is a clear sign of ownership of their issues by the local population.[49] In the former case, SISDUK empowered community groups by according them public recognition and by providing opportunities for sensitization, skills training programs, and access to financial support.

In the latter case, the demand for better schools was evident from interviews that revealed that, for some schools, parents and communities had already made voluntary contributions and undertaken school renovation and improvement on their own.[50] With this demand as a backdrop, improved transparency in school management committees through the introduction of democratic elections helped enhance school management practices. The pursuit of more effective rural infrastructure by Bangladesh's LGED also benefited from the people's strong

---

48. World Bank (2009).
49. Land (2004).
50. JICA (2002).

demand for rural development. A key driver, along with the creation of an efficient executing organization, was the ownership of the founding chief engineer and his associates and their strong commitment to rural infrastructure. They understood the importance of all-weather physical infrastructure in their flood-prone country and also that the elimination of bureaucratic procedures inherited from the colonial era would enable fast construction.[51]

SPECIFIC DRIVERS. Our three cases illustrate well that the capacities of stakeholders—community members, teachers, NGOs, and government—have been enhanced and sustained at various points by diverse triggers and drivers. The window of opportunity for creating momentum behind the CD process depends on the political, historical, and social context.

In the initial phase of the South Sulawesi case, the drastic decentralization policy and the democratic transition of the Habibi government were instrumental in widening the operating space for voluntary community groups to build on existing rural development activities. The policy change was also instrumental in providing strong motivation for local governments to undertake pilot community-driven, rural development initiatives.

In Niger the central government demonstrated a clear commitment to introducing participatory school management in conjunction with educational decentralization.[52] Such a degree of commitment at the highest political level was instrumental in creating the time and space to experiment and to develop locally suited SBM models without resistance or excessive political interference. The successes of the two general elections of 1999 and in 2004 as well as the local election of 2004 could produce an environment favorable to the introduction of democratic elections to select COGES members.

In Bangladesh rural development has consistently been one of the pillars of the country's economic growth and poverty reduction strategy. It has been realized against the backdrop of a large rural populace, which accounts for some three-quarters or more of the total population.[53] Similarly for donors, rural development has been one of the priority sectors for assistance to Bangladesh. These priorities have helped LGED gain resources for its CD and investment in rural infrastructure.

In addition to the specific drivers related to context as discussed above, we also observed other factors at work in our cases that promoted overall CD processes. In the case of South Sulawesi, CD efforts benefited from the availability of various training programs and timely financial support through the SISDUK system. In

---

51. Ministry of Foreign Affairs, Japan (2006); Fujita (2011).

52. Hamani Harouna, then minister of Basic Education and Literacy, commented in an interview in January 2006 that "we have found that the government cannot manage the schools alone. We thought it necessary to create a system that would allow collective management and sharing of responsibilities. We thought we should involve the residents and parents in running our schools." JICA (2006b).

53. Gaining the support of rural people has been an important policy objective for political leaders.

Niger the successful introduction of elected membership and the improved transparency that resulted were critical in activating COGES, while joint planning and more judicious execution of school activity plans further empowered the COGES members and other stakeholders, while strengthening trust among them.[54]

In the Bangladesh LGED case, several driving factors were instrumental in enhancing organizational capacity. The most important among them was the founding chief engineer, Q. I. Siddique, who established a strong base for LGED's subsequent organizational development. With his exceptional leadership and vast knowledge and experience in rural infrastructure, he was central to the overall design of the organization. His vision helped create its corporate culture. Siddique's ability to mobilize and make full use of external support further enhanced LGED's capacity. His vision and management style passed down to his associates and LGED staff after he retired.

MUTUAL LEARNING. Analysis of the three cases in this study confirms that enhanced and sustained CD is normally underpinned by a virtuous cycle of mutual learning that occurs through strengthened interactions among stakeholders, especially between public institutions and their beneficiaries.

In the South Sulawesi case, in which villagers were encouraged to participate actively in creating development initiatives, we find a clear illustration of this point. As part of the program, local stakeholders—villagers, government officials, and foreign experts—held discussions and, with encouragement from foreign experts, agreed to organize a "master-hand contest." Through this contest, villagers began to appreciate the value of their local knowledge, knowledge that officials and even some villagers had considered inferior to externally sourced knowledge. The event was an eye-opener for local officials and foreign experts, who found a greater store of local capacity than they had expected.[55] This mutual learning process led to the establishment by the Takalar government of SISDUK; foreign experts played only a supportive role.[56] Such co-creation through mutual learning of innovative solutions based on local knowledge should be at the heart of any sustained CD process.

Mutual learning is also apparent in the Niger school-based management case. COGES activities opened important opportunities for its members—including teachers, parents, and students as well as local education officials and other community members—to understand their respective roles and responsibilities vis-à-vis each other and to learn how to solve school-related problems collaboratively.[57]

54. JICA (2006c).
55. IDCJ/IC (2003).
56. Land (2004).
57. A school inspector at the district level commented that many teachers and education administrators were initially skeptical of COGES, as its establishment might weaken the authority they had enjoyed. But as they saw the improvement a year later, they came to accept that community participation in school management benefited them. A member of the community stated in an interview that local residents began

The LGED business model is conducive to organizational learning. Rural infrastructure, such as roads, village markets, and communal irrigation, are individually relatively small so can be implemented quickly (in one to two years) and are low risk to LGED, even if some fail. These characteristics enabled LGED to distinguish project successes and failures within a short period of time and to adopt new technologies, elements that contributed to knowledge and experience accumulation. A 1998 report on LGED's assessment exercise pointed out that "the organization has quickly adapted itself to new experiments, technologies," still is valid until now, reflecting a process of mutual learning among the agency's staff at various levels.[58]

Each of the three cases shows that mutual learning and trust are vital to discover locally appropriate solutions to meet the needs of beneficiaries and stakeholders. The mutual learning process typically begins with a joint identification of local needs, followed by an exploration of local knowledge and resources. During the learning process, innovative solutions to local issues are identified through a combination of external and local knowledge. The three cases also show clearly that the time and space for learning, or *Ba,* is valuable in promoting the co-creation of innovative solutions to local issues. In South Sulawesi, external actors facilitated and supported the creation of *Ba* for mutual learning and trust. In Niger, the *Ba* for experimenting with an improved School for All COGES model was created through deliberate effort by the joint team of government officials, a local NGO, and donor experts.[59] The government's commitment to a participatory school-based management policy was clearly evident in the education sector program of the PDDE, which also ensured time and space for COGES experimentation.[60] In Bangladesh the LGED's enhanced institutional autonomy following the change in its organizational status, together with the presence of strong and skillful leaders, created an excellent *Ba* for the organization.

SCALING UP. The SISDUK system, as a model approach to capacity development, was scaled up for use in all the other villages. Having learned from early difficulties, the local government strengthened the SISDUK office through its own initiative by recruiting field officers and gradually upgrading its organizational status.

With a strong government commitment to school-based management, Niger's School for All COGES approach deliberately placed government officials at the center of the implementation process while ensuring a participatory nature for COGES, one that involved parents, students, and community members. Local

---

to change their opinion due to their involvement in school management with COGES as their representatives. From a mind-set in which the government should take care of all school matters, they shifted to one in which local residents should and could contribute to school improvement. JICA (2006c, p. 223; 2009, p. 206).

58. ISO and others (1998).

59. JICA (2006c); EPT (2007).

60. PDDE (2002).

NGOs and foreign expert teams restricted themselves to catalytic and supportive roles from the very early stages.[61] Another feature of the initiative during the process of COGES' scaling up was the establishment of a COGES federation in each commune, for which the majority of the operational cost was borne by local contributions. Through the federation mechanism, the government and COGES officers at the district level were able to indirectly monitor large numbers of COGESs in their areas under the supervision of school inspectors and regional education offices.

In the Bangladesh case, rural infrastructure projects have now been spread nationwide. The LGED has worked closely with local stakeholders (such as governments and beneficiaries) to ensure broad participation at all stages of projects. It has also adopted labor-based technologies to create employment opportunities for the poor and uses local materials in construction and maintenance. In light of the LGED's success at CD, some donors are now considering replicating the LGED model in other GOB organizations.

DONOR AS AN EXTERNAL ACTOR. As described earlier, the donor as an external actor can play supportive roles in assisting local CD processes. We can draw examples from our cases to illustrate this.

All of our cases confirm that adequate assessment and identification of strategic entry points—the right time and place and the key targets for assistance, including individuals and organizations—are crucial for effective CD assistance. Assessment exercises provide external actors with information so they can decide the directions to take and the roles to play in respective CD support.[62] In the South Sulawesi community-driven, rural development initiative, the strategic entry points among stakeholders were communities and their members as beneficiaries, local government officials directly charged with providing public services to communities, and community facilitators responsible for interfacing between the community groups and local governments.[63] In Niger, in keeping with the policy of decentralized primary school management, intensive efforts to mobilize and enhance local collective practices through COGES produced tangible outcomes despite the limited financial and administrative capacity of the Education Ministry.[64] In Bangladesh, the LGED was a natural choice for development partners because it was already known to be a highly motivated executing organization in a sector badly needed by the rural poor.

In each of our case studies, external donors consciously respected local stakeholder ownership, although on occasion external donors proactively helped to

61. The Niger Ministry of Education and JICA jointly agreed from the onset that local education officials would be the key players in the EPT initiative. JICA (2003).

62. When they are jointly undertaken by both local stakeholders and external donors, as in our cases, such assessment exercises can become learning opportunities for local stakeholders.

63. JICA (2004).

64. JICA (2009).

nurture a sense of local ownership. In South Sulawesi, for example, external advisers provided training opportunities and relevant knowledge during the initial phase to foster awareness among local stakeholders and to ensure their commitment to community-driven rural development.

External donor assistance has often served to accelerate the CD process. For example, the LGED CD process benefited from assistance from the Swedish government in the 1980s in the early stages. Then in the late 1990s, MANCAPS' technical assistance (provided by ADB) helped the LGED to formulate a long-term strategy. In the Niger case timely technical advice and support were instrumental in the formulation and experimentation of the COGES' minimum package for the school management committee.

The participation of external actors in *Ba*, or mutual learning, was also instrumental in creating effective solutions in the cases studied. In the Niger case a series of joint meetings involving not only local officials and NGO staff but also donor advisers became one such *Ba*, which led to the development of locally grounded COGES minimum packages.

The important feature in all cases was that the role of in CD was catalytic and supportive. The case of South Sulawesi is illustrative: the donor patiently waited while sharing relevant information and encouraging *Ba* for discussion until such time as the local government took the initiative to institutionalize and scale up a community-driven rural development mechanism.

## Conclusion

We have focused thus far on five factors in conducting our comparative analysis of the three case studies. In past discussions, the CD process is usually considered to be a black box. We have tried to open that black box to better understand CD's complexity and dynamics.

First, our analysis confirms the relevance of the five basic CD factors, which we identify through the literature review. Thus our analysis demonstrates that strong ownership by beneficiaries and a willingness to take the initiative to resolve them are the basis for a sustained CD process.

Second, we observed that CD processes are essentially dynamic, and in each case there are a set of drivers that serve to trigger and sustain the dynamic process. Drivers created by political, historical, and social contexts are often critical in triggering and enhancing the CD process, as indicated by the decentralization process in Indonesia and its democratic transition. The introduction of a new policy or the enactment of a new law might also be an important CD driver, as was the case with Niger's school-based management policy for primary schools. A substantive improvement in the enabling environment for CD could have a similar effect. Organizational culture, well-designed institutional mechanisms, and enlightened leadership (as in the case of the LGED in Bangladesh) can also serve as important triggers in enhancing the organizational effectiveness for better service delivery.

Third, our analysis shows that mutual learning through interaction among stakeholders is vital for a clear understanding and identification of local needs. This enables local knowledge and resources to be identified and innovative solutions to be developed in partnership with local beneficiaries. This is exemplified, in particular, by the community-driven rural development system SISDUK in South Sulawesi.

Fourth, the pathways to scaling up a CD process are diverse, as observed across all three of our cases.

Fifth, the role of external actors in the endogenous CD process can be important. Our comparative analysis reinforces the principles that the role of external actors is to extend catalytic support to locally owned processes and that external support works best when it is furnished through mutual learning between local actors and external actors. More specifically, the nature of support will vary depending on the context, entry point, and timing. It is essential, therefore, that adequate assessments be done so that capacity for what, for whom, and in what context can be understood and appropriate entry points for effective CD support can be determined.

## Policy Implications

There are three policy implications involved in capacity development. One is to understand it as a dynamic process. Second is recognizing its centrality for enhancing and sustaining Millennium Development Goals. And third is building a process for supporting it.

A DYNAMIC PROCESS. The SISDUK system of Takalar Regency in South Sulawesi Province, Indonesia, adopted a genuinely community-driven approach, which put responsibility for the identification of their own priority issues on local groups and, with help from field officers, on available local resources. Such an approach, built as it is on local organization and social capital, is quite distinct from an approach geared toward speedy disbursement of cash grants to the rural poor.[65] The former approach is more sustainable than the latter, although it requires more time.[66] With regard to the School for All program in Niger, the COGES approach resulted in a highly sustainable and replicable effort to achieve basic education goals, including notable improvements in girls' primary school enrollment. These examples reinforce the point that treating CD as a dynamic process is mostly likely to lead to sustained development results.

---

65. JICA intentionally avoided this method. As its Evaluation Report mentions, "An approach focusing only on poverty reduction, which would achieve the goal in a short term, was not adopted." JICA (2004, p. 114).

66. We acknowledge that such relatively quick disbursement of cash grants to people in poverty and to members of vulnerable groups may be desirable, especially in postdisaster and postconflict emergency situations.

MILLENNIUM DEVELOPMENT GOALS. Our case studies suggest that focused CD efforts can enhance not only the technical capacity linked to a specific issue, but also generic capacity, which can then be mobilized to tackle other issues. Most of the MDGs—health, access to safe drinking water, education, gender equality—are interrelated, making multisectoral approaches more effective and efficient than vertical sectoral ones.[67] Multisectoral approaches, however, are often seen as slowing the development process, especially when there is vertical provision of services by separate sectoral ministries and public agencies, with little collaboration among them. In these cases, locally driven practices that engage multiple stakeholders can open up the dynamism of the CD process through mutual learning. If a community achieves one of the MDGs through the process of CD, this experience will render that community better able to attain other MDGs. Thus the advantages of reaching the MDGs through the CD process are multiplied.

BUILDING SUPPORT. Our analysis of the role of external partners shows that attention is urgently needed to develop and refine CD approaches, methods, and tools for more effective support. The long to-do list includes development and refinement of tools for effectively assessing country capacity at various levels and identifying appropriate support entry points. Another priority is the development of monitoring mechanisms with appropriate benchmarks and indicators to capture short-term and long-term outcomes, given the complex nature of CD. These priority actions should be jointly pursued by the development community, including partner governments, to ensure support at global and country levels.

## New Challenges, Emerging Actors, and Capacity Development

The lessons from this chapter apply equally to emerging development issues, such as climate change. To illustrate this point, take the example of an adaptation measure for climate change. We reviewed several encouraging cases of disaster prevention initiatives in Caribbean and Central American countries.[68] In these cases, CD processes at both community and local government levels strengthened capacity to effectively respond to disasters that may be linked to climate change, including floods and landslides.[69] The governments of these countries supported integrated, community-based field trials for disaster prevention management, which created a space (or *Ba*) for stakeholders to experiment with risk communication techniques using various concrete tools, such as hazard maps, early warning systems, and disaster prevention plans.

67. The Millennium Villages Project is an example that has succeeded in attaining the positive synergies of a multisectoral approach. Buse, Ludi, and Vigneri (2008, p. 17).

68. Several Caribbean countries have embarked on a joint initiative through the regional Caribbean Disaster Emergency Response Agency. Central American countries have been implementing the BOSAI project in coordination with the regional Centro de Coordinacion para la Prevencion de los Desastres Naturales en America Central. JICA (2010b).

69. JICA (2008a).

Parties involved in CD support are increasingly diversified, and newly emerging actors play large roles at both the country and international levels. For instance, non-OECD donors such as the Islamic Development Bank have been financing LGED's village infrastructure development project, which incorporates a local community capacity-building component for LGED staff.[70] Our case studies also demonstrate that local organizations are building their own capacity as local CD service providers. In the South Sulawesi case, for example, a local university and some NGOs have become important CD service providers to both local governments and communities on the basis of knowledge and experience acquired through their active involvement in donor-supported capacity development initiatives.[71]

Active involvement in CD support by emerging actors, especially those of the South with their fresh development experience, offers promise. However, the proliferation and diversification of CD support actors will call for better coordinating frameworks, especially at the country level.

## Recommendations

The Paris process and other UN forums, such as the recent UN MDG summit, confirm the centrality of CD in the aid effectiveness agenda. However, there is still a need to deepen our understanding of CD and to translate this into more informed and effective practices.

At both global and country levels, CD-relevant discussions and actions, constituting the global MDG framework, are ongoing. These include the global monitoring process of the Paris Declaration on Aid Effectiveness and the Financing for Development and Management for Development Results initiatives of the United Nations. In order to strengthen engagement among partner countries, stakeholders, and donors, global CD networks such as the CD Alliance and the Learning Network on CD (LenCD) have been launched and are becoming increasingly active.[72] CD is also being discussed in a number of sectors and thematic areas at the global level. In the education sector, this includes the preparation and dissemination of EFA-FTI "Guidelines for Capacity Development."[73] In the health sector, issues closely linked to CD, such as health systems and human resources for health, have become central to discussions over health reform. Global CD action on public financial management and statistics capacity are also under way.

Activities at the country level that promote CD have been started in several developing countries. Joint government and donor task forces on CD have been

70. LGED (2009).

71. International NGOs assist with the capacity development of local NGOs. See PACT (www.pact world.org) and the international NGO training and research center, INTRAC (www.intrac.org/pages/en/about-us.html).

72. The latest information on activities by the CD Alliance can be found at www.oecd.org/document/55/0,3343,en_2649_34565_43338103_1_1_1_1,00.html. A dedicated LenCD Web page provides detailed information (http://sites.google.com/site/lencdorg/).

73. EFA (2008).

formed in Ghana and Cambodia and other countries. Some countries have even produced national CD strategy documents, though they are of varying quality.[74] To ensure harmonized global platforms for CD, future action should build on these ongoing networks and processes.

We are of the view, however, that still more needs to be done to mainstream CD into global, regional, and country discussions and operations.

### GLOBAL AND REGIONAL ACTIONS

—Ensure that CD is prominent in both discussions and activities pertaining to the MDGs and in coping with emerging challenges.

—Strengthen global CD networks by engaging all relevant stakeholders in CD support, including governments of partner countries, donor organizations, and NGOs.

—Conduct and compile rigorous case studies, especially those linked to sectors and themes, and make them available to general CD practitioners, researchers, and sector/theme specialists by taking advantage of information and communication technology.

—Promote joint global effort to enhance and strengthen CD methodologies, tools, benchmarks, milestones, and indicators for more effective capacity assessment, monitoring, and evaluation of practices.[75]

### DONOR ACTIONS

—Promote better understanding of CD among staff, including those in leadership positions, by providing adequate learning opportunities.

—Further mainstream CD into policies, strategies, guidelines, aid delivery procedures, monitoring, and evaluation, including the development of benchmarks and indicators.[76]

—Promote CD understanding among the general public.

—Deploy timely and harmonized assistance including both financial and technical support instruments carefully programmed to enhance local CD.

—Consider what the most appropriate roles are for a donor as an external actor, given the local context, in order to enhance CD and produce sustainable results.

### PARTNER COUNTRY ACTIONS

—Promote capacity assessments for identifying "capacities for what for whom and in what context."

---

74. JICA (2008c).

75. Several donors, such as UNDP, the World Bank Institute, Germany's GTZ, and JICA, have introduced capacity development assessments and related practices. Their experiences are valuable for this purpose.

76. As several organizations are already proceeding with this, opportunities for sharing such experiences are planned in conjunction with preparations for the Busan High-Level Forum.

—Take full account of the results of initial capacity assessments and map out strategies for CD, including how to scale up in conjunction with other development interventions. Whenever possible, work jointly with other stakeholders, including external actors.

—Devise adequate monitoring mechanisms—including outcome indicators and CD process milestones—which will ensure *Ba* for mutual learning among country stakeholders and external actors.

## References

ADB (Asian Development Bank). 2008. "Practical Guide to Capacity Development in a Sector Context: Working Draft." Manila.

Baser, Heather. 2004. "Report: Tokyo International Symposium on Capacity Development: From Concept to Practice Exploring Productive Partnerships." Tokyo.

Brinkerhoff, Derick, and Peter Morgan. 2010. "Capacity and Capacity Development: Coping with Complexity." *Public Administration and Development* 30: 2–10.

Buse, Kent, Eva Ludi, and Marcella Vigneri. 2008. "Beyond the Villages: The Transition from Rural Investments to National Plans to Reach MDGs Sustaining and Scaling up the Millennium Villages Formative Review of the Millennium Villages." Project synthesis report. London: Overseas Development Institute.

Clarke, Peter, and Katy Oswald. 2010. "Introduction: Why Reflect Collectively on Capacities for Change?" *IDS Bulletin* 41, no. 3.

EFA (Education for All: Fast-Track Initiative Capacity Development Task Team). 2008. "Guidelines for Capacity Development in the Education Sector." Washington: World Bank.

ECDPM (European Centre for Development Policy). 2008. "Capacity, Change, and Performance: Study Report." Discussion Paper 59B. April. Maastricht.

Fisher, Catherine. 2010. "Between Pragmatism and Idealism: Implementing a Systemic Approach to Capacity Development." *IDS Bulletin* 14, no. 2: 108–17.

Fujita, Yasuo. 2011. "What Makes the Bangladesh Local Government Engineering Department (LGED) So Effective? Complementarity between LGED Capacity and Donor Capacity Development Support." Working Paper 27. Tokyo: JICA.

GOVNET/DAC. 2005. "Living up to the Capacity Development Challenge: Lessons and Good Practice." Draft.

GTZ. 2003. "Capacity Development for Sustainable Development: A Core Task of GTZ." Policy Paper 1. March.

Hartmann, Arntraud, and Johannes F. Linn. 2008, "Scaling-up: A Framework and Lessons for Development Effectiveness from Literature and Practice." Wolfensohn Center for Development, Brookings.

Harvey, Blane, and Jonathan Langdon. 2010. "Re-imagining Capacity and Collective Change: Experiences from Senegal and Ghana." *IDS Bulletin* 41, no. 3.

Hofman, Bert, and Kai Kaiser. 2002. *The Making of the Big Bang and Its Aftermath.* Atlanta: Georgia State University.

IDCJ/IC (International Development Center of Japan and IC Net Ltd). 2003. "Capacity Development and JICA's Activities: Cooperation for Promoting Knowledge Acquisition." JICA discussion paper. Tokyo.

ISO and others (International Standards Organization, Swedish Management Group, Interchain AB/Ltd.). 1998. *MANCAPS: Management Capability Strengthening Project.* Dhaka.

JICA (Japan International Cooperation Agency). 2010a. "Final Evaluation, Project on Support to the Improvement of School Management through Community Participation (School for All), Phase 2."

———. 2010b. "Joint Mid-Term Review on the Project, Capacity Development for Disaster Risk Management in Central America (BOSAI)."

———. 2009. "Midterm Review on the Project, Support to the Improvement of School Management through Community Participation (School for All), Phase 2."

———. 2008a. "Analyzing Community-Based Disaster Prevention Management from CD Perspective." CD case studies series.

———. 2008b. "Capacity Assessment Handbook: Managing Programs and Projects toward Capacity Development."

———. 2008c. "Synthesis Report: Effective Technical Cooperation for Capacity Development."

———. 2007. "Preparatory Study Report on the Project on Support for Improvement of School Management through Community Participation (School for All): Phase 2, Niger."

———. 2006a. "Capacity Development: What Is CD? How JICA Understands CD, and How-to Concepts for Improving JICA Projects."

———. 2006b. "Empowering Local Communities: Designing Development Aid in Emergency Situations, Africa." Promoting of Human Security in Practice 1. DVD audiovisual material.

———. 2006c. "Report of the Final Evaluation of the Project on Support to the Improvement of School Management through Community Participation (School for All)."

———. 2004. "Report of Final Evaluation on the Technical Cooperation Project on Strengthening Sulawesi Rural Community Development to Support Poverty Reduction Programs."

———. 2003. "Report of Preparatory Study on Support to the Improvement of School Management through Community Participation (School for All)."

———. 2002. "Basic Design Study Report."

Land, Anthony. 2004. "Developing Capacity for Participatory Development in the Context of Decentralization." Discussion Paper 57B. Maastricht: European Centre for Development Policy and Management.

Lavergne, Réal, and John Saxby. 2001. "Capacity Development Vision and Implications." Capacity Development Occasional Series 3. January. Ottawa: Canadian International Development Agency.

LGED (Local Government Engineering Department). 2009. "Annual Report of LGED Financial Year 2007–2008." Bangladesh.

Lusthaus, Charles, and others. 1999. "Capacity Development: Definitions, Issues, and Implications for Planning, Monitoring, and Evaluation." Occasional Paper 35. Montreal: Universalia.

Ministry of Foreign Affairs, Japan. 2006. "Government of Bangladesh Programme-Level Evaluation: Japanese Assistance to LGED-Related Sectors."

Nonaka, Ikujiro, Ryoko Toyama, and Toru Hirata. 2008. *Managing Flow: A Process Theory of the Knowledge-Based Firm.* New York: Palgrave Macmillan.

OECD (Organization for Economic Cooperation and Development). 2008. *Accra Agenda of Action.* Paris.

OECD/DAC (Organization for Economic Cooperation and Development, Development Assistance Committee). 2006. *The Challenge of Capacity Development: Working toward Good Practice.* Paris.

Otoo, Samuel, Natalia Agapitova, and Joy Behrens. 2009. *The Capacity Development Results Framework: A Strategic and Results-Oriented Approach to Learning for Capacity Development.* Washington: World Bank.

Projet EPT (Projet Ecole Pour Tous). 2007. "Minna no gakko dayori: Phase 1 Saishu-go" [EPT newsletter phase 1, final issue]. Tahoua, Niger.

———. 2010. *Monthly Report.* Multiple issues.

Qualman, Ann, and Joe Bolger. 1996. "Capacity Development: A Holistic Approach to Sustainable Development." *International Development Express*, no. 8.

PDDE. 2002. "Programme Décennal de Développement de l'Education au Niger." Niamey.

Suharyo, Widjajanti I. 2003. "Indonesia's Transition to Decentralized Governance: An Evolution at the Local Level." Working paper. Jakarta: SMERU Research Institute.

TFP Niger (Technical and Financial Partners of Education Sector in Niger). 2002. "Education for All, Fast-Track Initiative: Assessment of the Proposal from Niger." Report on the meeting of technical and financial partners. Niamey.

UNDP (United Nations Development Program). 2008. "Capacity Assessment Methodology User's Guide."

———. 2003. "Ownership, Leadership, and Transformation: Can We Do Better for Capacity Development?"

———. 2002a. "Capacity for Development: New Solutions to Old Problems."

———. 2002b. "Developing Capacity through Technical Cooperation."

———. 1998. "Capacity Assessment and Development in a Systems and Strategic Management Context." MDGB Technical Advisory Paper 3.

———. 1995. "Capacity Development for Sustainable Human Development."

Wilbur Smith Associates. 2008. "Final Report on the Technical Assistance Services to Support Implementation of the Institutional Strengthening Action Plan (ISAP) of LGED."

Woodhill, Jim. 2010. "Capacities for Institutional Innovation: A Complexity Perspective." *IDS Bulletin* 41, no. 2: 47–59.

World Bank. 2009. "Operational Risk Assessment for Local Government Engineering Department in Bangladesh: Final Report."

———. 2005. *Building Effective States: Forging Engaged Societies.*

———. 2003. "Decentralizing Indonesia: Regional Public Expenditure Review Overview Report." East Asia PREM Unit.

# 9

## Scaling Up with Aid: The Institutional Dimension

JOHANNES F. LINN

Official aid flows have significantly increased over the last decade, from about $80 billion in 1997 to about $130 billion in 2008, but this level remains well short of the goal set by the G8 at the Gleneagles Summit.[1] At the same time, aid has become increasingly fragmented, as the number of aid agencies and actors has rapidly grown.[2] New bilateral donors have appeared on the scene, new official aid organizations have been set up in traditional donor countries, and the number of multilateral donors has skyrocketed.[3] In addition, thousands of private aid donors—a few rivaling the largest official donors, but most very small—have joined, with total private aid reaching as much as $60 million to $70 billion a year.[4]

However, fragmentation is an issue not only of the number of donors and of the complexity of the organizational architecture of aid. It is also a matter of fragmen-

I wish to thank Jonathan Adams for his very effective research support, Homi Kharas for his steadfast encouragement to pursue the scaling-up agenda, and Arntraud Hartmann for contributing much to my thinking on scaling up. Thanks are also due to Angela Clare, Alex Shakow, and the participants in the Brookings workshop on aid effectiveness on July 19, 2010, for their comments. The financial support of the Japan International Cooperation Agency (JICA) and the Korea International Cooperation Agency (KOICA) is gratefully acknowledged.

1. OECD (2010).

2. Acharya, Fuzzo de Lima, and Moore (2006); IDA (2007); Kharas (2007); OECD (2008).

3. In 1910 there were reportedly 5 multilateral organizations. By 1950 their number had increased to 30, by 1980 to 130, and by 2008 to over 200. OECD (2009, 2010).

4. Kharas (2007).

Figure 9-1. *Project Numbers, Average Size, and Median Size for All Official Donors, 1999–2008*

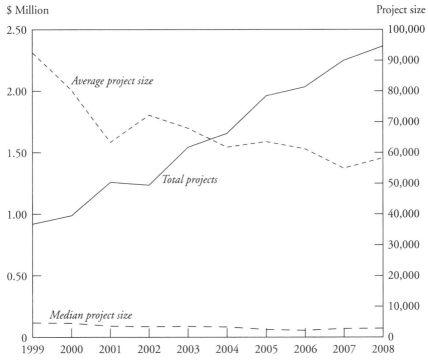

Source: Data compiled by Jonathan Adams, based on Findley and others (2010).

tation in the sense that the number of projects has multiplied while the average size of projects has dropped. In aggregate, new official aid initiatives a year grew by over two-and-a-half times over ten years (from about 35,000 to some 95,000), while the mean size of official aid projects fell to below $1.6 million in 2008, down from about $2.4 million in 1999. More striking yet, the median size of projects dropped from $120,000 to only $70,000 (figure 9-1).[5] More than half of all donor projects amount to less than $100,000. Although there is a tremendous variance across donors in terms of project number and size, the proliferation of agencies and ever-smaller projects is affecting bilateral and multilateral donors alike.

Transaction costs for recipient countries and donors depend significantly on the number of donor agencies and number of projects. Therefore the explosion of

5. Information on project numbers is difficult to establish, since for some donors single projects are listed under multiple identifiers in the original DAC database and have to be aggregated for an accurate project count.

agencies and project numbers has to be a major concern. This needs to be balanced against the benefits that small projects and new donors can add, if they bring and test innovative ideas, enhance effectiveness through competition, and provide responsiveness to country priorities, as well as additional money. However, as the number of projects has increased dramatically, as average project size has decreased—with a proliferation of small and even very small projects—chances are that the diseconomies of numbers and coordination are getting more severe, that many initiatives are one-time interventions only, disconnected from others, and that there is little lasting benefit from many of the activities beyond the immediate impact, limited as they are in size, scope, and duration. This inference is confirmed by case study evidence.[6] It also is consistent with the "macro-micro paradox of aid effectiveness," which refers to the disconnect between econometric estimates of the impact of aid (none or negligible) at the country level and the evaluations of the impact of individual aid-financed projects (substantial).[7]

One way to respond to this trend of rising project numbers and declining project size is to aim to reverse it. Each aid agency could reduce the number and increase the average size of its activities in recipient countries. This would be a start.

Another approach would be to improve coordination and harmonization among the growing number of aid agencies and projects. This has been pursued by the international community through the Paris Declaration on Aid Effectiveness and the subsequent Accra Agenda for Action, under which donor and recipient countries committed themselves to improve the effectiveness of aid through the pursuit of five principles: ownership, alignment, harmonization, results, and mutual accountability. However, implementation of this agenda, while carefully monitored by the OECD/DAC, has turned out to be difficult, especially as regards effective in-country coordination. One of the key problems is that, while governments and aid agencies have made commitments at the level of their leadership and have made progress in meeting their commitments through pursuing top-down, aggregate targets, there have been too few efforts to change aid agency procedures, processes, and incentives that operate inside donor institutions and on the ground in recipient countries. It is by addressing these institutional dimensions of the aid system that managers and staff will ensure that the many small projects ultimately translate into programs and policies that reach a significant portion of the target population.

This can be done by placing greater emphasis on scaling up—that is, by replicating smaller activities, by transferring the experience from small pilots to follow-up projects and programs funded by other aid donors or the government, or by helping to bring about systemic policy and institutional changes. While aid donors typically pay attention to innovation, experimentation, learning-by-doing,

---

6. Fengler and Kharas (2010).
7. Mosely (1987).

and evaluation—increasingly with a keen eye for achieving measurable impact from the individual projects—few focus on how to scale up their successful interventions. And, typically, project evaluations by aid agencies do not assess whether or not any steps have been taken to scale up successful interventions.[8]

This in effect means that the many projects and programs pursued by individual donor agencies remain isolated interventions with limited, if any, catalytic impact. Efforts aimed at coordination and partnership agreed and implemented top down at the international and even country levels remain pro forma and are pursued only sporadically at the project level, with generally no systematic handoff from one donor to another or from a donor to the recipient government or other stakeholders in country. In short, there is too little attention to scaling up aid-supported interventions.

The central tenet of this chapter is that donors will have to change their way of doing business from the bottom up and focus much more explicitly on scaling up—and on the institutional dimensions of scaling up—if they want to translate individual project success into substantial development results. Ultimately, of course, it is all about the scaling up of country-owned programs by the countries themselves. But aid donors have a special responsibility to support this scaling-up process, rather than—as is too often the case—to reinforce local tendencies for small, one-time initiatives.[9]

The next section takes stock of the state of the debate on scaling up.[10] Subsequent sections lay out a framework for approaching the institutional scaling-up challenge and review how selected individual donor agencies and initiatives have—or have not—pursued the scaling-up agenda. The chapter concludes with a summary of lessons and some recommendations for the 2011 High-Level Forum on Aid Effectiveness.

## Debate on Scaling Up

In recent years interest in scaling up has been on the rise. In 2004 the international community mounted a significant effort to put scaling up on the map of development policy and development assistance with a major conference in Shanghai, at the behest of James Wolfensohn (then president of the World Bank) and jointly hosted with the Chinese government. But neither the Paris Declaration in 2005 nor the Accra Agenda for Action in 2008 explicitly mentions scaling up as an objective.[11] Various specific actions to be undertaken under the declaration are

8. Hartmann and Linn (2008).

9. There are, of course, good examples of successful scaling up in developing countries, among them very notably Mexico's conditional cash transfer program, Progresa-Oportunidades. See Levy (2006).

10. This chapter focuses on the scaling up of successful developing interventions, not on increasing aid resources. In the aid literature and public debate, scaling up is often associated with the latter meaning.

11. See www.oecd.org/dataoecd/58/16/41202012.pdf.

potentially supportive of a scaling-up agenda (such as joint donor missions and programmatic approaches), but no systematic approach to scaling up was developed. The World Bank itself did not systematically pursue the scaling-up agenda after James Wolfensohn left in 2005.

The Wolfensohn Center for Development at Brookings picked up the challenge of promoting research on scaling up in 2005. As part of its program of work, Arntraud Hartmann and Johannes Linn review the literature and practice on scaling up and summarize the scaling-up debate as follows:

> The scaling-up debate goes back at least to the surge in development aid and attention to global poverty in the 1970s, spearheaded by Robert McNamara, and continued in the 1980s with efforts by NGOs and others aiming to achieve a development impact on a larger scale. While it has since broadened to include various dimensions of development interventions beyond the project level and has been linked to the debates on diffusion of innovation, the literature remains primarily focused on the scaling up of individual projects, with a particular focus on public service delivery programs, especially in the health sector and for community-driven development (CDD) programs, which typically are community based and involve NGOs. The literature offers less insight on the scaling up of policies, programs, and projects outside the health sector and CDD programs, and it rarely discusses scaling up from national to supranational (regional or global) levels.[12]

More recently, the Brookings Institution published a fascinating debate about the benefits of "thinking big versus thinking small."[13] As part of this debate, Lant Pritchett summarizes what appears to be an emerging consensus:

> Clearly, "thinking big" has led to centralized, top-down programs of the "big-push" variety against which "thinking small" has lashed back, calling for more local variation and experimentation and more marketlike mechanisms that would allow emergent properties of the small to transform the big. But if the system as structured creates no pressures or spaces for the scaling up of innovations, then thinking big must attend to systemic issues if the small is to have a chance.[14]

There is also evidence that the development assistance community pays greater attention to the scaling-up challenge:

—Perhaps most significantly, the newly created vertical funds, such as the Global Fund to Fight AIDS, TB, and Malaria and the Global Alliance for Vaccines

---

12. Hartmann and Linn (2008, p. 7).
13. Cohen and Easterly (2009).
14. Pritchett (2009, p. 162).

and Immunization (GAVI), represent a great push by the international community to scale up interventions in selected, narrowly defined areas of global concern.

—A number of multilateral donors have started to pursue the scaling-up agenda. Among them, the International Fund for Agricultural Development (IFAD) recently completed an institutional scaling-up review, and the United Nations Development Program (UNDP) is exploring whether and how to apply scaling-up considerations more systematically in its programs.[15]

—Some bilateral donors are pursuing at least a partial scaling-up agenda. In the United States the HIV/AIDS program PEPFAR and the Millennium Challenge Account are examples of this trend. In Germany the GIZ has pursued various aspects of a scaling-up agenda.[16] In Japan the president of Japan International Cooperation Agency (JICA) declared that her institution will be aiming to "speed up, scale up, and spread out" the impact of its assistance.[17] And in Australia, AusAID is exploring how to approach scaling up.

—Some of the large foundations have made scaling up one of their core concerns. This is perhaps most obvious for the Gates Foundation, whose guiding principles include this: "We take risks, make big bets, and move with urgency. We are in it for the long haul."[18] Other foundations with an explicit scaling-up mission include the MacArthur Foundation, the Rockefeller Foundation, and the Packard Foundation.

—New web-based initiatives, such as GlobalGiving and Kiva, bundle small-donor contributions electronically and distribute them directly to small projects and recipients in poor countries, in line with private donor preferences.[19]

—Finally, in the United States the Obama administration has elevated the scaling up of successful interventions as one of its core objectives in the field of domestic social policy.[20]

Hartmann and Linn conclude their review of the literature and experience with the observation that too little attention has been paid to the institutional dimensions of the scaling-up challenge; that is, governments and aid agencies have not sufficiently considered how their institutional goals, strategies, policies, processes, and incentives support or block their pursuit of a scaling-up agenda.[21]

15. For IFAD, see Linn and others (2010).

16. GTZ (2007).

17. Ogata (2008).

18. See www.gatesfoundation.org/about/Pages/guiding-principles.aspx. A Google search of "gates foundation scaling up" yields innumerable references to projects funded by the Gates Foundation in whose statement of goals scaling up plays a significant role.

19. Desai and Kharas (2010).

20. See for example the report on an interview with Sonal Shah, head of the White House Office of Social Innovation and Civic Participation, in *Alliance Magazine,* September 1, 2009 (www.alliance magazine.org/en/content/interview-sonal-shah).

21. Hartmann and Linn (2008). Pritchett (2009, p. 156) puts the institutional challenge as follows: "In nearly any other industry economists would be interested in the empirics of the 'inside-the-firm' production process . . . [but] somehow the most routine of production decisions of no economic relevance at

The purpose of this chapter is therefore to advance the debate on scaling up by focusing on the institutional dimensions of scaling up through aid and to develop some specific recommendations for the international development community on how to enhance aid effectiveness with more effective focus on, and implementation of, the scaling-up agenda.

## Framework for Analyzing Scaling Up

The framework of analysis that Hartmann and Linn designed and that is further developed in Linn and others starts with the recognition that there is a close link between innovation, learning, and scaling up.[22] It defines what scaling up is and identifies key dimensions of the scaling-up challenge. It then posits the question whether or not a particular intervention should be scaled up and defines pathways for scaling up to achieve impact at scale through a combination of drivers pushing the scaling-up process forward, while also creating the space for initiatives to grow.

### Innovation, Learning, and Scaling Up

Scaling up is part of a broader process of innovation, learning, and scaling up (figure 9-2). A new idea, model or approach is embodied in a pilot project with limited impact. By learning from this experience with monitoring and evaluation (M&E), organizational internal knowledge is created while organizational external knowledge is disseminated. This knowledge in turn can be used to scale up the model through expansion, replication, and adaptation with multiple impact. The experience from scaling up feeds back into new ideas and learning. Outside knowledge can also feed scaling-up efforts, if an organization picks up on the pilot experience and learning of another organization.

A number of observations can be made with regard to this innovation/learning/ scaling-up triad.

—Innovation, learning, and scaling up should be treated as separate, albeit linked, processes. Each of the three concepts refers to an important but separate stage in the development of an intervention at scale, and each requires its own appropriate process, skills, resources, and attention. Innovation and scaling up are often complementary, but there are also times when they compete in terms of resources, managerial attention, and political payoff.

—Development actors need to focus not only on innovation but also on learning and scaling up. The focus on innovation is endemic in the aid industry and the development business, usually to the detriment of an adequate focus on learning and especially on scaling up.

---

all (for example, about class size, textbook availability, or ability tracking) are somehow considered interesting areas for 'policy-relevant' research without any coherent explanation of how this knowledge will lead producers to change their behavior to scale."

22. This section draws substantially on chapter 2 of Linn and others (2010).

Figure 9-2. *The Links of Innovation, Learning, and Scaling Up*

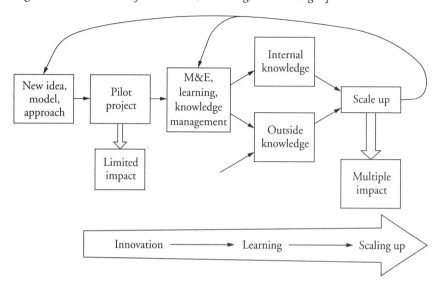

Source: Linn and others (2010).

—The innovation/learning/scaling-up process is not linear but is an iterative and interactive cycle. As indicated in figure 9-2, there are many feedback loops from learning and scaling up back to innovation. Indeed, M&E often generate new ideas for better design and implementation, and the scaling-up process will often require adaptation and innovation in the way the original model or idea is brought to scale. Nonetheless, it is useful to think in terms of the three main components of the process as distinct and separable phases, each with its own important role to play.

—Not every innovation can or should be scaled up, and not every scaling up needs to involve innovation. Many innovations may not be suitable for scaling up. It is precisely the experimental nature of the innovation process that needs to be recognized as important in its own right, and the risk of pilots not succeeding must be accepted as an integral part of the innovation and learning process. Failed pilots may offer as many and perhaps more lessons than successful ones. But of course failed or unsustainable pilots should not be scaled up.

—Scaling up involves two possible error types. A type 1 error is not scaling up at all or scaling up too little. A type 2 error is a wrong scaling up. Much attention in the scaling-up literature is on lack of scaling up. This is most typical with smaller aid organizations, which cannot hope to scale up interventions with their own limited resources and hence tend to focus on small and limited projects with limited impact. But there are also aid organizations that support scaling up or operate at a large scale but do so suboptimally or in a wrong way. Type 2 error is found more frequently in large development banks, such as the World Bank, which can and often do aim to go to scale in their country strategies and programs. Evaluations of their programs find insufficient piloting, testing, and learning as well as inappropriate phasing of approaches, which prevents operating at scale.

## Definition of Scaling Up

Hartmann and Linn define scaling up as "expanding, replicating, adapting, and sustaining successful policies, programs, or projects in geographic space and over time to reach a greater number of people."[23] This definition can be adapted as appropriate for the mission of the institution. For example, Linn and others use the term *rural poor people* instead of simply *people*.[24] The reference to "sustaining" in this definition is worth noting for two reasons. First, it makes no sense to scale up an intervention that is not sustainable. Hence the fact that many evaluations of aid projects give relatively low ratings on sustainability also raises questions about their scalability. Second, scaling up is not only about the process of scaling up but also about sustaining the scaled-up program once it has been scaled up. As Larry Cooley and Richard Kohl stress, different institutions or institutional capacities may be needed for the scaling-up process and the operation and maintenance of the scaled-up program once in place.[25]

## Pathways for Scaling Up

A scaling-up pathway is the sequence of steps that need to be taken in the innovation/learning/scaling-up cycle to ensure that a successful pilot or practice is taken from its experimental stage through subsequent stages to the scale ultimately judged to be appropriate for the intervention pursued. In general there are many possible pathways for scaling up a successful intervention. For each case an aid organization needs to explore potential pathways early on and take proactive steps to plan and prepare for scaling up in terms of dimensions, desired ultimate scale, drivers and spaces, the agency's operational modalities, intermediate results, and M&E.

—Selecting the dimensions: Scaling-up pathways can follow different dimensions. They may simply expand services to more clients in a given geographical space. They can also involve horizontal replication, from one geographic area to another; functional expansion, by adding additional areas of engagement; and vertical scaling up. The latter involves moving from a local or provincial engagement to a nationwide engagement, often involving policy dialogue and technical assistance to help achieve the policy and institutional conditions needed for successful national-level scaling up.[26]

23. Hartmann and Linn (2008).
24. Linn and others (2010).
25. Cooley and Kohl (2005).
26. Altenburg (2007) provides an excellent account of the experience of vertical scaling up in selected German aid projects.

---

Box 9-1. *Drivers of Scaling Up*

A few key factors drive the process of scaling up.

—Ideas and models: There must be an idea or model that works at a small scale and emerges from research or practice.

—Vision and leadership: A vision is needed to recognize that the scaling up of a (new) idea is necessary, desirable, and feasible. Visionary leaders or champions often drive the scaling-up process.

—External catalysts: Political and economic crises or pressure from outside actors (donors, EU, and others) may drive the scaling-up process.

—Incentives and accountability: Incentives drive the behavior of actors and institutions toward scaling up. They include rewards, competitions, and pressure through the political process, peer reviews, and other evaluations. Monitoring and evaluating against goals, benchmarks, and performance metrics are essential to establish incentives and accountability.

Source: Adapted from Hartmann and Linn (2008).

---

—Defining the desired scale: It is important to define up front the ultimate scale to which an intervention should or could be taken, given the needs of the target population and the nature of the intervention, and to consider realistically the time horizon over which the scaling process needs to extend in order to achieve the desired ultimate scale. Hartmann and Linn find that a successful scaling up of programs to national scale can take five to ten years or longer.[27]

—Focusing on key drivers and spaces for scaling up: Two sets of factors need to be considered in designing the appropriate pathway for any given case. Drivers are the forces pushing the scaling-up process forward (box 9-1). Spaces are the opportunities that can be created, or potential obstacles that need to be removed, to open up the space for interventions to grow (box 9-2). Not all drivers and spaces have to be considered or developed with equal depth. Indeed, identifying and focusing on the core factors applicable to a particular case is one of the requirements of effective scaling up.

—Defining intermediate results: Along the scaling-up pathway it is important that the program deliver intermediate results. This is necessary to allow for the testing and, where needed, the adaptation of the approach. But it also helps with ensuring the buy-in of community, government, and other stakeholders.[28]

—Selecting operational modalities for scaling up: Donor agencies have various options for applying their operational modalities in supporting the pathways for scaling up. They can use their own resources (top up, repeater projects,

27. Hartmann and Linn (2008).
28. See Schaffer and Ashkenas (2005).

---

Box 9-2. *Space for Scaling Up*

If scaling up is to succeed, space has to be created for the initiative to grow. The most important spaces are

—Fiscal/financial space: Fiscal and financial resources need to be mobilized to support the scaled-up intervention, or the costs of the intervention need to be adapted to fit into the available fiscal/financial space.
—Natural resource/environmental space: The impact of the intervention on natural resources and the environment must be considered, harmful effects mitigated, or beneficial impacts promoted.
—Policy space: The policy (and legal) framework needs to support scaling up.
—Institutional/organizational/staff capacity space: Institutional and organizational capacity must be able to carry the scaling-up process forward.
—Political space: Important stakeholders, both those in support and those against the intervention, need to be attended to through outreach/communication and suitable safeguards to ensure political support for a scaled-up intervention.
—Cultural space: Possible cultural obstacles or support needs to be identified and the intervention adapted to permit scaling up in a culturally diverse environment.
—Learning space: Knowledge about what works and doesn't work in scaling up needs to be harnessed through monitoring and evaluation, knowledge sharing, and training.

Source: Adapted from Hartmann and Linn (2008).

---

programmatic approaches), work in partnership with other agencies (co-financing and SWAps), or hand off to other donors, the government, or nongovernmental partners.[29] They can finance investments, provide technical assistance, or engage in policy dialogue. And they can scale up an intervention within a country or across countries.

—Putting M&E in place: M&E are key ingredients of a successful scaling-up strategy in various important respects. First, during the implementation of the pilot or experimental stage the intervention needs to be monitored to learn what are the drivers and spaces that may affect an eventual scaling-up process, and the impact of the pilot in terms of the lives of the poor needs to be evaluated (preferably against a control group). Second, during the scaling-up process monitoring will provide important feedback on any unforeseen aspects of the scaling-up pathway and permit the adaption of the pathway as needed. Intermittent evaluation of the impact of the scaled-up program during implementation and after completion is needed to ensure that the expected results actually materialize.[30]

29. SWAps (sectorwide approaches) bring together multiple donors in support of a multiyear sector program agreed with the government; they may or may not involve pooled funding or budget support.
30. Linn and others (2010) points out that there is an important feedback loop from scaling up to M&E. Evaluation evidence shows that most donor and recipient agencies face difficulties in implement-

Many methods of evaluation are available, with pride of place in recent years given to randomized impact evaluation, which may however not always be feasible, cost effective, or appropriate.[31]

—Risks of inadequate attention to scaling-up pathways: A number of problems can result from not paying due attention to scaling-up pathways. Opportunities for scaling up may be missed (type 1 error), or scaling up may be done badly (type 2 error). Lack of attention to costs may create "boutique" approaches that only work "in the small." Setting up special-purpose entities (for example, project implementation units) rather than working through ministries may limit institutional options later. Working with limited financing mechanisms, not identifying policy constraints, and working with small implementing partners (such as NGOs) may limit the potential for scaling up later. And lack of effective and timely M&E may lead to poor decisions in scaling up.

## Aid Agencies and Scaling Up

How have specific aid organizations addressed the scaling-up challenge? My sample of aid agencies is not complete or systematic. In essence, availability of information determined the choice.

I start with three midsized agencies or initiatives: IFAD, UNDP, and the UN's Millennium Villages (MV). This is followed by a review of selected multilateral development banks: the World Bank, the Asian Development Bank, and the Inter-American Development Bank. A third group involves vertical funds and global programs: the Global Fund to Fight AIDS, Tuberculosis, and Malaria; GAVI; the Education-for-All Fast-Track Initiative (EFA-FTI); and the Global Agriculture and Food Security Program (GAFSP). This leaves out very important segments of the donor community: DAC and non-DAC bilateral official donors, private foundations, and the large NGO community. More research is needed to explore the role scaling up plays, or should play, for these donors.

Even with this selective approach the evidence available is of varying quality. Only for one organization, the IFAD, has a detailed institutional scaling-up review been conducted. For the other official agencies, much of the evidence draws on evaluation documents of the agencies themselves. As mentioned above, few evaluations explicitly address the scaling-up question. Although key elements

---

ing effective M&E in aid-financed projects. One key reason is that when the focus is principally only on the project, not the scaling-up pathway of which the project is an integral and critical part, M&E, while costly, does not contribute much to the success of the project by itself. However, once project managers buy into the importance of the scaling-up pathway and recognize the contribution that the learning from the project experience can make to the successful pursuit of such a pathway, they will value the benefits of M&E and hence have an incentive to develop an effective M&E process.

31. See Cohen and Easterly (2009) for various contributions to the debate on whether, when, and how randomized evaluation can suitably be employed.

of the scaling-up approach, strengths, and weaknesses can be gleaned from these evaluations, the conclusions of this institutional review represent only one step in an ongoing research agenda.

### Midsize Development Institutions

Midsize donors are most obviously faced with the scaling-up challenge. They tend to be small but not insignificant relative to the scale of the development problems that they try to address.[32] In order to scale up they need to be selective (both in terms of country focus and in terms of sectoral focus), and they likely need to partner with others. For these aid agencies, the scaling-up challenge is mostly one of avoiding the type 1 error (not focusing enough on scaling up), although when they do focus on scaling up they will also need to avoid the type 2 error (scaling up the wrong way).

INTERNATIONAL FUND FOR AGRICULTURAL DEVELOPMENT. IFAD's mission is to reduce rural poverty.[33] It is unusual among the traditional aid donor agencies in that its corporate strategy documents for the last decade have clearly stated a scaling-up objective. In fact, the innovation/learning/scaling-up triad is a concept pervasive in IFAD's strategy. IFAD's "Strategic Framework, 2007–2010" states that "innovation without scaling up is of little value."[34] Moreover, there have been cases in which IFAD has supported successful scaling-up efforts. A particularly prominent example is IFAD's sustained program of support for rural poverty reduction in the highland communities of Peru (box 9-3).

In 2009 IFAD's management commissioned an external review of its approach to scaling up. The review concludes that IFAD's "scaling-up efforts are not the result of a systematic approach to this part of its mission. In fact, current operational guidance documents and procedures generally do not focus on scaling up."[35] The review also documents, based in part on evaluations done by IFAD's evaluation office, that many opportunities for scaling up were not pursued.

The key recommendation of the review is to shift IFAD's operational approach and culture from its traditional project focus to a country program focus. IFAD's country strategy documents should lay out the scaling-up pathways along which IFAD plans to support long-term rural poverty reduction at a significant scale, with effective consideration of the dimensions, drivers, and spaces for scaling up. In addition, all operational policy and process guidelines should explicitly focus on the scaling-up objective, while ensuring that they are kept simple and unbureaucratic.

For IFAD an essential element for successful scaling up is to work with partners, both government agencies and other donors, either to hand off successful

---

32. In a few countries a midsize donor may be the principal donor—and large relative to the scale of the national development challenge (for example, Australia in Papua New Guinea).

33. This section draws on Linn and others (2010).

34. IFAD (2007).

35. Linn and others (2010).

---

Box 9-3. *Scaling Up IFAD's Rural Antipoverty Programs in Peru*

IFAD has provided Peru with eight loans since 1980, for a total of $115 million. It supported the development of poor rural communities in the Peruvian highlands, reaching over 150,000 households in 30 percent of Peru's 5,000 poor highland communities. The programs have drawn on community involvement in generating demand-driven rural service provision by private contractors and using a competition-based approach to allocate resources to scale up successful interventions. Over three decades the program was scaled up horizontally (by covering addition highland districts), functionally (by adding other areas of engagement beyond agriculture, such as rural nonfarm development and housing), and vertically (by working with the government to create a national program of rural poverty reduction). Other donor agencies (the World Bank and GTZ) drew on IFAD's experience in developing similar programs.

The success of this program can be attributed to a fortuitous combination of local interests, a network of national champions, and IFAD's long-term, Peru-based, country program manager. These actors created the sense of mission and the financial, political, policy, partnership, learning, and cultural space required to permit the scaling-up process to take hold and proceed.

Source: Linn and others (2010).

---

interventions for replication or scaling up, to cooperate through co-financing, or to coordinate sectorwide donor support (such as SWAps). This could also help IFAD compensate for the very limited capacity it has to assist in vertical scaling up through policy advice and capacity building.

The review also recommends to IFAD a stronger focus on learning from experience by pursuing more effective M&E, by systematically reviewing its own successful scaling-up experiences, and by developing stronger in-house capacity for advising operational frontline staff on how to design and implement scaling-up pathways.[36] Also, while IFAD's evaluation office is one of the few among such offices in the donor community to evaluate the scaling-up performance, a more systematic approach, and one that explicitly separates innovation from scaling-up performance, would be desirable. The review also recommends that IFAD get together with other development partners to share scaling-up experiences.

In terms of organization, staffing, budget, and resource allocation, the review concludes that IFAD's country program managers need to focus on the scaling-up agenda and that more of them need to be located in country, rather than at headquarters, as is currently the case for most. The review also recommends that targeted grant funding and internal administrative budget resources be dedicated to support scaling up to incentivize stakeholders and IFAD staff. Finally, it rec-

---

36. As noted above, a focus on scaling up actually provides a better alignment of incentives for staff and project managers to carry out effective M&E.

ommends that IFAD aim to increase its loan size and explore how to introduce metrics that effectively track the progress with the implementation of its scaling-up agenda.

IFAD's management broadly accepts the assessment and recommendations of the external review and is in the process of formulating its plans for follow-up. Moreover, during the period of the review (2009–10) IFAD operational managers and staff were already giving increased attention to the scaling-up agenda in their day-to-day work.

UNITED NATIONS DEVELOPMENT PROGRAM. As a development agency, UNDP operates at many levels: at a global level, in supporting analysis and advocacy for global development objectives (including through support for the Millennium Development Goals and through its annual human development reports); at the regional level, in supporting regional cooperation in the developing world (such as Central Asia; see below); and at the national and subnational level, in funding country programs in support of national development and poverty reduction. UNDP's own resources are limited and it relies substantially on earmarked funding provided to it by other donors. It is in connection with its national and subnational activities that UNDP faces the challenge of scaling up, since most of its projects and interventions at the country level are small relative to other donors and relative to the needs that countries face.

No systematic assessment of UNDP's scaling-up approach and experience is available. However, a limited review of UNDP's country program evaluations shows that UNDP in the past has not explicitly focused on scaling up and has tended to support small and short-term project interventions. In Turkey a UNDP county program evaluation in 2004 found that the agency supported many worthwhile pilot initiatives that responded to local needs and interests but that it failed to follow up with evaluation, replication, and scaling up, which meant that there was little lasting impact of many of its activities.[37] A follow-up country program evaluation in 2010 concluded that, while the UNDP had reduced the number of small projects in Turkey and improved the sustainability of its intervention, the prevalent form of support remained small pilots with weak M&E and limited attention to follow-up and scaling-up opportunities.[38]

A 2008 country program evaluation for Tajikistan found a mixed picture in terms of UNDP's success in scaling up.[39] On the one hand some of its programs, such as the implementation of the ambitious Global Fund to Fight AIDS, Tuberculosis, and Malaria, reached substantial scale, although only limited efforts were made to strengthen the national health system capacity (that is, strong horizontal but weak vertical scaling up). Similarly, in its rural infrastructure program the

37. UNDP (2004).
38. UNDP (2010).
39. UNDP (2009a).

UNDP is reported to have addressed about 30 percent of local infrastructure requirements. However, the report concludes that many of UNDP's interventions remain at the pilot stage and need to be taken to a higher level through policy dialogue and capacity building.

UNDP's management has recently started to focus explicitly on the scaling-up challenge. It has commissioned a pilot review of the Tajikistan country program experience from the perspective of its scaling-up performance. This review is to be completed in early 2011.[40]

THE MILLENNIUM VILLAGES PROJECT. The MV project is an effort of the Millennium Promise, an initiative led by a prominent champion, Jeffrey Sachs of the Earth Institute at Columbia University, to demonstrate that the Millennium Development Goals can be reached by implementing a scalable, holistic model of village development. Starting with a number of pilot villages in Africa under a five-year start-up program, the project supports agricultural, health, educational, and infrastructure improvements, with strong community engagement. By strictly limiting the cost per capita to $120, of which $60 to $80 is contributed by the project, and by managing for clear and measurable results on the ground, project organizers hope to demonstrate that rural poverty can be eradicated if the model is replicated by governments on a larger scale and supported by donors within the envelope of financing commitments that they have made globally (0.7 percent of GDP).[41] According to a recent interim report by Millennium Promise and an earlier evaluation sponsored by the Overseas Development Institute (ODI), the project has demonstrated the feasibility of the model in the pilot cases and substantial impact in terms of poverty reduction at the village level.[42]

MV organizers have also embarked on pushing a multidimensional scaling-up strategy: horizontally (to more villages and countries), functionally (by diffusion of lessons in special areas of MV experience), and vertically (by getting countries to adopt a national MV strategy).[43] In the case of Mali, MV reports that the government, with its assistance, has developed a national MV strategy and that work is under way in Nigeria with the same intent.

The ODI evaluation specifically considered the sustainability and scalability of the MV experience. It regarded its strict cost limitation as a strong plus in this regard but notes that the success of the pilot villages depended on significant input by highly capable staff. Sustainability, the evaluation concludes, will depend on long-term commitment to the approach, integration of the MV model into

40. The author of this chapter is in charge of the Tajikistan scaling-up review. It is notable that the program shows significant recent progress in terms of its efforts to focus on scaling up. It is also worth noting that UNDP's new evaluation guidelines contain various explicit references to the need to evaluate the scaling-up aspects of projects and programs—in contrast to the previous guidelines (UNDP 2009b).

41. See Millennium Promise website (www.millenniumpromise.org).

42. Millennium Promise (2010); Buse, Ludi, and Vigneri (2008).

43. For a summary of the scaling-up approach, see the Millennium Promise website.

government structures, and more generally, engagement with the national government. For scaling up, the report notes that effective learning, adaptation, and simplification of the model and a move beyond the model (linking the villages to national infrastructure, value chains, and prevailing governmental rural development strategies) are critical. Also, continued and long-term donor support and dedication of national fiscal resources for the approach are also a sine qua non. This assessment is echoed in the subsequent assessment.[44]

Scaling up the MV approach at the national level thus requires additional fiscal and institutional space as well as effective coordination among the many governmental agencies and international organizations that need to come together to make this holistic approach work at a national level. The fact that the project has not been teaming up with IFAD, a long-established UN agency tasked specifically with the fight against rural poverty, is a striking reminder of how difficult it is to achieve interinstitutional cooperation, even among UN sister agencies, let alone to sustain it for the long haul.

### Multilateral Development Banks

In view of the large scale of their financial engagement and their focus on systemic, sectorwide, or countrywide issues, one would expect that the large multilateral development banks (African Development Bank, Asian Development Bank, Inter-American Development Bank, and especially the World Bank) would focus more explicitly on scaling up and operating at scale, in terms of their lending, their technical assistance, their analytical work, and the policy dialogue. Hence one would expect more type 2 errors (wrong scaling up) than type 1 errors (no or too little scaling up). In this section we review six sectorwide strategies or evaluations for the World Bank and one sector evaluation each for the Asian Development Bank and the Inter-American Development Bank to see how these big development banks have responded to the scaling-up challenge. The imbalance in evidence among the banks likely reflects not only different degrees of explicit consideration of scaling up but also differences in the availability of and ease of online access to sectorwide evaluations of their programs.

WORLD BANK. Following a major push by the World Bank to put scaling up on the agenda of the international development community with the 2004 Shanghai Conference, and even with its publishing the findings of this major event, the World Bank did not pursue scaling up systematically on an institutionwide basis.[45] However, at least two studies specifically address sectoral scaling-up strategies, and four sector evaluations shed light on the Bank's approach to scaling up.[46]

---

44. Millennium Promise (2009).
45. Moreno-Dodson (2005).
46. A fifth sector evaluation, on the Bank's engagement in the water sector, unfortunately did not focus on scaling-up issues in any systematic way. World Bank (2010).

This section briefly summarizes and interprets the findings of these studies and evaluations. A study on scaling up in watershed management reviews the experience of World Bank programs in this area and concludes that the overwhelming majority of bank-funded projects involved a micro-watershed approach.[47] As a result they did not allow for (macro) watershed-wide interactions, did not involve watershed-wide planning, and hence had few, if any, watershed-wide benefits. There are exceptions, such as the bank's support for the China Loess Plateau Program, which involved a large-scale watershed-wide development program, carefully developed and implemented by the Chinese authorities over a long time horizon supported by multiple, sequential bank loans.

Based on this experience, the study finds that the following key factors need to be explicitly considered in any scaling-up effort (aligned to a significant extent with the drivers and spaces defined earlier):

—Focus on incentives for improved water management (driver).

—Identify winners and losers (political space).

—Consider natural resource conservation implications (natural resource space).

—Develop participatory and partnership approaches (partnership space).

—Focus on institutions and the policy and legal framework (institutional and policy spaces).

—Ensure effective M&E (learning space).

The study also advises avoiding complexity in program design but concludes that most large-scale watershed management projects end up by necessity being complex and costly and, hence, need to pay special attention to careful planning and monitoring.

A study on scaling up in hydropower development provides a broad-gauged review of the global power sector's experience and lays out some core requirements for successful scaling up.[48] They include

—Ensuring sufficient scale of financing (financial/fiscal space).

—Promoting good technical practice and effective data collection (learning space).

—Incorporating sound environmental assessments (natural resource space).

—Engaging effective service firms and developing the country's institutional and planning capacity (institutional space).

—Building partnerships (partnership space).

—Leveraging supranational regional cooperation.

An evaluation of the World Bank's health, nutrition, and population (HNP) programs finds that between the 1990s and 2000s the bank's annual funding for HNP remained roughly constant, at about $1.5 billion, but since the number of

47. Darghouth and others (2008).
48. World Bank (2009a).

projects increased, the average size of HNP projects declined.[49] Key issues identified by the evaluation relevant from a scaling-up perspective include the tendency of bank-funded projects to be excessively complex, lacking adequate risk assessment, and suffering from weak M&E—all issues that reflect poor scaling-up practice (type 2 error).[50] The report also shows that there was a proliferation of pilots that were not effectively evaluated. In addition, the evaluation highlights two specific problems: difficulties in supporting health sector reforms and mixed outcomes of SWAps.

Regarding health sector reform—an objective of the World Bank's HNP strategy of 2007 and an instrument for vertical scaling up—the evaluation concludes that the bank's approach was hampered by political obstacles in the countries in which it operated and by a lack of political and stakeholder analysis (inadequate political space), adequate M&E (inadequate learning space), and appropriate sequencing of reforms (of the scaling-up pathway).

As for SWAps, the bank approved twenty-eight HNP projects, involving SWAps in twenty-two countries. The evaluation report concludes that these SWAps succeeded in achieving greater government ownership and in strengthening local capacity and donor coordination, but there is no evidence that sector outcomes of SWAps are better than under traditional approaches. The report cites the risk that, in the short term at least, the focus on SWAp preparation may distract the government and donors from focusing on program implementation. This result, if it holds up, is disappointing, since SWAps have an a priori appeal as an instrument for effective scaling up. The report points out that the SWAps typically lacked clearly articulated objectives and approaches and suffered like other projects in the sector from poor M&E.

Finally, the evaluation concludes that the bank's approach to communicable diseases remains caught on the horns of a dilemma, between a narrow focus on specific disease interventions (with the attendant difficulties of addressed systemic issues) and a broader focus on systemic reform and capacity development (with the resulting lack of focus, perceived or real, on specific diseases). In essence this is the tension between horizontal and vertical scaling up, to which we return below in discussing the experience of global (vertical) funds.[51]

An evaluation of the World Bank's HIV/AIDS program recounts the history of the bank's engagement in the HIV/AIDS area, which required the strong championship by Wolfensohn, who declared a "war on AIDS" in 2000, calling for the bank to marshal its forces to develop dedicated and large-scale HIV/AIDS interventions at the country level.[52] According to the evaluation, aside from substantially

49. World Bank (2009b).
50. The report points to the lack of incentives for project managers to engage in effective M&E but doesn't spell out what might be the right incentives.
51. The report also notes that the bank's HIV/AIDS projects have a very low success rate (only 29 percent of projects have been evaluated as at least moderately successful).
52. World Bank (2005).

ramping up its financial engagement, the bank was successful in building political commitment to meeting the HIV/AIDS threat at the country level, in setting up or strengthening national HIV/AIDS institutions, and in supporting complementary investments in other areas, especially by improving the capacity of the ministries of health. In this sense, the bank was able to provide for improved financial, political, and institutional space in support of scaling up HIV/AIDS programs.

However, the bank's programs also suffered from a number of weaknesses. It overestimated the strength of NGO and community institutions in supporting the delivery of relevant interventions, it suffered from cumbersome procedures, and it tended to design overly complex projects. A key constraint was the lack of effective information, due to weak M&E and research—a type 2 error, as reflected in this blunt quote from the evaluation: "By and large, what is being scaled up, has not been locally evaluated."[53] In addition, the evaluation notes a number of problems that impeded effective scaling up: limited country capacity and poor governance, weak national HIV/AIDS strategies (which can be interpreted as a lack of well-established scaling-up pathways), and a tendency by the bank and other donors to bias limited national health spending priorities and capacity in unbalanced support for HIV/AIDS to the detriment of other important health priorities.

An evaluation of the World Bank's primary education programs concludes that the scaling up of access, in particular enrollment, is a key objective of bank-funded programs.[54] In this regard, these programs made a significant contribution, with 70 percent of projects achieving or more than achieving their ambitious targets. The bank's policy development support notably helped to increase the budgetary resources allocated by governments to primary education and thus helped provide the necessary fiscal and financial space.

However, the evaluation points to a number of type 2 errors. There was little focus on reducing dropout or repeater rates, and insufficient attention was given to improving the quality of education, including consideration of management incentives as well as teacher recruitment and incentives. The lack of focus on quality was a problem especially for programs that involved broad-gauged social funds or conditional cash transfers. The report also critiques the fact that educational interventions supported by the bank were insufficiently anchored in prior evaluation and analytical work, although it notes that the bank's support for M&E led to improvements in countries' use of M&E capacity and tools. However, according to the evaluation, the links between policy and M&E lessons were insufficiently developed.[55]

---

53. Ibid., p. 62.

54. World Bank (2006).

55. The evaluation does not comment in any depth on the role or performance of the Education-For-All Fast-Track Initiative (EFA-FTI) or on the quality of sector strategies supported by the bank. In effect, there is no assessment therefore of whether the bank supported systematic scaling-up pathways with sustained or intermittent engagement.

Finally, an evaluation of the World Bank's municipal management programs starts with the observation that engagement by the bank was significant in scale, reaching about 3,000 municipalities, or an estimated 15 percent of all municipalities in borrowing countries.[56] But it also notes that the bank's project documents usually do not permit an assessment of how many people will benefit from the programs supported and hence that it is difficult to assess the scale of the intervention. The report has a number of highly relevant conclusions from a scaling-up perspective.[57]

—Wholesale projects (projects that cover a large number of municipalities and typically involve an intermediary agency supported by the bank) tend to be more successful than retail projects (projects that involve direct assistance to only one municipality or to a small number of jurisdictions). In other words a scaling-up approach is more successful than a limited-scale intervention. One of the implications is that smaller donors who cannot follow the wholesale approach may have limited scope for engagement in this area, unless they team up with other donors to scale up the resources they put in.

—One of the factors explaining the success of scaled-up interventions is the use of competitions in allocating resources. This confirms what Clifford Zinnes explores in detail in his book on the use of interjurisdictional competition as an instrument for effective scaling up.[58]

—The report also confirms the importance of vertical scaling up by taking a systemic approach to improved municipal development and management.

—The reports notes further that one of the strengths of bank-supported interventions is that they were effective in creating fiscal space through strengthening municipal financial policies and systems.

The evaluation also identifies a number of weaknesses in the bank's approach, which reflect type 2 errors (wrong scaling up). For example, the bank paid little attention to municipal planning and used few analytical tools (especially cost-benefit analysis) to identify priorities. This reflects a lack of explicit consideration of the scaling-up pathway. Also, the bank paid too little attention to operation and maintenance implications of municipal investments that it financed, raising questions about the sustainability of the programs at the scale intended. Further, M&E was weak, focusing mostly on project implementation and little on results.

INTER-AMERICAN DEVELOPMENT BANK. In 2006 the IDB's Office of Evaluation and Oversight carried out an evaluation of IDB's engagement in the health

---

56. World Bank 2009c.

57. The bank supported multiple follow-on projects in many of the countries. For example, for Indonesia the report refers to a ninth project (MDP IX), for China to MDP VII, and for Russia and Colombia to MDP IV. Unfortunately, the evaluation does not assess how the sequence of projects was developed and implemented or whether and how seriously the projects supported a programmatic, or scaling-up, approach over time.

58. Zinnes (2009).

sector from 1995 to 2005. It observed that IDB heavily focused on systemic public sector reform aimed at achieving structural changes in line with the prevailing belief that market-oriented, private-sector-driven solutions are generally preferable to those dominated by the public sector. In that sense, IDB scaled up vertically by supporting policy reform and horizontally across countries and by rolling out its standard prescriptions for reform across the region.

The main conclusion of the evaluation, relevant to the scaling-up challenge, is that the IDB's

> reform actions were not evidence based; they have, to a large extent, followed a set of consensual assumptions of the time that resulted from the belief that market-based mechanisms and incentives were the only solution to the problems and inefficiencies observed in the sector. Despite the lack of empirical and sometimes conceptual support, these assumptions were not seriously questioned: they were judged to be right because they were based on the "right premises."[59]

Accordingly, the bank's support for a standard package of reforms (contracting with private providers, promoting primary health care services, introducing performance-based incentives or contracts, introducing user fees and cost recovery mechanisms, and decentralizing sector institutions) was not a tested model and did not bring the expected results. The report also concludes that primary health care interventions were especially lacking in evaluation, and it recommends that "experiences with basic packages need to be evaluated and potential scaling-up alternatives assessed."[60]

ASIAN DEVELOPMENT BANK. A 2008 evaluation of ADB education sector programs does not specifically address the scaling-up challenge.[61] It does note the importance of long-term engagement in the education sector but does not comment on whether and how the bank was responsive to this need. Nevertheless, the report draws a number of lessons relevant to the scaling-up agenda. In particular it stresses the need for developing the fiscal and financial space for educational programs, along with institutional, political, and cultural space. It also notes the critical importance of effective M&E. However, it does not measure the performance of ADB educational projects against these specific requirements.

## Global Funds and Programs

The final set of donor entities reviewed here from a scaling-up perspective covers global funds and programs (also known as vertical funds), with a special focus on health sector programs.

---

59. IDB (2006, p. vi).
60. Ibid., p. 34.
61. ADB (2008).

GLOBAL HEALTH PROGRAMS. There exist seventy to ninety global health programs, but only two are significant in terms of funding: the Global Fund to Fight AIDS, Tuberculosis, and Malaria and the GAVI Alliance.[62] Together the two entities provided $2.7 billion in health finance in 2007, or some 12 percent of all aid in health. They are recent creations and ascribe their popularity among donors and recipients to the fact that they focus on specific high-priority areas and are results oriented, flexible, transparent, and inclusive in terms of their governance.[63] Perhaps their most attractive feature, however, is their undiluted aim to increase quickly the delivery of funding for interventions that make a large impact in narrowly defined areas: AIDS, TB, malaria, and immunization. They are in effect scaling-up facilitators, since they do not implement programs themselves but provide funding to implementing agencies in country on an incentive basis.[64]

In terms of their principal objectives—expanding rapidly the provision of targeted health services—the two funds generally have been remarkably successful. The Global Fund report is particularly emphatic and graphic in demonstrating its impact at scale.[65] Figure 9-3 shows the explosive growth of interventions in the three areas of the Global Fund's engagement. Despite these considerable achievements of going to scale quickly, the evaluations and crosscutting reviews identify a number of issues that the global health funds need to grapple with in their pursuit of scale. Five are discussed here.

First, and perhaps the most frequently mentioned: global health funds singlemindedly pursue horizontal scaling up in their areas of engagement. Traditionally they have not engaged in broader health system reform and capacity building nor pursued functional scaling up by branching into other health areas. The simplicity of their approach, compared with the complexity of World Bank health programs, has been a great strength but also has meant that other health priority areas have been shortchanged due to the heavy engagement by the global funds.[66] In response to this concern, the global health funds have started to devote substantial funds for strengthening health systems—in the case of the Global Fund, almost one-third of its funds.[67]

Second, global health funds have not participated in broader health sector strategy formulation and implementation, including SWAps. However, here too

62. Isenman and Shakow (2010).

63. Isenman, Wathne, and Baudienville (2010). It also helps that global health funds provide grants, rather than loans. Many countries, especially middle-income countries, do not want to borrow from the multilateral development banks at market terms for health interventions. This gives the funds a clear competitive advantage.

64. For evaluations of the funds, see Global Fund (2009a); GAVI Alliance (2008); World Bank (2008); Isenman and Shakow (2010); Isenman, Wathne, and Baudienville (2010).

65. Global Fund (2009b).

66. Isenman and Shakow (2010); World Bank (2008).

67. Global Fund (2009b).

Figure 9-3. *Rapid Progress with Top Three Indicators for HIV, TB, and Malaria,
2004–08*

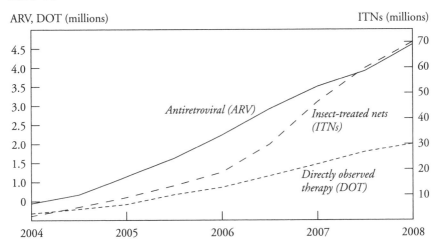

Source: Global Fund (2009b).

there has recently been progress, since the Global Fund now supports SWAps (in
Ghana and Malawi, although not in Tajikistan).[68]

Third, global health funds have not yet found ways to partner with other international donor partners on the ground.[69] This is not surprising, since the funds
have no local representation but work through implementing agencies. Moreover, developing and sustaining interagency collaboration is always a difficult,
time-consuming chore, which all partners tend to eschew unless there are very
clear benefits.

Fourth, and directly relevant to the scaling-up agenda, the financing modalities of the global health funds are relatively short term and the competitive selection process of funding applications creates uncertainties about the ability to roll
over and extend funding arrangements.[70] This makes it difficult for countries and
their implementing agencies to plan for sustained funding and long-term scaling
up. Moreover, since scaled-up interventions require incremental recurrent cost
funding and since local fiscal resources often do not permit sustained funding, the
sustainability of the programs is in serious doubt. The Global Fund, however,
maintains that it can provide long-term predictable funding due to its ability to
provide indicative and potential funding envelopes beyond its short-term

approval process. It has been proposed that the global health funds adopt a longer term country allocation approach to strengthen the predictability of their resources from the recipient country point of view and, specifically, that the challenge fund approach of the Global Fund is "well suited to encouraging innovation and piloting and should be used for that purpose. But this approach should be avoided in new funds and modified in existing ones when the objective is longer-term support for country programs."[71]

Finally, the evaluation documents consulted for this study do not allow an answer to the question whether the global health funds encourage the development of a scaling-up pathway rather than merely the specification of short- to medium-term delivery goals without a longer term vision and systematic consideration of alternative scaling-up options. This would be a critical aspect of a longer term, successful, country-based approach to scaling up the specific health interventions supported by the global health funds.

EDUCATION-FOR-ALL FAST-TRACK INITIATIVE. The EFA-FTI was launched in 2002 as a partnership among donors and recipient countries to accelerate progress toward universal primary school completion by 2015.[72] The main idea was to support the development of primary education strategies in developing countries and provide adequate funding to help countries achieve their strategic goals. However, aside from an initially small catalytic fund, all donor funding was to be provided by donors through their regular education sector financing on a country-by-country basis rather than through a separate funding mechanism administered by the EFA-FTI's secretariat, in contrast to the Global Fund for AIDS, TB, and Malaria and GAVI.

While in principle the scaling-up idea is firmly embedded in the basic mission of EFA-FTI, in practice the initiative has not achieved its goals so far. According to a recent evaluation a number of factors have contributed to the relatively weak scaling-up performance of the EFA-FTI:[73]

—Standards of sector strategies were set too high ("gold-plated"), making for protracted negotiations and frustration among the recipient countries, some of which withdrew from the program.

—Limited funding was provided by donors through their regular education programs, leading to underfunding of sector strategies.

—The EFA-FTI was unable to overcome internal disincentives within donor agencies for working in effective partnership with others.

—M&E of program implementation were weak.

—The EFA-FTI secretariat had very limited capacity.

71. Isenman, Wathne, and Baudienville (2010, p. vii); Global Fund (2009b).

72. EFA-FTI (2004).

73. Cambridge Education and others (2010).

—The governance structure of EFA-FTI was heavily tilted toward donor participants.

THE GLOBAL AGRICULTURE AND FOOD SECURITY PROGRAM. The newest of specialized global programs with a scaling-up agenda is GAFSP. It was founded in January 2010 to "provide readily available additional financing to scale up agricultural and food security assistance on a coordinated basis in response to demonstrated commitment to results by countries."[74] Based on initiatives by the G8 and G20 summits in 2010 in response to the global food crisis of 2007–08, and with inputs from a wide array of stakeholders, the design of GAFSP is somewhere between those of the Global Fund and the EFA-FTI.

A steering committee, consisting of equal numbers of donor and recipient country representatives, and with representation also from civil society, allocates available funds to countries that have submitted acceptable proposals for investment or technical assistance based on a national agriculture and food security sector strategy and investment plans. All funding is channeled through existing multilateral agencies (such as the World Bank, regional development banks, and IFAD) with the intention of providing additional, immediately available, resources that are complementary to, and reinforcing of, existing initiatives.[75] An innovative aspect of the GAFSP is that it includes a public and private sector funding window. By October 1, 2010, GAFSP had attracted $880 million in pledges from the United States, Canada, Spain, Korea, and the Bill and Melinda Gates Foundation and had allocated $224 million to five countries (Rwanda, Bangladesh, Sierra Leone, Haiti, and Togo).[76]

It is too early to tell how the GAFSP will work out in practice. Major success factors will be its ability to attract additional donor funding, the ability of governments to develop effective scaling-up pathways as part of their national sector plans, the implementation capacity of recipient countries, and the readiness of the multilateral agencies to support the GAFSP scaling-up agenda. Three developments have the potential to support a successful outcome. First, the U.S. bilateral Feed the Future Initiative is complementary to GAFSP in purpose, approach, and resource deployment, based on President Obama's pledge of at least $3.5 billion for agricultural development and food security over three years.[77] Second, in 2010 a group of over one hundred organizations, involving the major multilateral and bilateral donors, recipient country governments, foundations, NGOs, and academic institutions, endorsed an initiative on scaling up nutrition interventions,

74. See GAFSP Questions and Answers (http://siteresources.worldbank.org/NEWS/Resources/GAFSPQuestions/Answers_ext042210.pdf).

75. The GAFSP Q&A specifically states, "It is important to note that GAFSP will not be a 'vertical fund' or new institution." Ibid.

76. See interview with Assistant Secretary of State Marisa Lago, October 5, 2010 (http://fpc.state.gov/148636.htm).

77. Feed the Future, "Feed the Future Guide," 2010 (www.feedthefuture.gov.FTF_Guide.pdf).

including in agriculture, health care, and social protection, under the banner of Scaling up Nutrition (SUN).[78] The principles of SUN (county-level focus and ownership, scaling up evidence-based cost-effective interventions, multisectoral engagement, and increased external funding) are complementary to the goals of the GAFSP.[79] Third, the World Bank and IFAD are exploring close cooperation in ensuring an effective partnership for scaling up in the agricultural and rural development area.

## Conclusions and Recommendations

This review of the institutional dimension of scaling up in aid is limited in coverage of donor agencies. More research and evaluation is needed to generate a complete picture of how donors support—or do not support—the scaling-up agenda in the countries where they work. Of course, the ultimate question is to what extent major development actors in the developing countries themselves accept the scaling-up agenda.

Nonetheless, some preliminary conclusions can be drawn based on what we know so far, and some tentative recommendations can await consideration during the preparation of the fourth High-Level Forum on Aid Effectiveness in Busan, Korea, in 2011.

### Conclusions

First, with the rise in project numbers and the decline in average project size the need for systematically pursuing opportunities for scaling up successful projects and interventions has become even more important than it was in the past. As a start, donors should aim to limit the rise in project numbers and to increase the average size of their projects.

Second, in recent years the scaling-up agenda has been gaining traction in the international development community, especially in connection with the rapid growth of specialized global funds and programs.

Third, more analytical and operational tools are now available to those who are interested in pursuing the scaling-up agenda. This includes the operational framework proposed by Arntraud Hartmann and Johannes Linn (and applied by Linn and colleagues) and the managerial framework proposed by Larry Cooley and Richard Kohl and applied in various health programs in developing countries.[80] Detailed manuals for scaling up in specific areas are also available in the work by Hartmann and Linn.

---

78. See "Scaling up Nutrition: A Framework for Action," 2010 (www.unscn.org/files/Activities/Endorsements_to_the_SUN_Framework_200810.pdf).

79. However, judging from the available documentation, coordination among the GAFSP and SUN initiatives remains in its infancy. Whether and how they will act in synergy is not yet clear.

80. Hartmann and Linn (2008); Linn and others (2010); Cooley and Kohl (2005).

Fourth, the information base on the approach of the aid "industry" to scaling up remains at best incomplete. Most important, we know little about the internal institutional goals, processes, results and evaluation metrics, and incentives that the many aid agencies employ and what their impacts are on the way agencies do or do not pursue a scaling-up agenda. This chapter aims to begin to fill this gap. Much more needs to be done.

Fifth, based on the evidence collected in this chapter, medium-sized and large multilateral development organizations have no systematic approach to scaling up. To the extent that they scale up or operate at scale, they do so without explicit consideration of the specific procedural, managerial, and M&E design challenges that they confront. As a result, type 1 and type 2 errors are common. The cursory evidence on bilateral official and private donors is that they are in a very similar, and perhaps even less satisfactory, position regarding their approach to scaling up. In contrast, the global (or vertical) funds and initiatives very explicitly focus on scaling up.

Sixth, a pervasive observation from all the cases reviewed in this chapter is that the evidence base for scaling up is generally extremely weak or nonexistent. Organizations either do not systematically pilot new innovations, or if they do, M&E is generally weak and not specifically focused on the lessons relevant for scaling up. The evaluation agencies of aid donor organizations generally do not focus on the scaling-up dimension of project and institutional performance (with the exception of IFAD). Research and evaluation findings, to the extent they do exist, are not systematically fed into the scaling-up process, where there is one.

Seventh, aid agencies do not generally explore appropriate scaling-up pathways for the interventions that they support. The increasing use of programmatic approaches, of SWAps, and of sector strategies and investment programs as a guide for individual projects is a step in the right direction, but the experience to date shows that unless there is a specific focus on the scaling-up agenda and unless scaling-up pathways are explicitly explored as part of these programmatic approaches, key aspects of the scaling-up agenda will be lost. The mixed experience with health sector SWAps is a case in point.

Eighth, and finally, there are a number of conclusions for the scaling-up process that can be gleaned from the institutional case studies presented in this chapter:

—Scaling-up pathways need to be designed flexibly and need to avoid undue complexity and ambition. Aiming for sectorwide approaches may be overly ambitious.

—There is a need to balance horizontal, vertical, and functional scaling-up approaches (such as in health).

—The tension between quantitative scaling up and quality objectives needs to be managed carefully (as in education).

—The cost dimensions of program replication and scaling up need to be explicitly considered, in terms of ensuring not only that the individual package is replicable in terms of cost but also that the cost and institutional requirements of systemic and network investments and support are fully considered (such as for global funds and Millennium Villages).

—Incentives are critical for scaling up. Competitive approaches to resource allocation and incentive provision may be useful instruments to support scaling up, but the specific application of challenge grants in the case of the Global Fund also demonstrates some risks.

—M&E is essential for an effective scaling-up approach; the pursuit of a scaling-up agenda can help create the incentives for project managers to take M&E seriously.

—Ultimately it's all about country-led, not donor-led, scaling up. The role of donors as intermediary or external drivers of the process should be the exception and self-limiting.

### Recommendations

Specific proposals for the High-Level Forum on Aid Effectiveness in Busan and for inclusion in a Busan Declaration on Aid Effectiveness are as follows:

—Donors commit to a moratorium on creating new multilateral agencies and to consolidate multiple national agencies (as done recently by Japan and Germany). Furthermore, donors commit to reducing the number and increasing the average (median) size of activities (projects).

—The declaration explicitly addresses the scaling-up agenda.

—Official donors and large private donors agree to introduce the objective of scaling up into their mission statements and operational policies and processes.

—Donors commit to introducing incentives and funding mechanisms to provide incentives for scaling up.

—Official evaluation procedures are amended to include scaling up as an explicit criterion. Private donors commit to evaluate their activities, including their scaling-up performance and to make the evaluations available publicly.

## References

Acharya, Arnab, Ana Teresa Fuzzo de Lima, and Mick Moore. 2006. "Proliferation and Fragmentation: Transactions Costs and the Value of Aid." *Journal of Development Studies* 42, no. 1: 1–21.

ADB (Asian Development Bank). 2008. "Education Sector." Manila: Operations Evaluation Department. December.

Altenburg, Tilman, ed. 2007. "From Project to Policy Reform: Experiences of German Development Cooperation." *Studies* 27. German Development Institute.

Buse, Kent, Eva Ludi, and Marcella Vigneri. 2008. "Beyond the Village: The Transition for Rural Investment to National Plans to Reach the MDGs. Sustaining and Scaling up the Millennium Villages." London: Overseas Development Institute.

Cambridge Education, Mokoro Ltd., and Oxford Policy Management. 2010. *Mid-Term Evaluation of the EFA Fast-Track Initiative: Final Report*. Vol. 1, *Synthesis Report Executive Summary*. Cambridge, U.K.

Cohen, Jessica, and William Easterly, eds. 2009. *What Works in Development? Thinking Big and Thinking Small*. Brookings.

Cooley, Larry, and Richard Kohl. 2005. "Scaling Up: From Vision to Large-Scale Change." Washington: Management Systems International.

Darghouth, Salah, and others. 2008. "Watershed Management Approaches, Policies, and Operations: Lessons for Scaling Up." Discussion Paper 11. Washington: World Bank, Water Sector Board.

Desai, Raj M., and Homi Kharas. 2010. "Democratizing Foreign Aid: Online Philanthropy and International Development Assistance." *Journal of International Law and Politics* 42, no. 4: 1111–42.

EFA-FTI (Education-for-All Fast-Track Initiative). 2004. "Accelerating Progress toward Quality Universal Primary Education: Framework." Washington: World Bank.

Fengler, Wolfgang, and Homi Kharas. 2010. *Delivering Aid Differently: Lessons from the Field*. Washington: Brookings.

Findley, Michael G., and others. 2010. "AidData: Tracking Development Finance." Paper prepared for conference, Aid Transparency and Development Finance: Lessons and Insights from AidData. Oxford, U.K., March 22–25.

GAVI Alliance. 2008. "Evaluation of the GAVI Phase 1 Performance, 2000–2005." Cambridge, Mass.: Abt Associates (www.gavialliance.org/resources/GAVI_ Phase1_Report_ FINAL_to_SC_Oct21.pdf).

Global Fund. 2009a. "The Five-Year Evaluation of the Global Fund to Fight AIDS, Tuberculosis, and Malaria: Synthesis of Study Areas 1, 2, and 3." Geneva.

———. 2009b. "Scaling up for Impact: Results Report." Geneva.

GTZ. 2007. "Scaling up Capacity Development." Draft. September. Eschborn, Germany.

Hartmann, Arntraud, and Johannes Linn. 2008. "Scaling Up: A Framework and Lessons for Development Effectiveness from Literature and Practice." Working Paper 4. Wolfensohn Center for Development, Brookings.

IDA (International Development Association). 2007. "Aid Architecture: An Overview of the Main Trends in Official Development Assistance Flows." Washington.

IDB (International Development Bank). 2006. "Health Sector Evaluation, 1995–2005." Report RE-324. Office of Evaluation and Oversight. Washington.

IFAD (International Fund for Agricultural Development). 2007. "Strategic Framework, 2007–2010." Rome.

Isenman, Paul, and Alexander Shakow. 2010. "Donor Schizophrenia and Aid Effectiveness: The Role of Global Funds." Practice Paper 5. Institute of Development Studies.

Isenman, Paul, Cecille Wathne, and Geraldine Baudienville. 2010. "Global Funds: Allocation Strategies and Aid Effectiveness." Final report. London: Overseas Development Institute.

Kharas, Homi. 2007. "Trends and Issues in Development Aid." Working Paper 1. Wolfensohn Center for Development, Brookings.

Levy, Santiago. 2006. *Progress against Poverty: Sustaining Mexico's Progresa-Oportunidades Program*. Brookings.

Linn, Johannes F., and others. 2010. "Scaling up the Fight against Rural Poverty: An Institutional Review of IFAD's Approach." Working Paper 39. Global Economy and Development, Brookings.

Millennium Promise. 2010. "Harvest of Development in Rural Africa: The Millennium Villages after Three Years." New York: Earth Institute.

————. 2009. "The Millennium Villages Project." Annual report 2008. New York: Earth Institute.

Moreno-Dodson, B., ed. 2005. *Reducing Poverty on a Global Scale—Learning and Innovating for Development: Findings from the Shanghai Global Learning Initiative.* Washington: World Bank.

Mosley, Paul. 1987. *Foreign Aid: Its Defense and Reform.* University Press of Kentucky.

OECD. 2010. "2010 DAC Report on Multilateral Aid." Paris.

————. 2009. "2008 DAC Report on Multilateral Aid." Paris.

————. 2008. "Scaling Up: Aid Fragmentation, Aid Allocation and Aid Predictability." Report of 2008 Survey of Aid Allocation Policies and Indicative Forward Spending Plans. Paris.

Ogata, Sadaka. 2008. "Present Conditions and Perspective of African Development from the Viewpoint of Human Security." Address. African Union, February 20.

Pritchett, Lant. 2009. "The Policy Irrelevance of the Economics of Education: Is 'Normative as Positive' Just Useless, or Worse?" In *What Works in Development? Thinking Big and Thinking Small,* edited by Jessica Cohen and William Easterly. Brookings.

Schaffer, Robert H., and Ron N. Ashkenas. 2005. *Rapid Results.* San Francisco: Jossey-Bass.

Sommer, Felix. 2009. "Immer weitere Kreise ziehen." *Akzente* 3 (GTZ).

UNDP. 2010. *Assessment of Development Results: Turkey.* New York.

————. 2009a. *Assessment of Development Results: Tajikistan.* New York.

————. 2009b. *Handbook on Planning, Monitoring and Evaluating for Development Results.* New York.

————. 2004. *Assessment of Development Results: Turkey.* New York.

World Bank. 2010. *Water and Development: An Evaluation of World Bank Support, 1997–2007.* IEG Study Series. Washington.

————. 2009a. "Directions in Hydropower: Scaling up for Development." Water Working Notes 21. Washington.

————. 2009b. "Improving Effectiveness and Outcomes for the Poor in Health, Nutrition, and Population." Washington.

————. 2009c. "Improving Municipal Management for Cities to Succeed." Washington.

————. 2008. "Global Program Funds at Country Level: What Have We Learned?" Washington.

————. 2006. "From Schooling Access to Learning Outcomes: An Unfinished Agenda." Washington.

————. 2005. "Committing to Results: Improving the Effectiveness of HIV/AIDS Assistance." Washington.

Zinnes, Clifford. 2009. *Tournament Approaches to Policy Reform.* Brookings.

# 10

## Transparency: Changing the Accountability, Engagement, and Effectiveness of Aid

HOMI KHARAS

Transparency and accountability are essential elements for development results. They lie at the heart of the Paris Declaration. . . . We recognise that greater transparency and accountability for the use of development resources—domestic as well as external—are powerful drivers of progress.

—Accra Agenda for Action, 2009

Lack of transparency is the single biggest obstacle to engagement of the public.

—Ad Council, 2010

One of the great scandals in development is the lack of good statistics to measure progress; this area needs much more investment.

—John Githongo and Jamie Drummond, 2010

Development cooperation, in an information age, is not only about whose projects and programs are most successful but also about whose stories are most compelling.[1] Transparency in aid is a critical part of promoting a story of successful development. Through transparency, donors and recipients can be held accountable for what they spend, more players can become actively engaged in development efforts by identifying underserved areas and niches, and aid can be made more effective through learning.

I would like to express thanks to Anirban Ghosh for his assistance with this chapter. Financial support from the Japan International Cooperation Agency (JICA) and the Korea International Cooperation Agency (KOICA) is gratefully acknowledged.

1. This is a paraphrase of Joseph Nye's observation that "politics in an information age is not only about whose military wins but whose story wins." Joseph S. Nye Jr., *Boston Review*, February/March 2005 (www.bostonreview.net/BR30.1/nye.php).

Transparency has long been recognized as a vital component of aid effectiveness, dating back all the way to the Marshall Plan and the founding of the OECD's Development Assistance Committee (DAC). Back then, however, information exchange was a much simpler endeavor. There were relatively few actors (in 1960, for example, the United States government provided 40 percent of ODA, with France and the United Kingdom accounting for another third), working toward a narrow goal (replacing infrastructure that had been destroyed in World War II) in well-defined locations (areas where infrastructure had been lost). Under these circumstances, transparency could be achieved simply by meeting around a table and sharing information among a half dozen actors working on similar projects in similar places. The urgency for transparency comes from the fact that the aid ecosystem has changed dramatically from its early incarnation, while the traditional systems of information exchange that operated on a need-to-know basis have proved unable to provide the data required for effective aid.

The new ecosystem of aid actors covers not just a few donors but many actors: emerging economy donors, multinational corporations, megaphilanthropists, high-profile advocates, and a vocal and energized global public. Engagement of these multiple actors has brought considerable energy and resources to bear on development, but it also adds to the difficulties of information sharing, as many of these new actors have little incentive to share data. Agreements on responsibilities and accountabilities are needed to change their behavior, as explored below. These actors are not working on one narrow goal, like postwar infrastructure rehabilitation, but rather on the broad goal of development, which is a much more complex affair. Development aid encompasses not only the financing of productive and social sectors but also cross-cutting issues such as gender, governance, anticorruption, urban development, and environmental and social sustainability. The creditor reporting system (CRS) of the DAC has 197 sector and topic codes to describe the purposes of aid interventions. Furthermore, many interventions are multipurpose, making it sometimes difficult to pin down what exactly is being funded even after the fact.[2]

In the Marshall Plan the spatial allocation of physical dollars was simple—reconstruction dollars flowed to where infrastructure had been destroyed. Today, development seeks to lift large geographic areas out of poverty. Country programs are important as an overarching guide, but within-country allocations are also important. Just as some countries have become donor darlings or donor orphans, there are spatial inequalities within countries in aid allocations and even within

2. As one example, major practical difficulties have surfaced with identifying a baseline of how much aid is already being provided for climate mitigation. There is a consensus that international negotiations on financing of climate mitigation should focus on additional amounts of aid, but without an adequate baseline, even if an agreement was reached, it would be problematic to implement.

families. When aid takes the form of delivery of public services like immunizations, rural health clinics, and basic education, where dollars are spent is an important consideration.

This preamble points to the three Ws of transparency—knowing the who (which donor gives money to which recipient), the what (what project is being funded and for what purpose), and the where (where is the project located) of funding. These three aspects of transparency, along with information on results, are crucial for mobilizing support and dollars, ensuring accountability, and maximizing effectiveness. At present, the three Ws apply to a diminishing share of total public and private aid, lessening accountability and effectiveness because information on emerging economy donors and private development assistance is poor. At the same time, information at the recipient country level is also poor, with inconsistencies in donor reports to local and global databases weakening credibility in the quality of the information and perversely resulting in more ad hoc requests for information. Beneficiary feedback and formal project evaluation are also lacking, limiting the learning that is needed to improve development effectiveness.

## A New Model for Aid Transparency

Aid transparency can be defined as "the comprehensive availability and accessibility of aid flow information in a timely, systematic, and comparable manner that allows public participation in government accountability."[3]

The Accra Agenda for Action, a document summarizing the deliberations of the third High-Level Forum on Aid Effectiveness held between September 2 and 4, 2008, called on all donors to disclose aid information in a timely manner. The agenda concludes: "We recognise that greater transparency and accountability for the use of development resources—domestic as well as external—are powerful drivers of progress."[4]

The OECD/DAC is the main source of aid data and the gold standard for international data. The main objective of the DAC Working Party on Aid Statistics is to "collect and publish timely statistics of official and private flows to all countries." Its data are comparable and accessible to the public, but they do not meet the highest standards of timeliness and comprehensiveness:

—Its data are incomplete, lacking details on emerging economy donors and private aid.

—Its data are inaccurate, with donors in the field reporting different data than their headquarters for aid to particular countries.

—Its data are not timely, with availability subject to over a year's delay.

---

3. Moon and Williamson (2010, p. 2).
4. Accra Agenda for Action final statement is available at www.paris21.org/pages/other/?id_news=109.

—Its data are neither forward looking nor compatible with budget accounts, limiting the ability of recipient countries to plan spending appropriately and to link aid with multiyear expenditure frameworks.

—Its data do not have sufficient geographic granularity to determine gaps in meeting needs.

The aid system of today still revolves around a centralized model of a few large agencies doing a few large projects. That model is now redundant and is having difficulty adapting to new demands for transparency. Tens of millions of people are providing expertise, resources, and technology toward solving development problems.[5] These people are connected via mobile phones, computers, and the Internet to each other and to the people they are trying to help. In this world, transparency is the mechanism through which development organizations have their ideas tested (via customer feedback loops), funded (by potentially millions of donors when impact and results can be demonstrated), and disseminated to other practitioners.

The promise of the new transparency is that the relationship of citizens and governments to aid institutions is changing in both donor and recipient countries. Citizens in rich countries are advocating for better spending of their taxes; governments in donor countries are demanding greater accountability and impact from aid agencies and aid programs; citizens in recipient countries are demanding their rights to oversee and comment on spending on development projects that ostensibly are for their benefit; and recipient country governments are keen to link aid with their own budgets and priorities.

The key change in transparency in the future will be to adapt information release from a controlled approach that enhances advocacy of the institution to an open approach that provides raw data that can be accessed by others for multiple purposes.[6] That approach puts a premium on the quality, coverage, timeliness, and accessibility of data. The advantage for the providing institution is that its influence can be expanded as the number of people using its data expands.

The disadvantage of such a system is that an open and voluntary approach is subject to misinformation and statistical inaccuracy depending on how data are compiled. Although some variation in data quality is inevitable, this is no more problematic than in other areas, such as national income accounts of developing countries, where data come from each individual reporting country. As long as source notes are well documented and there is openness to clarifications that data users might ask for, it is better to have more complete data with the risk of some inconsistency than missing data. Over time, peer review and user pressures will provide incentives for improvements in data quality.

---

5. About half of all American households are reported to have contributed to relief efforts in Haiti, for example.

6. IATI already provides for data to be published in a common, open format.

## Gaps in Transparency for Mutual Accountability

In 2008 Mary Robinson, the former president of Ireland and of the UNHCR, called transparency a basic expression of mutual accountability.[7] Mutual accountability can only work if there is a global culture of transparency that demands provision of information through a set of rules and behavioral norms. These rules and norms are moderately well established among official DAC aid agencies but are in a nascent stage for emerging economy donors and private development assistance. Both supply-side norms (harmonized standards and definitions) and demand-side norms (minimum expected provision of data) need to be further articulated.

Aid transparency in the future should be driven by the needs of mutual accountability processes. *Mutual accountability* here refers to an agreed-upon set of norms through which partners build commitments to collaborative actions that result in improved outcomes. Such a system, which is voluntary in nature and designed to enhance relationships and cooperation between development partners, is not amenable to a set of rigid rules with sanctions for noncompliance. This approach borrows from the concept of regulation through information pioneered by Giandomenico Majone in the context of European integration.[8] Majone explains that when rule enforcement is difficult, as is the case between development partners, traditional command-and-control regulation based on mandatory rules does not work. Instead, if transparent, relevant, accurate, and reliable information is made available, it can be used to reward or sanction individual agencies according to their performance.

In simple terms, rules that donors should provide specified information are a supply-side mechanism that has long been the preferred route to increasing aid transparency, but this is a route that is slow and tortuous. It needs to be supplemented by a demand-side mechanism: we need people to act on good information and to demand the provision of such information. That puts a premium on listening more closely to aid recipient country needs for data and on heeding calls for serious evaluations of accomplishments. It also means establishing a stronger culture of accountability within aid, which rewards aid successes and penalizes aid failures. Transforming the transparency agenda into one that focuses on action and outcomes, as opposed to processes, is key.

The framework of mutual accountability developed by Oxford Policy Management identifies three mechanisms for mutual accountability: independent third-party reviews, peer reviews, and mutual reviews (table 10-1). Table 10-1 emphasizes the demand for transparency. Too often, transparency has been approached from the supply side, with agencies supplying information that is never used, or databases being established without clear understanding of what is

7. OECD (2008).
8. Majone (1997).

Table 10-1. *How Accountability Depends on Transparency*

| Mechanism | Process description | Transparency challenges |
|---|---|---|
| Independent third-party reviews | Spotlights, or independent third-party reviews, based on benchmarking and analytical reviews are typically carried out by civil society organizations, legislatures, and other stakeholders. They are largely used in donor countries but are increasing in aid recipient countries. | Spotlights on donor agencies have been hampered by inadequate data at both global (donor) and local (recipient) levels. Emerging economy donors and private aid donors are absent from this picture. |
| Peer reviews | Mirrors, or peer reviews, of donors (as in the DAC peer review process) and recipients (as in the Africa peer review mechanism) are based on dialogue and qualitative judgments as well as empirical data. | Multilateral aid agencies, emerging economy donors, and private aid donors do not participate in significant peer reviews but operate on the basis of accountability to their boards, which have access to proprietary agency information. |
| Mutual reviews | Two-way mirrors, or mutual reviews at country or international level, are designed to foster a dialogue in which collaboration can be debated to improve aid effectiveness. Surveys are often used to provide additional information. | Only a handful of recipient countries conduct systematic mutual reviews with development partners. These reviews are often hampered by the lack of quality data at local levels, lack of evaluation, and lack of beneficiary feedback. |

Source: Droop, Isenman, and Mlalazi (2008).

required. Overreporting is costly and has led in many cases to reporting fatigue and an unwillingness to tackle urgent issues in the provision of information. Prioritization of exactly what is needed is therefore the first step toward better transparency; this should be firmly rooted in accountability procedures at the global, donor, and recipient levels.

The key priorities for improving mutual accountability processes are summarized in table 10-2. The first row shows a need for systematic data at the global level in order for countries and agencies to make strategic choices over their assistance. For example, the issue of country selectivity and the problems that emerge with herd behavior toward some countries have been well documented.[9] In the same vein, analysts looking at global data find some sectors have been underfunded compared to need: agriculture, nutrition, and climate-smart development

9. Marysse, Ansoms, and Cassimon (2007); Levin and Dollar (2005); Rogerson and Steenson (2009).

Table 10-2. *Gaps in Aid Transparency Today*

| Level | Issue | Impact | Action needed |
|---|---|---|---|
| Global | Coverage of new donors | Better strategies | Expand donor coverage |
| | Quality of data | Understanding of global effort | Encourage IATI participation or similar voluntary disclosure of high-quality data |
| Local | Accountability mechanisms | Predictability, allocative efficiency, harmonization | Gather high-quality local aid data on needs, resources, standards and link to budget |
| | Beneficiary feedback | More effective projects | Expand based on new information technology capabilities |
| | Evaluation | Learning on development | Organize more recipient country evaluation offices for all public spending |

are examples.[10] But these conclusions depend on data from an increasingly small subset of total aid. The DAC reports about $122 billion in net ODA for 2008 (DAC donors and multilaterals), but total aid is estimated at over $200 billion, with private aid accounting for at least $52.6 billion and perhaps as much as $75 billion, while emerging economy donors probably contribute over $14 billion.[11] Without better data on these players, identification of underserved recipients or sectors is less credible.

Even among traditional donors there is considerable scope to improve the quality of data. To bolster efforts at transparency, a voluntary group of donors, partner countries, aid experts, and civil society launched the International Aid Transparency Initiative (IATI) at the Accra High-Level Forum. IATI aims to create a common and universally agreed method of sharing aid information among all stakeholders.[12] The Accra agenda committed donors to "publicly disclosing regular, detailed and timely information on volume, allocation and, when available, results of development expenditure to enable more accurate budget, accounting and audit by developing countries." IATI can help donor signatories meet this commitment. As of January 2011, eighteen donor agencies were members of the IATI.

While a valuable endeavor, IATI is not the only way forward; other voluntary standards with similar objectives would be equally useful. What is important

10. Zoellick (1999); World Bank (2010).

11. Private aid estimated by Center for Global Prosperity (2010); emerging economy figure from Park (2010).

12. Details of IATI's role and member information are available on its website (http://aid transparency.net/).

about IATI is the functionality it supports, among them more regular, detailed, and timely data on the volume, allocation, and results of development expenditure and better integration with budgets and accounting systems. What is significant about IATI is that recipient countries are a major driving force behind the design of what improvements in aid quality are most critical to their needs (although only eighteen partner countries are active participants in IATI at present). They are eager to ensure that aid information is published in a way that is compatible with their budgets, that has indicative future projections, and that publicly announces all agreed conditions. With these in place, recipients can more easily "own" the aid programs that other development partners are supporting. Phase 1 of IATI already moves the details of this agenda significantly ahead. What remains is to get the largest donors to join this initiative or develop their own compatible approaches to improving the quality of aid data.

There are also serious issues at the recipient country level. It is clear that mutual accountability must be based on solid information covering, at a minimum, development needs, resources, and minimum standards. Pilot country experiences suggest that, with these in place, significant gains to aid effectiveness emerge from improving the predictability of aid, reallocating resources to geographic and sectoral areas with the greatest priority, and harmonizing the work of donors. Recipient countries are starting to provide independent reviews of partner performance, but experience with these is still limited, implying a critical feedback loop is not operating well.

The local level is also where most learning from aid projects should be done, as development is increasingly seen as an interactive process involving institutions and behaviors that are country and context specific. But that recognition has not resulted in a commensurate increase in beneficiary feedback or formal evaluation in country. The costs of beneficiary feedback have fallen dramatically, and participatory approaches to development design and implementation have been shown to have significant effects in aid projects as well as in private sector commercial applications.

Formal evaluation is largely construed as an opportunity for each aid agency to draw lessons for its own operations (although the number of independent evaluation offices is small), rather than lessons for each recipient country. Evaluations rarely comment on the systemic change associated with a development intervention.

In summary, this assessment suggests two tracks for the aid transparency agenda. First, at the international level, there is a need to expand the scope of coverage to incorporate new development partners (such as Korea, China, and India) and large private NGOs and foundations, as well as to improve the quality of data provided by traditional aid providers. These donors should be encouraged to provide data in a format that is easily downloadable and with sufficient disaggregation that it can be adjusted to permit comparisons with other aid data.[13] Second, at the country level, there is a need for more systematic reporting to recipient governments and their citizens in a way that can harmonize and align aid behind recipient government programs and contribute to broad public debate. In this, spending of aid dollars should be treated in parallel with spending of domestic tax resources—governments need to be accountable to citizens and parliaments for setting spending priorities, executing in the most effective fashion and learning and adapting based on success and failure as measured by the impact on beneficiaries.

## Expanding the Scope of Transparency at the International Level

Transparency at the international level requires information on the aid and other development activities of non-DAC donors and private development actors.

### Non-DAC Donors

Nineteen emerging economy donors already report to the DAC. However this list excludes several of the largest Southern donors, such as China, India, Brazil, and Venezuela. These countries have few incentives to report. Unlike the small new European emerging economy donors, they do not necessarily subscribe to the broader norms of aid effectiveness represented by the DAC. Nor do they feel a need for harmonization with existing donors—non-DAC donors deal directly with recipient governments. Further, their aid is often in the form of turnkey projects and technical assistance rather than in the form of cash.

Such aid is difficult to value on a comparable basis across countries. For example, an Indian doctor may provide the same services as a French doctor, but if both are paid by their respective aid agencies, there could be a difference in "aid" provided by as much as ten to one. These same differences in cost are far less extreme among DAC donors, enabling them to simplify their aid recording in money-equivalent terms without too great a distortion. The point is simply that greater detail needs to be provided on aid as the scope of reporting broadens to include more disparate donors. The detail then allows for a variety of comparisons and studies to be done.

Non-DAC donors are an emerging force in development assistance. Most developing country members of the G20 have their own aid agency or ministerial office. While it is difficult to be precise about the scope of their assistance, one UN-commissioned study estimated net ODA disbursements of around $10 billion in 2006.[14] A more comprehensive assessment of their aid in 2008 puts the

13. For example, most aid data define eligible countries and specific purposes for aid. If individual donors provide only aggregates without identifying the details and using different definitions, the data cannot be comparable with others.

14. Hammad and Morton (2009).

figure at $14.5 billion, and even this is likely to be a significant underestimate.[15] Over time, these figures are likely to grow. For example, if the G20 developing country members alone were to disburse just 0.15 percent of their GDP in aid in 2015, they could account for $26 billion (in constant 2007 terms). In other words, even if non-DAC donors are relatively minor in overall aid today, they are likely to be a very significant share of total aid in the medium term. Once they start to operate at scale, the pressure on non-DAC donors to reveal more information on their development activities will become stronger. It is in their interests to develop approaches for providing data now, rather than being forced into it in an unprepared way in the near future.

Lesson: Obtaining better data on non-DAC donors must be a priority for the transparency of the overall aid system. Non-DAC donors should be encouraged to outline their plans for release of aid information at or before the Busan High-Level Forum.

## Private Development Actors

Little is known about the aggregate volumes of private aid, although the amounts are believed to be substantial. It is estimated that private development assistance (PDA) from fourteen developed countries totaled $52.6 billion in 2008.[16] The U.S. portion of PDA, $37.3 billion (71 percent of the identified total), is composed of flows from diverse groups, including NGOs, foundations, religious organizations, corporations, universities, and individuals. Since the above estimates are for only fourteen countries, global PDA is even higher. PDA is most visible in response to humanitarian and emergency crises. In the aftermath of the Haiti earthquake, it is estimated that more than half of American families contributed to the relief effort. But detailed work on U.S. NGOs suggests that only about one-third of their programs are for humanitarian work. Another 8 percent is diverted into overhead and administrative expenses, leaving about 56 percent for actual development purposes.

NGOs have decades-long experience with assessments of projects and foundations routinely monitor the impact of their grants. This field-based knowledge is the basis for considerable NGO advocacy, but many of the data are unpublished, hard to aggregate, and based on internal self-reporting rather than on independent studies and formal evaluations meeting professional standards.

During the reconstruction effort in Aceh after the tsunami of 2004, all actors, including NGOs, were asked to provide information on their activities to the local relief and reconstruction agency (BRR). The detailed concept notes that were requested were specific, generating local standardization of reported data. A similar system is being implemented in Haiti. Information on existing and future

---

15. Park (2010); *The Economist,* July 15, 2010, estimates Brazilian ODA at $1.2 billion in 2008, compared to $437 million officially reported by Brazil to the DAC for 2007.

16. Center for Global Prosperity (2010).

planned projects by all actors including NGOs and businesses is supposed to be submitted to the Interim Haiti Reconstruction Commission. However, recent reports suggest that, looking back over the last six months, the lack of transparency by relief groups has caused much of the coordination problems that continue to plague the response. Most NGOs appealed to emotion and positive anecdotal accounts to bolster fund-raising rather than reporting facts on the progress of actual activities.[17]

The reality is that there are few incentives for NGOs, foundations, or private corporations to provide systematic data on their operations. Costs of data provision are perceived to be high and to add to administrative overhead, while benefits are seen as small. When PDA was small and scattered, overlap with others and the need for coordination was low. It is only now that PDA has swelled to non-marginal amounts that more systematic information is required.

A start is being made but on a voluntary basis. For example, InterAction, an umbrella organization of U.S. NGOs and foundations, has started mapping its members' projects in Haiti and, more broadly, its members' projects on food security to show the benefits that can come from overarching geographic and sectoral perspectives. But it is unclear if this leadership-by-example model will be sufficiently powerful to overcome the collective action and incentive problems facing the PDA community.

Lesson: The PDA community has the size and the field experiences to play a more constructive role in the global aid architecture. But it cannot do this without shouldering at least a minimum responsibility for providing transparent information about its activities. A plan that would give the PDA community greater voice in the global aid architecture (perhaps representation in the DAC ministerial and high-level forums) in return for greater transparency might provide the incentive to more participation between private and official development assistance. The target should be to document most PDA, at least in terms of broad aggregates, by the time of the Busan High-Level Forum and to reach agreement on reporting standards among the largest providers of PDA.

*Improve Data Quality*

Together, IATI members accounted for just over half of total ODA in 2008, or less than one-third of all aid. Several major ODA donors, including the United States, France, and Japan are not members. Only one private foundation is a member. It is critical to ensure that the scope of reporting on aid is broadened to include more donors—preferably all. Such reporting does not need to happen through joining IATI itself and adopting all its standards for sharing information. Some donors may prefer to achieve a similar functional equivalent by

---

17. Andrew C. Revkin, "Report Faults Haiti Aid Groups on Openness," *New York Times,* July 12, 2010.

reporting in other ways or directly to recipient countries rather than to central-ized, global databases like the CRS. The key is to have sufficient information available to build a better process of mutual accountability on aid and develop-ment results.

Lesson: A high-level push, perhaps through the G20, would be desirable to have all major advanced country donors subscribe to IATI or adopt functionally equivalent standards and to implement transparency improvements before the Busan High-Level Forum.

## Expanding Reporting at the National Government Level: New Tools

Tracking development finance data at the recipient country level consists of three basic steps. These are categorized into data in, data management, and data out (figure 10-1). There are issues with each step in the current setup. First, some data are simply not collected (a data-in problem). Feedback from poor people in devel-oping countries is an example. Collecting information on control groups that did not receive aid in order to isolate the impact of a specific aid intervention is another example. This kind of baseline data is crucial for evaluation but is often an after thought in aid projects. Here, the problems lie in cost (data gathering can be expensive) and in agency incentives and culture.

Second, some data are available but need to be reformatted to align with inter-national standards and be published in ways that permit easy merging of the information into a global database (a data management problem). An example might be disbursement data from some large aid agencies that have developed dif-ferent purpose codes for their own internal use. Here the problems are harmo-nization of standards and the transition costs of moving to a new system. In fact, work on transparency suggests that donors do actually publish or make available large amounts of information but not in a standardized form, making it hard to access and to compare with similar information across different agencies.

Third, some data are collected by agencies but not published (a data-out prob-lem). Examples of this include significant information from private aid donors and emerging economy donors like China. Official DAC donors do not ade-quately report on internal projections of aid or within fiscal-year disbursements, for example. Here the problem is political—an unwillingness to lose control over information and a fear of being held accountable. Table 10-3 demonstrates the complexity of a standardized database and suggests why existing databases at recipient country levels have been hampered by persistent poor data quality.

What is needed is a single agency in each partner country with authority and control over all the issues identified as important to a database. Typically, partner country views are ignored. For example, the Paris Declaration monitoring survey

Figure 10-1. *Key Considerations, Data Management and Information Process*

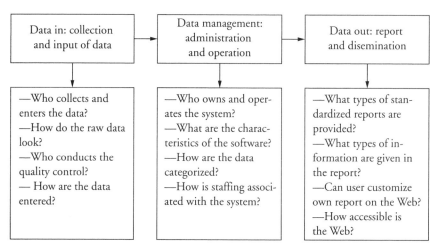

Source: Agustina and Zaki (2010).

asks recipient governments only three questions about aid quality, compared to nineteen questions asked of donors.[18]

Adequate attention also needs to be paid to the demand for information. The systemic structures of mutual accountability for aid, within which transparent information is used, are still evolving. Considerable focus has been placed on developing country accountabilities, and a variety of global information bases now track and compare developing country outcomes on such things as revenue transparency, governance, ease of doing business, and development-friendly policies. These data are linked directly or indirectly to the provision of aid and other development resources, creating an incentive system for improvement. But comparable indexes tracking donor performance on aid projects are lacking.[19] Hence, donors have little incentive to provide high-quality aid information, nor do they systematically seek feedback from aid recipients (either countries or actual project beneficiaries).

At the same time, there has been an explosion of tools to improve transparency if the system generates adequate demand for their adoption. These tools range from recipients' in-country databases on aid flows to data systems based on mobile telephony and georeferencing and geomapping software. The availability of new tools offers practical options for systemic change that would otherwise have been merely theoretical.

18. OECD (2008, pp. 140–41).
19. Birdsall and Kharas (2010) is a recent attempt at constructing indexes of donor aid performance.

*Recipient Country Databases*

Today, over thirty developing countries have established local databases on aid. Several in-country aid management databases exist, most notably the aid management platform (AMP) and the development assistance database (DAD). The AMP platform uses the AiDA (accessible information on development activities) standard and relies on data-harvesting techniques. The recipient country database is automatically linked to the OECD/CRS database and several other international donor databases, such as those of the World Bank and the U.K. Department for International Development (DFID). With implementation of IATI, the power of the AMP will expand.

On the other hand, DAD relies on in-country reporting mechanisms by aid agencies. The advantage of the DAD approach is that data are based on what is actually happening in the field and so, in theory, should be more reliable. The DAD can also be linked more closely to recipient-country budget classifications. Because it is web based, the DAD is accessible to the public at large. However, the disadvantage of this approach is that sectoral classifications may vary among countries, so discrepancies may appear between the data at the country level and data reported at the aggregate level. The DAD is also complicated with requests for data covering many fields, and questions have arisen as to the reliability of the data in the system. Without credibility, development partners have become weary of supplying information to the DAD, reducing effectiveness still further.

The poor quality of information in local databases can be a serious problem. If one of the main uses of aid data is to feed into donor strategies and help them identify gaps between needs and resources, then data accuracy is important. An example of differences in reporting from Pakistan's DAD and the same donor's reporting to the CRS is shown in table 10-3. The first row shows that DFID reported a disbursement of $36.8 million in 2006 in its CRS submission but that it informed the Pakistanis that it has disbursed $69.9 million. The second row shows that local DFID officials reported support for tax administration reform but that the CRS had no record of such a project. The last two rows show a similar issue for the World Bank support of the NWFP Development Policy Credit and for ADB's Private Participation in Infrastructure project. Other rows show discrepancies either in commitment or disbursement data.[20]

This single example shows that discrepancies arise for many donors and many types of information. The pattern is repeated over and over again. When assessing the performance of development partners, the government of Mozambique felt obliged to have two indicators of transparency: whether information was delivered to the government and whether government standards for the full disclosure of the

20. These examples should not be taken as an indication that the agencies are less transparent than others. In fact, they score in the middle of the pack on transparency indicators. Ibid.

Table 10-3. *Discrepancies between Pakistan's Development Assistance Database (DAD) and OECD's Creditor Reporting System (CRS), 2006*
U.S. $ billion

| Donor | Project title | Commitment | | Disbursement | |
|-------|---------------|------|-----|------|-----|
| | | DAD | CRS | DAD | CRS |
| DFID | Poverty Reduction Budget Support, 2005–06 to 2007–08 | 139.8 | 110.4 | 69.9 | 36.8 |
| DFID | Tax Administration Reform Project | 21.7 | . . .[a] | 4.3 | . . .[a] |
| Netherlands | Water, Environment, and Sanitation Response in earthquake-affected areas | 14.0 | 14.5 | 14 | 5.8 |
| Australia | Pakistan Earthquake ADB Trust Fund | 14.0 | 8.05 | 7.9 | 8.05 |
| ADB | Private Participation in Infrastructure Program | 400 | . . .[a] | 200 | . . .[a] |
| World Bank | NWFP Development Policy Credit | 90 | . . .[a] | 93.04 | . . .[a] |

Source: Agustina and Zaki (2010).
a. No commitment reported to the CRS.

portfolio were met by the donor. The World Bank, Belgium, Portugal, and Canada were named as problem donors with respect to transparency in Mozambique.

Much of the time recipient governments simply do not know what donors are doing in their country. For example, an official at the Ministry of Finance in Afghanistan, when interviewed by Oxfam America, said that since 2001 the United States had pledged $32 billion in aid but that less than 20 percent ($6 billion) had been recorded in the government databases.[21] When the Nigerian Planning Commission reviewed the volume and quality of an estimated $6 billion of ODA between 1999 and 2007, it found many donors uncooperative and only USAID and the EU (with a delay of three months) were able to provide the requested information on what they had spent and where. The report comments that the Chinese were asked to provide information but does not say whether any response was forthcoming.[22]

The challenges of local database management are several. The systems must be able to provide reports and deal with multiple priorities, which needs an institutional capacity to operate and sustain them. For example, in the case of the Recovery Aceh Nias database, the government priority was to identify geographical gaps between needs and resources, while donors were more concerned about

21. Oxfam America (2010, p. 7).
22. Steven (2010).

tracking aggregate financial flows. Local databases need an explicit methodology for data entry and reporting covering sector classification, separation of data into type of aid, treatment of multipurpose projects, double counting, needs assessments, archives for analyzing trends, and auditability. Links with domestic budgets are also important to enhance accountability and coordination.

Without good data on what donors are doing, few developing countries have a robust way of holding donors accountable. A few countries, including Mozambique, Ghana, Tanzania, and Zambia, have experimented with reviews of development partners, with some success at improving aid effectiveness, but the power imbalance between donors and recipients is so large that there are natural limits on what can be achieved in these reviews. Citizen reviews, however, are less constrained, and if information is accessible to them, then there is more potential for forceful advocacy. That puts a premium on the quality of local databases.

Lesson: Few local databases on aid provide accurate data. Several platforms exist, creating difficulties with integration into international databases. Without better local databases, aid recipient countries cannot hold donors accountable. A standardized format for local databases should be developed, perhaps through IATI, by the time of the Busan High-Level Forum, and major donors should commit to improving local databases with technical, financial, and informational support.

### Georeferencing

One exciting new tool is georeferencing, or geomapping. Examples of aid projects whose location can and should be coded include physical infrastructure like roads, bridges, schools, and clinics as well as locations where safety net programs like cash transfers or food distribution are active. From being a specialized tool, geomapping has become more readily available thanks to advances in technology. This technology is being extensively used in the Haiti reconstruction effort. A free and public mapping software, GeoCommons, was made available to allow users to visualize the geographic distribution of aid data. With its open architecture, data from different donors can be readily combined to compile collaborative maps.

During the January 2010 earthquake in Haiti, FortiusOne (the developer of GeoCommons) partnered with Google and used its satellite imaging capabilities to piece together an evolving image of what Haiti and its capital city, Port-au-Prince, would look like after being rocked by the magnitude 7.0 earthquake. The maps were able to overlay earthquake zones, building collapses, wrecks, shelters, hospitals, and development projects. Relief workers were also able to see any obstacles that might inhibit their progress. Using the interactive platform, any NGO was able to input information to be shared by everyone, giving real-time updates on relief progress. Many agencies have indeed used the system, including InterAction, the Crisis Project, Direct Relief International, World Vision, the Climate Project, SRI International, National Alliance to End Homelessness, American Rivers, Sierra Club, United Nations Environmental Program, CARE, and UNICEF.

The Haiti example demonstrates something that development workers have long known. Development assistance is most effective when it fills a gap between needs and resources. Identifying these gaps at the national level is only part of the story. Given the significant inequality in the spatial provision of public services in most developing countries, it is essential to drill down to local areas to identify need. Indeed, there is a growing body of data that is representative at the subnational level: maps showing poverty, health indicators, transport networks, population and demographic distributions, and other vital economic characteristics can be overlaid with maps showing development projects if the latter are georeferenced. Unfortunately, most existing development projects do not have geographic coordinates listed. One study suggests that at least 25 percent of development projects have enough information to be geocoded.[23]

Geocoding is a first step toward more engagement of communities and local recipients in providing feedback on development projects in their area, and because it identifies the totality of projects it can be used to redirect resources. For example, the geocoding in the Recovery Aceh Nias database allowed the Reconstruction Agency for Aceh and Nias to identify where donors were planning on locating projects and to compare that with its needs assessment (see figure 10-2). The financing-to-needs ratio was calculated in a number of provinces, and resources were reallocated accordingly to even out the gaps. As another example, UNICEF has built its strategy in Brazil based on targets at the municipality and facility levels because of the significant intrastate inequality in outcomes it identified.[24]

Lesson: The georeferencing of development projects allows for integration of development resources with development needs obtained from other sources. Minimizing the gap between needs and resources is vital for achieving allocative efficiency in development. Maps showing the location of development assistance should be developed for the Busan High-Level Forum.

### Expanding and Disseminating Evaluation Lessons and Feedback Loops

Both private and official development communities would benefit from more systematic attention to learning from their experiences. The PDA community offers new approaches, long-term engagement within countries, links with communities and subnational government levels, and new forms of partnerships.[25] The ODA community can help scale up and provide links with state service providers. Both typically pass through phases from actually delivering services in countries

23. Aidinfo.org (2010).
24. UNICEF (2009).
25. Many INGOs routinely plan to spend PDA as ten-plus-year investments into a particular program area or civil society organization. Worthington (2010).

Figure 10-2. *Aceh: Financing-to-Needs Ratio Post-Tsunami, Based on Geocoding of Projects*

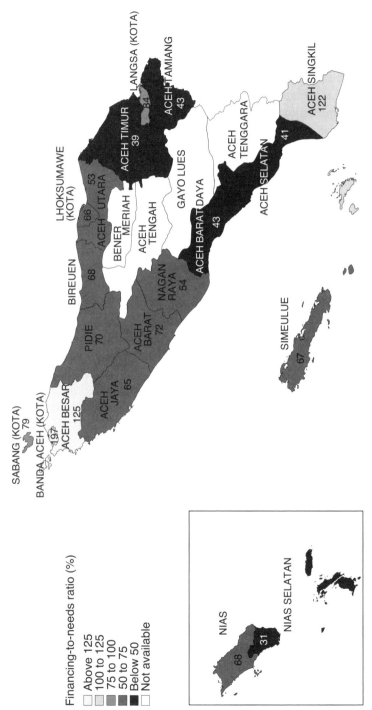

Financing-to-needs ratio (%)

Above 125
100 to 125
75 to 100
50 to 75
Below 50
Not available

with the least capacity to being catalytic agents in countries where capacity is stronger. But rigorous evaluations and assessments of the most effective approaches along this chain are in short supply.

One indicator of the limited state of shared knowledge and agreement on effective interventions is that the views of academic experts and development practitioners appear to vary widely. The Copenhagen Consensus of 2008 reflects the judgments of eight expert economists (five of whom are Nobel Laureates) on the most cost-effective development solutions. Five of the top ten interventions are in the field of malnutrition. One would imagine that this would therefore be a high priority for development practitioners. Yet Robert Zoellick, president of the World Bank, has called nutrition "the forgotten MDG."[26] ODA for nutrition has averaged only $300 million a year, according to the OECD—less than 0.3 percent of all ODA.

The same pattern of differing views on development priorities is observed at local levels. There, beneficiary feedback is essential (box 10-1). The ability to provide real-time information on projects can result in better planning, better funding, and better implementation. And when beneficiaries see that action follows from transparency, the demand for and supply of good feedback goes up.

Almost all evaluation is done in donor agencies, with the idea that lessons should be drawn by that agency to improve its work. But development outcomes are highly context and country specific. Evaluation is as much a challenge for national governments in developing countries as for the partnering aid organizations. In fact, in some countries there appears to be a significant difference between the findings of beneficiary assessments and donor evaluations.[27] The largest gap in the current evaluation structure is the limited number of beneficiary assessments.

That is starting to change, but slowly. Following the success of Mexico's introduction of mandatory evaluations for all social programs, other countries have started to follow suit. India is establishing a new independent evaluation office, catalyzed by the Planning Ministry, and taking advantage of its sophisticated IT sector to provide real time data to improve the monitoring and evaluation of public services. A few standards can help ensure good evaluations, such as having a registry so unpleasant findings cannot be swept under the rug, publication of all evaluations, transparency of evaluation methods and data replicability, counterfactual data and possible conflict of interest of evaluators.

Rigorous evaluation is a necessary component of mutual accountability and should be embraced by all development partners. Evaluation by recipient countries is of high importance. An International Development Evaluation Initiative

26. Ross (2010).
27. Ezra Suruma, former minister of finance, Uganda, conversation with author.

Box 10-1. *How Feedback Can Improve Aid Effectiveness*

One of the most promising aspects of increased transparency is the ability to create feedback loops. Experiments are under way to use new technologies and approaches to find out what communities care most about—before aid projects are even designed—and to seek their input during project implementation.

In one recent experiment in Kenya, the private aid marketplace GlobalGiving asked community members to tell stories about the development issues that were most important to them. Only one out of sixty-five local and foreign civil society organization leaders working in the area were able to accurately guess all of the top concerns of the community, and on average these leaders guessed only three of the top six community concerns.

Another experiment tried to find out how well a development project was working by asking the community in real time for honest feedback. For example, youth belonging to a Kenyan sports organization suspected that its leader was stealing from them, but they became the driving force for transparency *only* when they were convinced that GlobalGiving would do something about it. The result was the dissolution of the old organization and the birth of an alternate organization.

These are just two examples of how transparency initiatives can catalyze better development. Technology and a real commitment to address feedback from stakeholders are transforming how projects are implemented.

Source: Dennis Whittle, CEO of GlobalGiving.

should be launched at the Busan HLF4, to provide assistance in undertaking specific evaluations and building evaluation units in aid recipient countries.

## Costs and Benefits of Transparency

If transparency is so important, why are there so many data gaps? One answer is that provision of data is a classic collective action problem. The benefits of a good information system are multiplied if everyone contributes. But if any one agency improves its data, while others do not, then that agency will have incurred potentially substantial costs while not gaining any benefits in terms of a better understanding of the system as a whole.[28]

A second answer is that transparency requires timely and useful information. There are many costly examples of information being requested for information's sake, leading to waste, duplication, and reporting fatigue. For example, in the case of Aceh post-tsunami, Claude de Ville de Goyet and Lezlie Moriniere found that a needs assessment conducted by the UN Disaster Assessment and Coordination

28. This is already happening to some degree. Funders of data collection, such as the Gates Foundation, are questioning the value added from improved transparency and have shifted strategies away from aid tracking efforts.

office failed to affect decisions, largely because of late delivery, unsatisfactory methodologies, and incentives to justify existing programs.[29] Other reports contained faulty baseline information, creating confusion.[30]

A third answer is that transparency permits outside stakeholders to become more involved and vocal about agency accountability. For aid agency managers, transparency could potentially reduce flexibility and expose agency shortcomings. Meanwhile, the benefits largely accrue to others, not to the agency itself. Top leadership is needed to change the culture and internal incentives in favor of transparency.

Transparency therefore needs to be managed carefully to be provided in standardized, broadly accepted formats with an understanding of how the information will be used. Under these conditions, it can be highly beneficial.

One study calculates the costs and benefits of implementing the IATI recommendations and finds that the costs are largely one-off, relating to standards, information technology, training, and management.[31] For the eighteen IATI signatories, the costs are estimated at $6 million. Globally, this would imply up-front costs of around $10 million to $15 million. Of course, if aid data are provided at the recipient level, as recommended above, there would be incremental costs for data maintenance that might require support from donors.

In contrast, the benefits of implementing IATI are far more substantial, amounting to billions of dollars annually (over $11 billion by some estimates).[32] These can be divided into efficiency savings and effectiveness gains. Efficiency savings arise from the fact that at present information requests are frequent and often have to be manually accommodated, at high cost. Donor agencies employ around 350 full-time staff at a country level just to meet ad hoc country requests. Standardizing and streamlining information could save $7 million annually just by eliminating duplicative reporting.

In addition to the pure savings described in the previous paragraph, there are numerous examples of effectiveness gains attributable to increased transparency. Transparency has been shown to improve service delivery. For example, community-based monitoring was shown to be effective in raising the quality of health services provided by rural health clinics in Uganda.[33] Large improvements in utilization of clinic services, in weight-for-age measures, and in large declines (up to a third) in under-five mortality were recorded just by having better engagement between the service provider and the community. A series of meetings and published report cards led to joint agreement on actions to be taken to improve the clinic's operations. However, a follow-up study by the same researchers also reveals

---

29. De Ville de Goyet and Moriniere (2006), p. 11.
30. Masyrafah and McKeon (2008).
31. Collin and others (2009).
32. Aidinfo.org (2009).
33. Björkman and Svensson (2009).

that the gains in effectiveness were lower in ethnically heterogeneous communities, presumably because of a lower level of trust and a lack of agreement on needed actions (and trust in the credibility of the data) in these communities.

Previous studies have shown that traceability of funds can reduce the opportunities for diversion. The now-famous public expenditure tracking surveys (PETS) of education grants in Uganda showed that the diversion of funds was reduced from 80 percent to 20 percent over a decade. But this is only partly due to the provision of better information. It is also due to the systemic improvements in public expenditure management in Uganda during this period. PETS and civil society monitoring of resources have had more limited impact in other cases. Overall, transparency may be a necessary, but not sufficient, condition for better expenditure controls. Broad public debate and citizen engagement in strategies and follow-up actions are also needed.[34]

Forward-looking predictability of aid is critical for it to be effectively used. Some studies have found that aid is often saved or used for paying down domestic debt rather than for productive investment or for delivery of public services, because too often they simply fail to materialize. A Kenyan finance minister is quoted as saying, "Consistent with our financial independence strategy, we have not factored in uncommitted budget support."[35] In other words, vague pledges of aid are less useful than transparent commitments.

Benefits can also accrue to donor countries. ODA is a voluntary transfer that, in democracies, ultimately depends on the support of donor country taxpayers. In theory, ODA should be aligned with constituent preferences through a political economy process. Aid transparency allows taxpayers to understand how their taxes are being used and thus to become more engaged in and supportive of aid. A 1995 survey conducted by PIPA (Program on International Policy Attitudes) found that Americans on average overestimate by as much as fifteen times the amount their government spends on foreign aid.[36] When asked the ideal amount that the government should spend on aid, the median response was five times actual government spending. Follow-up surveys in 2001 and 2010 found no change in the public's extreme overestimation of the amount of the federal budget that goes to foreign aid.[37]

As another example, there is a significant disconnect between taxpayer preferences and actual aid allocation channels. A strong majority of the U.S. public prefers to give aid through multilateral institutions rather than bilaterally, but the U.S. share of aid going through multilateral institutions fell to 11 percent in

---

34. Sundet (2008, p. 8).

35. Mwega (2009).

36. PIPA (1995). The *Washington Post* conducted a follow-up survey in 1996, and the attitudes had not changed much. In a 1997 PEW poll, 63 percent of the respondents thought that the United States spent more on foreign aid than on Medicare.

37. PIPA (2001, 2010).

2008, half the level of a decade before (and one-third the level of other major donor countries). These examples suggest that there is a wellspring of public support for development assistance in the United States that has not been fully tapped because of the lack of clear communication of the magnitude of official aid and the channels through which it is provided.

The new USAID administrator, Rajiv Shah, articulated this vision on May 5, 2010:

> I am convinced if we can be the most transparent development agency in the world that the American people will accelerate their support of our work. . . . We need to make this work much more transparent. We need to have much more rigorous evaluation systems. We need to invest more in collecting real baseline data and understanding counterfactuals because much of our current M&E portfolio, frankly, is retrospective storytelling as opposed to rigorous analysis.[38]

Greater transparency will also foster better coordination between agencies within a donor country. In several countries, aid is provided through multiple agencies, often with overlapping responsibilities. Without transparency, there is little clarity in the United States on the links between foreign assistance objectives, legislation, presidential initiatives, and foreign assistance organizations.[39] With benefits accruing to all major stakeholders—recipient governments, recipient civil society, donor governments, and donor civil society—the demand for a major push on transparency is both clear and urgent. The question has shifted from if there should be greater focus on transparency to what priority should be given to each improvement on the long list being sought.

## Conclusion

Transparency in aid data is a priority—both an end in itself, as an ethical use of public money and private donations, and an instrument for achieving better development outcomes. The ability to trace aid from the money flow to results, evaluation, and learning can improve aid effectiveness at low cost. This does not require full standardization, nor perfection, but it does require acceptance by donors of their responsibility to provide basic information on their activities. New IT tools have reduced the cost for doing this. Official donors have long pledged to increase the transparency of their aid, a commitment that was reiterated in Accra.

But while donors agree on the principle of transparency, they have been slow to move in practice. The supply-side route of urging donors to improve transparency, while useful, is proving to be slow. Country ownership and mutual

38. See www.usglc.org/USGLCdocs/Shah%20Transcript%205%275%2710.pdf.
39. Brainard (2007).

accountability provide an impetus for greater demand for transparency, if taken seriously, and can change the incentives of donors. At present there are strong incentives not to report bad outcomes and, indeed, to report minimally to avoid the risk of unfavorable comparisons. That is changing as improved accountability structures raise demand for better data. For instance, parliamentarians and civil society are demanding more transparency from their governments, both those providing and those receiving aid. Organizations like Philanthropedia provide comparative data on charities to allow private donors to make more informed choices. Finally, independent agencies like the International Initiative for Impact Evaluation provide evaluations across a number of donor projects. These forces need to be strengthened.

While improved transparency standards have now been developed through the IATI, many donors have yet to sign up. They should either do so or develop appropriate alternatives. A high priority is to launch a campaign to get all DAC donors and multilateral agencies to provide, at a minimum, better aid data functionality either through becoming IATI signatories or by other means.

It is likely that non-DAC donors and PDA will remain outside the detailed data framework proposed by IATI for the present. These donors are of sufficient scale that they need to take responsibility for providing information in a fashion that meets their own needs but that also responds to the global nature of transparency, which is a public good. Defining transparency, while allowing flexibility for the manner in which data are made available as long as they are accessible and sufficiently fine grained to be merged with global data sets, is the next step. At the same time, incentives and political commitment may be needed to get action, if the experience of DAC donors is any guide. Forums like the G20 and the Busan High-Level Forum can be useful for mobilizing this political support.

In many ways, the call for aid transparency is a handmaiden of the call for greater ownership by recipients. The voices of aid beneficiaries are still muted. Haiti's prime minister, Jean-Max Bellerive, says the country is committed to transparency.

> We have a government that wants to give the service that the population is entitled to . . . [We] have to prove to all the people we are working with that we have transparency . . . that we are working towards progress, really, and that everybody [understands] what we are going to do in the short- [and] mid-term, and that we are putting in place a system for accountability and evaluation. . . . So the key word is transparency, and we are willing to do that.[40]

Unfortunately such commitments to transparency are easier said than done. Despite many efforts to build local databases, few provide adequate information.

---

40. NPR, "Prime Minister: Haiti Committed to Transparency," April 1, 2010 (www.npr.org/templates/story/story.php?storyId=125463818).

There is little donor attention to these efforts, and individual countries are developing their own customized versions.[41] These customized databases are not always compatible with global databases, and data accuracy is a concern. They may also be inaccessible to local civil society and be in a form that does not permit a match with geographical needs assessments.

Finally, it is worth remembering that transparency is a good with significant positive externalities and increasing returns to scale. The more provided, the greater the benefits. As information becomes more comprehensive, more timely and fine-grained, it becomes more valuable. Benefits are dispersed among many stakeholders in development, but costs are concentrated largely in the providers of development assistance. While these conditions lead to an underinvestment in transparency, they also suggest that the payoff from increased focus on transparency would be significant: the benefit/cost ratio would appear to be enormous.

Because of the externalities associated with provision of information, the full benefits of transparency will only be realized if progress is made on multiple fronts. Therefore, in addition to advocating for continued progress of the IATI and other such voluntary data transparency programs, the following four actionable items are recommended for the Busan High-Level Forum:

—Non-DAC donors should be encouraged to outline their plans for release of aid information at or before the forum.

—A target should be set to document most PDA, at least in terms of broad aggregates, by the time of the forum and to reach agreement on reporting standards among the largest providers of PDA. In return, representatives of civil society would be fully consulted in the forum's outcome document and would be invited as partners to major events at which aid and development policy is discussed. This bargain would change incentives for PDA organizations.

—A standardized format for local databases should be developed, perhaps through IATI, by the time of the forum, and major donors should commit to improving local databases with technical, financial, and informational support. These databases should be linked to budgets and, to the extent possible, geocoded so as to permit overlays with needs assessments.

—An international development evaluation initiative should be launched at the forum to build evaluation capabilities in aid recipient countries, help inform public debates on aid effectiveness, and systematically collect beneficiary feedback.

## References

Agustina, Cut Dian, and Ahmad Fahmi Zaki. 2010. "Tracking the Money." In *Delivering Aid Differently: Lessons from the Field,* edited by Wolfgang Fengler and Homi Kharas. Brookings.

41. Cambodia and Bulgaria have locally developed customized aid databases.

Aidinfo.org. 2010. "Show Me the Money: IATI and Aid Traceability." Briefing paper, March.
————. 2009. "The Costs and Benefits of Aid Transparency."
Birdsall, Nancy, and Homi Kharas. 2010. "Quality of Official Development Assistance Assessment." Center for Global Development.
Björkman, Martina, and Jakob Svensson. 2009, "Power to the People: Evidence from a Randomized Field Experiment on Community-Based Monitoring in Uganda." *Quarterly Journal of Economics* 124, no. 2: 735–69.
Brainard, Lael, ed. 2007. *Security by Other Means*. Brookings and Center for Strategic and International Studies.
Center for Global Prosperity. 2010. "Index of Global Philanthropy and Remittances."
Collin, Mathew, and others. 2009. "The Costs and Benefits of Aid Transparency" (http://aid info.org/files/aidinfo-Costs-and-Benefits-October-2009.pdf).
De Ville de Goyet, Claude, and Lezlie C. Moriniere. 2006. "The Role of Needs Assessment in the Tsunami Response." Tsunami Evaluation Coalition (http://www.alnap.org/pool/files/ needs-assessment-final-report.pdf).
Droop, James, Paul Isenman, and Baki Mlalazi. 2008. "Mutual Accountability in Aid Effectiveness: International-Level Mechanisms." Briefing Note 2008-03. Oxford Policy Management.
Hammad, Lama, and Bill Morton. 2009. "Non-DAC Donors and Reform of the International Aid Architecture" (www.nsi-ins.ca/english/pdf/Non-DAC%20donors%20&%20aid%20 architecture.pdf).
Levin, V., and David Dollar. 2005. "The Forgotten States: Aid Volumes and Volatility in Difficult Partnership Countries (1992–2002)." Paper prepared for DAC Learning and Advisory Process on Difficult Partnerships (http://siteresources.worldbank.org/INTLICUSSPANISH/ Resources/34687926.pdf).
Majone, Giandomenico. 1997. "The New European Agencies: Regulation by Information." *Journal of European Public Policy* 4, no. 2: 262–75.
Marysse, Stefaan, An Ansoms, and Danny Cassimon. 2007. "The Aid 'Darlings' and 'Orphans' of the Great Lakes Region in Africa." *European Journal of Development Research* 19, no. 3: 433–58.
Masyrafah, Harry, and Jock McKeon. 2008. "Post-Tsunami Aid Effectiveness in Aceh Proliferation and Coordination in Reconstruction." Working Paper 6. Wolfensohn Center for Development, Brookings.
Moon, Samuel, and Tim Williamson. 2010. "Greater Aid Transparency: Crucial for Aid Effectiveness." Project Briefing 35. Overseas Development Institute.
Mwega, Francis M. 2009. "A Case Study of Aid Effectiveness in Kenya: Volatility and Fragmentation of Foreign Aid, with a Focus on Health." Working Paper 8. Wolfensohn Center for Development, Brookings.
OECD. 2008. *Survey on Monitoring the Paris Declaration*.
Oxfam America. 2010. "Information: Let Countries Know What Donors Are Doing" (www.ox famamerica.org/publications/information-let-countries-know-what-donors-are-doing).
Park, Kang-ho. 2010. "Korea's Role in Global Development." *Northeast Asia Commentary* 36. Brookings.
PIPA (Program on International Policy Attitudes). 2001. *Survey: Americans on Foreign Aid and World Hunger*.
————. 1995. *Survey: Americans on Foreign Aid and World Hunger*.
Rogerson, Andrew, and Suzanne Steensen. 2009. "Aid Orphans: Whose Responsibility?" OECD Development Co-operation Directorate.
Ross, Julia. 2010. "Scaling Up Nutrition: Remembering the 'Forgotten MDG'" (http://blogs. worldbank.org/meetings/scaling-up-nutrition-remembering-the-forgotten-mdg).

Steven, David. 2010. "Nigeria: Do Donors Know What They're Spending?" (www.globaldash
    board.org/2010/03/19/nigeria-donors-spending).
Sundet, Geir. 2008. "Following the Money: Do Public Expenditure Tracking Surveys Matter?"
    U4 Issue 2008:8 (www.cmi.no/publications/file/3195-following-the-money.pdf).
UNICEF. 2009. "The State of Children and Adolescents in Brazil."
World Bank. 2010. *World Development Report.*
Worthington, Sam. 2010. "The Relationship between Official Development Assistance and
    Private Development Assistance." Policy brief. Brookings–Blum Roundtable on Develop-
    ment Assistance Reform in the Twenty-First Century.
Zoellick, R. 1999. "Congress and the Making of US Foreign Policy." *Survival* 41, no. 4: 20–41.

# 11

## Promoting South-South Cooperation through Knowledge Exchange

HYUNJOO RHEE

Over the last decade, South-South cooperation in development assistance (SSC) has increased markedly. Although it has a long history, having emerged as a result of the decolonization movement in the 1950s and 1960s, South-South cooperation has expanded recently thanks to the rapid industrialization of key countries in the 1990s, the subsequent increase in South-South trade, and the progressive emergence of the South's private sector. Today SSC is viewed as an emerging, yet powerful, game changer in global politics, trade, commerce, and development assistance.

The role of South-South cooperation in development has two aspects. The first aspect focuses on the volume of development financing and mostly involves large middle-income or upper-income donors, which are capable of providing sizable assistance. The BRICs (Brazil, Russia, India, and China) and other dynamic, emerging economies—often referred to as new development partners— are the key players. Their contributions outweigh a considerable number of traditional donors in terms of scale. Mostly provided in the form of large-scale infrastructure projects, their contributions make up most of the global volume of SSC, amounting to $15 billion today and growing by at least 7 percent a year (see chapter 2, this volume).

Another aspect of SSC lies in the exchange of knowledge and practical experiences as an effective means of capacity development. The famous case of Bangladesh spreading microfinance initiatives throughout the world has proven that knowledge, even from a least-developed country, can be highly influential. The historical connotation of development assistance as a flow of resources streaming exclusively from rich Northern countries to poor Southern countries is not relevant for knowledge exchange, which blurs the traditional distinctions separating aid providers from recipients. SSC knowledge exchange encompasses not only big, emerging donors but also the resource-deprived and poverty-stricken countries that constitute most of the global South and that would never have been thought of as development providers in traditional frameworks. As a concept, SSC therefore democratizes participation in development cooperation. Small-scale technical cooperation is the main modality.

This chapter focuses on this second aspect of South-South cooperation: knowledge exchange and innovations in aid modalities (box 11-1). What is the impact of these innovations on the evolving global aid system today? And what are the resulting challenges and issues? Because of limited information, the methodology used here is to review existing case studies and experiences, complemented by an in-depth assessment of how one poor country, Lao PDR, has used SSC to deepen its development.

## Assessing the Impacts of SSC: Unpacking the Current State of Play

The essence of South-South knowledge exchange is its diversity across a large number of developing countries and the understanding that many countries can contribute to capacity development. Previously, technical cooperation was mostly understood as a vertical transfer of skills from the developed to the developing world, on the basis of assumptions that developing countries do not have enough technology and knowledge to push forward development agendas. An "injection" or "transfer" of know-how from the developed world, therefore, was a suitable approach.[1] The notion of development simply meant a process in which developing countries mimicked the developed world.

Then in the 1990s, as questions about what makes aid effective began to be asked, there was a major paradigm shift in technical assistance and capacity development. This included a country-driven and ownership-based process of knowledge acquisition rather than vertical transfer.[2] Capacity development today is understood as an endogenous process.[3] The issue is therefore to provide an enabling environment conducive to generating locally grown solutions. This has brought with it greater appreciation of the value of Southern knowledge in terms of capacity development.

1. Fukuda-Parr (2002).
2. OECD (1991); UNDP (1993); Fukuda-Parr (2002).
3. OECD (2006); UNDP (2008).

---

**Box 11-1.** *Normative Issues of South-South Cooperation*

Currently there is no universal definition of South-South cooperation. Even though there are a handful of widely accepted definitions, terms and usages differ from organization to organization. It is extremely controversial, if not contradictory, to describe what actually demarcates the South and the North. Being derived from a composite of geographic, historic, political, and socioeconomic backgrounds, the distinction has been usually connotative rather than logical and has shifted according to changing global political environment.

As used in this chapter, South-South cooperation means developing countries working together to foster sustainable development and growth by sharing technical knowledge and financial resources. The term therefore entails both technical cooperation and financial assistance, in the form of either grants or loans. The definition of triangular development cooperation follows the United Nations Economic and Social Council's definition: "OECD/DAC donors or multilateral institutions providing development assistance to Southern governments to execute projects/programs with the aim of assisting other developing countries." In addition, the North refers to members of the Organization for Economic Cooperation and Development's Development Assistance Committee (OECD/DAC), whereas all other countries, regardless of income groups or status as aid provider, are referred to as the South.

Source: United Nations (2008, p. 3).

---

## The Value of Southern Knowledge

Developing countries may need not only cutting-edge knowledge but also ideas that are more attuned and applicable to their context. This is not to diminish the importance of the many successes and tangible contributions of developed countries in providing technical cooperation over decades but rather to recognize that other experiences are also useful for development. Southern case studies are powerful tools to transfer skills and generate successful solutions. Such case studies can be highly useful in development cooperation, as countries look for practical lessons learned in similar development contexts.

There are many examples of developing countries successfully solving the same challenges as others. One that is frequently cited is agriculture. Knowledge and expertise required for rice growing and for food production and preservation in a tropical location, for example, can be more easily found in countries with similar climatic conditions than in industrialized countries with temperate climates.[4] Successful SSC cases in this area include the Brazil-Africa agriculture projects and knowledge sharing on rice paddies in Southeast and East Asia countries.[5] Other

---

4. Kumar (2008) argues that it might be one of the reasons that agriculture became the sector most prone to South-South exchange; the exchange is usually concentrated within a region.

5. See the OECD Task Team on South-South Cooperation (TT-SSC) case stories in www.south south.info.

---

Box 11-2. *Lao-Thai-ADB Program on Strengthening the Capacity of Provincial Water Supply Enterprises*

The Asian Development Bank provided $60,000 for the staff of three provincial water supply enterprises in Lao PDR, in the field of water treatment, water quality control, water distribution, and leak detection. The Provincial Waterworks Authority (PWA) in Thailand provided resource persons and trainers for the program. The training program was undertaken in four localities: the Training Center at Chinamo Water Treatment in Vientiane; selected water supply systems in northeast Thailand for on-the-job training; the Training Center at the PWA's Khon Kaen regional offices in Thailand; and on-site training at selected water supply systems in provincial Lao PDR. Training at each locality was of one to two weeks' duration. The courses were carried out in the Thai language, because the Lao staff are more conversant with that language than with English.

The PWA trainers evaluated the trainees' acquisition of knowledge and skills and concluded that it was sufficient to carry out their daily work smoothly, albeit some needed more training in conjunctive areas of work. They expressed confidence that the trainees could subsequently develop more skills to deal with more complex problems in the future.

The trainees reported that the skills and knowledge they had acquired would be sufficient for them to perform their daily work smoothly and would be used most directly in their daily work. They were confident about further development of skills to solve complex problems in the future. They also felt that the PWA trainers' explanations in Thai were helpful.

Postevaluation results concluded that the training "overachieved" the operational and technical targets initially set out by the ADB. A high level of satisfaction with regard to the PWA of Thailand was noted as well, and the report recommends it be considered again for similar sets of training programs for the next ADB water supply improvement program.

---

cases focus on sharing technology and equipment. For instance, the knowledge and skills of Thai technicians in the Northern provinces (with whom Lao PDR shares a commonality in water management systems and equipment) have proven to be effective in Lao PDR water management (box 11-2).

Other similarities include sociopolitical background and development capacities and challenges.[6] The Lao-Vietnam-Japan cooperation in local administration reform, the Vietnam-Nepal exchange on development strategies, and the study visits assisted by the UNDP on how to reach the Millennium Development Goals have amply proven the effectiveness of SSC when it builds on the exchange of experiences in similar development contexts (boxes 11-3, 11-5).[7]

6. For example, current local governance reform in Lao PDR, a heavily centralized ex-Soviet socialist country, has benefited from Vietnam's experiences, which proved to be more effective than those of Japan and other developed countries. Lao PDR and Vietnam share socialist traditions, a centralized governance system, and foremost, a single-party political system, in which Japan or any Western country could hardly have expertise.

7. See the OECD TT-SSC case stories in www.southsouth.info.

Box 11-3. *Lao-Vietnam-Japan Cooperation in Local Administration Reform*

In conjunction with the current local administration reform in Lao PDR, Lao-Vietnam cooperation has been carried out with financial and technical assistance from Japan. It is well known that Vietnam and Laos share similarities in political systems and governance structures and have maintained a close relationship since the 1970s. Recently, Vietnam has successfully accomplished milestone projects in restructuring the local administration system, which motivated the Public Administration and Civil Service Authority (PACSA) from Lao PDR to draw lessons from the Vietnamese experience.

Initiated by PACSA, a study visit to Vietnam was organized in August 2009 with assistance from JICA. During this study visit, themes for knowledge exchange were identified and elaborated. Based on this, a workshop was organized in November 2009 in Lao PDR with the leadership of PACSA, during which PACSA and Vietnamese counterparts mirrored each structure and reform process and distilled lessons for the ongoing reform process in Lao PDR.

A performance review rated the workshop to be successful not only in the usefulness of contents but also from the capacity development perspective—for Lao PDR and Vietnam to mirror the situations, draw lessons, and identify further actions. From this exercise, the possibility of Lao-Vietnam-Japan third-country technical cooperation projects has been explored, and in the meantime PACSA has invited Vietnamese experts to visit and intends to host a series of seminars in the future.

Exchanging innovative ideas furthers capacity development in the South and allows technical cooperation to be more interactive and easily absorbed. Speaking the same language and distributing support materials often prompts and facilitates exchange. Correlations among language fluency, the quality of interaction, confidence building, and the outcomes of learning have been proven by many empirical studies in linguistics. Some examples include intra-LAC technical cooperation and the South-South HIV/AIDS program between Brazil and Lusophone Africa.

The flexibility and diversity of modalities are also meaningful assets. In South-South knowledge exchange, varied modalities ranging from invitational training, study visits, and on-the-job training are applied with flexible lengths, in contrast to traditional North-South technical transfers that can be somewhat constrained due to geographic distance. Box 11-5 shows one successful case that built on the comparative advantages of various development partners to deliver an effective solution for Laos.

*Implications of South-South Knowledge Exchange*

As noted, South-South exchange is a horizontal process of experience sharing and knowledge co-creation rather than a vertical transfer in traditional North-South relations. As such, it can result in highly effective capacity development. In addition, positive spillovers, such as self-confidence, mutual learning, and partnership

Box 11-4. *Triangular Cooperation and Trilateral Cooperation*

Triangular cooperation and trilateral cooperation are not identical, although both types of cooperation involve three partners and include the South-South element. Triangular development cooperation, often referred to as TDC, is generally understood as a type of development cooperation in which Northern donors and multilateral institutions support South-South exchange (although see different definitions in box 11-1). Therefore, the objective is to assist Southern countries to further cooperate and gain a maximum of positive spillovers from mutual learning processes. Notwithstanding its primary goals—building capacities for recipient countries—there is a complementary focus on what Southern partners acquire through learning by doing.

For trilateral development cooperation, Germany suggests the definition of "cooperation projects which are jointly planned, financed and carried out by an established donor country which is already a member of OECD DAC together with a cooperation country which, although itself a recipient of development cooperation and not (yet) a member of DAC, is emerging as a New Donor, and a third country as the recipient" (for the German definition, see DIE 2007). An essential feature is that knowledge exchange is jointly financed and processed by the established donors and the cooperation country. In practice, it usually operates within a parent North-South bilateral program or project and serves as a means of enhancing the overall performance of the program and project. A fundamental difference with the aforementioned TDC is whether South-South cooperation is understood as a goal in itself or as a means of achieving something else. Many three-party cooperation projects known as TDC are actually trilateral cooperation. In this regard, horizontal study visits of Lao officials for the MDGs planning framework in Bhutan (by the UNDP), and for road maintenance funds in Ghana, Zambia, and Cambodia (by the World Bank), should be understood as trilateral cooperation.

development, as well as endogenous solution-seeking skills, are conducive to effective capacity development, as expressed in the Bogota Statement towards Effective and Inclusive Development Partnerships.

However, in spite of the proven effectiveness in specific instances and the potential for capacity development, South-South exchange has remained limited. A year-long case study led by the OECD/DAC Task Team on South-South Cooperation (TT-SSC) documents about 120 cases of South-South technical cooperation undertaken in the course of the last five years. The sample is not exhaustive, but it represents the most comprehensive list of what is actually occurring in SSC around the world. One finding from the study is that the number of projects and their size remains small. Moreover, these exchanges are usually one-off and random. SSC is highly fragmented.

The variety of case studies also shows the extent to which Southern knowledge can be effective in meeting a variety of development challenges today. South-South knowledge exchange has considerable potential for impact, if managed

---

**Box 11-5.** *Lao-Thai-German Cooperation on Vocational Education and Training*

To better tailor the vocational and technical education and the number of school graduates to the demands of the labor market, the Lao Ministry of Education has set up the National Technical Vocational Education and Training strategy. GIZ provides a vocational training and capacity development program to support the strategy, with the German Development Bank financing the construction and extension of six Integrated Vocational Education and Training (IVET) schools across northern provinces in Lao PDR.

To train Lao vocational teachers for the schools, GIZ has implemented trilateral training courses in northern Thailand since 2008, in collaboration with the Thai Office of Vocational Education Commission. Entailing a comprehensive range of areas covering agriculture, hotel services, restaurant management, automotive, electrical power, and construction, the training courses have been organized for one-month training on technical subjects followed by one-month practical training in didactics in Thai colleges, by Thai instructors. Having successfully completed courses, the trainees can benefit from supplementary coaching by Thai mentors at IVET schools in Lao PDR upon availability.

Training was conducted in the Thai language, in accordance with the curriculum plans as agreed among three parties. Course materials were produced by institutions in Thailand, fully reflecting the context of the northern Thailand/Lao region. As the project manager at GIZ mentioned, this Thai-Lao component was necessary, given the fact that any counterpart, even from Germany, could not excel because of language differences and because of their limited understanding of local market demand for labor skills. Further, the levels (practicing teachers) and numbers (around 200) of the trainees, in addition to a relatively long duration (two months) of training, required the training be cost effective, which precluded the use of Northern experts.

The evaluation reports a successful outcome. The trainees expressed high satisfaction rates of over 70 percent, in terms of the course contents, didactics, and materials. Scores ranked over 80 percent satisfactory for the appropriateness of equipment, the level of training, language, and the usability of materials received for their own teaching work. In terms of costs, the per-head budget was about $1,000, excluding training fees and accommodations, which were provided voluntarily by institutions in Thailand. As of May 2010 over seventy Lao teachers from three of six IVET schools have been trained.

---

properly and provided with adequate resources. The key question, therefore, is how to optimize its potentialities and promote the practices globally.

## Pioneering Ideas for Solutions

The solutions can be found as readily at the regional dimension as at the global dimension.

## Putting Regional Dimensions at the Fore

Regionalism has been a key to leveraging South-South activities since the very beginning of the notion of SSC itself. Regional and subregional entities were created as long ago as the 1960s and have subsequently evolved into major region-wide or subregionwide organizations, forums, and platforms with considerable influence in global politics, economy, and trade.

For South-South relations the commonality of history, language, culture, and ethnicity among neighboring countries has played a key role. In the course of the past decade, intraregional trade has increased and helped to foster regional relationships. The growing need for a larger platform to address cross-border issues, such as infrastructure, climate change, disaster risks, and pandemics, has also strengthened relations on a whole range of aspects. The recent acceleration of regional integration efforts across the globe is a sheer reflection of countries sharing commonalities and trying to deal with common issues together.

Many regional organizations have sprung up to deal with cross-border issues. Much infrastructure in roads, energy, and communications is transnational. In other words, there is considerable overlap between projects in infrastructure and trade-related projects and those referred to as regional public goods, which have a regional dimension of purpose, consequence, and impact. Infrastructure and trade-related sectors are also where Southern cooperation has been most pronounced, at least in terms of the volume of aid and other development cooperation flows.[8] In Africa, the South provides about the same volume of resources as traditional DAC donors that invest via the Infrastructure Consortium for Africa.[9] The same is true in Latin America, where neighboring countries are investing in linking their economies together, and in East Asia. This provides one rationale why regional organizations offer a convenient platform for SSC: they are active in the very sectors that are of interest to Southern aid providers.

In fact, regional frameworks to coordinate actions around infrastructure issues have existed for a long time. Table 11-1 lists a few frameworks for infrastructure, currently operating at the regional and subregional levels.

Regional frameworks have proven to be effective despite different forms, modalities, arbitration mechanisms, and member composition. One can pinpoint successes and failures. For the successes, the frameworks have greatly contributed to improving data transparency among members, providing common tools and methodologies for joint actionable items, raising funds, and enhancing policy coordination. A few successful frameworks have even covered a full range of activity scopes and functions, creating platforms that are extendable into the future.

---

8. Woods (2008); UNCTAD (2010); Lum (2009).
9. OECD Development Center (2008).

Table 11-1. *Examples of Infrastructure-Focused Regional and Subregional Frameworks, Initiatives and Programs*

| Infrastructure framework/program/initiative | Geographic coverage | Sector | Governance | | Activity scope | | | Function | | Funding |
|---|---|---|---|---|---|---|---|---|---|---|
| | | | Secretariat | Member | Planning | Implementation | M&E | Advisory | Operational | |
| GMS | Southeast Asia | Transport, energy, others | ADB | RNSO | V | V | V | V | V | V |
| CAREC | Central Asia | Transport, trade, energy | ADB | RMSO | V | V | V | V | V | V |
| HAPUA (ASEAN power grid) | Southeast Asia | Energy | ASEAN | RS | V | ... | ... | V | ... | (V) |
| ASEAN highway network | Southeast Asia | Transport | ASEAN | RS | V | ... | ... | V | ... | (V) |
| ALTID | Asia | Transport | UNESCAP | RNSO | V | ... | ... | V | ... | (V) |
| BDP | CLMV | Water | MRC | RNMO | V | V | ... | V | V | (V) |
| IIRSA | South America | Transport, Energy, ICT | IDB/INTAL | RSO | V | V | V | V | V | V |
| PIDA | Africa | Transport, energy, water, ICT | AfDB | RMO | V | V | V | V | V | V |
| EAC road network project | East Africa | Transport | EAC | RMO | V | ... | ... | V | ... | (V) |

Source: Author's compilation.

Abbreviations: ADB: Asian Development Bank. AH: Asian Highway. ALTID: Asian Land Transport Infrastructure Development. ASEAN: Association of Southeast Asian Nations. BDP: Basin Development Plan. CAREC: Central Asia Regional Economic Cooperation. CLMV: Cambodia, Lao PDR, Myanmar, Vietnam. EAC: East African Community. GMS: Greater Mekong Subregion. HAPUA: Heads of ASEAN Power Utilities/Authorities. IDB: Inter-American Development Bank. IIRSA: Initiative for the Integration of Regional Infrastructure in South America. INTAL: Institute for the Integration of Latin America and the Caribbean. M: Multilateral institutions, including UN agencies and the World Bank Group. MRC: Mekong River Commission. N: Northern bilateral donors. O: Regional or subregional entities, including regional banks. PIDA: Programme for Infrastructure Development in Africa. R: Regional aid recipient countries. S: Southern aid provider countries, including regional aid providers. TAR: Trans-Asian Railway. V: Provided with an own-funding mechanism, such as trust funds or funding by members. (V): Lacking predisposed funding capacity or funding is procured externally.

Although these experiences offer meaningful insight for what a regional coordination framework should be, existing frameworks have hardly examined the reality of rising Southern involvement. As of now, Northern actions for infrastructure inevitably overlap with analogous, existing activities by Southern partners. Operational and policy consistency would make sense. The coordination framework therefore should be inclusive, with greater coordination between the North and South.

There is now an opportunity and a necessity to accelerate a merger of the fragmented regional frameworks that have sprung up over the last couple of years. Examples include the Programme for Infrastructure Development in Africa (PIDA) and the Initiative for the Integration of Regional Infrastructure in South America (IIRSA) that is merging with the Union of South American Nations (UNASUR). These trends set the groundwork for enhanced coordination in the regions and subregions. The question now is how to use such initiatives for better North-South coordination and to transform a de facto division of labor, which exists in terms of randomly different outcomes but not in terms of a structured operational plan, into a real, operationally effective division of labor that captures the evolving dynamics of SSC.

It may not be realistic to expect all Southern donors to join in the investment programming done by regional organizations: they have operated largely through direct bilateral programming to date. But many regional organizations are now realizing that they need to pay more attention to the soft infrastructure aspects of their programs in order to maximize benefits. The rules, regulations, workings of local governments, development of cross-border supply chains, and other aspects of what makes for effective cross-border commerce may be best supplied by neighbors. Hence using regional platforms to advance SSC knowledge exchange may be a way to significantly increase the volume of SSC and triangular cooperation.

### Creating an Enabling Environment for South-South Knowledge Exchange

Globally, South-South knowledge exchange needs a more effective enabling environment so that countries can optimize the potential of the exchanges. Field observations and interviews with practitioners give insights into what constrains Southern countries from becoming involved in SSC and what triggers their interest.

WHAT CONSTRAINS SOUTH-SOUTH EXCHANGE? The first important constraining factor seems to be a lack of recipient capacity to articulate their needs and expectations from SSC in a practical way. Second, developing countries do not seem to have a sufficient understanding of global practices; who does better in the field and what experiences could be usefully shared. Third, given the many bilateral combinations of South-South cooperation that exist, the lack of procedural knowledge can be an obstacle: How to proceed? Which organization, entity or staff to address? Fourth, the scarcity of financial resources of both provider and recipient is a problem: Who should pay for the exchange? While in principle this could be resolved through triangular cooperation, in practice the size of projects is small compared to transaction costs, so opportunities are lost. Overall, there exists a systemic discrepancy in matching demand with supply and providing the resources to execute South-South knowledge exchange. What can be done to mend the current situation?

WHAT TRIGGERS SOUTH-SOUTH EXCHANGE? Triggers prompting South-South exchange work at different levels. At the uppermost part of the chain of command, political commitments make things happen. In this case, South-South knowledge exchange can be part of wider cooperation strategies among countries, rather than stemming from specific needs from the ground.

Exchange could also be prompted at the institutional level. For example, research in tropical agriculture is prompted by research centers, associations, universities, and the ministries of agriculture of Southern countries. Preestablished cooperation frameworks among institutions, previous experience of exchange, and mutual knowledge of counterpart institutions would be enabling factors.

Individuals can also be important triggers. Leaders and key personnel can bridge the interested partners and match the demand and the supply. For the famous South-South microfinance exchange of the 1980s and 1990s, it was the professional acquaintance between Muhammad Yunus, the managing director of Grameen Bank in Bangladesh, and David Gibbons, who had been advocating the expansion of credit access in rural Malaysia, that played a crucial role in prompting Project Ikhtiar, a Grameen program in Malaysia. Similarly, Governor Daniel Lacson of the province of Negros Occidental in the Philippines and Cecilia del Castillo, the director of the Negros Women for Tomorrow Foundation, were jointly inspired by the Bangladesh model and together devoted themselves to learning the operating principles and skills in order to implement a program in the Philippines.

As experience shows, however, individual endeavors alone would not have been sufficient. Even for the microfinance exchange, political and institutional support was necessary. But to complete the circle, institutional triggers would not have generated tangible results without devoted individuals, nor would they have had a chance to flourish if not accompanied by political support. In other words, all three triggers need to be present to achieve positive impact.

LESSONS FROM EXISTING FRAMEWORKS. To leverage South-South knowledge exchange more, available knowledge, resources, and people would need to be brought together in a better combination. Table 11-2 draws an overview of existing frameworks promoting South-South exchanges. Governance structures, funding modalities, and operational characteristics vary greatly from one framework to another, with differing accomplishments, shortcomings, and challenges. The strengths and weaknesses of these frameworks should be weighed carefully against each other. These are summarized in table 11-3. On balance, sector-based and regional-based frameworks seem to be more effective than global multisector frameworks.

Existing frameworks do not pay sufficient attention to the South-South matching process. The current models presuppose an effective match of demand and supply and focus more on the funding decision. In addition, frameworks should be aimed at facilitating and brokering the matching process so as to ensure effective, feasible outcomes. Brokering the match should be proactive, rather than retroactive. Another deficiency is the dearth of proper monitoring and evaluation (M&E). Performance monitoring and results management should be addressed as part of South-South cooperation. The impact of SSC so far has tended to be narrowly measured by number of trained participants and size of budgets, not the ex post performance of operations and achievement of objectives. Those lessons are important to improve the effectiveness of SSC in the future.

Last, promoting South-South knowledge exchange has to embrace Northern partners in order to reach adequate scale and scope. The financing and partnership broadening synergies with the North through trilateral and triangular cooperation have been effective but, so far, limited.

## Recommendations for Future Actions

My recommendations fall into three categories: regional coordination, attention to the global ecosystem, and looking to the Busan High-Level Forum for additional momentum toward designing effective policy frameworks.

### Coordinating Actions Regionally

To ensure an appropriate level of inclusive coordination for Southern assistance in infrastructure to further leverage South-South exchange, regionwide or subregionwide frameworks should be conceived.

First, it is important to build regionally inclusive infrastructure coordination frameworks. The structures should have adequate levels of policy, clear mandates, and sufficient capacities to transform the current de facto division of labor into an effective division of tasks, responsibilities, and impacts among Northern and Southern development partners.

Second, experiences and lessons from the existing frameworks should be followed. Existing frameworks have proven their success and should be a basis for future actions. Creating a brand-new structure for SSC is not recommended. Although such a structure would guarantee a fresh start, it would risk further compromising effectiveness and only add to the proliferation of frameworks. In Africa, for instance, the Infrastructure Consortium for Africa (ICA) and the PIDA could be a good base from which to improve. Made up of G8 bilateral donors and multilateral agencies, the ICA aims to accelerate progress to meet Africa's infrastructure

Table 11-2. *Examples of Existing Frameworks Promoting South-South Knowledge Exchange*

| Example | Characteristics | | Governance |
| | Scope (sector/ geography) | Main interface | |
|---|---|---|---|
| GFDRR South-South program | Sector (disaster risk) | On+offline | GFDRR Secretariat (World Bank) |
| Alliance for Financial Inclusion | Sector (microfinance) | On+offline | GTZ Thailand |
| Africa-Brazil agricultural innovation marketplace | Sector (agriculture) | On+offline | EMBRAPA |
| Program for South-South Cooperation Benin-Bhutan-Costa Rica | Sector (biodiversity, sustainable development) | On+offline | National Mechanism of Costa Rica for Sustainable Development |
| SEETF | Multisector/global | On+offline | World Bank |
| UNDP/Japan Partnership Supporting South-South Cooperation | Multisector/global | Offline | UNDP SU/SSC |
| J-SEAM (ex-JARCOM) | Geographic (Southeast Asia) | On+offline | JICA Thailand mission |
| ACMECS | Geographic (Southeast Asia) | Offline | TICA |
| South-South Info | Multisector/global | Online | WBI, OECD TT-SSC |

Source: Author's compilation.
Abbreviations:
ACMECS: Mekong Economic Cooperation Strategy
AFI: Alliance for Financial Inclusion
EMBRAPA: Brazilian Agricultural Research Corporation
GFDRR: Global Facility for Disaster Reduction and Recovery
J-SEAM: Japan-Southeast Asia Meeting for South-South Cooperation
OECD TT-SSC: OECD/DAC Task Team on South-South Cooperation
SEETF: South-South Experience Exchange Trust Fund
UNDPSU/SSC: UNDP Special Unit for South-South Cooperation
WBI: World Bank Institute

| South-South promotion | | | |
| --- | --- | --- | --- |
| *Knowledge repository (people, institutions, practice cases)* | *Brokering S-S technical matching* | *Financing S-S projects* | *Project advisory services* |
| No | Implicit | Multidonor trust fund type, with specified budget ceiling | Established manuals, tools and document template (online) |
| Partially (cases) | Implicit | Multidonor trust fund type, with specified budget ceiling | Unspecified (online) |
| Partially (cases) | Explicit | Multidonor trust fund type, with specified budget ceiling | Established guidelines, tools and document template (online) |
| Partially (institutions, cases) | Explicit | The Netherlands' multiyear fund, with specified budget ceiling | Established guidelines, tools and document template (online) |
| Partially (cases) | Implicit | Multidonor trust fund, with specified budget ceiling | Established guidelines, tools and document template (online) |
| No | Implicit | Japan-contributed trust fund | Unspecified |
| Yes | Explicit | JICA's country assistance budget | Established guidelines, tools and document templates (online) |
| No | No | TICA | Unspecified |
| Yes | No | No | No |

Table 11-3. *Strengths and Weaknesses of South-South Knowledge Frameworks*

|  | *Strengths* | *Weaknesses* |
|---|---|---|
| Sector based | Contents can be technically thorough. Sector knowledge cocreation and regeneration are possible over repeated operations. Interregional cooperation possible. Institutions and people can know each other. | Multisector activities might have operational limits. |
| Geography based | Regional integration agendas can be mainstreamed with framework. Geographic, linguistic, and cultural commonalities can be maximized. Institutions and people can know each other. | Exchange might be limited to within the region. |
| Multisector and global | Sectoral and geographic coverage can be comprehensive | Sector expertise lacking. Practicalities lacking, because people and institutions often do not know each other. Matching process could risk being superficial. |

Source: Author's compilation.

needs in support of economic growth and development and addresses both national and regional infrastructure in water, energy, transportation, and communications. The more regional country-driven PIDA, on the other hand, actually provides a strategic framework and programs for transportation, energy, water, and ICT sectors. Other examples include IIRSA and FONPLATA in South America (box 11-6). These frameworks have provided a solid foundation for infrastructure coordination for over a decade. Once the convergence with the newly established Union of South American Nations (UNASUR) is completed, the frameworks are expected to effectively perform subregionwide coordination that is more in tune with regional integration efforts. In Southeast Asia, the Greater Mekong Subregion (GMS) could be a foundation for further SSC. The GMS has one focus on developing new corridors within and among countries in the subregion by building domestic infrastructure that is linked across international borders.

Third, adjust governance to make the inclusive frameworks work. Generating inclusive regional coordination frameworks should be accompanied by significant governance reforms. Regional country ownership would need to be reinforced. Necessary reforms include inviting stakeholders onto the board and steering committees, improving data transparency, and undertaking joint operations. These must be underpinned by a substantial political commitment. Adjusted policy, clearer mandates, adequate operational capacity, and sufficient financial and human resources are needed to scale up the activities of more inclusive regional frameworks.

Fourth, enforce monitoring and evaluations regionally. M&E issues require immediate action.[10] Based on current experience, solutions must address two challenges: the lack of knowledge about impact and an unwillingness to measure performance in a way that could reflect poorly on development partners providing the service. One option is to include or strengthen M&E functions within existing regional platforms. For example, IIRSA does environmental assessments and results monitoring for key activities, providing common tools and methodologies as well as advisory services. Another option is to establish a dedicated regional M&E function. A good model is the Regional Centers for Learning on Evaluation and Results in Africa, operating in association with the African Development Bank, the Asian Development Bank, the International Development Bank, and other bilateral and multilateral donors, and managed by the World Bank.[11]

Fifth, emphasize the leadership role of regional banks. Regional banks seem to be well disposed to lead SSC frameworks. So far, GMS, ICA, and IIRSA have all been led or supported by respective regional banks, and have been evaluated as performing well. Among the banks' strengths are policy coordination capacity, financial resources, operational know-how on regional public goods, and local knowledge. Additional advantages are the relatively well-balanced voices of the South and the North and responsiveness to the region's own issues.[12]

## Toward a Global Ecosystem of South-South Platforms

To enable more and better South-South knowledge exchange, a global ecosystem of facilitating forums, networks, and platforms should be established. Rather than starting from scratch, this chapter recommends that SSC platforms be established in regional, geographic-based organizations, including those established primarily to manage infrastructure as well as the emerging sectoral platforms.

---

10. The development of systematic M&E would have tremendous impact. Foremost, if project performance is measured, clear targeting and deployment of appropriate measures becomes possible. Subsequently better value for money positively affects the target beneficiaries in recipient countries as well as the taxpayers in donor countries. Because a considerable portion of Southern aid often comes at the expense of a country's own social needs, there is a high premium on documenting results. Also, given the fact that Southern aid has heavily focused on infrastructure development, which potentially involves environmentally damaging operations, it is important to demonstrate the mitigation measures implemented thanks to environment impact assessments.

11. The Regional Centers for Learning on Evaluation and Results (CLEAR) is a multiregional initiative, whose goal is to contribute to strengthening the monitoring and evaluation (M&E) and performance management (PM) capacity of countries and their governments to achieve development outcomes. In association with AfDB, ADB, and IADB, CLEAR supports regional centers (to provide in-region capacity development and technical assistance services) and global learning (to strengthen practical knowledge-sharing on M&E and PM across regions). See details on the website www.worldbank.org/ieg/clear.

12. Griffith-Jones, Griffith-Jones, and Hertova (2007).

Box 11-6. *Initiative for the Integration of Regional Infrastructure in South America*

The IIRSA was established in 2000 as a forum for coordination of intergovernmental actions, with the aim of promoting the development of transportation, energy, and communications infrastructure to strengthen the physical integration of the twelve South American countries. The IIRSA works on the basis of a two-tier approach, with geography-based integration and development hubs, supplemented by a sectoral process addressing transportation, energy, and communications. It aims to facilitate coordination mechanisms and exchange of information among governments. The strategic partners of the IIRSA include the Inter-American Development Bank, the Corporación Andina de Fomento, and the Financial Fund for the Development of the River Plate Basin (FONPLATA), which work to support infrastructure projects costing up to $40 million for the physical integration of Argentina, Bolivia, Brazil, Paraguay, and Uruguay. The Institute for the Integration of Latin America and the Caribbean, a unit of the International Development Bank, serves as the secretariat for the IIRSA Technical Coordination Committee. In 2010 the IIRSA was incorporated into the newly established Union of South American Nations.

A GLOBAL ECOSYSTEM. Sectoral and geographic frames could become the building blocks of a global ecosystem of knowledge exchange platforms. Sector-based frames would be effective in joining sector knowledge, experts, institutions, and available resources together, thereby coming up with immediately applicable, sufficiently practical, and fully feasible solutions. Geography-based frameworks would complement this sector-based model, particularly in terms of intraregional cooperation. Priority would have to be given to the sectors that affect the South the most and where Southern knowledge can make a tangible contribution, such as in microfinance, agriculture, sustainable development, climate change adaptation, disaster risk reduction, HIV/AIDS, and pandemic management.

A FOUR-PILLAR FRAMEWORK. To effectively promote South-South knowledge exchange, the platforms should be comprehensive one-stop shops, encompassing four pillars.

—Knowledge marketplace and networking: connect institutions, people, and knowledge. The platform should be able to serve as a sectoral or regional repository and marketplace of available knowledge, people, and institutions as well as practice cases. The repository function is fundamental for effective technical and financial matching processes in the future. Streamlined knowledge should also include extensive information on bidding, employment, and other networking devices, as connecting would have to occur not only at the institutional level but also at the practitioner level to gain maximum sustainability and practicality. Benchmark gateways, marketplaces, communities of practice, and other interfaces are examples of how this repository function works in current platforms. A good practice example is the Microfinance Gateway (box 11-7).

---

Box 11-7. *The Microfinance Gateway*

A comprehensive online resource for the global microfinance community, the Microfinance Gateway website (www.microfinancegateway.org), features research publications, articles, institution profiles, consultant profiles, and the latest industry announcements, news, events, and job opportunities. The website seeks to create an interactive platform for knowledge exchange for, of, and by the entire microfinance industry. The diverse user base includes microfinance practitioners, donors, networks, consultants, service providers, academics, and policymakers. Users can consult articles and documents and share views by rating and commenting on them. The flagship articles, in *Microfinance Voices,* provide monthly reviews of practice cases and lessons learned. The website is provided as a service of the Consultative Group to Assist the Poor, a consortium of thirty-three donors supporting microfinance.

Source: Consultative Group to Assist the Poor and Microfinance Gateway.

---

—Technical matching of demand and supply. Building on this knowledge base, an effective technical matching of demand and supply should take place. Online and offline devices and modalities offer promise here. For example, the Africa-Brazil Agricultural Innovation Marketplace (box 11-8) and Benin-Bhutan-Costa Rica Program could be useful prototypes.

—Financial matching. This pillar would provide funding for technically matched South-South proposals using preapproved resources from the North, either as trust funds or via an ad hoc request system.

—Project advisory service. A technical advisory function would help Southern partners to develop convincing, attractive, and practical projects. The advisory function would support feasible and strategic South-South project formulation and appraisal and help development partners cope with the complex project management processes of potential donors. It should also include M&E related assistance, because getting DAC donors engaged in SSC promotion through trilateral and triangular cooperation will be increasingly contingent on the proven quality of the South-South project. Existing frameworks make use of online methodologies and document templates. Some countries additionally dispatch experts to country offices as in the case of the Japan-Southeast Asian Meeting for South-South Cooperation.

ONLINE TOOLS AND OFFLINE DEVICES. The four pillars identified above should fully explore diverse technologies and devices, such as virtual meetings, online study courses, and the use of mobile devices. It should operate with an appropriate mix of online and offline interfaces. For instance, knowledge exchange and technical matching could occur online, whereas resource matching can be facilitated through offline stakeholder forums and technical advisory services implemented through a mixture of online tools and physical dispatch of experts.

Box 11-8. *EMBRAPA: Brazilian Agricultural Research Corporation*

In response to the agricultural challenges facing Benin, Burkina Faso, Chad, and Mali (known as the Cotton-4 countries), Brazil provides technical assistance through EMBRAPA. One of the visible projects of EMBRAPA in Africa is the Cotton-4 project. The main objective of the project is to increase productivity and production in the cotton sectors of the recipient countries through the transfer of Brazilian agricultural technology. It is expected that this will raise the incomes of producers, create jobs, and contribute to the mitigation of food insecurity in the Cotton-4 countries.

Source: UNCTAD (2010).

MANAGING THE PLATFORMS. Developing a global ecosystem of platforms would not imply creating a new independent organization. Instead, small units would be necessary to manage the pillars and coordinate overall actions online and offline, which could be hosted by multilateral organizations that have global expertise in specific sectors of work. Many sectoral knowledge platforms currently being managed by the multilaterals could be a starting point (figure 11-1).

Figure 11-1. *Model Framework of South-South Cooperation Platform*

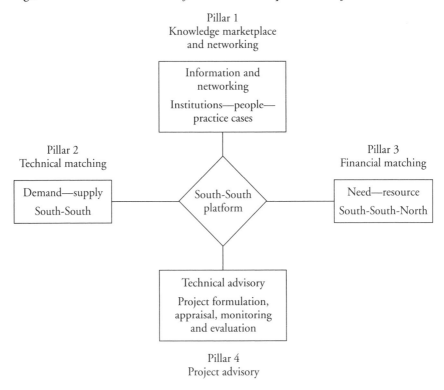

Pillar 1
Knowledge marketplace
and networking

Information and
networking

Institutions—people—
practice cases

Pillar 2
Technical matching

Demand—supply
South-South

South-South
platform

Pillar 3
Financial matching

Need—resource
South-South-North

Technical advisory

Project formulation,
appraisal, monitoring
and evaluation

Pillar 4
Project advisory

## Laying Down Milestones and Policy Frameworks

The Busan High-Level Forum on Aid Effectiveness offers an opportunity to establish the political support for an enabling environment that encourages more, and more effective, SSC. The role of new development partners and SSC was only briefly discussed at earlier forums in Paris and Accra. Although the Accra Agenda for Action took preliminary steps to acknowledge the growing importance of the issue, it spelled out only the basic principles of SSC in terms of complementary features to North-South aid and partnerships built on mutual benefits and respect for sovereignty. Only a brief reference was made in relation to capacity development.[13]

There have been major steps forward since that time. Most recently, the Bogota High-Level Event in March 2010 provided a significant opportunity to take stock of what has been achieved and to chart the way forward for South-South exchange and inclusive partnerships. Global efforts to compile evidence of the effectiveness of South-South operations continue today. Taking the reins, the Busan High-Level Forum could provide additional political momentum behind SSC as a major approach to better deal with the development challenges of our time. The viability of the four-pillar approach suggested above could be the basis for discussion at this meeting.

## References

DIE (Deutsches Institut für Entwicklungspolitik). 2007. "Trilateral Development Cooperation with 'New Donors.'" Briefing Paper 5/2007. Bonn.

Fukuda-Parr, S. 2002. "Operationalising Amartya Sen's Ideas on Capabilities, Development, Freedom, and Human Rights: The Shifting Policy Focus of the Human Development Approach." UNDP.

Griffith-Jones, S., D. Griffith-Jones, and D. Hertova. 2007. "Enhancing the Role of Regional Development Banks: The Time Is Now." Paper prepared for the G24.

Kumar, N. 2008. "South-South and Triangular Cooperation in Asia-Pacific: Towards a New Paradigm in Development Cooperation." RIS-DP 145. New Delhi: Research and Information System for Developing Countries.

Lum, T. 2009. "China's Assistance and Government-Sponsored Investment Activities in Africa, Latin America, and Southeast Asia." Congressional Research Service Report.

OECD. 2006. *The Challenge of Capacity Development: Working towards Good Practices.*

———. 1991. *Principles for New Orientations in Technical Cooperation.*

OECD Development Center. 2008. *Emerging Public and Sovereign Fund Investors in Africa's Infrastructure: Challenges and Perspectives.*

UN (United Nations). 2008. *Background Study for the Development Cooperation Forum: Trends in South-South and Triangular Development Cooperation.*

13. The Accra Agenda recognizes the importance of South-South exchange and its interrelations with capacity development (article 14-b), while suggesting a set of principles, including the complementary role of SSC to traditional North-South aid (article 19-e).

UNCTAD. 2010. "South-South Cooperation: Africa and the New Forms of Development Partnership." Report 2010. Economic Development in Africa.

UNDP. 2008. *Supporting Capacity Development: The UNDP Approach.*

———. 1993. *Rethinking Technical Cooperation: Reforms for Capacity-Building in Africa.*

Woods, N. 2008. "Whose Aid? Whose Influence? China, Emerging Donors, and the Silent Revolution in Development Assistance." *International Affairs* 84, no. 6: 1–17.

# Contributors

*Kemal Derviş* is Vice President and Director, Global Economy and Development, Brookings Institution.

*Shunichiro Honda* is Research Associate, Japan International Cooperation Agency Research Institute.

*Akio Hosono* is Senior Research Fellow, Japan International Cooperation Agency Research Institute.

*Woojin Jung* is Policy Analyst, Korea International Cooperation Agency.

*Homi Kharas* is Senior Fellow and Deputy Director, Global Economy and Development, Brookings Institution.

*Johannes F. Linn* is Senior Resident Scholar, Emerging Markets Forum, and Nonresident Senior Fellow, Global Economy and Development, Brookings Institution.

*Koji Makino* is Senior Adviser to the Director-General, Operations Strategy Department, Japan International Cooperation Agency.

*Ryutaro Murotani* is Research Associate, Japan International Cooperation Agency Research Institute.

*Jane Nelson* is Director, Harvard Kennedy School's Corporate Social Responsibility Initiative, and Nonresident Senior Fellow, Global Economy and Development, Brookings Institution.

*Mai Ono* is Research Assistant, Japan International Cooperation Agency Research Institute.

*Kang-ho Park* is Director-General, Ministry of Foreign Affairs and Trade, Korea.

*Tony Pipa* is Senior Adviser, Bureau for Policy, Planning and Learning, U.S. Agency for International Development.

*Sarah Puritz Milsom* is Senior Research Assistant, Global Economy and Development, Brookings Institution.

*Hyunjoo Rhee* is Policy Analyst, Korea International Cooperation Agency.

*Mine Sato* is Research Associate, Japan International Cooperation Agency Research Institute.

*Shinichi Takeuchi* is Senior Research Fellow, Japan International Cooperation Agency Research Institute.

*Keiichi Tsunekawa* is Director, Japan International Cooperation Agency Research Institute.

*Ngaire Woods* is Professor of International Political Economy and Director of the Global Economic Governance Programme, University College, University of Oxford.

*Samuel A. Worthington* is President and CEO, InterAction.

# Index

AAA. *See* Accra Agenda for Action

ABONG (Associação Brasileira de Organizaciones No Gubernamentales, Brazil), 72

Accessible information on development activities (AiDA), 246

Access to Medicines Index, 103

Accountability: aid and, 24–25, 237; civil society organizations and, 62; climate change and, 24–25; corporate governance, responsibility, and accountability, 95–96; definitions and concepts of, 237; evaluation and, 251–52; of foundations and INGOs, 69–70; of governments, 77; mutual accountability processes, 237–41, 245; official development assistance and, 78; outside stakeholders and, 253; peer, party, and mutual reviews and, 237, 238t; priorities of, 238–39; private development assistance and, 78; public accountability mechanisms, 87; public support for aid and, 117; transparency and, 28, 237–41. *See also* Information; Transparency

Accra Agenda for Action (AAA; *2008*): aid architecture and, 63; capacity development and, 26; commitments by donors for better practice, 121, 204; country ownership and, 124; coverage of, 11; effectiveness framework of, 61; fragmentation and duplication of aid and, 122; private sector and, 100; scaling up and, 205; South-South coordination and, 277–78; tied aid and, 103; transparency and, 28, 233, 239; trust and, 78; view of new development partners, 41, 52

Accra High-Level Forum on Aid Effectiveness (Accra HLF; *2008*), 2

ACFID (Australian Council for International Development), 72

Aceh (Indonesia), 242, 247–48, 250, 252–53

Acumen Fund, 89

Adaptation Fund (AF), 165, 168, 165, 170

ADB. *See* Asian Development Bank

Ad Council, 104, 233

AF. *See* Adaptation Fund

AFD. *See* Agence Française de Développement

Afghanistan: aid to, 44, 45, 128, 129, 138; as a capacity trap country, 130, 132, 133f; community development councils in (CDCs), 140–41; corruption and inefficiency in, 139; delivery of services in, 136–37, 138, 139; dispersion of armed power, 135; economic issues in, 138; health services in, 138n41;